Terrorism, War, and the Press

Nancy Palmer, Editor

The Joan Shorenstein Center on the Press, Politics and Public Policy

ISBN 1-884186-21-1

Library of Congress Cataloging-in-Publication Data available

Table of Contents

Introduction

As we watch press coverage of the war in Iraq, issues surrounding the role of the journalist during wartime arise again. Embedded reporters, decisions about printing or broadcasting gruesome images, and the impact of patriotism on press coverage are just some of the topics being debated. At the Shorenstein Center, we have benefited enormously from the wide range of experiences and thoughtful research by visiting Fellows from Iran, Northern Ireland, India, Russia, Israel, Burundi, the United States, and elsewhere who have lived through, reported on, and studied situations outside the normal realm of experience for most Americans. The publication of *Terrorism, War, and the Press* is part of an effort to share their fine work with a wider audience.

The Joan Shorenstein Center on the Press, Politics and Public Policy has been home to more than 150 Fellows since its beginning in 1986. The Fellows are distinguished scholars and reporters who come to Harvard for one semester and spend their time researching and writing a paper on a topic related to the press and politics. This book is a collection of writings by former Fellows and current faculty on a topic we wish were more remote.

In the first section of the book, *September 11, 2001*, veteran journalists Matt Storin, Ramindar Singh, and Andy Glass discuss the terrorist attacks from their unique vantage points. Matt Storin, former editor of *The Boston Globe*, examined press coverage by *The New York Times* and *The Washington Post* between the time of the first bombing of the World Trade Center in 1993 and the second attack in 2001. He found that the papers did increasingly well over the time period in covering the potential for terrorist attacks within the United States, but very little was published about the wider view of America's role in the world. Ramindar Singh and Andy Glass were Fellows at the Shorenstein Center at the time of the September 11 attacks. We found Singh's observations as an Indian journalist illuminating. His research and analysis of Indian and Pakistani newspaper coverage gave many of us in Cambridge a different perspective on the news that we were receiving from the U.S. press. Andy Glass, a Washington-based journalist and technology enthusiast, understood September 11 as the first major test of today's online communications systems. He discusses the role of the Internet in broadcasting breaking news, providing public health information, empowering independent journalists, and its impact on national security issues.

Chapters by Tim Cooke, Nachman Shai, Nik Gowing and Gadi Wolfsfeld comprise the second section of the book, *Lessons Learned from Northern Ireland,*

Israel, Bosnia, and the Gulf War. Tim Cooke's chapter on Northern Ireland explores the particular challenges for news organizations and journalists in the reporting of sustained conflict at home. Journalists in a society impacted by long-term political violence operate in an environment where news judgments are fraught with contradictions and play out before a contentious backdrop. Cooke's chapter draws on his experiences as a reporter for the BBC. Nachman Shai, former chief spokesperson for the Israel Defense Forces, had a unique role during the Gulf War. His authoritative voice told Israelis when to retreat into their safe room and when to put on their gas masks. The chapter he wrote, reflecting on the role of the spokesman, has become a classic teaching tool at the Shorenstein Center, and his advice about telling the truth during a crisis is a valuable lesson to be remembered for the future. Nik Gowing's chapter, written during his Shorenstein Fellowship in 1994, was based on his experiences as a reporter in the former Yugoslavia and wide-ranging interviews with officials in the United States and Europe. He challenges the conventional assumption of an automatic cause-and-effect relationship between real-time TV coverage and foreign policy making. Israeli scholar Gadi Wolfsfeld writes about the role of the news media in unequal conflicts such as protests, terrorist acts, and war between a powerful country and a weaker one. He examines the likelihood of the media playing an independent and significant role through changing times and circumstances, with third parties emerging as powerful actors.

The last section of the book concerns *Freedom of the Press.* Fred Schauer, Harvard's Frank Stanton Professor of the First Amendment, takes a rather contrary view on the constitutional rights guaranteed reporters. Schauer discusses press demands, government and military uses of the press, and the extent to which the First Amendment requires the state to provide assistance to the press. Pulitzer Prize–winning reporter Jack Nelson has covered every U.S. president since Richard Nixon. In his chapter on U.S. government secrecy, he looks carefully at the administration of President George W. Bush and discusses new efforts to create an ongoing dialogue between reporters and representatives from the intelligence and defense communities.

Each chapter in this book has been published previously as a Shorenstein Center research paper, discussion paper, or working paper. Fred Schauer first presented his chapter as part of a Center-sponsored press briefing on terrorism in Washington, D.C., soon after the September 11th attacks. (See www.shorensteincenter.org for a complete listing of Shorenstein Fellows and Center publications.)

The Jessie B. Cox Charitable Trust, the Goldsmith-Greenfield Foundation, and Walter H. Shorenstein have all provided generous financial support for the Shorenstein Center's Fellows Program, the initial research and writing of the papers included here, and the book project.

I would like to thank Alex Jones, Director of the Shorenstein Center, for giving me the freedom to undertake this project. I am very grateful to Tom Patterson, Bradlee Professor of Government and the Press, for his guidance and support. Parker Everett and Tami Buhr provided editorial and technical assistance. Edie Holway has infused the Fellows Program with warmth, good humor, and professionalism and is responsible for much of our success. Finally, I would like to thank Fred Lyford and his wonderful staff at Puritan Press for their help on this book and so many other publications over the years.

Nancy Palmer
Executive Director
Joan Shorenstein Center on the Press, Politics and Public Policy

While America Slept
Coverage of Terrorism from 1993 to September 11, 2001

Matthew V. Storin

S O FAR AS IS KNOWN, the traumatic attacks of September 11, 2001, were not foreseen by U.S. intelligence services, and they certainly were not predicted in the media. Yes, some government commissions warned of terrorist attacks within American borders sometime in the future. But the events of 9/11 shocked virtually all Americans, including the President of the United States. So it is useful to consider whether American news outlets utterly failed to prepare the public for this trauma, or raised at least some flags of caution. To date, there has been almost no detailed study that could answer this question. This chapter attempts to do so.

I. Methodology

The research spans an eight-and-a-half-year period from the bombing of the World Trade Center on February 26, 1993, through the coverage of September 10, 2001, concentrating on *The New York Times* and *The Washington Post*. The stretch of time being studied required the limitation to the two American newspapers that arguably devote the most resources to the coverage of public policy at home and abroad. But I made this limitation reluctantly. As the former editor of a large regional newspaper, *The Boston Globe*, I am well aware that much good work is done by other top newspapers and there is an inordinate amount of attention given to these leading papers by analysts of American media. Time constraints also prevented me from considering televised coverage. But, while most Americans get their news from television, it is well understood that the vast majority of such coverage as the networks might undertake in international news is greatly influenced by what appears in *The New York Times* and *The Washington Post*.

As for the time period chosen, the 1993 bombing of the World Trade Center, though it resulted in relatively few casualties, was a dramatic signal that terrorism would no longer be something that happened to other people, other nations. So it seemed a logical point at which to begin the study.

I set out to evaluate content published in the *Times* and *Post*, including on the editorial and OpEd pages, that would meet either of two criteria:

1. The published information would help a reader understand that there was a realistic and perhaps likely threat of a major terrorist attack by Islamic militants against a target within American borders.
2. The published information would help a reader understand that attitudes toward the U.S. within the Islamic world were often hostile and, at the extremes, very dangerous and violent.

I reviewed more than 2,300 news stories, editorials, commentaries and even letters to the editor in this pursuit, using Lexis-Nexis and Dow Jones Interactive search systems, utilizing such key words as terrorist, terrorism, anti-American, threat, bombing, anti-terrorism, Islam, jihad, Muslim, and, certain proper nouns such as Hart and Rudman (for former Sens. Gary Hart and Warren Rudman, cochairs of an important commission on national security). Hundreds of other stories were searched out solely for statistical purposes, e.g., the frequency with which Osama bin Laden merited front-page mention. The organization of the chapter is chronological, with sections devoted to key events and the coverage that followed.

For two years of the study period, a smaller paper, *The Tampa Tribune*, (September 2001 circulation 242,938) was evaluated to compare the "trickle down" results as reflected in a paper that generally would do no original reporting on policy issues at the international or national level. Also, I searched for books, magazine articles and unclassified government reports that indicated the level of intensity in addressing the terrorist threat and the underlying attitudes of the Islamic world outside the realm of journalism.

II. Summary of Findings

The research led to these findings:

- The glaring weakness of both newspapers was their inattention to the underlying causes of terrorism and scant coverage of frustrations within the Islamic world, including opinion or analysis pieces that prompt debate.
- Generally, the newspapers did solid reporting on the growing threat of international terrorism against targets within American borders, though it was done inconsistently, and without ever elevating the story to levels of urgency achieved by some other contemporaneous issues, e.g., security at the Los Alamos National Laboratory in New Mexico.
- An article in *The Columbia Journalism Review* (November-December, 2001) arguing that the media "missed" the story of the terrorism threat was misleading, particularly regarding *The New York Times*, which it singled out for criticism.

Key Dates	
February 26, 1993	bombing of World Trade Center
June 27, 1993	missile attack on Baghdad
March 20, 1995	Japanese cult, Aum Shinrikyo, stages chemical attack on Tokyo subways; later in 1995 Iraq revealed it had built a large biological warfare arsenal and had contemplated using it during the Gulf War
April 19, 1995	Oklahoma City blast
June 25, 1996	bombing of Khobar Towers in Saudi Arabia near Dhahran, killing 19 U.S. soldiers
July 17, 1996	TWA 800 crashes, killing 210 passengers and 18 crew, and creating suspicions of terrorism that were never proved.
July 27, 1996	bomb goes off at Olympics in Atlanta; post-midnight blast in Centennial Park kills one and injures more than 100
August 7, 1998	bombing of U.S. embassies in Kenya and Tanzania
August 21, 1998	U.S. launches Cruise missile attacks against suspected terrorist camp in Afghanistan and suspected chemical weapons plant in Sudan
December 17, 1998	U.S. begins bombing raids against Iraq
October 12, 2000	attack against the U.S.S. Cole in the port of Aden, Yemen, killing 17 American sailors

Findings

I. February 26, 1993: The Bombing of the World Trade Center

The bomb that exploded in the parking garage of the twin towers killed five and brought the horror of terrorism to the U.S. Coverage was massive and dramatic. As might be expected for coverage of a local calamity, *The New York Times* published more than a dozen stories the next morning. Over the course of the calendar year, the *Times* would present over 600 news stories, editorials and OpEd pieces relating to the blast. The *Post*, though not covering a local event, would do more than 170 stories.

On Thursday, March 4, the arrest of Mohammed Salameh, who was said to associate with Islamic militants, shifted the focus of terrorism coverage in the direction of the Middle East. Two days later the *Times* gave a reasonably comprehensive look at the growth of "Islamic terror groups" in a piece by Youssef M. Ibrahim on page A24. Referring to the recruits for these groups, Ghassan Salame, an expert on the Middle East from the Paris Institute of Political Studies, was quoted as saying:

They differ from the older generation in three crucial ways. First, their impatience with the status quo is stronger. Second, their willingness to use force is palpable. Third, their list of enemies is much longer.[1]

On March 28, the *Times* disclosed that the newspaper had received a letter, linking the bombing to U.S. support of Israel.[2] In that same edition would appear the earliest mention of Osama bin Laden found in this study, a reference deep in a 1,200-word story on page A14 that Yemeni officials suspected the Sudan-based militant of financing terrorism by Afghanistan veterans in Yemen.[3]

My research over the next eight years of coverage, leading to 9/11, would reveal few pieces like Ibrahim's that probed at the origins of what appeared to be a growing Islamic terrorist threat. On May 1, the *Post*'s Caryle Murphy, reporting from Cairo, took up an even rarer topic: the role that Western policies might have played in igniting Islamic passions. She cited ". . . the psychological and political repercussions on the Islamic movement of the 1991 Persian Gulf War, a perception by Islamic militants that the West has a double standard when it comes to enforcing U.N. resolutions . . ."[4]

The following day a *Times* story by Richard Bernstein made the point that the security Americans might have felt against terrorism was now gone. The headline was: "Blast Shatters the Illusion that U.S. Soil Is Immune from Assault." One source was Bruce Hoffman from the RAND Corporation, who said the bombing seemed to be the work of amateurs. He added, "We have the illusion that we are immune to terrorism and terrorists abroad see us that way. Now terrorists abroad may say 'If this is what the second string was able to accomplish, imagine what a first-string terrorist group could do.' This incident may ironically make the United States a more attractive target for terrorism than in the past." This was one of the earliest direct references in either newspaper to a changing threat of terrorism *within* American borders.

In the years covered by this research, statements that directly addressed the threat of additional terrorist acts within the U.S. appeared occasionally and not always prominently. The Bernstein piece ran on page A39. But on July 3, the *Times* did publish on page A1 a report that the "Islamic Group," the followers of Sheik Omar Abdel Rahman, who had just been arrested in the U.S., pledged to hit new American targets, including some in the U.S. (Later in July, the *Times* made one of its infrequent references to aviation security with a report on page A16 that a system that had been in place for 20 years, primarily to block hijackers, might "not be adequate against a growing terrorist threat." Despite what was a prophetic statement, the paper apparently did not initiate any enterprise reporting on the system before 9/11.)

Also, in the category of assessing preparedness, a story in the Outlook section of the Sunday *Post* on June 13, by freelance terrorism specialist Steven Emerson, said the FBI had received a "general warning" from German intelligence agents that

Islamic terrorists were shifting their emphasis to U.S.-based targets. The FBI disregarded the warning, Emerson charged.[5] The next month the *Post* also took a look at what appeared to be lax rules at the Immigration and Naturalization Service (INS) that allowed terrorists to easily enter the country. At this point, many of the elements that would come together in the attacks of 9/11, eight years later, were at least being touched upon by both papers—aviation security, entry into the U.S. by dangerous persons, domestic targets and enflamed passions.

Newspaper coverage is, by its nature, free flowing and bound to include contradictions, especially when viewed in hindsight. For example, in its editions of June 27, 1993, the *Times* quoted a private security official, the former Police Commissioner of New York City Robert J. McGuire, saying "the world has changed ... (in light of the terrorist bombing of the World Trade Center)." But on December 20, 1993, the *Times* reported that the Port Authority was searching for a new advertising agency "to encourage the leasing of office space, tourist visits and the use of the shops and restaurants at the complex." In this regard, the newspaper may well have been accurately reflecting a return to complacency on the part of New Yorkers following the February 1993 blast.

On April 14, 1994, the *Post* reported on a development indicating that the farther removed from a terrorist event, the lesser the vigilance. Reporter Roberto Suro revealed that the INS was no longer running routine fingerprint checks on immigrants in an attempt to prevent known terrorists from entering the country. Previously, the Suro article said, "thousands" of people a year had been blocked from entry.[6]

Even people who visited the World Trade Center near the one-year anniversary of the blast were forgetting the shock. N.R. Kleinfield reported on page A1 of the *Times*:

> People scurry through the two towers untouched by year-old ghosts. 'I feel safer here in this place than on the streets of New York,' remarked a cheery Matthew Dillard, a 25-year-old computer consultant from Annandale, Va., who was interviewed on the observation deck the other day. 'I have for the most part forgotten about that attack.'[7]

A review of the *Post* and *Times* in 1994 reveals little intensive reporting or analysis of terrorism beyond coverage of the trial. The *Times,* perhaps particularly preoccupied with coverage of the trial, did less analysis of the terrorism threat than the *Post* in 1994. One exception was a prescient piece in *The New York Times Magazine* by Tim Weiner on March 13, 1994, looking at the consequences of the war in Afghanistan in which the U.S. had aided the rebels against the Russians.

Weiner reported on the many training camps for militants, though he did not link them to international terrorism at that time. But there was one chilling passage in which an old Afghan man told the reporter that the pre-Taliban leadership had been put in place by the Americans. "Now," he said, "we want the United States to shake these leaders and make them stop the killing to save us from them." He concluded, "There is a fire burning in Afghanistan. Now, if there is a fire in my house, and my neighbor won't help put it out, what kind of neighbor is he? Doesn't he understand that his own house may burn?"

There was also a story in the *Post* that was predictive of an attitude that would gain prominence during the post-9/11 period. Daniel Pipes, writing in the Sunday Outlook section of the *Post*, reported on the disbelief in the Middle East over terrorist deeds that to more objective eyes seemed almost certainly the work of Islamic militants.[8]

In a New York City courtroom, four Middle Eastern men had been found guilty of planting a bomb in the World Trade Center in 1993, and they had admitted that they hated the U.S. Pipes wrote, "Few Middle Easterners saw things so simply. For them the real question is: Which government was the gang working for? The American or the Israeli?"

So in the aftermath of the February bombing, the nation's two leading newspapers on public policy were touching on most of the important questions, though not often and not prominently.

II. 1995–97: Oklahoma City, Tokyo Subways, Khobar Towers and Atlanta Olympics

This was a quiet period as measured by anti-American terrorism attacks that were international in origin. The Oklahoma City explosion, which killed 168 people on April 19, 1995, was a horrific event that dominated the news for weeks, but it was quickly determined to be domestic terrorism. There were other events in the time period (see Key Dates box, page 3), but none appeared to have an impact on the national psyche. The chemical attack on the Tokyo subways on March 20, 1995, would resonate most strongly in cities that have underground transportation and was deemed domestic terrorism. The blast of the Khobar Tower residential building near Dhahran was shocking with its death toll of 19 American servicemen, but deaths of military abroad on a one-time basis have limited staying power on front pages. Finally, the bomb that went off after midnight on July 27, at Centennial Park in Atlanta, killing one and injuring more than 100, has never to date been tagged as international terrorism and took place during a special event that was soon over.

The mood of the period was perhaps symbolized by a quote from a *Post* story on April 21, following bomb threats that involved federal buildings in 11 cities the day before. Mike Ackerman, managing director of a security firm in Miami, noted: "For three to six months after the World Trade Center bombing, they really paid attention to security in New York. The problem is that after nothing happens, you tend to lose focus. In some ways terrorists can almost predict when we're going to lose focus." In the story, New York City Police Commissioner William Bratton said it is "almost impossible" to secure any building, particularly one with parking nearby. He said good intelligence is the best defense.[9]

One analyst who did not lose sight of the larger issues was Harvard's Graham Allison who, writing for the *Post* on the threat of "loose nukes" in the post–Cold War period, made this chilling point:

> What prevented the Oklahoma City bombers or the terrorists who sought to topple the World Trade Center two years earlier from causing much greater damage? Certainly, no moral or humane inhibition about killing children. The operative constraint was the technical capacity for destruction that they could readily acquire.[10]

At this point, Allison's thinking was ahead of any seen in the two newspapers. In fact, at a Harvard forum in the spring of 2002, Allison made an observation that he had been studying Osama bin Laden "since 1993," a time in which the Saudi Arabian militant had yet to surface in the American press.

At various times in the study period, the academics studying terrorism seemed to be ahead of the reporters in the intensity of their efforts. For example, judging by what appeared in print, no reporter on either the *Post* or *Times* between 1993 and 2001 talked directly to terrorists in the Islamic world nearly so much as Harvard's Jessica Stern.[11]

III. 1998: The Embassy Bombings and U.S. Retaliations

In this year, the threat of international terrorism moved closer to center stage in the *Times* and *Post,* but, alas, center stage was already occupied: Congress was engaged in impeachment proceedings against the President of the United States. Nexis is not suitable for exact numerical comparisons, but it is worth noting that a search for articles that prominently mentioned "terrorist" or "terrorism" and "threat" in the two newspapers produced a total of fewer than 150 returns for 1998. Searching the same newspapers for the words "impeach" or "impeachment" in prominence ran afoul of the system's limits. There were more than 1,000 examples for each newspaper that year.

Terrorism was not much in 1998's headlines until August 7, when U.S. embassies in Kenya and Tanzania were bombed. But in hindsight from the attacks of 9/11, a few of the articles before August 7 are notable.

The *Post* reported on January 6, that federal officials were offering a training course to prepare local institutions for the perceived growing threat of chemical or biological attacks within the capital: ". . . [F]ederal and city officials acknowledged that a lack of preparation and planning means the capital remains especially vulnerable to massive casualties in such an attack."[12]

Meantime, in the *Times* on February 25, a small Reuters story on page A11 reported that U.S. intelligence officials were warning about "Islamic edicts" calling for attacks on U.S. civilians throughout the world. The edict was published "in the name of a group headed by Osama Bin Ladin [sic]."[13]

On April 23, the *Times* reported that Attorney General Janet Reno had floated the idea of creating a "national stockpile" of antidotes and vaccines to protect the civilian population against chemical or biological attacks.

Further on germ warfare, the *Post* reported on page A1 on May 21, that President Clinton had ordered that vaccines and antibiotics be stockpiled by the U.S. to protect American civilians against a germ attack.[14] The *Times* followed the next day with coverage of the formal speech by Clinton.[15]

Unlike some other White House announcements on terrorism (see reference to fire department equipment, page 20–21), this one was followed up aggressively by the *Times*. In a piece that coincidentally ran on August 7, the day the embassies were hit, William Broad and Judith Miller dissected the defects and controversies in the administration's germ warfare plan in a 3,400-word piece on page A1. Early in the year and again at year's end, the *Times*' Broad and Miller kept a bead on the weaknesses of the germ warfare defense and the rising fears of vulnerability. In the latter of these two excellent pieces was a quote that would have greater resonance three years later. Robert M. Blitzer, who had recently left the FBI after being in charge of its domestic terrorism sector, said of the germ warfare threat, "Eventually, this is going to hurt us. There is no question in my mind."[16]

Also in the spring, the *Post* broke an exclusive report on a federal interagency study of the more general terrorism threat, from both domestic and international sources. Commissioned by Attorney General Janet Reno after the Oklahoma City bombing, the study found "widespread deficiencies in the federal government's ability to combat terrorism, from a lack of intelligence-sharing on domestic plotters to the need for smaller tracking devices that will escape detection when placed on people and cars." It also proposed various actions aimed at combating the threat of germ and chemical warfare.[17]

Less than a month earlier, the *Post* reported on page A3 that Defense Secretary William S. Cohen was adding 10 new emergency teams to cope with chemical or biological attacks within the U.S.[18] Compared to the previous three years, the intensity of anti-terrorist coverage was at least somewhat higher, though it fell far short of dominating the news pages.

On May 22, President Clinton picked up on some of these same themes in delivering the commencement address at the U.S. Naval Academy. He specifically mentioned international terrorists as the type of nontraditional threats to U.S. security that needed to be considered in defense policy. He issued security directives that included the establishment of a national Coordinator for Security,

Infrastructure and Counter-terrorism, arguably the precursor for the Homeland Security position filled by Tom Ridge after 9/11. The *Post* story ran on page A3.[19] A few weeks later, the *Post* reported on a major disaster drill planned for Washington, D.C., with a focus on chemical and biological warfare.[20]

With the exception of the *Times* report on germ warfare, most of the stories at this point in 1998 had reflected that government appeared to be working harder on the terrorism issue than the press, which is probably better than the converse.

For much of 1998, the Clinton administration was pressuring Iraq to allow United Nations weapons inspectors full access. There were repeated threats of bombing attacks against Iraq. (These ultimately took place in mid-December.) On February 14, the *Post* published a letter from a retired professor of international affairs at George Washington University that reflected a view seldom found in news accounts or even OpEd pieces in either the *Post* or *Times*. The letter writer stated in part:

> Crushing the disarmed and starved Iraq is likely to enrage Arab masses, boost Muslim fundamentalism and fuel terrorism. If Saddam is as devilish as he is presented, his agents may already be sitting in a number of places clutching the jars of anthrax to be released at a proper time.[21]

It was a sentiment that may have seemed alarmist regarding bioterrorism in early 1998 but far less so in late 2001. In any event, it was rarely expressed in these two leading American newspapers.

On August 7, U.S. embassies in Kenya and Tanzania were bombed, killing 218 people, including 10 Americans. On August 21, the U.S. launched retaliatory strikes against a suspected terrorist camp in Afghanistan and a suspected chemical warfare facility in Khartoum, Sudan. This news merited considerable front-page coverage and from this point until 9/11, terrorism was a more prominent topic in major newspapers. The attention was further fueled by the apparent attempts at terrorism in conjunction with the millennium celebrations at the end of 1999 and the water-borne bomb that left a gaping hole in the side of the destroyer, U.S.S. Cole, in the port of Aden, Yemen, on October 12, 2000.

In the *Post* at least three front-page stories between August 13 and 21 focused on Osama bin Laden as the prime suspect in the embassy bombings.[22] The *Times* Week In Review section on Sunday, August 23, included a taste of Osama bin Laden in his own words. The text in part:

> . . . After World War II, the Americans became more aggressive and oppressive, especially in the Muslim world . . . American history does not distinguish between civilians and the military, and not even women and children. They are the ones who used the bombs against Nagasaki. Can these bombs

distinguish between infants and the military? America does not have a religion that will prevent it from destroying all people.

The attacks on the embassies provoked a degree of introspection about international terrorism that was almost never seen in these newspapers between 1993 and September 11, 2001. There was little news reporting on people who held these views, but their sentiments were found in pieces on the opinion pages of both papers.

In its Outlook section on Sunday, August 30, the *Post* published one of those rare pieces that went beyond the "threat" of terrorism to the underlying conditions that might breed it. Echoing in some ways the letter from the retired professor at George Washington, former CIA official Raymond Close made these observations, among others:

> Most of us accept the premise that terrorism is a phenomenon that can be defeated only by better ideas, by persuasion and, most importantly, by amelioration of the conditions that inspire it. Terrorism's best asset, in the final analysis, is the fire in the bellies of its young men, and that fire cannot be extinguished by Tomahawk missiles.

and

> . . . In declaring a full-scale war on terrorism, the Clinton administration seems tempted to emulate Israel's failed example. This is understandable, but wrong. Israel's situation is totally different from ours in every imaginable way. The state of Israel has been committed for 50 years to a policy of massive and ruthless retaliation—deliberately disproportional. 'Ten eyes for an eye,' the Israelis like to say. And still their policy fails, because they have not recognized what the thoughtful ones among them know to be true—that terrorism will thrive as long as the Palestinian population is obsessed with the injustice of their lot and consumed with despair. Wise and experienced Israeli intelligence officials have conceded to me that the brilliantly 'successful' assassination of a Palestinian terrorist leader in Gaza a couple of years ago led directly to the series of suicide bombings that helped bring Israel Prime Minister Binyamin Netanyahu to power—and may thereby have set back Israel's chances for peace for many years to come.

In the *Times* on August 16, Robert M. Gates, who was Director of Central Intelligence under President George H. W. Bush, outlined his ideas on how to fight terrorism at its roots:

> We can pursue a peace in the Middle East that does not kowtow to Israeli Prime Minister Benjamin Netanyahu's obstructionism and betrayal of

Yitzhak Rabin's legacy . . .

We can promote human rights and political freedom in the Middle East as we did in the Soviet Union and try to now in Asia. We can use force against the sponsors of terrorism, whether governments or groups, or, in the case of individuals, we can arrest and try them to show that our reach is, in fact, as long as our memory.

Times columnist Thomas L. Friedman also took a broader, step-back view. On August 22, he wrote,

The key to make the problem better is by a three-pronged policy: mercilessly attacking anyone, anywhere, who attacks our citizens or diplomats, embracing those who would be friends by constantly trying to build a moderate political center, particularly in the Muslim-Arab world, and always showing a road map to a better future for those who waver in between.

Getting at underlying causes, he quoted historian Ronald Steel:

The cultural messages we transmit through Hollywood and McDonald's go out across the world to capture and also undermine other societies. We are the apostles of globalization, the enemies of tradition and hierarchy.

One does not have to agree with any or all of these opinions to nevertheless believe that this kind of analysis belongs in America's leading newspapers, and in greater prominence than letters to the editor and freelance OpEd pieces.

Meantime, in the *Post* on September 4, 1998, a detailed, 1,500-word piece by correspondent Pamela Constable told of different sides of life under the Taliban in Afghanistan. She interviewed those who chafed under their strict rules and those who admired the Taliban in general and Osama bin Laden as well. It was published on the front of the Style section.

The *Post* also published an unusual piece on November 5, by Washington-based reporters Michael Grunwald and Vernon Loeb, that quoted sources, named and unnamed, who questioned whether the role of Osama bin Laden and al Qaida [sic] were being overemphasized in the investigation of the embassy bombings.

The reporters cited terrorist expert Harvey Kushner who said the emphasis on bin Laden might be overdone. He said even the capture of bin Laden would not solve the problem of "why people like bin Laden get created, and why they have followers." Again a quick reference, deep in a 1,400-word story, to the broader issues of terrorism.

A more conventional approach to the problem was articulated in a *Post* Outlook section piece on Sunday, August 30, by Ralph Peters, a retired Army intelligence officer who wrote a novel, "The Devil's Garden," about terrorism. He urged military commitment beyond Clinton's missile attacks to get at terrorists. The scenario he painted, including the use of Special Forces on the ground, closely mirrored the approach ultimately pursued in Afghanistan in the closing months of 2001.

The *Times* did publish, on August 25, an account of how the missile attacks of August 21 were seen by a moderate Muslim in Sudan. A critic of bin Laden, this scholar said the attacks would only enhance the militant's status. For the news columns of either the *Times* or the *Post*, this was a very broad worldview that was rarely reported on during the eight and a half years covered by this research.[23]

So overall, the reporting and, to a lesser extent, the analysis on terrorism intensified in 1998, but the Clinton saga was preoccupying America, so the prospect of educating even the more careful reading public was remote.

IV. 1999: Bin Laden's Higher Profile

Between the attacks on the embassies in Africa in 1998, and the attack against the U.S.S. Cole in 2000, there were no major terrorist attacks against American targets at home or abroad in 1999 and coverage of the topic in the *Times* and *Post* was unremarkable. But there was far more notice made of Osama bin Laden. He was mentioned in the *Times* 162 times and in the *Post* 144 times. In 1997, the year before the bomb attacks against the embassies in Kenya and Tanzania, which were ultimately linked to bin Laden by authorities, there were three mentions in the *Post* and six in the *Times*.

In addition to the Osama interest, there was a smattering of articles that related in other ways to what would become the traumatic events of 9/11:

- In a front-page interview with the *Times*, published January 22, 1999, President Clinton said it was "highly likely" that a germ or chemical attack would be launched against Americans at home within the next few years.[24]
- Another front page story in the *Times* by Judith Miller revealed on September 22, 1999, that the Clinton administration was seeking money to develop a laboratory for fighting germ warfare at the Plum Island Animal Disease Center on Plum Island, off Long Island.
- In the *Post*, on March 16, appeared a story that again demonstrated that the White House could put the media spotlight on a topic but that that was no guarantee of further attention. An article on page A11 reported that President Clinton would commit millions of dollars to "equip and train" firefighters around the country so they could better respond to acts of terrorism. It was reported that the Justice Department would provide nearly $70 million in grants nationwide. A Nexis survey of the *Post* from that date until September 11, 2001, did not turn up a further mention of this program.[25]

- The *Times* reported on a growing fear that New York City's public and private institutions could be targeted by terrorists, particularly as a result of the trials that would take place in 2000 of the suspects in the African embassy attacks.[26]
- In the *Post*, a Stephen S. Rosenfeld commentary on the OpEd page focused on "homeland defense," a precursor of "homeland security," which would become a household term in 2001. The piece questioned whether a missile defense system made sense in an age when threats might come in many other forms as compared to during the years the U.S. centered its defenses on the Soviet Union.[27]

In March and July there were significant pieces in the *Post* on bin Laden, including in March a warning from one terrorist that the deaths from the missile attack against a suspected training camp in Afghanistan the previous August would be avenged. The unnamed member of the terrorist group Harkat, which was linked to bin Laden, said, "For each of us killed or wounded in the cowardly U.S. attack, at least 100 Americans will be killed . . . I may not be alive, but you will remember my words." The July story, on page A3, said bin Laden was still a threat. "We haven't killed him off," said Robert Oakley, a former counterterrorism official in the State Department. "But we've clearly reduced his ability to do things."[28] The *Times* reported on page A1 on April 13, 1999, that American commandos were trying to capture bin Laden near the Pakistani border with Afghanistan. Some administration critics questioned his importance.[29]

Both papers covered the fears of terrorist attacks in connection with the coming millennium celebrations at year's end. On December 16, the *Post* said it had obtained a copy of a report by a commission on the threat of terrorism, headed by Gov. James S. Gilmore III of Virginia. The commission, noting that terrorists with weapons of mass destruction were a "genuine threat," questioned whether governments were prepared to deal with the results, particularly the issue of federal vs. state responsibilities. The story was published on page A6.[30] The *Times* did not report on the Gilmore document.

When pulled out of a larger context, these articles—viewed through a rear view mirror from 9/11—seem significant. But spread across a whole year, they probably had much less impact on most readers.

V. 2000–2001: First the Post and Then the Times Give the Threat at Home New Attention

This was a curious period in which the *Times*, during 2000, seemed to lose sight of terrorism as a priority, though it covered extensively the attack on the U.S.S. Cole in October of that year. Then the newspaper's focus returned in 2001 with some probing work on bin Laden and Afghanistan that was ultimately part of a Pulitzer Prize–winning effort.

In 2000, while the *Times'* attention to terrorism appeared to wane, the *Post* reported a significant number of *de facto* warnings concerning terrorism within U.S. borders. Among them:

- "Although New Year's celebrations have passed safely and Clinton administration officials are relieved, federal law enforcement leaders say it is not time to relax—based on threats not directly tied to the year 2000 coming out of the Middle East and elsewhere. 'It is clear and should be clear to all Americans that the risk of terrorism will continue,' said Attorney General Janet Reno."[31]
- "Key to Clarke's [Richard Clarke, counterterrorism specialist in the National Security Council of Clinton administration] thinking is the idea that a new breed of global terrorist—embodied by bin Laden—has developed the ruthlessness and resources to carry its war to American soil. He said in an interview that America's new enemies are certainly not going to repeat Saddam Hussein's mistake of lining 'his tanks up in the desert' for U.S. forces to destroy. 'They will come after our weakness, our Achilles heel, which is largely here in the United States.'"[32]
- "At the same time, the report said, the United States faces new threats from loosely organized terrorist networks operating out of lawless 'swamps' such as Afghanistan, whose ruling Taliban movement, while professing no grudge against the West, continues to harbor fugitive Saudi extremist Osama bin Laden."[33]
- "'The United States has no coherent, functional national strategy for combating terrorism,' [Virginia Gov. James S.] Gilmore said. 'The terrorist threat is real, and it is serious.'" (Gilmore headed a federal commission on terrorism.)[34]
- "The report [by the National Intelligence Council] . . . also concludes that terrorist attacks against the United States through 2015 'will become increasingly sophisticated and designed to achieve mass casualties.'"[35]

But there were some mixed messages in the pages of the *Post*, not necessarily a bad thing for a newspaper. Former State Department counterterrorism official Larry C. Johnson, who would write a *Times* OpEd piece in July 2001 expressing similar opinions, was cited as playing down the terrorist threat. Johnson said the National Commission on Terrorism (yet another anti-terrorism panel, this one known as the Bremer Commission) had greatly exaggerated the threat. "We need a little bit more mature approach to this," he said. "Is there the potential for mass casualties? Yes, but we don't have to reinvent the wheel in counterterrorist policy."

Reporter Vernon Loeb, on June 23, paraphrased Johnson and said that a global counterterrorist campaign had been "effective at disrupting the activities of terrorist groups linked to Saudi exile Osama bin Laden . . ."[36]

But in the *Times* in 2000, there was perhaps the most uninhibited commentary seen in the two newspapers during the eight and a half years spanned by this research. It was published on October 14, two days after the attack on the Cole in Yemen. An OpEd piece, it was by Reuel Marc Gerecht, a former Middle East specialist in the Central Intelligence Agency. He wrote in part:

> The Clinton administration has tenaciously pursued a peace process that Muslims regard as an insult to their pride. Muslims from Tangiers to Tehran may be willing to concede that Israel exists because, as the Soviets used to say, the correlation of forces allows no other alternative. But they rebel against the idea that Jews have a legitimate, historic right to a state west of the Jordan River, which is, after all, the ultimate objective of the peace process. For decades, the State Department has operated under the assumption that with the right batch of Israeli concessions the Arab world would tire, cut a deal, and recognize the legitimacy of the Jewish state.

He also wrote:

> Though esteemed for their knowledge, Jews are usually characterized in Islamic tradition as cowardly and weak. Losing to Christians over the last 300 years has been bad enough, losing to Jews since 1947 has been especially galling.

He said further,

> . . . the Muslim reluctance to concede that "Muslim lands" can ever legitimately be relinquished to infidels is age-old. Imbedded into Islamic law and custom.

Whether he was right or wrong, Gerecht was taking straight on the issues of ethnic conflict in a way that was almost never seen in the American media.

But as the 11th of September dawned, there had been no notable public debate in America on any of the issues relating to terrorism, e.g., were we sufficiently prepared, or was there anything we should be doing in the Middle East to combat hatred of the U.S., whether in evaluating foreign policies or even in paying more attention to telling our story to the Islamic world.

What Were They Reading in Tampa?

The Tampa Tribune is a quality regional paper of medium size. Its daily circulation is 242,938 (September 2001). Comparisons by Nexis search are not necessarily definitive, but I wanted to choose one smaller paper to compare in general terms what was available to readers who do not buy *The New York Times* or *The Washington Post* on a regular basis. Indeed, it would be difficult to find the *Post* on a same-day basis in Tampa, except perhaps in the high tourism months of mid-winter.

A comparison for four years of the study period—1995, 1996, 1997 and 1998—was done using the key words of "terrorism" or "terrorist" and "threat." When these words were used in searches of the *Times* they turned up 299 articles, editorials, columns or letters. The comparable total for the *Post* was 258. For the *Tampa Tribune,* the four-year total was 46.

Obviously, the "trickle down" effect for serious news with an international aspect may be very limited. Although television news was not a part of this study, any observer of the major networks in the past decade would not be optimistic about finding much there, though the coverage after 9/11 was very strong. To its credit, ABC News broadcast an exclusive interview with bin Laden in May 1998.

Although the *Tampa Tribune* numbers are not impressive, the newspaper did do many of the 46 stories with its own staff reporters, concentrating on local aspects of the terrorism threat, an apt role for a regional paper. The total does include one column by the *Times'* Thomas Friedman.

Conclusions

In the Introduction of this chapter, two standards were articulated for evaluating the content:

1. The published information would help a reader understand that there was a realistic and perhaps likely threat of a major terrorist attack by Islamic militants against a target within American borders.
2. The published information would help a reader understand the broader aspects of the terrorism issue—for example, why attitudes toward the U.S. within the Islamic world were often hostile and, at the extremes, very dangerous and violent.

I. Coverage of the Threat

In the wake of the 9/11 attacks much was made of the perceived failure of the press to publish clear warnings that terrorists might strike. Forget that the more crucial performance of the CIA could not have been much better, the critics homed in on the failure of *The New York Times* in particular to report on the conclusions of the United States Commission on National Security when it issued its final report at the end of January 2001. Harold Evans, the distinguished former editor of the *Times* and the *Sunday Times* of London, excoriated *The New York Times* in the November-December issue of the *Columbia Journalism Review* under the headline, "WHAT WE KNEW: WARNING GIVEN . . . STORY MISSED."

In his *CJR* piece, Evans said, "We were warned." He quotes the commission's warning, "Americans will likely die on American soil, possibly in large numbers." Evans failed to note that this and other predictions by Hart-Rudman were in an extended time frame—"over the next quarter century." Not the kind of stuff that energizes headline writers.

The commission, co-chaired by former Senators Warren Rudman and Gary Hart, issued a report that was crammed much more with proposed changes in government policies than with warnings. The particular alarm Evans quoted had been made initially in the panel's "phase one" report in 1999. (Though that report also got scant press coverage.)[37]

In fact, that same month that Evans was writing about, January 2001, the staff of *The New York Times* produced an impressive three-part series on the terrorist threat that, with all due respect to the members of the Hart-Rudman Commission, was more compelling in its exposure of the threat.

The first piece, a 6,200-word examination of Osama bin Laden and his Al Qaeda network, tied bin Laden to both the World Trade Center bombing and the embassy attacks. It noted, "Al Qaeda trains 'sleeper' agents, or 'submarines,' to live undetected among local populations," and that attacks are planned "months or years in advance."[38] In part three of the series, a reporter visited training camps for terrorists in Afghanistan.[39]

This doesn't excuse the curious oversight of the *Times* in ignoring the commission. But it does undermine the contention that they "missed" the story. In fact, the three-part series was part of a *Times* package that was awarded the Pulitzer Prize for Explanatory Reporting in 2002.

So now that we've put that little contretemps to rest, does that mean that America's elite press was up to the task of preparing its readers for anything approximating the attacks of 9/11? As the Hertz commercial puts it, not exactly.

Despite some patches of excellent work by both the *Post* and the *Times*, particularly the latter, this detailed study of the content from those years demonstrates what the veteran CBS reporter, Bob Schieffer, meant when he said of the months before 9/11, "Terrorism was not on anyone's front burner in those days."[40]

In 2000, for example, readers of the *Times* would know that the newspaper was far more energized by the question of whether Wen Ho Lee, a scientist at the Los Alamos National Laboratory, had passed nuclear secrets to the Chinese government. Dr. Lee was eventually cleared, but during 2000, there had been 15 front page stories in the *Times* on his case.

This does not mean they were wrong to actively pursue the Wen Ho Lee story (though the *Times*' aggressiveness on this story did become an issue after Dr. Lee was released from custody), but by comparison the newspaper published only four pieces on page A1 that year that prominently mentioned Osama bin Laden, despite the attack on the U.S.S. Cole that occurred on October 12. The following year, between January 1 and September 10, 2001, there were 10 front page stories in the *Times* that prominently mentioned bin Laden, although only half of them referred directly or indirectly to the terrorist leader in headlines.

For the 11 months, between October 12, 2000, and September 11, 2001, a Nexis search indicates that the *Times* published only six stories on page A1 that prominently mentioned a threat of terrorists or terrorism.[41]

So the general conclusion of the research is reflected in these numbers. By no means was the newspaper ignoring the issue of bin Laden or the terrorist threat. But one could argue that the newspaper never sent a strong signal of priority regarding terrorism through sustained page one attention. And while the January piece put the threat of bin Laden in high profile, a piece several months later poked holes in the menacing image of his terrorist group (to paraphrase the headline of a May 31 story on page A1). Reporter Benjamin Weiser said the embassy bombings trial "made clear that while Mr. Bin Laden may be a global menace, his group, Al Qaeda, was at time slipshod, torn by inner strife, betrayal, greed and the banalities of life . . ."[42]

As the findings indicate, the *Post* also did solid work on terrorism, though not with the intensity with which the *Times* covered the germ warfare threat in 1998 and bin Laden's terrorism network in early 2001. Occasionally the performance of the *Post* was more consistent than that of the *Times*. For example, for calendar year 2000, a search of key words depicting the terrorist threat yielded 12 significant stories from the *Post*, none from the *Times*.[43]

Both newspapers extensively covered several major terrorism attacks during the study period, which included events stretching from the 1993 bombing of the World Trade Center to the 2000 attack against the U.S.S. Cole. The news stories were not included in the research, because such coverage was not optional. On the other hand, the examples of excellent reporting and analysis that are included in this study must be considered in the context of the whole newspapers in which they were published. These are comprehensive publications that put an average of seven stories on page A1 every day, 365 days a year, or a total of nearly 22,000 front page stories over eight and a half years. And if one assumes about 30 national or foreign stories totally in each edition of the *Times* and *Post* for the same period, they appeared among more than 90,000 articles in each paper over the study period. Each newspaper also would have published more than 12,000 OpEd pieces. The *Times* would have presented a similar number of editorials and the *Post* about 8,000. So it is noteworthy that within a universe of perhaps 224,000 articles, this research focused on about 2,300, or little more than one percent, that fit minimal criteria for review. So despite the good work that was found, one is again reminded of Bob Schieffer's remark, quoted earlier, that terrorism was not on anyone's "front burner."

It must also be noted that during all the years of this study, a large body of work concerning terrorism was being compiled in the academic community. Though there was not time to review all of it, one must note the work at Harvard of Graham Allison, Ashton B. Carter, Laura K. Donohue, Richard A. Falkenrath, Juliette Kayyem, Joseph S. Nye and Jessica Stern, among many others. The John F. Kennedy School of Government lists more than 35 papers and articles on terrorism by members of the faculty just since 1998. Martha Crenshaw of Wesleyan University and Brigitte Nacos of Columbia University are just two of many others who were doing significant studies of terrorism during these years, and surely there were many others throughout the U.S.

One could argue whether in the natural order of things it isn't unsurprising that the academic community would be ahead of the press in at least the intensity of its attention to the topic, but as a journalist I still must confess some surprise at the comparative large volume of academic work that was being done prior to 9/11.

Still, as Crenshaw has found, the academic work generally occurred in a relatively narrow field regarding "loose nukes" and other weapons of mass destruction. Attacks such as those against the Khobar Towers and the U.S.S. Cole, which bore more resemblance tactically to the attacks of 9/11, did not seem to fire the passions of the academic world.

In March 2002, Crenshaw observed, ". . . [T]errorism was not generally considered an important national security threat unless it combined two dangers: a threat to the U.S. homeland *and* the use of 'weapons of mass destruction,' defined as nuclear, chemical, biological or radiological weapons" (emphasis in original).[44]

(As noted earlier, Jessica Stern did impressive work on attitudes of Islamic militants, much of it through personal interviews.)

One paper, published by the Strategic Studies Institute of the U.S. Army War College in 1995, did predict that American foreign policy operations (this was during the Clinton Administration) were inviting a response from terrorists against targets within U.S. borders. Stephen Sloan, a professor of political science at the University of Oklahoma, wrote:

> . . . [E]ven if Washington is motivated by the highest of ideals, i.e., democratization, humanitarian assistance, or nation-building, those who will be the objects of such efforts might resent it. Their use of terrorism on American soil is a likely response."[45]

News coverage in the *Post* and *Times* during the research period tended to concentrate on the most likely terrorists and potential targets rather than the potential weapons, except for work done on germ and chemical threats, particularly by the *Times* in 1998. So as Crenshaw's research indicates, there was a difference in emphasis between the work of academics and the reporting in these two newspapers.

II. *Coverage of Attitudes Toward U.S./Roots of Terrorism*

As to the second standard used in evaluating press content for this study—the relevance to attitudes toward the U.S. and other possible roots of terrorism—this is largely a barren landscape over the eight and a half years of the research.

This study yielded an occasional piece—most notably the OpEd piece by Robert Gates and an occasional column by the redoubtable Tom Friedman—that looked at terrorism or terrorists in a broader, geopolitical context. But they were by far the exceptions.

Even the publication in 1997 of "The Clash of Civilizations" by Samuel P. Huntington (Touchstone Books), expanding on a summer 1993 article in *Foreign Affairs,* prompted little more than book reviews in the *Times* and *Post*. My searches of the two newspapers found no prominent links between the points Huntington raised on conflict between religious cultures and the seeming growth of terrorist threats against the United States. (The *Foreign Affairs* article followed by only a few months the bombing of the World Trade Center.) But Huntington himself did the kind of analysis that was almost never seen in those newspapers:

> The West, and especially the United States, which has always been a missionary nation, believe that the non-Western people should commit themselves to the Western values of democracy, free markets, limited government, human rights, individuals, the rule of law and should embody these values in their institutions . . . What is universalism to the West is imperialism to the rest.[46]

Understandably, this is tricky terrain on which to write for the public prints. One person's efforts to explain conditions that might provoke enough rage to fuel a suicide bomber is another person's apologia for those who would murder innocent people.

Concern for what one might call "Patriotic Correctness" in the U.S. was so strong in the aftermath of the 9/11 attacks that the five major television news organizations agreed to follow Bush administration guidelines for handling videotapes of Osama bin Laden.[47]

At times these inhibitions gave me pause in my own research. Was this a reasonable quest to find such content?

I was inspired at a midpoint in my work by a remarkably generous statement from Mariane Pearl, widow of the murdered journalist, Daniel Pearl. On February 22, 2002, when her husband's death had been confirmed, she said:

> Revenge would be easy, but it is far more valuable in my opinion to address this problem of terrorism with enough honesty to question our own responsibility as nations and as individuals for the rise of terrorism.

This kind of introspection had been almost totally absent in the American press, particularly before 9/11. There was not time to make a fair analysis of the academic efforts in this area, or to know the classified work of the U.S. government. It is noteworthy that three of the better OpEd pieces on what drives terrorists were written by former CIA officials (Gates, Close and Gerecht). Also, *The Atlantic Monthly* did a number of thoughtful articles related to terrorists and motivations in the 15 years prior to 9/11.[48]

Perhaps not surprisingly, these inhibitions in newspapers flared up particularly in the immediate aftermath of the attacks on the World Trade Center and Pentagon. T.R. Reid, a London-based correspondent for the *Post*, told Christiane Amanpour on CNN International on October 6, 2001, that he worried about writing on the topic of how much the U.S. was hated in the Islamic world.

"I think we can explain why people wanted to do this to our country," Reid said, "without being apologists for terror." But he cautioned, "If I wrote this story now, thousands of people would write into the *Washington Post* and say, 'Fire the guy.'" He said that eventually such stories would be written, and they were.

One senses that the taboos, to the extent they existed, continue to ease. At a conference at Harvard's John F. Kennedy School of Government in May 2002, there were panels on "Root Causes of Terrorism" and "What Can Be Done to Address the Root Causes of Terrorism."

In the weeks after 9/11, *Newsweek* and *The Boston Globe* both published major presentations under the headline "Why They Hate Us." Other publications, including the *Los Angeles Times,* did similar stories.

Timothy Garton Ash, director of the European Studies Centre at St. Antony's College, Oxford, and a senior fellow at the Hoover Institution at Stanford, wrote an OpEd piece in the *New York Times* in April 2002 that carried the headline, "The Peril of Too Much Power." He said, "Contrary to what many Europeans think, the problem with American power is not that it is American. The problem is simply the power. It would be dangerous even for an archangel to wield so much power." There is no way to prove or disprove that this piece would have appeared in the *Times* before 9/11. But it's certainly debatable.

One does not have to believe that U.S. policies are necessarily misguided to advocate that there be an uninhibited debate in the pages of the American press. It is always possible that there might be better policies for the U.S., whether in its use of military and diplomatic power or the purveying of our culture—our "soft power," as Joseph S. Nye, Jr. writes.

But how will we know if we don't ask?

III. Practical Lessons

No one would argue that more aggressive press coverage could have prevented the attacks of 9/11. So what importance can be attached to the coverage of terrorism before that infamous date, and does it teach us anything?

At a minimum, the quality media don't want to be surprised by historic events any more than government does. In the case of media, it is a challenge that must be met to some degree in order to hold readership and audiences. Beyond that, it could be argued that accurate, predictive coverage, if of necessity generalized, can provide some benefit to prepare the nation for change. It might not alter history, but it could minimize some of the impacts, perhaps even loss of life. Surely it is possible that government and media combined to increase vigilance and possibly thwart danger from additional terrorist attacks in the immediate months after 9/11.

It would be easy to point the finger at editors and say they should have been more concerned about terrorism from 1993 to September 2001. I could point the finger at myself. Yes, and throw in all the governments of the free world as well. But more realistically, the coverage in the *Times* and *Post*, as outlined in this paper, demonstrates the value of well-resourced newspapers that have expert journalists who can follow areas of coverage that are not necessarily an immediate priority. The work of such journalists as Judith Miller and Stephen Engelberg of the *Times* and Caryle Murphy of the *Post* could be cited as an example. The question facing even the best newspapers in America, given economic pressures, is whether they can continue to afford these kinds of specialists who may be probing important issues even when they are not front-page news. As flawed as the overall coverage of terrorism might have been between 1993 and 2001, it would have been almost negligible without the expertise of these experienced, dedicated reporters. One can only hope that the *Times*, *Post* and other news outlets will continue to support this kind of work.

Finally, it behooves editorial page and OpEd editors to be sure their pages meet issues head-on, even those that run the risk of drawing criticism from super patriots and others with strong opposing views. Indeed, publishers and editors might consider expanding the space they devote to opinion pieces. A free and vigorous debate almost always serves the nation best.

Endnotes

1. Ibrahim, Youssef M., "Throughout Arab World, 20 Years of Growth of Islamic Terror Groups," *The New York Times*, March 6, 1993, p. A24.

2. Mitchell, Alison, "Letter Explained Motive in Bombing, Officials Now Say," *The New York Times*, March 28, 1993, p. A1.

3. Hedges, Chris, "Muslim Militants Share Afghan Link," *The New York Times*, March 28, 1993, p. A14.

4. Murphy, Caryle, "West Has Helped Fuel New Islamic Militancy," *The Washington Post*, May 1, 1993, p. A15.

5. Writing in *The Wall Street Journal* on May 31, 2001, Emerson, along with Daniel Pipes, probably came as close as any American journalist in predicting the events of September 11, 2001. They said, "Indeed, recent information shows that Al-Qaeda is not only planning new attacks on the U.S. but is also expanding its operational range in countries such as Jordan and Israel," p. A16.

6. During 1994, the *Post* published 54 stories that mentioned at least once each the terms "World Trade Center" and "bombing." The *Times*, not surprisingly, had a considerably larger number of stories, 182 in total.

7. Kleinfield, N.R., "Reverberations: Aftermath of a Bombing—A Special Seport; Trade Center Blast's Legacy: Security Improved, and Lost," *The New York Times*, February 20, 1994, p. A1.

8. Pipes, Daniel, "The Paranoid Style in Mideast Politics; From the Gulf War to Somalia, Fear of a Sinister Uncle Sam, *The Washington Post*, November 6, 1994, p. C1.

9. Gugliotta, Guy, and Barr, Stephen, "Preemption of Terrorists Is Urged; Government Place on 'Moderate Security Alert,' Bomb Threats Close Buildings." *The Washington Post*, April 21, 1995, p. A22.

10. Allison, Graham, "Must We Wait for the Nuclear Morning After?" *The Washington Post*, April 30, 1995, p. C7.

11. See, for example, Stern, Jessica, "Meeting with the Muj," *Bulletin of the Atomic Scientists*, January/February 2001, p. 42, and Stern, Jessica, "Pakistan's Jihad Culture," *Foreign Affairs*, November-December 2000, p. 113.

12. Graham, Bradley, "Local Authorities Train to Handle New Threat; Program Shows Emergency Crews Procedure in Germ, Chemical Strike," *The Washington Post*, January 6, 1998, p. A1.

13. Weiner, Tim, "Reno Says U.S. May Stockpile Medicine for Terrorist Attacks," *The New York Times*, April 23, 1998, p. A14.

14. Graham, Bradley, "Clinton to Order Reserves of Germ Weapon Antidotes," *The Washington Post*, May 21, 1998, p. A1.

15. Miller, Judith, "Defense Dept. to Spend Millions to Bolster Germ-Warfare Defense," *The New York Times*, May 22, 1998, p. A18.

16. Miller, Judith, and Broad, William J. "Exercise Finds U.S. Unable to Handle Germ Warfare Threat," *The New York Times*, April 26, 1998, p. A1; William J. Broad and Judith Miller, "THE WORLD: LIVE AMMO; The Threat of Germ Weapons Is Rising. Fear, Too, p. A1.

17. Suro, Roberto, "U.S. Lacking in Terrorism Defenses; Study Cites a Need to Share Intelligence," *The Washington Post,* April 24, 1998, p. A1.

18. No byline, "Military Adding 10 'Chem-Bio' Response Teams," *The Washington Post,* March 18, 1998, p. A3.

19. Lippman, Thomas W., "Clinton Pushes New U.S. Security Focus," *The Washington Post,* May 23, 1998, p. A3.

20. Fehr, Stephen C., "Major Disaster Drill Planned for D.C. Area; Focus to Be on Chemical, Germ Threats," *The Washington Post,* July 2, 1998, p. A12.

21. Petrov, Vladimir, emeritus professor of international relations at George Washington University, Letter to the Editor, *The Washington Post,* February 14, 1998, p. A28.

22. Vernon Loeb and Walter Pincus, "Bomb Suspect Has been a Target; Aides Say bin Laden Had Motive, Means to Attack Embassies," *The Washington Post,* August 13, 1998, p. A1; Kamran Khan and Pamela Constable, "Bomb Suspect Details Anti-U.S. Terror Force; Muslim Radical Said to Lead Thousands," *The Washington Post,* August 19, 1998, p. A1; Howard Schneider and Nora Boustany, "A Barrage of Criticism in Mideast; U.S. Accused of 'State Terrorism,'" *The Washington Post,* August 21, 1998, p. A1.

23. Perlez, Jane, "AFTER THE ATTACKS: IN SUDAN; A Moderate Thinks U.S. Shot Itself in Foot," *The New York Times,* August 25, 1999, p. A6.

24. Miller, Judith, and Broad, William J. "Clinton Describes Terrorism Threat for 21st Century," *The New York Times,* January 22, 1999, p. A1.

25. Charles Babington, "Clinton Plans Training for Firefighters on Terrorism," *The Washington Post,* March 16, 1999, p. A11.

26. Weiser, Benjamin, "Death Threats Against Mayor Said to Rise," *The New York Times,* October 6, 1999, p. B1.

27. Rosenfeld, Stephen, "Hard Choices in Homeland Defense," *The Washington Post,* March 5, 1999, p. A33.

28. Cooper, Kenneth J. "Muslim Militants Threaten American Lives," *The Washington Post,* March 7, 1999, p. A21; Loeb, Vernon, "Bin Laden Still Seen as Threat; U.S. Harassment Campaign May Backfire, Boost Fugitive's Image," *The Washington Post,* July 29, 1999.

29. Weiner, Tim "U.S. Hard Put to Find Proof bin Laden Directed Attacks," *The New York Times,* April 13, 1999, p A1.

30. Melton, R.H. "Panel Criticizes U.S. Anti-Terrorism Preparedness," *The Washington Post,* December 16, 1999.

31. Adams, Lorraine, and Vise, David A. "Border Arrests Yield Little Calm; Scope of Possible Terrorism Threat Remains Unknown; Probe Is Far-Flung," *The Washington Post,* January 10, 2000, p. A3.

32. Dobbs, Michael, "An Obscure Chief in U.S. War on Terror," *The Washington Post,* April 2, 2000, p. A1.

33. Lancaster, John, "U.S. Study Finds Terrorist Shift to South Asia, *The Washington Post,* May 2, 2000, p. A24.

34. Vise, David A. "Panel Calls for Creating Counterterrorism Agency," *The Washington Post,* December 15, 2000, p. A8.

35. Loeb, Vernon, "Global Threats Against U.S. Will Rise, Report Predicts; Experts Assess Future World Conflicts, Economic Trends," *The Washington Post,* December 18, 2000, p. A3.

36. Loeb, Vernon, "Terrorism Panel Faulted for Exaggeration," *The Washington Post,* June 23, 2000, p. A29.

37. The Hart-Rudman Commission (The U.S. Commission on National Security/21st Century) was one of three blue-ribbon commissions studying the threat of terrorism to the U.S. The others were the so-called Bremer Commission (named for Ambassador L. Paul Bremer and officially the National Commission on Terrorism) and the Gilmore Commission (named for former Virgina Governor James S. Gilmore III and officially the Advisory Panel to Assess Domestic Response Capabilities for Terrorism Involving Weapons of Mass Destruction). The Bremer group issued a report in June 2000, the Gilmore Commission issued reports in December 1999 and 2000, and Hart-Rudman issued reports in 1999, 2000 and 2001. All made recommendations for improvements in federal government organization and policy, though Hart-Rudman was arguably the most comprehensive.

38. Engelberg, Stephen, "One Man and a Global Web of Violence," *The New York Times,* January 14, 2001, p. A1.

39. Miller, Judith, "Killing for the Glory of God, In a Land Far From Home," *The New York Times,* January 16, 2001, p. A1.

40. Schieffer made the remark at a conference at the Brookings Institution in Washington, D.C., on February 6, 2002, "Rudman-Hart Commission Warns of Terrorist Attack: Why Did the News Media Ignore It?" Brigitte L. Nacos of Columbia University, who has done extensive research on media coverage of terrorism, including television, noted in a March 2002 paper, "Most news organizations (prior to 9/11) simply did not buy the premise that international terrorism was a major threat unless there were specific alerts for explicit time periods as was the case with the Y2K predictions."

41. These were keywords for the search used most frequently in this research.

42. Weiser, Benjamin, "Trial Poked Holes in Image of bin Laden's Terror Group," *The New York Times,* May 31, 2001, p. A1.

43. Nexis search using "terrorism" or "terrorist" and "threat" for each newspaper.

44. Crenshaw, Martha, "Terrorism, Strategies and Grand Strategies: Domestic or Structural Constraints?" presented at the International Studies Association Convention, March 24–27, 2002, New Orleans, LA.

45. Sloan, Stephen, "Terrorism: How Vulnerable Is the United States," *Terrorism: National Security Policy and the Home Front,* The Strategic Studies Institute of the U.S. Army War College, May 1995.

46. Huntington, Samuel P., *The Clash of Civilizations,* Touchstone Books, 1996, p. 184.

47. Carter, Bill, and Barringer, Felicity, "Networks Agree to U.S. Request to Edit Future bin Laden Tapes," *The New York Times,* October 11, 2001, p. A1.

48. Among the pieces done in *The Atlantic Monthly* were: "Thinking about Terrorism" by Conor Cruise O'Brien, June 1986; "The Roots of Muslim Rage" by Bernard Lewis, September 1990; "Blowback" by Mary Anne Weaver, May 1996; "The Counterterrorist Myth," by Reuel Marc Gerecht, July/August 2001.

Author's note: The title of this paper, "While America Slept," appeared as a cover line in *Time Magazine*'s edition of May 27, 2002. For the record, as my colleagues at the Shorenstein Center can attest, I chose this title for my paper at the time of our first internal presentations in early February.

Covering September 11 and Its Consequences
A Comparative Study of the Press in America, India and Pakistan

Ramindar Singh

The September 11 attack on the World Trade Center in New York confronted the press with a supreme challenge in America where the earth-shaking event happened and in South Asia which continued to experience violent aftershocks months later.

September 11 affected Americans in a most fundamental way; it forced them to re-assess their role in the world and question why they become a target for disaffected groups in faraway lands. Similar reassessments were underway on the other side of the globe, with the press in India and Pakistan asking a different set of questions about how this event would affect and alter the lives of people in the South Asia region.

This chapter is an attempt to analyze how the press in America responded to the need to understand and report what happened on September 11, analyze why it happened and to present this information and analysis in a professional manner untainted by emotion, sentiment or jingoism. Simultaneously it examines how the press in India and Pakistan handled a similar challenge in their region.

It would be tempting, while analyzing the performance of the press in these three countries, to cover a wide spectrum of newspapers and television stations. But to make this exercise manageable, I have limited the scope of these inquiries to one leading newspaper from each country, though my general observations about the press in each country are based on an overview of local press there. I have specifically examined *The New York Times* as representative of the American press, the *Times of India* of the Indian press, and from Pakistan I have studied *Dawn*, the authoritative Karachi paper which in my view, represents the best of Pakistani journalism. This limited sample opens this analysis to the danger of over-generalization, but I hope these findings broadly reflect journalism trends in these countries.

One trend that emerged clearly is that location affects perspective, and perception: What you see depends on where you stand. The picture of the world that you see from the vantage point of New York or Washington is radically different from the view one gets in New Delhi or Islamabad. Geography not only colors the picture but often transforms it.

For example, let us look at how the press in the US, India and Pakistan has portrayed three major players in this drama: George Bush, Pakistan's leader General Pervez Musharraf and Indian Prime Minister Atal Behari Vajpayee. How these leaders appear to their home audiences is radically different from the image you get from afar, and distance distorts the image as you move away from home turf.

America's view of itself and its president, as reflected by the American press, is quite different from the view one sees from South Asia. It's not only a different perspective, but a totally different picture. Within South Asia too, the view from Islamabad as filtered through the eyes of the Pakistani press is quite different from what is projected by the Indian press. And there are subtle but interesting shifts in the way in which India and Pakistan, traditionally hostile neighbours, see their respective leaders in the light of their altered relationships with the US.

Before September 11, George W. Bush was regarded by large numbers of his countrymen as a wimp, an intellectual pygmy. I remember the poster that greeted me when I walked into one office at Harvard University at the start of the fall term in September 2001: it portrayed George Bush as Alfred E. Neuman, the moronic mascot of MAD magazine. The nationwide call to arms after September 11 changed all that, particularly after Bush's stirring address to Congress on September 21. That speech transformed Bush from a lack-luster, tentative leader into Mr. President. Several months later, in January 2002, 83 percent of Americans still viewed him as a wartime president who led his country effectively up until the ouster of the Taliban regime in Afghanistan. Even though his presidency was rescued from ordinariness by momentous events, he retained tremendous popular support at home and at one point his approval rating had soared to 92 percent.

It was inevitable that the press in America, increasingly sensitive in recent years to market sentiments, would let its treatment of the president and their judgment of his actions be affected by these approval ratings. Like members of Congress, journalists allowed themselves to be swept along in the countrywide upsurge of nationalistic sentiment. For nearly three months after the fall of the World Trade Center, they raised no questions about the missteps and omissions of the Bush administration: The president was allowed to get away with policies for which his predecessors would have been flayed.

It's not that the President was consciously portrayed as a heroic figure to cover up his lack of charisma or other infirmities. But by consciously withholding criticism and unquestioningly applauding his actions and speeches, and splashing his photographs all over the news columns, the press in the US contributed to turning him into a virtual hero.

Move away from the US and the view changes, and also the tone of reporting. The American press had begun to see Bush in a new light, but this personality transformation is not reflected in India's leading English-language newspaper, the *Times of India*, a proAmerican paper which proclaims its empathy with American values and beliefs. The *Times of India* remains cynical about George W. and the policies of the American government. And in the view of the *Times of India* editorial writers, Mr. Bush has yet to transcend his failings: they still see him as a bumbling dyslexic, a "Saturday Night Live" caricature co-authored by Jay Leno and Conan O'Brien. In the American press Bush had gained stature; to the *Times of India* he was Rodney Dangerfield playing John Wayne.

Nowhere is this illustrated better than in a comic strip *Dubyaman*, that the *Times of India* has run every day since September, initially on the front page and later on the international page. In this spoof of Superman, a weepy Dubyaman goes

around trying to save the world but has to be saved from embarrassment by his sturdy sidekicks Colin Powell and Dick Cheney who read to him every night to improve his English and geography.

This cynical Indian view of the American leadership and its lofty-sounding objectives in the war against terrorism is due in part to the avowedly anti-war policy of the *Times of India*. In both cases it appears to be a case of the wish fathering the thought. American opinion, its confidence badly shaken, *wanted* to see him as a wartime leader in the hour of crisis and therefore *invested* him with these qualities. India's snobbish intellectuals saw him as a lightweight and no demonstration of firepower in Afghanistan could convince them to see him as anything else. The overblown caricature painted by the *Times of India* is as much of an exaggeration as the heroic dimensions attributed to Bush by the American press. But by continuing to satirize him as Dubyaman, the *Times of India* made the mistake of persisting with a stereotype whose relevance had ended with September 11. Some commentators on the *Times of India* staff who had earlier been trenchant critics of the US changed their tune and started seeing benefits for India in the American intervention in Afghanistan, but the lasting impression that the *Times of India* left on the minds of its readers is of Bush as Dubyaman. The medium (comic strip) had become the message.

The View From Islamabad

The Pakistani press was more practical: it virtually ignored the personality of Bush and concentrated instead on the US president's tremendous power, exercised through political and military actions, to alter the lives and futures of the people of Pakistan and its neighbors. Unlike their Indian counterparts, leading Pakistani commentators were reluctant to parody Bush: it's difficult to see someone as a joker when that joker is holding a gun to your head. So the columnists of *Dawn* vented their vitriol on their own leader, General Pervez Musharraf, and his military predecessors, whose Taliban policies led to Pakistan's humiliation and whose involvement in Kashmir terrorism led to a brink-of-war military standoff with India.

It wasn't always so. In the summer of 2001 Musharraf was a hero to scribes at home. He had returned triumphant after a summit meeting at Agra with the Indian Prime Minister; he was generally seen in Pakistan and India as having staged a media coup by going on Indian TV and defending the jihad in Kashmir as a freedom struggle. And even though the summit had collapsed because of his outspokenness he was, by and large, lionized by the Pakistan press as a tough-talking patriot who had told the Indians where they got off.

But in American eyes he was regarded as something of a villain, a usurper. Before September 11 the US government and media painted of Musharraf in negative terms. Most stories in the American press about Musharraf began with a judgmental description of Musharraf as "Pakistan's military ruler who captured power in a coup two years ago. . ." He was virtually shunned by the international community, and treated as an outcast by the United States, Britain and the countries of the Commonwealth.

Time, terrorism, and the Taliban changed all that.

September 11 provided General Musharraf with an opportunity to dramatically end Pakistan's isolation as well as his own. The moment Pakistan joined America's War on Terrorism, Pakistan's status changed from that of a virtual pariah to a friend. Overnight Musharraf became America's most-quoted ally, second only to Tony Blair. This turnaround was captured by Celia Dugger of *The New York Times* who wrote (on November 30, 2001) that "Pervez Musharraf, the military ruler who has been transformed from a dictator scorned by the West, to the darling of the American-led anti-terror coalition."

In the month before September 11, *The New York Times* had mentioned him in only ten stories, mostly in negative terms. In the month after September 11, he figured in *New York Times* stories 70 times, almost always with sympathetic references to the difficulties he was facing because of his decision to join the alliance against terrorism.

Reviled in the West but lauded at home before he jettisoned the Taliban, Musharraf now found himself being applauded abroad but pilloried at home. The same Islamists and right-wing radicals who had lionized Musharraf for his support to their Jihad against India in Kashmir, saw his abandonment of Osama bin Laden, the big-daddy of all jihadis, as a stab in the back. Now he was a quisling, a puppet of the Americans, not only by people in the streets but also by independent columnists. Ayaz Amir has repeatedly argued in *Dawn* that Musharraf sold Pakistan short by his eagerness to jump onto the American bandwagon.

"It is a moot point what crumbled faster," he wrote, "the twin towers of the World Trade Centre or the imposing ramparts of Pakistani pride? Just a few threatening statements from President Bush and General Powell and Pakistan's military government, usually so tough at home, conceded everything the Americans were asking for."

USA Today reported with barely concealed glee that the general's opponents inside Pakistan had taken to calling him Busharraf.

But to be fair to the general, his change of heart had come at the point of a gun. Patrick Tyler of *The New York Times* narrates (Nov. 13) the dramatic circumstances of the general's conversion: "Within 48 hours of September's terrorist strikes, Secretary of State Colin Powell telephoned General Pervez Musharraf of Pakistan and said, 'General, you have got to make a choice.' After several conversations with Powell, *New York Times* columnist Bill Keller narrates (Nov. 25) how Powell's "most trusted deputy Richard Armitage had already called in the Pakistani

intelligence chief . . . (and) delivered a seven-point, with-us-or-against-us ultimatum calling on the Pakistanis to close their border with Afghanistan, open their
intelligence files and provide access for American forces." In the memorable words
of the Godfather, the general had been made an offer he could not refuse.

Writing on September 14, *Dawn*'s Ayaz Amir confirmed that Armitage had
threatened "it was for Pakistan to decide whether it wanted to live in the 21st century
or the Stone Age." What precisely was Pakistan afraid of, he asks? "That the US in
blind anger would make an example of us, flatten our airfields, destroying our installations, taking out our nuclear strategic assets? We are being told to be wise. Wisdom
does not lie in acting cravenly . . . there is no reason for us to sully national honour
by behaving in too supine a manner . . . a measure of self-serving calculation is
involved in the decision General Musharraf has taken on behalf of the nation . . . "

In subsequent columns Amir applauded the leaders of Iran and Lebanon for
showing more guts in the face of American bullying. In his November 23 column,
"Who's held a gun to the nation's head?", Amir challenged Musharraf's contention
that "a tiny minority of unenlightened, obscurantist and backward-looking religious extremists" were holding the majority of Pakistanis hostage.

> . . . after the change of political climate in Pakistan it is near-treason to sug-
> gest that prior to September 11 General Musharraf subscribed to the same
> philosophy he now so stoutly berates. His own words on numerous occa-
> sions testify to the fact that on Afghanistan, Kashmir and the great strategic
> space provided to Pakistan by its nuclear capability his views were no differ-
> ent from that of the Beards (mullahs). Both sides, the army and the Beards,
> swore by the same strategic orthodoxy.

> It goes to General Musharraf's credit that he changed his mind quickly when
> circumstances changed . . . Even so, he could try putting Pakistan's peculiar
> brand of obscurantism in perspective. When the very bastions of national
> security are infected by the spirit of holy war, does obscurantism reside in
> the madrassas or in the bastions standing guard against the enemy?

> . . . Who held whom hostage? It was not the madrassas which forced any gov-
> ernment to support the Taliban. This was a decision taken by the national
> security establishment in pursuit of "strategic depth" and similar notions
> which have characterised our Afghan policy. The madrassas had it not in
> their power to hold the nation hostage. It was the army and the intelligence
> services which brooked no assault on the "obscurantist elements" because
> they were seen as serving the "national interest"—a bogey in whose name
> every last lunacy can be justified.

What is clear to Ayaz Amir is clear also to the Bush administration: that the
general was grandstanding, making a virtue out of necessity. So while paying fulsome

tributes to the general in public, Powell and Defense Secretary Rumsfeld did not allow Musharraf's objections to change the way in which the war in Afghanistan was being prosecuted.

Musharraf first declared that no American troops would be based on Pakistani soil; a few days later he opened his airports for use by American helicopters and other aircraft. In December 2001 and January 2002 he even permitted American troops to extend their hot pursuit of the Taliban into Pakistani territory. By January 2002, he had also permitted the American/allied forces a permanent base in Karachi.

He made it clear in October 2001, he would like the bombing of Afghanistan to last no more than a few days. It went on until January 2002. He had asked the US to suspend bombing during the holy month of Ramadan. The bombing continued.

When he visited the US in November 2001, he pleaded with President Bush and Colin Powell to release the 60 F16 planes whose shipment had been banned after sanctions were imposed on Pakistan. His request was rejected by Powell. He warned there would be chaos unless the Northern Alliance was stopped from entering Kabul, but when he returned home a few days later it was in time to see Northern Alliance troops pouring into Kabul.

This prompted the press to note that Pakistan's red carpet was fraying at the edges. On November 16, Amir wrote: "with the Northern alliance entering Kabul. . . . the mood in Islamabad is anything but celebratory. . . . Overestimating our importance , we had convinced ourselves that our frontline status gave us a virtual veto over the shape of things to come in Afghanistan. If not that, then at least our objections regarding the Northern Alliance would be respected."

"We forgot that the Americans were working to a different deadline. . . . Pakistan is reduced to delivering dire warnings of further strife in Afghanistan. Let us express our fears by all means. But with no leverage to back up our warnings we only underline our impotence . . . At the root of our distress lies our strange obsession with Afghanistan. Why don't we leave Afghanistan alone . . ."

So as the war went well for America, the outlook for Pervez Musharraf kept getting bleaker at home. Reporting from Islamabad on November 24, John Burns, in *The New York Times,* encapsulated the general's predicament: "the sense that the United States has failed to keep its side of the deal is rife. . . . General Musharraf has bitten his tongue. . . . He does so knowing that his own standing in Pakistan would be seriously undermined if he were to say that the United States had broken a promise to him."

The *Times of India* construed these rebuffs as deliberate punishment. Washington correspondent Chidananda Rajghatta argued on November 28 that some of the rebuffs were intended and that in all but name, the US was at war with Pakistan:

Despite all the protestations about military ruler General Pervez Musharraf's "bold and courageous stand" and Islamabad's status as a front-line ally, there is a growing sense in Washington that Pakistan has worked against US interests in Afghanistan. There is also anger in sections of the administration over what is seen as Pakistani perfidy over issues ranging from deployment of its troops, agents and private militia in Afghanistan to its dangerous game of nuclear weapons proliferation.

As a result, the Bush administration has begun to quietly punish Pakistan even while publicly upholding a facade of goodwill, just as Islamabad is also maintaining a pretense of cooperation in the fight against terrorism while pursuing its own agenda. Several incidents bear this out, including the latest episode involving two prominent Pakistani nuclear scientists, who have now been detained again at Washington's insistence over suspicion that they were involved in planning an "Anthrax Bomb."

The US has also allowed the Northern Alliance to decimate those euphemistically known as "foreign fighters"—who it now turns out are mostly Pakistani irregulars and jihadists with some serving army personnel and agents directing them.

Western journalists in the region have now exposed the smokescreen that referred to these fighters as "Arab, Chechen and Pakistani," by reporting that they are almost exclusively Pakistani. In some cases, Washington itself has joined in by using air power to bomb the Pakistani fighters.

While publicly continuing to endorse and applaud the military regime of General Musharraf—to the extent of ignoring his announcement that he will continue to be Pakistan's president even after the proposed October 2002 elections—Washington has begun to ignore a growing list of Pakistani gripes . . .

In each case, the US has gone ahead and done pretty much what suits its war aims, forcing Musharraf to fall in line and handle the domestic fall-out.

. . . In one instance at least, accounts by Northern Alliance fighters that they executed scores of Pakistani fighters "before the eyes of US military personnel," after they refused to surrender, have enraged Islamabad. . . .

The strange dissonance between the official positions of the two sides and the private differences is the subject of much discussion in Washington . . . "It's like a bad marriage. Or like two colleagues who mistrust each other but are forced to work together," a Congressional aide who works on regional issues said.

The View From New Delhi

The third player in this drama, Indian Prime Minister Vajpayee, was for the first few months pushed to the sidelines primarily because India was seen as a marginal player, not directly involved with the great events unfolding in Afghanistan. After initially sulking over America's coddling of Pakistan, Vajpayee later felt it was inevitable that the US alliance of convenience with Pakistan would come in for re-examination. And after that happened, Vajpayee turned the heat up on Pakistan, to bring international attention back to the fact that instead of being viewed as part of the solution to the problem of terrorism, Pakistan was part of the terrorism problem in South Asia.

After joining the alliance against terrorism Musharraf immediately brought Kashmir into the equation, saying he had aligned with the US to protect Pakistan's interests regarding Kashmir and its nuclear assets. And India had reacted with a show of pique when foreign minister Jaswant Singh cancelled a meeting with Senate Foreign Relations Committee Chairman Joe Biden on a visit to Washington. South Asia expert at the Brookings Institution Stephen Cohen thinks India was seething. In an interview published on December 2, 2001 he said:

> Many Indians resent the manner in which Pakistan has been transformed from being part of the problem to its new status as an essential element in the solution. I think the Indians seethed with anger as they saw US rebuilding a relationship with the one country, Pakistan, that they identified fully with international terrorism, and seeing the US trying to accommodate their other strategic rival, China, which is, incidentally, the real winner in this whole affair.

Seething is too strong a word but it serves to illustrate India's initial disappointment with the West's willingness to forget Pakistan's role in supporting terrorism in Kashmir. But India pinned its hopes on the American president fulfilling his commitment "to go after terrorism in all its forms all over the world . . . to destroy it without geographic constraints and without time limits." Colin Powell reiterated President Bush's pledge, adding that this included "terrorism which affects India. The war against terrorism can leave no room for exceptions...There are no good terrorists and bad terrorists." Powell had told Bill Keller (*New York Times Magazine*, November 25) that one of his main objectives in the future was to defuse the explosive border dispute in Kashmir.

The Indian prime minister kept away from the spotlight hoping that American leaders would be true to their words. India also received with great happiness the news that the US was playing a significant role in securing Pakistan's nuclear weapons following the arrest and interrogation of half a dozen retired Pakistan nuclear scientists who had been traveling to Afghanistan and meeting with Osama bin Laden.

What's more, after the embarrassing collapse of its Afghanistan policy, sensible voices in Pakistan have begun to raise the question whether its Kashmir policy needs to be reassessed. One such voice is Amir, who feels that Pakistan "must recognize that after Afghanistan the freedom struggle in Kashmir is bound to come under greater American scrutiny. In the new global climate now forming there will be less patience for such extra-territorial organizations as Lashkar-i-Taiba and Jaish-i-Muhammad."

"So how best to support the Kashmir cause? By letting the Kashmiris carry on their own struggle or by raising the flag of militancy within Pakistan? Sooner rather than later we will have to answer this question."

The answer to that question was provided by the US, which banned these organizations after the December 13 attack on the Indian Parliament by militants suspected to belong to these organizations.

So, with Bush and Powell echoing India's sentiments and Pakistani commentators calling for a reassessment of Pakistan's Kashmir policy, Vajpayee was content to wait on the sidelines. It is little wonder, therefore, that between September 11 and November 21, when both of them visited New York and met with Bush and other world leaders attending the United Nations General Assembly session that Musharraf made it to the pages of *The New York Times* 173 times versus only 32 times for Vajpayee. But Vajpayee realized that after America's immediate objectives were achieved in Afghanistan, the US ardor for Musharraf would cool.

The Nuclear Question

And cool it did, primarily because of US worries about unsecured Pakistani nuclear materials passing into the hands of Al Qaeda. The US appears to have intervened directly to ensure the security of Pakistan's nuclear weapons.

Battalions of reporters and analysts who had been scouring the tinderbox region of South and Central Asia since the start of the bombing of Taliban and Al Qaeda hideouts in Afghanistan began on October 7 missed the significance of this and other big stories unfolding right under their noses in Pakistan.

Consumed with immediate concerns, the bombing of Afghanistan and the pursuit of Al Qaeda, few reporters looked ahead to what these actions could mean in the near future when Al Qaeda jihadis on the run from Kabul, Kunduz and Kandahar would sneak into Pakistan and ultimately into Kashmir to continue their jihad there. Apart from a couple of articles, *The New York Times* too did not see the implications for South Asia as a result of the rout of Al Qaeda. The likelihood of the flight of the Taliban leading to increased India-Pakistan tensions was foreseen at the Shorenstein Center's Theodore White seminar and again at the New Directions for News seminar organized by the Nieman Foundation around the end of October and early November, 2001.

Given the prevailing circumstances, there was only one place for the Taliban to run to, Pakistan, and given the existing connection between Al Qaeda training camps and the Kashmiri insurgency, it was almost pre-ordained that Pakistan would allow/encourage the fleeing Taliban to wend their way to Kashmir to continue the proxy war/jihad against India.

Any student of sub-continental history could have predicted this possibility, but few among the Pakistan-based journalists covering the War against Terrorism strayed from their pre-determined beat. It's only after the world's biggest concentration of military forces actually happened on the India–Pakistan border in mid-December that these journalists took notice.

Similarly unnoticed was the nuclear development relating to America's direct intervention to prevent Pakistan's nuclear weapons from passing into the hands of terrorists. This story too had been there all along in the shape of small, unconnected bits of information floating around in the newspapers of Pakistan and the United States. All it needed was for someone to piece this information together from tell-tale items which appeared regularly in the columns of *Dawn*. But American and Indian reporters either didn't see the story or deliberately avoided writing it as disclosure would hurt the interests of America, Pakistan and India. It was a development which raised the chilling specter of political instability in Pakistan since every Pakistani regime to date has projected the possession of nuclear weapons as a matter of national pride and as a security against India.

Understandably, neither Pakistani nor U.S. officials have so far officially admitted this has happened but the first hint of this development came from none other than the Pakistan Foreign Minister Abdul Sattar himself.

Addressing a press conference in Islamabad on November 1, Sattar disclosed that Pakistan had accepted an offer made by the US Secretary of State Colin Powell for training Pakistani experts "for security and protection of nuclear assets." His choice of words in the next sentence is very telling. He said "Pakistani experts would be apprised of the *security measures being applied by the United States* (emphasis added)."

If Sattar is to be believed, even before Pakistani personnel had been informed or trained, the US was *applying security measures* with regard to Pakistan's nuclear assets.

Three factors appear to have forced Sattar to make this admission. One was a spate of stories in the American press suggesting that a coup by fundamentalist generals sympathetic to the Taliban and Al Qaeda may unseat Musharraf and hand over nuclear material to Osama bin Laden.

Musharraf quickly scotched any talk of a coup in an interview with *USA Today*, which carried alongside its Musharraf interview a report of a Gallup poll in Pakistan that suggested that the majority of the Pakistanis supported his actions.

(The parent Gallup organization in the US quickly denounced the Pakistan poll as unreliable.)

The second was an unexpected, tongue-in-cheek endorsement by the Indian Defense Minister George Fernandes on October 30 that Pakistan's nuclear assets were in safe hands. "Those concerned with Pakistan's nuclear weapons are responsible people," Fernandes said.

Surprisingly, Fernandes' certificate raised no eyebrows. Sattar, however, appears to have got the message that the Indian Defense Minister may spill the beans, so, according to a report in Karachi's newspaper, Sattar "surprised" local and foreign correspondents by walking down to the Foreign Office briefing hall to read out a statement, which said, among other things, that "Pakistan's strategic assets are under foolproof custodial controls" without specifying whose custody it was. After paying tribute to the professionalism of the Pakistani armed forces, he said any apprehension that these assets "might fall into the hands of extremists was entirely imaginary."

He then proceeded to mention the offer made by Colin Powell to train Pakistani experts. He explained that the Pakistani experts would be apprised of the security measures being applied by the United States.

The third reason why Sattar made this admission was to deny a story in *The New Yorker* in which Seymour Hersh suggested that US special operations troops were training with Israeli commandos for a possible mission into Pakistan to "take out" Pakistan's nuclear warheads to prevent them from being transferred to Al Qaeda.

Now, Sattar is a seasoned diplomat who has spent several decades in the Pakistan Foreign Service and has held the most prestigious postings that the service had to offer. He chooses his words with extreme care and precision, as I discovered when I interviewed him when he was Pakistan's ambassador to India in the early 1990s. He is very particular when speaking on the record to journalists and has an uncanny knack of conveying the precise sense of what he wants to communicate.

His choice of words is telling and significant. He talks of "custodial control" of the nuclear assets, leaving open the interpretation that the custodial control was being exercised by someone else. He said "dedicated formations of specially equipped forces have been deployed for ensuring the security of Pakistan nuclear installations and assets" without specifying whether these specially equipped forces were all Pakistani or there were elements of outside forces that had come in to guard these nuclear assets. Interestingly, the words used by George Fernandes two days earlier are telling: they reveal as much as they conceal. "I would like to give them credit. Those concerned with Pakistan's nuclear weapons are responsible people," he said.

On the same day as Sattar made the statement in Islamabad, US Deputy Secretary for Disarmament John Bolton quoted George Fernandes to quell doubts about the safety of Pakistan's nuclear weapons.

It is intriguing how, all of a sudden, the US and India, which had been leaking like crazy to the press about their misgivings about the safety of Pakistan's nukes and the likelihood of their being transferred to Al Qaeda, started reassuring all and sundry that they were in safe hands. Were they acting in tandem?

Just as Abdul Sattar has a reputation for precision in his choice of words, Fernandes too has a reputation for speaking out of turn and revealing things that cause embarrassment to his government and other governments.

Some years ago he let slip in an interview the government's assessment that India's main strategic threat came from China rather than Pakistan. The Indian government was forced to say that these were Fernandes' personal views and the Chinese government objected.

Three years ago, after Indian and Pakistan military clashed at Kargil, Fernandes let it be known that this military misadventure was the handiwork of the Army chief Musharraf and that the then Prime Minister Nawaz Sharif was not aware of it. That too was confirmed by later events.

It could well be that on October 30 too he was trying to embarrass Musharraf and this is why Sattar took the unusual step on November 1 of coming down to the foreign office briefing in Islamabad and disclosing that the Americans were applying security measures to Pakistan's nuclear assets.

Powell's offer of help in securing these assets was disclosed after the US secretary of state visited Islamabad and Delhi on October 15, but it probably was an undisclosed part of the seven-point ultimatum that the US had issued to Pakistan in the first few days after September 11. Bob Woodward's behind-the-scenes revelations in *The Washington Post* in the end of January 2002 confirmed that the no-choice-but-to-comply ultimatum was sanctioned by Bush himself.

Did the ultimatum mention nuclear weapons security? *Dawn*'s columnist, Ayaz Amir, respected equally in Pakistan and India, appears to think that it did. He made this connection in a piece published on September 14:

> He said Armitage had threatened "it was for Pakistan to decide whether it wanted to live in the 21st century or the Stone Age. What precisely was Pakistan afraid of? That the US in blind anger would make an example of us, flatten our airfields, destroying our installations, taking out our nuclear strategic assets?

By the time the bombing of Afghanistan began on October 7, Musharraf had, according to a report in *The Washington Post*, ordered an "emergency redeployment" of the nuclear arsenal to at least six new locations. He also began relocating critical nuclear components. The threat to his prized weapons was patently manifest. He used this opportunity to also reshuffle his top generals and create a strategic planning division within the nuclear program.

The *Sunday Times* of London went so far as to suggest that he had even thought of moving his nuclear warheads for safekeeping to a friendly neighbor—China, which had clandestinely aided Pakistan's nuclear weapons and missile development programs. Further confirmation of this was provided by the arrival in Islamabad on December 2 of two Italian arms control scientists, to "prepare a report on the status of nuclear security in Pakistan" as blandly reported by *Dawn*:

> Sources said the visiting scientists, Prof Paolo Cotta-Ramusino and Prof Maurizio Martellini, would be looking at certain key questions relating to safety of Pakistan's nuclear weapons, the percentage of nuclear weapons that are assembled, effects of the September 11 attacks and the Afghan crisis on the nuclear posture of Pakistan, Pakistan's reaction to possible Indian attack and the public perception of the nuclear weapons. The report would later be submitted to the Italian government, they said.
>
> The scientists, visiting under the auspices of the foreign ministry of Italy, have held deliberations with foreign ministry officials and think-tanks to assess the safety of nuclear weapons and the risks of proliferation of weapons of mass destruction to terrorists and rogue states, the sources said . . .

The newspaper quoted from a report prepared by the two scientists which said:

> The situation has raised serious concerns about the possibility that terrorist groups have acquired weapons of mass destruction or may be striving to acquire such weapons. . . .

It then went on to comment that some of the questions being asked by the two "have raised concern in the security establishment."

Here then was Pakistan's leading English-language newspaper reporting that two European scientists were going around the country questioning Pakistani scientists about the extent to which the country's nuclear assets were weaponized and whether some of these weapons could have been passed on to Al Qaeda terrorists.

The Pakistan government did not deny this report or its contents just as there had been no denial of the Sattar statement that the United States was applying security measures to Pakistan's nuclear assets.

The United States has apparently gone about the task of verifying the status and number of Pakistan's nuclear weapons in a roundabout but clever manner calculated to save Musharraf from embarrassment at a time when America still needs his help to sort out the mess in Afghanistan. Just as the Bush administration had used the good offices of British Prime Minister Tony Blair to convince the international alliance about the evidence against Osama bin Laden and used a representative of the United Nations Secretary General to cobble together an alternative government for Afghanistan, in the same way it appears to have drafted two of Europe's best known and energetic disarmament experts to help verify the status and disposition of Pakistan's nuclear weapons. More remarkable is the fact that a Pakistani newspaper was allowed to report this by the military government in Islamabad.

The two scientists on the team are known campaigners for disarmament. Maurizio Martellini is the Secretary General of the Landau Network-Centro Volta, based in Como near Milan, which, according to the Centro's website, collaborates with UNESCO and the Italian Ministry of Foreign Affairs in promoting "research programs in science and international security, including proliferation of weapons of mass destruction, disarmament. . . . and use and misuse of biotechnologies."

The other scientist, Paolo Cotta Ramusino, was the Secretary General of the Italian Union of Scientists for Disarmament (USPID). Centro Volta and USPID work closely with the Non Proliferation Project of the Carnegie Endowment for International Peace in Washington. Both Martellini and Ramusino know Abdul Sattar, who attended one of their disarmament-related seminars in Como in May 1999.

The scope of their inquiries in Pakistan left nothing to the imagination. One need only quote a few paragraphs from the report published on December 6, 2001:

> . . . in terms of nuclear proliferation risks the scientists are exploring the possible links of Pakistani nuclear scientists with the Afghan Taliban and the Arab Afghans in the past and present scenarios, effectiveness of control over Pakistani fissile material storage and production facilities, possible transfer of illicit nuclear material through Pakistan and Afghanistan and the effectiveness of control of Pakistan's radioactive sources and their potential illicit traffic.

> They said that in terms of chemical and biological weapons the scientists have questions about effective control of materials of concern for chemical and biological weapons transfer and diffusion, Pakistan/Afghan border in recent history and transfer of illicit biological, chemical agents and dual use equipment through the border.

> Some of the questions being asked relate to transfer of nuclear scientists and experts to Afghanistan or any other country and the impact of recent events on the scientific community, particularly on the community of scientists involved in military and defence activities. The sources said the scientists would also report the impact of Pakistan's nuclear programme on the role of Islamic countries in the international arena and whether Pakistan's nuclearization has contributed to any change in the role of the Islamic countries.

Are these then the "security measures being applied by the United States," which Sattar had spoken of on November 1? It sounds suspiciously so, and the Landau Network-Centro Volta team was sent in to confirm that the measures were still in place.

It is therefore not surprising that the Indian defense minister should express happiness that "those concerned with Pakistan's nuclear weapons are responsible people": he probably knows that these "concerned, responsible people" are not Pakistanis.

Subsequent developments on the India/Pakistan border since mid-December, leading to the biggest and most dangerous military face-off on the subcontinent in the last 30 years, confirm this hypothesis. India's aggressive rhetoric and military drumbeating, which is totally out of character with its mild conduct toward its neighbors in the past few decades, would appear to suggest that India realizes that it can fight and win a conventional war with Pakistan now that the nuclear factor has possibly been neutralized. Hence the massive military mobilization on the border and also the January 25 test-firing of its Agni ballistic missile at a time when the world community was counseling restraint.

Just a few years ago, in 1998, when the two armies clashed at Kargil, India resisted the temptation to expand the Kargil confrontation into a general war partly because of the danger of Pakistan's nuclear weapons. Now, hardly a day goes by without a statement by the prime minister, or the home minister, or defense minister or foreign minister saying that India is prepared to go to war. Apart from putting pressure on the United States to pull India's chestnuts out of the fire lit by terrorists from across the Kashmir border, these statements also indicate a genuine readiness on the part of India's political leadership to fight a conventional war with Pakistan because the nuclear risk has now been either eliminated or minimized.

There are a large number of people in India who think that this aggressive posture is justified after the December 13 attack on the Indian parliament by militants strongly suspected to be linked to Pakistan-based agencies. The popular support for this political belligerence is what scares world leaders like US Secretary of State Colin Powell and brings them rushing to the subcontinent when such threats as India's are aired. After September 11, the definition of self-defense used by the US to bomb the Taliban in Afghanistan has changed the rules of international behavior. It is easier for countries like India, itself threatened by terrorism, to say if the US could bomb Afghanistan which provided sanctuary to Al Qaeda, how can India be blamed for wanting to take out the staging posts in Pakistan which are sending terrorists into its territory?

It is equally possible that having neutralized Pakistan's nuclear option, Powell feels it is incumbent upon the US to protect Pakistan from a military defeat at the hands of India.

This brings me to the question of why all this has gone virtually unreported. Is it because the US press believes the country is at war and has therefore unquestioningly accepted "war-time" restraints on reporting sought by the Bush administration?

Since the early days after September 11, much of the American press had convinced itself that since the nation was at war, it became the patriotic duty of the press not to dilute that war effort. For the bulk of the press this meant not criticizing the administration for what it was doing and, luckily for the administration, accepting unquestioningly all that the administration was putting out. Immediately after September 11 it appeared that the American press, caught up in the nation's grief over the loss of several thousand lives in the WTC bombing, had suspended disbelief and the kind of skeptical questioning that is one of the basic functions of a free press.

There were several results of this suspension of disbelief. Having allowed itself to be co-opted into the administration's war on terrorism, it did not feel compelled to go beyond the surface events that were unfolding. Any criticism of the press' refusal or hesitation to question the administration brought forth an angry retort from journalists: "You don't understand we are at war," or "this is war we are talking about," suggesting as it were that in a warlike situation the American press takes on a patriotic duty which overrides and supercedes its professional duties.

Few people would admit this, but in effect this is what was happening.

In the first weeks after 9/11, very few reporters and writers in the newspapers questioned how this undeclared war against a non-state entity could be used by the administration to curtail civil liberties, justify the use of military tribunals to try suspected terrorists, and request the press not to telecast videos of bin Laden.

From September through December there was hardly a question asked about the failure of the intelligence agencies in preventing the 9/11 attack. In a populistic paroxysm of patriotism, the US Congress suspended judgment of the administration and so did the press. It might make sense for the president, in his desire to maintain cohesiveness in his administration, not to sack the intelligence agency heads while a "war" is being waged, but should that absolve the president of the responsibility of asking for accountability?

The first detailed news report speaking of the possibility of an investigation into the intelligence failure appeared in *The New York Times* on November 23, nearly two and a half months after September 11. After that token offering, the issue went into hibernation again for several months.

Popular support for the President, which at one point touched 92 percent, seems to have colored the judgment of Congress but should it also have swayed the American press? Marvin Kalb explains this by saying that journalists who were hired during the Cold War felt they owed a responsibility to the news, and news organizations to the public. The public was later replaced by the market and market share.

This dilemma of patriotic duties versus professionalism at a time of crisis was voiced in a stark way at the seminar following the annual Theodore White Lecture at the Kennedy School on November 1, 2001. Judy Woodruff, who delivered an excellent lecture on how the electronic media had covered 9/11, was asked why the press was not asking the obvious questions about the failings of the administration. She replied that among other things American journalists had to be conscious of their duties as citizens.

In that remark Ms. Woodruff, a thoughtful journalist, paraphrased the American journalists' essential dilemma in the aftermath of September 11: Should their duties as citizens of a country which had been attacked and their consequent feelings of nationalism and patriotism change the parameters and rules of professionalism by which journalism is practiced? If so, then what about truth? Does truth become optional in times of national crisis? Is that press then *free*?

There has, I think, been insufficient or no debate in the American media on this question of the journalist's fundamental duties and responsibilities. If nationalistic feelings are allowed to color press coverage then one can hardly expect balance and detachment from journalists in countries that are perpetually in crisis.

At the root of this dilemma is the question of what defines national interest, and whether at a time of crisis or national emergency, national interest means supporting what the government of the day is doing. If that is so, then a journalist who criticizes the actions and policies of the government because he genuinely believes these policies are hurting the nation would be open to the charge that he is antinational. Behind this is the larger question: Is the government the only body which has the power and the ability to define what is in the national interest? And should the press complicity allow the government's judgment to supercede its own?

All these questions could legitimately be posed to the American press in the aftermath of September 11. It would appear that even news organizations that had fought all the way to the Supreme Court to defend their right to determine what is in the public interest to publish were only too willing to put that right into storage for some months after September 11 and to let public interest be determined by a government that was intent on curtailing civil liberties and setting up military tribunals for trial of terrorists.

Whatever little questioning of the administration's actions did take place was on the op-ed pages of the major newspapers and op-ed writers like Thomas Friedman, Anthony Lewis, Maureen Dowd and Paul Krugman (in *The New York Times*) and James Carroll of *The Boston Globe* among a handful of others, who saved the day for the American press. Outside the columns of the newspapers it was left to media pundits like Marvin Kalb to argue that patriotism and concerns of citizen's duties do not change the basic rules of journalistic functioning. "Patriotism," he said at a seminar in the Shorenstein Center in October 2001, "is wonderful for the citizen but not for the journalist. Patriotism inhibits skepticism and a good journalist has to subject all statements and claims by the government to skeptical inquiry." But for the initial months after September 11, in the lull between the catastrophe and its consequences, the voices of people like Kalb were merely cries in the wilderness.

The roots of this acquiescence probably go back to the Gulf War in which the US press allowed itself to be shackled by Pentagon-enforced limits on access to the war zone and combatants. The US press then had to depend on official releases and briefing for much of their information on how the war was going. This enabled the creating of myths about the accuracy of smart bombs and the success of Patriot missiles. Says Kalb, "80 percent of the smart bombs missed their target but the press was told they were 100 percent accurate."

Probably stricter controls were in effect in Afghanistan, which the press accepted without demur. As in the Gulf War, so also in Afghanistan, civilian casualties were allowed to be garbed as collateral damage, an inoffensive description which camouflages the maiming and mutilation that war heaps on non-combatants.

Lacking credible firsthand action-reports from the war zone *The New York Times* and *The Boston Globe* often took recourse to full-page descriptions of the zap-em fry-em abilities of the munitions and weapons that the US was using in Afghanistan. The war in Afghanistan was turned into a show window for the technological wizardry of America's munitions industry: Bombs 'R Us for the grown man! Or How the Daisy Cutters Tamed Afghanistan's Poppy Growers.

This list of omissions should not obscure the fact that in most other areas *The New York Times* and other newspapers did a superb job of reporting the tragedy and its aftermath. *The New York Times* and other papers like *The Boston Globe* provided compelling reading in the months after September 11, and they were rewarded by a clutch of Pulitzer Prizes and other journalism awards. Since the purpose of this chapter was to critically evaluate the functioning of these papers, it has of necessity focused on the shortfalls. The examples of professional excellence in the reporting of 9/11 are so numerous and so obvious that they do not need recounting.

The War on Terrorism Goes Online

Andrew J. Glass

All the headline-making events that have happened since the terrible Tuesday in September on which the United States was successfully attacked by foreign terrorists have occurred during the Internet Age. While the parameters of today's online communications systems were in place during the 1991 Persian Gulf War, that relatively brief struggle occurred shortly before the advent of the World Wide Web and, consequently, before millions of people across the planet could access and exchange information in real time on Internet-enabled computers.

This chapter investigates the multifaceted role that the Internet has played in the initial phases of the equally multifaceted campaign against global terrorist networks in what Defense Secretary Donald Rumsfeld called this "so-called war." It is an effort that, necessarily, seeks to evaluate a moving target. Nevertheless, some of the unique aspects of the post-9/11 Internet environment were already evident three months after the attacks.

Moreover, the broader questions of U.S. information policy have strong implications for the Net, which can be made to respect national borders only under the kind of draconian conditions that have yet to be widely imposed in the West and that, in any event, would pose significant technical, legal and administrative challenges were they to be implemented.

In theory at least, a terrorist based in the Middle East equipped with a satellite-enabled link to the Internet could read today's issue of *The New York Times*—replete with uncensored strategic and tactical battle reports—online in the same time frame as any Manhattan-based reader. (Making such a satellite-based data phone call, to be sure, could also attract the interest of the National Security Agency.)

Conversely, one of the hottest Internet sites in the hours that followed U.S. military retaliation against the then Taliban rulers in Afghanistan in early October 2001 was a site based in Qatar, the small oil-rich nation on the Persian Gulf.

The first pictures of the October 7 bombing strikes on Kabul appeared on aljazeera.net, the Arabic world's equivalent of CNN and MSNBC. Although the site

47

is in Arabic, enterprising netizens could make out the gist of the stories through an Arab-English translation site such as *tarjim.ajeeb.com/ajeeb*.

Said Peter Brown, an editorial page columnist for the *Orlando Sentinel:* "In this Internet age, when the terrorists can read the *Washington Post* instantaneously in Kabul, there is reason to carefully limit logistical information about U.S. forces. This is a new kind of war. If the changes that this new kind of warfare requires limit the news media's ability to do their job, then that's too bad. However, let's not whine about it. It would be nice if everyone understands that we are in this together."

In comparison to other recent military operations, President Bush and his advisors appear to have gone to greater lengths to conceal information, which has direct implications for the freewheeling Net culture. Even while it identified Osama bin Laden as its primary suspect, the White House initially refused to provide any of the evidence it possessed linking bin Laden's organization to the attacks. Instead, Americans got their information indirectly when British Prime Minister Tony Blair outlined the case in a speech to Parliament and immediately posted a dossier on the evidence on the Internet, which was then widely linked to news sites around the globe.

As illustrated by the Blair posting, the potential use and misuse of cyber-technology has become integrated into the post–September 11 world. Thus, the Internet has also served as the source of many, if surely not all, of the more than 250,000 tips received by the FBI since the attacks. Persons interested in collecting the $25 million reward for Osama's capture are able to download the full particulars of the offer on the Justice Department's anti-terrorism website.

Another Internet staple application—chat room logs that record Web data transfers—could be, and probably already have been, used by the FBI and CIA to locate the terrorist networks. There are also indications that the U.S. government is seeking to use highly sophisticated cyber techniques to deplete the terrorists' financial networks, although, in most cases, foreign governments need to cooperate with such endeavors.

In sum, all this suggests that, in more ways than one, the Internet nowadays is serving as a double-edged sword, an information tool that at once both propagates and ameliorates these high crimes.

Crisis News on the Net

For some Americans, the Internet proved to be an immediate boon in helping them to deal with the horrific events of September 11. Instant web sites and "white pages" were set up as a means to help search for and identify missing persons. News groups, listservs and newsletters became beacons of guidance seeking to cut through the chaos.

In the ensuing hours after the attacks, American Data Technology Inc., one of the nation's largest dedicated Web host firms, posted a notice on its site that pleaded with its clients of Internet service providers "to limit [their connections] to the network as much as possible" in order to allow critical voice and data traffic to get through. Nevertheless, on the whole, the Net did not fail even as the weakest links in the system proved to be the servers that support major news websites.

Meanwhile, clogged telephone lines—which utilize a big chunk of the same Net infrastructure that served news sites—prevented family members from reaching loved ones feared missing or dead. In some poignant cases, e-mail proved to be the last resort and the final means of communication from the World Trade Center twin towers before their catastrophic collapse.

The big picture, however, reveals that the terrorist attack on U.S. soil immediately increased Internet usage of online-enabled Americans. According to a study by Jupiter Media Metrix, an authoritative source of online demographics, an average of 11.7 million Americans visited online news sites on each day in the week after the September 11 attacks—nearly double the 6 million who had visited news sites in the week before the attack. A follow-up Harris Interactive survey found that two weeks after the attacks, the number of wired Americans logging onto news sites had more than doubled. (In addition to news sites, the Red Cross website [www.*RedCross.org*] averaged 398,000 unique visitors a day during the week.)

The chart below, extracted from the Jupiter data, reviews the viewership response at major news portals that drew a million or more unique visitors during the week:

Online Site	Number of unique visitors	% increase from previous week
CNN	17,247,000	23.2
MSNBC	14,994,000	20.2
ABC News	5,469,000	7.4
CBS	4,842,000	6.5
New York Times	4,536,000	6.1
Washington Post.com	4,430,000	6.0
Slate	3,443,000	4.6
USAToday.com	3,367,000	4.5
Fox	2,934,000	4.0
BBC	2,624,000	3.5
Los Angeles Times	1,343,000	1.8
Associated Press	1,221,000	1.6
Boston Globe	1,006,000	1.4

Another study by the Pew Research Center for the People & the Press—conducted between September 12th and 13th among a sample of 1,226 adults, 18 and older—revealed that Americans mostly relied on television in the immediate aftermath of the attacks—even as they sharply raised their Internet usage in order to stay in touch with loved ones, friends and business associates.

Given the networks' collective response to the first instance of megaterror on American soil, it is not at all surprising that the Internet initially played a second-fiddle role as an information medium. The "Big Four" networks suspended all of their regular programming and substituted wrap-around news coverage for at least the first 90 hours of the crisis—exceeding the continuous airtime they had devoted to the assassination of President John F. Kennedy in 1962 and the start of Operation Desert Storm in 1991.

Nevertheless, for millions of Americans with access to the Internet, cyberspace played an important, paramount or supplementary role as an effective communications tool, furnishing both e-mail and instant messaging services in addition to access to news sources within the United States and abroad.

However, according to Pew, only 3 percent of Internet users said that they had gotten most of their information about the attacks from the Internet. By contrast, 81 percent of all Americans got most of their information from television. Interestingly, there was no measurable statistical difference between Internet users and non-users in their reliance on TV news.

Some 11 percent got most of their information from radio. Again, there was no statistical difference between the responses of Internet users and non-users. (A quarter of Internet users multitasked on that fateful Tuesday by having their TV sets or radios on while they surfed or dealt with their e-mail.)

On September 11, the day of the attack, 15 percent of all Internet users sent e-mail messages concerning that traumatic event to family members and 12 percent sent e-mail to friends. In addition, 6 percent of Internet users sent instant messages on that Tuesday—about the same level of usage of instant messaging services that takes place on any given day online.

On an overall basis, 36 percent of Internet users sought news online in the first two days in the immediate aftermath of the attacks. On that Tuesday alone, 29 percent of Internet users—some 30 million people—sought news online. That is one-third greater than the normal news-seeking online audience on a normal news day.

In the first 48 hours after the crisis, 13 percent of Internet users logged into virtual meetings or participated in virtual communities by reading or posting comments in chat rooms, online bulletin boards, or e-mail list servers. On a typical day, only 4 percent of online Americans visit chat rooms.

Of the Internet users who sought to obtain news of the crisis online on the day of the attacks, 43 percent of them said they experienced problems reaching their desired sites. Within this group, 41 percent kept on trying; 38 percent went in search of news to other sites and 19 percent gave up entirely.

In sum, the Pew survey concluded that while the Internet was not a primary resource for news or outreach for most Americans immediately after the terror attacks, it still served as a useful supplement, particularly through the use of e-mail and instant messaging, and as a news source.

No doubt, a lack of accessibility was one reason why online news services failed to measure up in the immediate wake of the attacks. The average "reachability" of the Internet dropped just over 8 percent from 96 percent to 88 percent around 10 A.M. EDT, about one hour and 15 minutes after the attacks began, according to Jupiter Metrix.Net.

At major news sites, which normally take between 2.5 and 3.5 seconds to access a Web page, the access time proved to be between 20 and 40 seconds. Moreover, for nearly three hours after the attack, some of the Internet's foremost news sites—including MSNBC, CNN and ABC—were unavailable because their primary servers had been destroyed in the collapse of the World Trade Center towers.

Once they were viable again, some news sites, such as CNN, recognized their backup servers' overload problems and redesigned their pages to strip out graphics, ads, and other time-consuming downloadable features, thereby increasing their throughput capacity. Once back in operation, CNN saw record traffic, reaching 9 million page views an hour, compared to their ordinary volume of 11 million page views per day. Having streamlined its site, CNN was able to connect effectively to the enormous online community thirsting for up-to-the-minute news of the crisis and resume some kind of service.

The Harris data closely tracked the Pew findings. Thus Harris reported that on September 12, 2001, television proved to be the primary source of information for 78 percent of Americans with online access in the 24 hours immediately following the attacks—followed by radio at 15 percent and the Internet at 3 percent.

However, a Harris poll completed three weeks later showed that the Internet achieved statistically significant gains, with 8 percent of the population using the Internet as their primary source of news, while both television (at 76 percent) and radio (at 8 percent) experienced a modest decline.

"There can no longer be any doubt that, for Americans who have online access, the Internet is second only to television as the medium of choice for news and information," said Michael Zimbalist, acting executive director of the Online Publishers Association. "And unlike any other medium, the Internet audience continues to experience rapid worldwide growth."

According to Harris, the percentage of people using the Internet as one of their information sources, if not their primary source, jumped from 64 percent to 80 percent in the two weeks after the attacks, overtaking radio (72 percent) and second only to television, with 98 percent. The top reasons given for using the Internet as a news and information source were:

- It provides information users want when they want it (63 percent of the respondents).
- It delivers more detailed information (43 percent).
- It offers more up to date information (42 percent).
- The news is accessible at work (42 percent).

Harris reported that in the wake of the attacks 35 percent of the people interviewed said their number of visits to news websites had increased and that 47 percent said the amount of time they spent on news websites had also risen appreciably.

Yet another metric came from MeasureCast Inc., which reported that AM News/Talk stations that streamed their programs over the Internet pumped out more hours of coverage to larger audiences as various aspects of the crisis enfolded.

Evidence of this growing trend occurred on Monday, November 12, 2001, when American Airlines flight 587 crashed in Queens, New York, near John F. Kennedy International Airport and was at first suspected to be another terrorist act. MeasureCast chief executive Edward Hardy said "many terrestrial AM News/Talk stations streaming their programs over the Internet streamed more hours that day than they did the previous Monday. We saw the same thing happen on September 11th, but the . . . audience size increases were more dramatic."

Online Journalism

"The Internet has had a good war," says David Brooks, senior editor of *The Weekly Standard,* a Washington-based opinion journal which, quite typically nowadays, puts its own work online for subscribers to its paper edition.

Online journalism may be sponsored by a parent cable or print outlet, such as CNN or *The Wall Street Journal.* Or it may be a stand-alone effort, such as *Slate,* which is wholly owned by Microsoft Corp., or *Salon,* which solicits both ads and $6-a-month subscriptions in order to read the full content. Or it may take the form of an independent website that is maintained by an already well-known journalist such as Andrew Sullivan (*www.AndrewSullivan.com*), or Michael Barone (*www.MichaelBarone.com*). Sometimes, the cyber-based news material is duplicated in another medium, either in the same form or in an altered form.

Online journalism has been around for nearly a decade. It is yet another example of "re-positioning"—the effort of media owners to diversify their holdings with interlocking and competing media. Nearly every major U.S. newspaper has hedged its investments by creating its own online site, with news as a key element in the cyber mix.

San Diego's "Sign On" carries a full share of crisis-related reports to a local audience that is heavily engaged in military affairs. Launched in 1996,

"SignOnSanDiego" set up its own desk operation within the *Union-Tribune* newsroom in 2001, linked to newsroom staff of 20 in a separate building.

"SignOn," said Gene Bell, chief executive of the Union-Tribune Newspapers, a member of the Copley newspaper chain, "is simply a different way of providing our content. We are no longer limited to print. We can add value for readers with this synergy. Newspapers must grow beyond the print product."

"Online coverage of the anti-terrorist effort reflects both our strengths and weaknesses," David Plotz, *Slate's* Washington bureau chief, told a Shorenstein Center audience in November 2001. "Without a doubt," Plotz added, "from bad times come good stories."

Plotz noted "an enormous surge of traffic" to the *Slate* site. The weeks following the September 11 attack brought some 10 million unique visitors to the online service, against 3 million who would normally visit in a month.

On the plus side, Plotz said, the Internet has raised the velocity of news coverage. "The rate at which people demand news is becoming faster and faster," he observed. "The Web is able to provide more substance than the all-news cable outlets. People want analytic information very quickly. They are being barraged with disparate facts from all over the world."

Accordingly, within 24 hours of the terrorist strikes, *Slate* provided a detailed civil engineering explanation of why the twin towers had imploded in lower Manhattan after being struck by jumbo jets. During that early time frame, the web site was also able to offer up a full profile of Osama bin Laden, then still a shadowy figure in the minds of many people.

"It is very reassuring for people to have their news in synthesized form and not just images of towers falling and planes crashing," Plotz said. "We're able to be there more quickly than the traditional news magazines. In fact, there's an increasing feeling out there that [the news weeklies] are always a week out of date."

"Online stories must be short," Plotz said. "People don't have the patience to read long-form journalism online. The best we can hope for is a 'conceptual scoop'"—one which he defined as "the ability to put a set of facts together in a different sort of way so that they make sense to people." But, he added, "there's an inherent tension between how fast you should do something and how well you should do something."

Despite *Slate's* high viewer volume, Plotz reported that it was much harder for him to get his calls returned than is usually the case for journalists who work for more established press outlets. Plotz noted that at times he had to call upon Michael Kinsley, *Slate's* founding editor—who was based in Washington state (but who is well known in the other Washington) and who writes a weekly column for *The Washington Post*—to run interference for him with top government officials.

There are some other negative aspects to online journalism as well, particularly in wartime. Thus, Plotz lamented "how little original material we are able to contribute to the facts" involving the American-led war in Afghanistan. "Most of the news gathering," he said, "is still being done by the wires, the large national newspapers and the television networks."

"There's very little original reporting online. That's still the Achilles heel of Web journalism. We are mainly a re-packaging operation, rather than a primary gatherer of news. It would be great to be driving White House coverage but we're not doing that." Moreover, Plotz added, as a group "we're still adolescents. At least sometimes we behave as adolescents."

In this respect, Plotz possibly had in mind Ann Coulter, a onetime contributing editor and columnist for *National Review Online.* Coulter was dropped after writing a column that recommended the United States invade Muslim countries, kill their leaders and convert them to Christianity.

Reflecting on that action, Kathleen Parker, a columnist for the *Orlando Sentinel,* wrote: "One might expect to lose some readers with that kind of commentary. Like [Bill] Maher [former host of the cancelled late-night television talk show "Politically Incorrect"], Coulter is provocative—especially when she appears on 'Politically Incorrect' in those microscopic skirts. But," Parker asked, "was she fired for her commentary, or was she fired for calling her editors wimps for declining to run her next 'swarthy-male' column?"

Life online, it seems, mirrors the more traditional news world. For, as Parker concluded, ". . . [If] I liked my job and wanted to keep it, even though I might disagree with an editor's decision (it happens), I probably wouldn't publicly insult the guy cutting my paycheck. That's called self-censorship, also known as being a grown-up."

Purported signs of "adolescence" aside, Plotz believes that in a crisis setting online journalism "forces everybody else to keep up with the same pace. There's very little patience, the people driving the system constantly demand a new story."

As he put it at the Shorenstein meeting: "Now things have to run on Internet time. The big downside of that is we're demanding that this war be fought on Internet time. And that's just not reasonable. You want to throw up big headlines very fast—even before you've reported it. CNN throws up a headline and you have to wait for the [real] story."

Plotz characterized the situation as "The Drudge Effect," in keeping with the website maintained by Matt Drudge, which is devoted in large part to breaking exclusive stories that are often gleaned, however, on a derivative basis. To some extent, online news coverage is caught up in that whirlwind as well. But, as Plotz noted, while in television news the words and pictures flash by quickly, "things live longer on the Web." In fact, since storage in cyberspace is essentially infinite and free, such accounts are often archived or stored on repositories maintained by secondary sites for months and even years on end.

The Wall Street Journal maintains an extensive free-of-charge site for columns and other features that mirror the editorial page of the newspaper's print edition (*OpinionJournal.com*). James Taranto, the online editor and former deputy editorial features editor of *The Wall Street Journal,* also prepares a "Best of Web" compilation that can only be found on the Internet. The result is a hybrid form of journalism that seamlessly combines hard reporting, news analysis and personal commentary.

The posting for December 7, 2001, discussed in detail the encounter between a CIA agent named John Spann and an American Taliban fighter named John Walker in a form that did not appear in any U.S. newspaper. Spann was killed shortly after the interview in a Taliban prison uprising.

In a dispatch entitled "The Voice of Treason Goes Mute," Taranto wrote: "Well well. It turns out John Walker, the Marin County weirdo whose 'spiritual journey' led him to join the Taliban, was interrogated by two CIA officers, the late Johnny 'Mike' Spann and another man identified only as Dave, at the Qala Jangi prison in Afghanistan. *Newsweek* has a transcript of the videotaped confrontation, in which Walker said . . . nothing":

> **Spann:** What's your name? Hey. [He snaps his fingers twice in front of Walker's face. Walker is unresponsive]
>
> **Spann:** Who brought you here? Wake up! Who brought you here? How did you get here? Hello?
>
> Later, Dave walks up. Spann and Dave speak to one another, within a few feet of Walker, loudly enough for the prisoner to hear them.
>
> **Spann [to Dave]:** I explained to him what the deal is.
>
> **Spann [to Walker]:** It's up to you.
>
> **Dave [to Spann]:** The problem is, he's got to decide if he wants to live or die. If he wants to die, he's going to die here. Or he's going to f——ing spend the rest of his short f——ing life in prison. It's his decision, man. We can only help the guys who want to talk to us. We can only get the Red Cross to help so many guys.

Taranto concludes: "Sad to say, the wrong American died—though this encounter raises the intriguing possibility of charging Walker in connection with Spann's death. . . ."

The fight against the terrorists began at a time when the economics of the Internet were in a perilous state. *Salon,* often cited as *Slate's* main competition, is in

David Plotz's words, "just clutching the edge of the cliff." (*Slate* itself is protected by Mircosoft's deep pockets and is, Plotz reported, close to breaking even.)

The wide-ranging iconoclastic nature of online commentary can be further exemplified by an article entitled "Round up the Jews!" and written for *Salon* by Ron Unz, a theoretical physicist and founder and chairman of Wall Street Analytics, Inc.

Unz' point is that if it's all right to racially profile Muslims and Arabs in the wake of the September 11 attacks as potential fifth-columnists, then it should have been all right also to single out Jews during the 1950s Communist-spy panic.

Unz notes that "[i]t's an undeniable historical fact that Jews made up an extraordinarily high fraction of America's leading Communist Party members and Communist spies even though the overwhelming majority of Jewish Americans were loyal and law-abiding patriotic Americans . . ."

But, he points out, "no figure of authority even on the extreme right ever did so publicly. Sen. Joseph McCarthy, whose name is synonymous with extreme anti-Communism, actually appointed a young Jewish aide, Roy Cohn, as his most prominent lieutenant. Similarly, American leaders ensured that both the prosecutors and the judge who sent Julius and Ethel Rosenberg to their deaths for spying were themselves Jewish."

So Unz concludes "intellectual honesty requires that anyone calling for the ethnic profiling of Arabs and Muslims as possible terrorists today should retrospectively endorse the ethnic profiling of all American Jews as possible traitors 50 years ago. And if such a statement chokes in his throat, perhaps he should reconsider its present-day analogue."

So-called "hyperlinks," which enable people to easily surf between sites, are a vital aspect of online journalism and can be found in nearly all the examples cited in this discussion. "You may lose a few people who never come back to the original site," Plotz noted. "But, in general, people are resentful if you don't give them the original documentation on which your account is based."

Online press criticism of crisis-related news accounts can also often be found at *InstaPundit.Com.* Thus, on December 7, 2001, writer Glenn Reynolds took on a front page *New York Times* piece by Fox Butterfield alleging that "the Justice Department has refused to let the FBI check its records to determine whether any of the 1,200 people detained after the September 11 attacks had bought guns." (Reynolds also reprinted the entire section of the penal code that governs this situation.)

As David Brooks noted, also online, Reynolds' analysis "highlights a fact that Butterfield conveniently left out of his story: U.S. law specifically forbids the Justice Department from allowing such checks." (According to Reynolds, the law allows law enforcement to trace a firearm captured at a crime scene, but it does not allow officials to go fishing through the gun records in search of somebody who owns a gun and might have committed a crime.)

Brooks concludes: "If true, this explodes the whole ideological intent of Butterfield's story," although Brooks felt that the language in the penal code "is less open and shut than Reynolds makes out."

The complex online relationships in the press among Brooks, Reynolds and Butterfield comes to the fore in Brooks' overall summary. Reynolds, Brooks tells us, "provides some historical background on Butterfield. Those of us in the media know that Butterfield is someone who often lets his ideology shape his reporting, but there's no reason others shouldn't know this. The web links it all together."

Independent Journalists

In conducting his tour of online news and opinion sites, the *Weekly Standard's* David Brooks said he found "truckloads of absolutely essential information every day." A separate search of news- and opinion-oriented websites in the second week of December related to the crisis confirms the accuracy of Brooks' comment.

Among the more valuable virtual news clearinghouses in cyberland is Hotline World Extra, a compendium of most that has been written, said, or thought about the war in Afghanistan in the English-language press over the past 24 hours. As Brooks noted, "the 'Hotline' has a domestic edition which is a depressingly exhaustive bible of the pundit class and carries a hefty subscription fee. But the war edition is free."

One of the independent online journalists whom Brooks admires is Andrew Sullivan, a former editor of the *New Republic*, who still frequently contributes to that journal as well as to the *New York Times Sunday Magazine*.

Sullivan prepares a virtual concoction which he calls the "Daily Dish," heavily laced with press criticism that is unavailable elsewhere and that, along with similar sites, serves to deepen and enrich the crisis coverage.

For example, on December 8, 2001, Sullivan tore into one of his favorite targets, the British-based *Guardian* newspaper, which he described as "the leading Western anti-war newspaper." In this instance, Sullivan, whose political slant is difficult to pigeonhole, dissected a *Guardian* editorial which conceded that while the war in Afghanistan isn't all over, humanitarian problems will no doubt continue.

While all that he says is true, Sullivan nevertheless declaims in cyberspace that the *Guardian* editorial "absolutely misses the bigger picture, which is that the U.S.-led campaign in Afghanistan continues to be far more successful than the pessimists, and even most optimists, ever thought possible." Sullivan concludes, "moderate liberals are now denying that there ever was an anti-war left; and left-liberals are now announcing that they were wrong about the war. Does it get any sweeter than that?"

Mickey Kaus is another such independent online journalist, albeit one with a liberal bent, whose often provocative reports, known as the "Kausfiles," are rarely mirrored or even widely cited in the mainstream press.

On December 6, 2001, in a typical posting, Kaus raised the question of whether it is in Bush's political interest to prolong the war in Afghanistan. Before the September 11 attacks, Kaus argued, "it seemed pretty clear that President Bush, though popular, might have trouble getting re-elected. Having passed his tax cut, and almost passed his education reform, he'd essentially run out of things to do on the domestic front . . . Worse, he faced a potential independent presidential campaign by Sen. John McCain."

Kaus postulates that the Arizona senator would have challenged Bush and won. But, he adds, "all that is moot, of course, thanks to the terrorist attacks. It's inconceivable that a military man like McCain would challenge Bush now while there's a war on."

The Kaus online filing argues: "What is becoming increasingly, glaringly clear—even as, with U.S. troops engaged in combat, it remains unmentionable—is that the continuation of the war works in Bush's political interest. It's not just that Bush, as an effective wartime leader, is popular. It's that as long as there is a war, Bush doesn't have to worry about McCain. As long as there is a war, he doesn't have to worry about anyone focusing too intensely on his nonexistent domestic agenda."

While such observations may or may not be "unmentionable" in the mainstream press, they are patently mentionable online. Thus, Kaus concludes "if Bush doesn't want to repeat his father's mistakes—which does seem a guiding principle of his administration—he'll be leery of a too-early termination of the current conflict. Not just for policy reasons, but also, if he thinks about them, for sound political reasons. As long as the war against terrorism is going as well as it seems to be going, then the longer it goes on, the better the chances that Bush will be a two-term commander."

In closing his essay, Kaus predicts that his online site "will be roundly condemned as unpatriotic" for having run a controversial political analysis of Bush's wartime strategy. Nevertheless, Kaus forecasts that "within two months the essential point—that it's in Bush's political interest to keep the war going—will be such a staple of punditry that you will switch channels when you hear it."

Andrew Ferguson, among others, represents a conservative viewpoint in what is a broad ideological spectrum of wartime coverage to be found online. Along with Brooks, Ferguson writes regularly as a contributing editor for the *Weekly Standard* and is an online columnist for Bloomberg News (*www.bloombergnews.com /columns/*) His commentaries are preceded by the disclaimer that "[t]he opinions expressed are his own." As several other such writers in cyberland, Ferguson also devotes a good deal of attention to press criticism of war-related events.

For instance, on December 4, 2001, Ferguson filed a 900-word report entitled "John Ashcroft Becomes All-Purpose Bad Guy." Quite typically, Ferguson's file amounts to a commentary-laced essay on recent news events.

"I've never been much of a fan of Attorney General John Ashcroft," Ferguson begins. "But anybody who gets trashed by four—yes, four—*New York Times* columnists over the course of a single weekend can't be all bad.

"He's not a particularly appealing figure on his own," Ferguson continues. "As a politician he's poorly suited to the tastes of the television age. His voice rolls out in a sleepy monotone, and let's not talk about the haircut. When he ran for re-election to his Missouri Senate seat last year, he lost to an opponent who had been dead for a month. Voters couldn't tell them apart."

"Ordinarily such men are dismissed as dull. But Ashcroft has managed to excite a large number of public people—not merely *New York Times* columnists but also professional activists, his fellow politicians, and civil libertarians of the left and the right. Cartoonist Pat Oliphant depicts him as a Taliban mullah. Bill Goodman of the Center for Constitutional Rights last week called Ashcroft and his Justice Department the Constitution's 'main enemies right now.' Osama bin Laden comes in second, I guess."

Ferguson goes on to cite the anti-communist raids of the 1920s conducted by a prior Attorney General, Mitchell Palmer, as an unseemly precedent. He argues that the best argument against implementing the new Ashcroft anti-terrorist rules revolves around the constitutional separation of powers—noting, "Ashcroft's tactics will have a better chance of passing the inevitable legal challenges if they're undertaken with congressional consent." Ashcroft, he concludes, should meet these unilateralist objections to his policies squarely "as a dull defender of the Constitution rather than the enemy that his more hysterical critics imagine him to be."

Irreverency can play a role in cyber-journalism as well, even when it comes to such acknowledged serious issues as national security. Jonah Goldberg, one such practitioner on the light side of the news, filed a "non-column column" on December 7, 2001, on his Web niche (*www.nationalreview.com/goldberg/goldberg.shtml*) reporting that he would be skipping his regular offering because on the due date, he would be "on a secret assignment for *National Review*."

As Goldberg explained it: "I will be at an undisclosed airport or airports somewhere on the Eastern seaboard reporting on the current state of our homeland security. (I will be carrying one *National Review Online* T-Shirt for anybody who comes up to me and says 'the fat man bathes in dirty moonlight'—World War II code for 'give me the damn t-shirt you dork.')

"I wouldn't even tell you this much, except for the unfortunate fact that I do not trust the suits at NR to pay for what would be my exorbitant legal expenses should I get put in an airport jail without my trusted readers knowing I went missing on official business."

Virginia Postrel, another independent (and independent-minded) online columnist takes on such issues as alleged Saudi discrimination against female U.S. military personnel.

In a December 7 posting, Postrel describes in detail the suit filed by Air Force Lt. Col. Martha McSally, the service's highest-ranking female fighter pilot, against the U.S. Department of Defense for sex and religious discrimination. Its genesis: a Pentagon rule that requires American servicewomen to wear the abaya, a full-length robe, and sit in the backseat of cars when they go off base in Saudi Arabia. McSally, an active Christian, objected not only on the basis of sex discrimination but also to being required to wear a garment that is a mark of Muslim faith. A full copy of her legal action is available on the website, an extra service that would not to be possible in a common newspaper or magazine setting.

Postrel concludes: "I'm wary of dress-code suits, particularly in a military context, but this one strikes me as a good 'don't throw me in the briarpatch' case. The regulations exceed even restrictive Saudi laws, don't apply to non-military personnel, and are basically designed to kiss up to the Saudis. The suit could give the administration a good excuse for ending the obsequiousness. Alternatively, we could require Muslim women visiting this country to wear crucifixes or dress like Britney Spears."

The idiosyncratic liberal-left viewpoint online is represented by such writers as Joshua Micah Marshall, a former Washington editor of the *American Prospect* who is currently completing his doctoral dissertation in Colonial American history at Brown University. Marshall is also the editor of the "Talking Points Memo," a website (*www.j-marshall.com/talk*) that serves up well-written commentary about the current crisis that is available only online.

For example, in a December 7, 2001, posting, Marshall termed John Ashcroft's performance before the Senate Judiciary Committee on the previous day as "offensive (and) even disgusting." Marshall added: "On attitude and lack of forthcoming-ness alone, it was bad. But to argue that those who raise questions about civil liberties are somehow aiding the terrorists is offensive and, frankly, requires an apology."

"Even if you don't think the Justice Department has done anything wrong or over-stepped on any count, you should still be glad that some people are raising these questions."

"Wartime and crisis often require steps that would be unwarranted and even unacceptable in peacetime. But there must be some counter-balance to the government which, in the nature of things, will try to push the ball as far as it can. . . ."

Marshall concluded: "Anti-war critics are always permissible, but I'm not sure they're always necessary. Civil liberties critics are always necessary. Even when they're wrong. This is the problem with Ashcroft. Both in his penchant for secrecy and his intolerance of criticism, his flaws of character and untoward belligerence get him in trouble even when he's right on the merits."

The War for Public Opinion

Since September 11, the Internet has played a useful role as an alternate source of news and opinion. While all the available evidence as 2001 wound to an end indicated that the Bush administration was continuing to prevail in what might be termed "the war for public opinion," it was equally evident that the Internet gave people a meaningful choice of viewpoints.

"The Bush administration has had to contend with a new set of media forces arising from the 'Information Revolution,'" said Tamara Straus, senior editor of *AlterNet.org*, one such online alternative voice.

As Straus saw it, "the war on terrorism is the world's first war for the Internet and foreign news outlets. Never before have so many people ostensibly had access to so much news and opinion from so many sources. Never before has it been possible to gauge so many views—not only in the United States—but from Europe and the Middle East . . . Public opinion is now vulnerable to what is reported outside the [America's] news borders."

Straus' own December 10 online essay illustrates her point. "The Pentagon's tactics in the media war have been less than subtle," she wrote. "For starters, they bought up access to all commercial satellite photographs of the region, preventing any news outlets from obtaining them. They also have prevented journalists from accompanying soldiers or airmen on most missions, or even from interviewing them afterward."

"Meanwhile, television news has been behaving more like a wing of the military than an objective Fourth Estate, with anchors like CBS' Dan Rather pledging his allegiance on air: 'Wherever [Bush] wants me to line up, just tell me where.'"

I. The Steganographic Scene

In ensuing months after the September 11 attacks, many accounts appeared in newspapers, news magazines and on-the-air reporting that the suicidal terrorists had cloaked their planning through coded Internet messages. Steganographic messages do not need to be encrypted—they are hidden in plain sight in the vastness of cyberspace.

Thus CNN.com cited a "law-enforcement theory about how the al-Qaeda network disseminates instructions to operatives in the field"—suggesting that Osama bin Laden had been hiding messages to his operatives on pornographic websites, where investigators presumably were less likely to spot them (CNN.com 11/12).

The CNN report and similar ones alleged that computers and the Internet were used in some unspecified covert ways to facilitate the first mass terrorist attacks on U.S. soil of the digital era. For the most part, the accounts cited as sources independent analysts and security consultants who had left their governmental posts.

Ever since the Internet became a mass communication medium, the potential use by terrorists of online encryption techniques has been a central concern of intelligence agencies. Those concerns have been echoed by lawmakers pressing to close digital loopholes through further legislation. Well before the September 11 attacks, in both open and closed testimony on Capitol Hill, officials from within the Department of Defense, the Central Intelligence Agency, the Federal Bureau of Investigation and the National Security Agency demanded legislative curbs on Internet privacy. Some even called for an outright ban of all encrypted messages that could not be successfully decoded by government monitors.

Throughout the 1990s, the information technology community largely focused on the question of whether security software that employed encryption techniques should also be subject to so-called "escrow" methodology. Such techniques require special "keys" which allow private messages to be decoded by the government—presumably only after in-place judicial rules had been followed.

In December 1999, however, the federal government abruptly scuttled its efforts to impose monitoring controls on the use of supposedly unbreakable encryption techniques as technologically unfeasible. They did so after privacy champions, joined by such security software programmers as Microsoft Corp., had persuaded key members of Congress that banning exports of American-made "strong encryption" could not prevent terrorism but that it could—and, indeed, probably would—significantly damage e-commerce. They argued that it would do so by triggering a wholesale shift of the multi-million-dollar online security business to overseas suppliers unbound by any ground rules that the U.S. government might seek to enforce. In short, the inherent trans-national nature of the Internet had seemingly undermined the would-be code breakers' agenda.

II. Terrorism and Internet Encryption

Within hours of the September 11 carnage, however, the pre-2000 debate resumed. It was widely asserted that Internet encryption must have been used to coordinate the attacks. Attorney General John Ashcroft demanded that Congress plug the loopholes. And Congress rapidly and dutifully sought to do so by passing on October 26 the so-called USA Patriot Act.

Even earlier, on September 13, just two days after the attacks on the World Trade Center and the Pentagon, Congress also passed the Combating Terrorism Act of 2001 (CTA), which significantly lowered the legal standards necessary for the FBI to deploy a surveillance system once known as Carnivore—currently the government's most potent device for spying on the private e-mail of American citizens within the confines of the United States.

Still pending on the legislative agenda is the proposed Mobilization Against Terrorism Act (MATA). If enacted in its present form, the law would empower U.S.

attorneys throughout the nation to order up a Carnivore installation without first obtaining a court order. It would also permit federal prosecutors to use electronic evidence gathered abroad, including Internet files, even when that evidence failed to follow Fourth Amendment guarantees against unreasonable search and seizure.

"These are the kinds of things that law enforcement has asked us for," said Sen. Jon Kyl, Republican of Arizona and a co-sponsor of the already enacted CTA. "This combination is relatively modest in comparison with the kind of terrorist attack we have just suffered," he added.

Much of the early reporting on these issues reflected a seven-month-old story in *USA Today* which claimed that bin Laden and his followers operated an Internet communications network based on encrypted messages that were concealed within pornographic pictures. (Jack Kelley: "Terror groups hide behind Web encryption." *USA Today,* February 5, 2001). These techniques, known as steganography (from the ancient Greek word for hidden writing), enable users to mask a coded message within a digital, picture, or music file by making small changes to data that are then nearly impossible to detect without employing special sophisticated software.

In the wake of the attacks, reports appeared on several Internet privacy-related websites to the effect that FBI agents had ordered EarthLink, the nation's third-largest Internet service provider (ISP), to install Carnivore. These reports said that the ISP, long a strong advocate of online privacy, had refused to do so.

The reality, however, differs somewhat from these accounts, and, in fact, had been widely reported in the trade press well before the attacks occurred. In December 1999, shortly after the FBI rolled out its Carnivore software, EarthLink told the agency that it would not allow the technology to be installed on its network. Subsequently, the parties, seeking to avoid a protracted court battle, cut a deal. That bargain permitted EarthLink to use its own software, rather than Carnivore, to monitor its e-mail traffic. At the same time, the ISP agreed to turn over all the data the FBI was entitled to inspect under any relevant subpoenas or court orders that the agency produced.

III. U.S. Government Response

A week after the attacks occurred, Ronald Dick, an assistant FBI director and chief of the U.S. National Infrastructure Protection Center, a coordinating body, informed reporters that the hijackers had used the Internet, and had "used it well."

Dick said FBI investigators—by obtaining records from ISPs and by reviewing computer files stored in various public libraries—had been able to locate hundreds of e-mail communications dispatched some 30 to 45 days before the attacks took place. These messages, written in both English and Arabic, were sent from both within the United States and abroad.

   Both in open briefings and in background sessions, Dick and other FBI officials repeatedly stressed that bin Laden's terrorist gang knows its way around the Internet. The supposed ringleader, Mohamed Atta, who flew the hijacked Boeing 767 into one of the World Trade Center's twin towers, reserved his seat on *Americanairlines.com*. Others communicated through Yahoo and Hotline e-mail accounts. Both services enable anonymous "handles," one reason, presumably, for their early adoption and continued popularity.

   The terrorist cell members, the government also let it be known, went online to research the possibility of utilizing the chemical-dispersing facilities of crop dusting planes to engage in urban chemical or bioterrorism. At the same time, the government briefers took care to note that all of these messages were sent "in the clear," without resorting to any encryption techniques.

   Dick also accused civil libertarians of, in effect, aiding and abetting criminals: "Quite simply," he told reporters, "the balance described in the Constitution, which provides the government with the capacity to protect the public, is eroding. In its place, the privacy of criminals and foreign enemies is edging toward the absolute."

   While the government avowed otherwise, a *Time* magazine story in mid-November reported that "secret Internet messages, known as steganography, may be the most insidious way that bin Laden has taken his terrorist movement online" (Adam Cohen, "When Terror Hides Online," *Time*, 11-12-01).

   The *Time* article speculated that "a terrorist mastermind" could insert plans for blowing up a nuclear reactor in, say, the digital image of a nose of a puppy posted on a pet-adoption web site. Operatives in the field, when told which nose to look for, "could then check for their marching orders."

   Time deduced that bin Laden's followers may have learned about steganography "when it burst on the pop-culture scene in such recent movies as "Along Came a Spider," in which a detective locates a key piece of evidence in a digitized picture of Charles Lindbergh's nose.

   The magazine further reported that the "FBI has been close-mouthed on whether it has found any steganographic images from bin Laden's al-Qaeda network." As noted above, that reporting contradicted the FBI's official stance, which held that none of the conspirators had used encryption technology or otherwise sought to conceal their messages. Once located, the FBI had said, their e-mails could be easily and openly read.

   The unnamed *Time* source who linked bin Laden's followers to steganographic techniques was a "former government official in France [who] has said that suspects who were arrested in September for an alleged plan to blow up the U.S. embassy in Paris were waiting to get their orders through an online photo." Many other accounts that took a similar tack cited no official sources in alleging that terrorists were using encryption methods.

As it happened, only a few days before the September 11 attacks, a computer team from the University of Michigan reported they had searched for Internet images that might have contained terror-laden plans. They did so by using a network of computers to look for the tell-tale digital "signature" of steganography. Researchers at the university's Center for Information Technology Integration said they "analyzed two million images but have not been able to find a single hidden message" (*www.citi.umich.edu/techreports/reports/citi-tr-01-11.pdf*). The pre-attack Michigan study has been widely ignored in the mainstream press.

Nevertheless, there are indications that law enforcement authorities, armed with the new antiterrorism statute that broadens their powers to intradict Internet communications, have stepped up their targeting of technology that could prove useful to terrorist organizations and that, if spotted in a timely way, could conceivably help foil further plots.

To be sure, these Internet sweeps are also subject to deliberate attempts to spread disinformation. It is known in the intelligence community that the terrorist networks are familiar with disinformation techniques—a favorite ruse of clandestine agencies in the Cold War era. What's not known is how sophisticated the anti-terrorist watchdogs are in ferreting out any disinformation they may encounter.

IV. Internet Privacy Concerns

For their part, civil libertarians continue to contend in the wake of the September 11 attacks that in due course Americans may come to regret having granted law enforcement agencies too much power to monitor American citizens and legal aliens. In the view of John Perry Barlow, co-founder of the Electronic Freedom Foundation and an Internet pioneer: "These provisions may seem semi-innocuous taken separately by the government we have at the moment. But it has the possibility of turning into a massive surveillance system, where anything you do online can be used against you by a government that is not as benign" (Adam Cohen, *Time*).

Recent surveys suggest that the Bush administration's anti-terrorist thrusts, with their online aspects, enjoy wide public support. The prevailing mood appears to hold that if you're not doing anything wrong, you have nothing to worry about and that if you are doing something wrong, the government has some new-found tools to find you and punish you.

Nevertheless, a vocal minority in the press—from both the new libertarian right and the more traditional liberal left—have spoken out against the post–September 11 legislative and administration actions. Their common meeting point appears to be privacy—what a Supreme Court justice once called "the right to be left alone."

Thus, in the December 2001 issue of *Yahoo! Internet Life*, Robert Scheer wrote: "Big Brother is back big-time, and Americans are welcoming him warmly."

"The fact is," Scheer added, "ordinary citizens will be affected far more by the Internet-oriented parts of this legislation than will terrorists."

Privacy advocates note that under the newly enacted legislation the federal government has gained expanded powers to spy on web surfing activities of all Americans, including specific terms that are entered into Internet search engines. The government need merely inform any federal judge of its choosing that its spying activities could conceivably lead to information that is "relevant" to an ongoing criminal investigation. The person being spied upon need not be a target of the investigation. The new law removes all judicial discretion: the application must be granted. Furthermore, the government is not obligated to report to the court or tell the person spied on what it has done.

The USA Patriot Act also raises the threshold of how much information the government may obtain about users from ISPs, such as Yahoo!, or others who handle or store their online communications. First, it permits ISPs to voluntarily hand over all "non-content" information to law enforcement without the need for any court order or subpoena. Second, it expands the records that the government may seek with a simple subpoena, without the requirement of a court review, to include records of specific online session times and durations, temporarily assigned network Internet Protocol (IP) addresses and the means and sources of payments, including credit card and/or bank account numbers.

One big winner in the new national climate will be the aforementioned Carnivore. Originally named for its ability to get at the "meat" in large quantities of e-mail and instant messaging, it has recently been renamed DCS1000 because the original name sounded so creepy. The DSC1000 technology was spawned in the FBI's own labs. The FBI is close-lipped about how it works, and ISPs that install it are under court order to keep quiet about its technological gizzards. It has been reported in the trade press to be a stealthy looking black box dedicated computer that runs on an Intel Pentium III chip under the Windows NT operating system. Its sole dedicated task is to "sniff out" Internet packets, the building block of all non-wire online communications. When the FBI has a suspect in its sights whose e-mail it wants to poke through, it gets a court order similar to traditional ones used for phone wiretaps employed with traditional point-to-point circuit-switched networks. It then takes the DSC1000 out of storage in its Quantico, Va., technical field headquarters and works with an individual ISP's engineers to hook it up to that server's packet-switched network. Once it's hooked up, the computer can search through e-mail traffic in a variety of ways—by names on "To" and "From" lines, by trolling for an Internet Protocol (IP) address and by filtering for keywords within the header or body of an e-mail message. In its official description of the DSC1000, the FBI insists that its software was designed to spy with "surgical" precision (*www.fbi.gov/hq/lab/carnivore/carnivore2.htm*) on specific individuals.

But the machine's critics are not so sanguine. They say that once the device is hooked up to an ISP's network, it can be used to do keyword searches—for, say, "hijack" or "bin Laden"—on every single e-mail which passes through the data-stream. "They're sucking on the hose," said Lee Tien, senior staff attorney with the Electronic Freedom Foundation. "It's conceivable they're taking every bit and deciding whether they're entitled to it or not, but maybe they're looking at every bit."

It's a fair bet that there will be a lot more DSC1000's installed in the weeks and months ahead. After September 11, according to widespread trade press accounts, the FBI fanned out and installed the data-capturing devices on ISPs throughout the country, without any further publicity and without any vocal opposition from the ISPs.

Just what information the FBI can collect in the altered national climate depends on what kind of court order the agency has procured. For circuit-switched phone wiretaps, routine orders call for so-called "trap-and-traces," which allow law enforcement authorities to record the phone numbers that a suspect dials, and to perform "pen-registers," which log the phone numbers and the time of incoming calls. Similar secret court orders, it is widely believed, are currently being issued for the DSC1000 in order to obtain e-mail addresses. But to actually gain access to the substance of a packet-switched e-mail message, under current law the FBI needs a full-blown content wiretap order, which the courts have been more wary in granting.

When the DSC1000 was first introduced as Carnivore, civil libertarians hoped to stop it cold. But after EarthLink settled with the FBI, for fear of losing its court case on appeal—and in the absence of any groundswell of popular opposition—privacy advocates have increasingly redirected their efforts to halting what they see as potential abuses in how the FBI might deploy the technology.

"We're not trying to stop them from doing their jobs," said Ari Schwartz, a policy analyst at the Center for Democracy & Technology. "What we're talking about is oversight."

These critics would like to be sure that when the DSC1000 is installed on an ISP the data collection that is done is truly the equivalent of a "surgical strike"—so that the FBI avoids any "collateral damage" by further downloading information about non-targets that it also happens to intercept. Moreover, the critics charge that the FBI is already misusing pen-registers and trap-and-traces. The government has argued that those limited wiretaps entitle it to e-mail headers—the brief subject headlines at the top of each message aimed at summarizing the contents. To get access to headers, Carnivore's critics say, the FBI should have to meet the higher standard for a content wiretap. They would also like to see rules instituted that would require the FBI to throw out collected evidence once an investigation is over, rather than allowing the government to store the data in a semi-permanent database.

The terrorist attacks will also probably increase the use of "computer foren-sics," detective work that turns criminals' own computers against them. One of the hottest tools in the field right now is keystroke logging—law enforcement's surrep-titious installation of software, or even a rigged keyboard, to log every keystroke a suspect types into his or her computer. Computer forensic techniques are usually kept under wraps. But keystroke logging techniques became public in the trial of Nicodemo S. Scarfo, an accused New Jersey bookmaker. The FBI used keystroke log-ging to ascertain the password to an Internet encryption program Scarfo allegedly used to relay gambling and loan-sharking data. Nevertheless, keystroke logging is hard for law enforcement to employ because it's usually a "black-bag job"—an agent must actually show up and install the monitoring device. Those techniques could yet prove to be a crucial asset in uncovering terrorist plots before attacks actually occur.

V. Online Community Response

Privacy advocates say they will keep fighting these battles—before judges, in Congress and in the media. But they also realize it's become a hard sell to try to rein in the carnivorous beast, a situation that is likely to persist for some time. "No mat-ter how you feel about Carnivore, if the smoke is still coming off the World Trade Center, no one is going to tell the FBI they can't install it," said David McClure, president of the U.S. Internet Industry Association.

"Laws made in crisis mode seldom vanish once the wartime footing ends," notes Brendan I. Koerner, a Markle Fellow at the New America Foundation. For example, in response to rumors that TWA Flight 800 had been downed by a ter-rorist bomb, Congress made it easier to expel legal aliens. However, when mechan-ical failure was revealed to be the culprit, the law remained on the books. Said Koerner: "Even if Al Qaeda is somehow dismantled in the coming years, one sus-pects that technology's carefree days were also a victim of September 11."

"We were probably poised to have much better privacy protections, and I think this is going to create a lot of resistance," said Jamie Love, executive director of the Consumer Project on Technology. He foresees a backlash against programs that enable anonymous Web browsing—and, perhaps, even an end to all anony-mous surfing on U.S.-based public-access terminals.

In the aftermath of the attacks, one prominent remailer operator shut down his system. In a note to his fellow operators, Len Sassaman explained his move by writing: "I don't want to get caught in the middle of this. I'm sorry. I'm currently unemployed and don't have the resources to defend myself. At this point in time, a free-speech argument will not gain much sympathy with the Feds, judges, and gen-eral public."

In hindsight, some of the privacy alarms that went off after the September 11 attacks now appear to have been false. In the hours after the attacks, there were scattered reports that several anonymous proxies—services that allow users to surf the Internet or send e-mail without revealing their identity—voluntarily shut down or cut back on services. Privacy advocates were concerned that the government might start to force anonymous proxies to stop operating, in the name of national security.

But so far, no evidence has emerged that the terrorists used anonymizers. In fact, they may have intentionally avoided them. "If you're a terrorist, your main goal is not to be noticed at all," says Lance Cottrell, president of Anonymizer.com. "Using an anonymizer gets you noticed." Investigators now believe some of the hijackers accessed the Internet through computers in public libraries in Florida and Virginia. Those personal computers offered them anonymity because they do not require log-ons or passwords. Their sign-in sheets are (or at least were until recently) thrown out at the end of the day, and at least some of the computers came with wrap-around "shields" that prevented other patrons from reading what was on the screen.

VI. Foreign Operations

The drive to root out radical Islamic terrorist cells is also likely to give a boost to an even more sweeping eavesdropping system: Echelon, the National Security Agency's (NSA) top-secret global wiretapping network. Echelon grew out of a 1945 agreement to share information obtained by bugging hostile powers, particularly the Soviet Union. It was developed and is now operated as a joint effort of the NSA and the intelligence operations of England, Canada and New Zealand. Echelon has been shrouded in mystery—so much so that its very existence was long doubted. But a report by the European Parliament in July confirmed that it is quite real. That report suggested the technology is able to intercept virtually any telephone conversation, e-mail, Internet connection or fax on a worldwide basis. Echelon is believed to work somewhat akin to a global police scanner. It is reportedly able to search out specific keywords like "hijack" or "bomb." Not surprisingly, the biggest stumbling block to the system is said to be the gigantic volume of data that is being collected—upwards of 3 million messages a minute, according to the estimates in the European Parliament report—that must then be sorted and analyzed. Clearly, if Echelon was working before September 11, it didn't prevent what occurred in Lower Manhattan, Northern Virginia and the Pennsylvania countryside.

The American Civil Liberties Union and other privacy advocates have long fought Echelon. Among their chief concerns is that Echelon will be used to spy on Americans, even though Americans are outside the NSA's jurisdiction, because Internet traffic takes such roundabout paths. For its part, the NSA, which has reportedly had to lobby Congress hard for Echelon funding, will now presumably have a far more receptive audience. Included in the items likely to be high on the NSA's wish list: funding to hire large numbers of staff, especially Arabic speakers, to sift through voluminous data.

VII. The Road Ahead

Immediately after the September 11 attacks, when rumors were rampant that the terrorists had encrypted their e-mail messages, it appeared that there would be a crackdown on encryption programs. Sen. Judd Gregg, Republican of New Hampshire, began drawing up legislation that would require encryption programs to contain a "backdoor" that would be accessible to U.S. law enforcement. But the anti-encryption campaign gained little momentum.

In part, it was because law enforcement began to doubt that the terrorists had bothered to use encryption. But just as important, the last prior attempt to crack down on encryption, during the Clinton administration, was abandoned when even its supporters began to doubt it would help. One key flaw: there's no way for the U.S. intelligence authorities to ensure that every encryption program sold in the world has a backdoor accessible to American law enforcement. "Why would terrorists use encryption with a backdoor we had access to?" asked Dorothy Denning, a Georgetown University computer-science professor who has abandoned her past support for rules requiring backdoors. "There are a lot of good encryption companies outside the U.S. they could go to."

Besides, as noted above, there's little evidence that terrorists have used encryption. Brian Gladman, who once headed up electronic security for Britain's Ministry of Defense and NATO, argues that the September 11 hijackers probably eschewed encrypted messages because they would have stood out and been more likely to have been picked up by the National Security Agency. (Although texts may not be able to be deciphered in a timely way by even the most powerful computers, other information, such as routing addresses, which cannot be encrypted on a packet-switched Internet network, could prove useful to the authorities in locating terrorist cells.)

In the wake of the September 11 attacks, the Internet community braced for a truly draconian privacy crackdown. Cottrell, the "atomizer" provider, heard talk of requiring Internet users to have an Internet ID card, with a smart-card reader or bio-optic identification, to go online, or imposing an affirmative duty on all ISPs to track their users. Richard Smith, chief technology officer of the Brookline, Mass.-based Privacy Foundation, talked of his fears that the government would require websites to log and save visitor IP addresses, and ISPs to save e-mail, for a period of years.

As a result of the post–September 11 crisis, there will almost certainly be some changes on the margins in privacy on the Internet. There will likely be more e-mail and Internet monitoring of specific suspects, pursuant to court orders. Echelon is likely to spy more than ever on overseas communications. And ISPs and other Internet players are already approaching requests from law enforcement with altered attitudes. "In the old days it was easy to take a stand and say anything goes on our ISP," says Internet association president McClure. "Now they're going to be quicker to say, 'unless there's a reason to think you're breaking the law.'" Still, some privacy advocates hope the changes won't be overwhelming. "There seem to be a lot of voices out there saying, 'Wait a minute, take this a little slower,'" says Cottrell. "We don't want to trample our civil liberties, particularly if there's no gain."

Some civil libertarians argue, in fact, that as the war on terrorism continues, there could even be a renewed appreciation for privacy. After all, secrecy can also help the good guys. Anonymizer.com is making its service available for free to investigators. That will allow law enforcement at all levels to look at terrorist websites without tipping off the groups that they're being watched. And there's another group that has traditionally relied on privacy: informants.

Anonymizer.com has created a special gateway to the FBI website where anonymous tips can be left about bin Laden and his terror network. It's something legislators may want to keep in mind when they reconsider the laws of cyberspace in the years ahead. After all, private e-mail, anonymized Web surfing and encrypted messages could hide not only terrorists but a wavering member of a terror network seeking to summon up the courage to turn them in.

VIII. National Security Issues

Free speech faces the strongest challenges during times of crisis. So it should come as no surprise that the U.S. government's response to the terrorist attacks of September 11, 2001, has had a chilling effect on the availability of information on the Internet as well as on some of the people who seek to provide information through that powerful medium.

On the other hand, a wealth of specific military and intelligence information is available online. One such content-rich site is Globalsecurity.org, which is based in Alexandria, Va., near the Pentagon. (On October 15, ABC News quoted John Pike, the site's proprietor, as having received a request from low-level military officials that he remove data he had gathered from military websites.)

To be sure, a Web search in early December found no websites that had been shut down by a direct federal order. Such an action, on its very face, would violate the First Amendment since U.S. courts have repeatedly ruled that the Internet, as a mass medium of communication, is subject to constitutional protection.

Commercial Internet service providers have been more active in shutting down sites. For example, Yahoo, one of the largest such providers, has unilaterally removed 55 "jihad-related" sites since September 11.

Similar rights may not be found in other nations, however. For example, in early October, the British government shut down qoqaz.net on the grounds that the site was run by London-based Azzam Publications, which it said advocated support of Muslim-run terrorism in the Caucasus, the donation of funds to the Taliban and military training for battling the West.

A cached copy of the British website, preserved by Google, includes an illustration captioned "Jihad in Afghanistan." Superimposed over a map of Afghanistan is a black cross dripping with red blood. A blue Star of David is positioned over the center of the cross. (Google has told both government agencies and private organizations that it will delete, at their request, cached versions of their Web pages where the originals have been removed.)

Assam.com has also been shut down by multiple ISPs in the United States, although it is still available via some others, particularly those affiliated with educational institutions such as Harvard. The dead links are explained on the still-active site as "due to freedom of speech being taken away in the West."

The U.S.-based Assam site contains an English-language version of Osama bin Laden's 13,000-word "Declaration of War Against the Americans Occupying the Land of the Two Holy Places," subtitled "Expel the Infidels from the Arab Peninsula," and written in 1996. The manifesto is preceded by a disclaimer stating, "Azzam Publications has provided this document for information purposes and as a reference for other media organizations only. It does automatically mean that we agree with or endorse everything written in this document."

To be sure, the Internet site enables people to read and evaluate bin Laden's polemic in toto, without editing or commentary. (A typical passage reads: "It should not be hidden from you that the people of Islam had suffered from aggression, iniquity and injustice imposed on them by the Zionist-Crusaders alliance and their collaborators; to the extent that the Muslims' blood became the cheapest and their wealth as loot in the hands of the enemies. Their blood was spilled in Palestine and Iraq . . .")

Here are some other examples of post-crisis self-censorship:

- Amazon.com, the leading bookseller on the Internet, deleted a photograph of a Arabic book jacket that shows a plane flying through the top of a building under construction in Riyadh, Saudi Arabia, that has a top shaped like the eye of a needle. The sole link to the World Trade Center is that the building in Riyadh was being financed by Prince Alwaleed bin Talal bin Abdul Aziz al-Saud, whose $10 million donation to the Twin Towers Fund was refused by Mayor Rudolph Giuliani of New York, because along with expressing condolences, the prince urged the United States to re-examine its policy toward Israel.
- Actress Barbra Streisand removed anti-Bush articles from her website, explaining that "in light of recent events, I strongly believe we must support our government despite our disagreements on certain policies, such as those relating to environmental, educational, social and other specific issues. My past concerns about such matters still pertain, but at this point

in time, I have removed several articles from my website in an effort to encourage national unity instead of partisan divisions."

- Steven Aftergood, who administers the Project on Government Secrecy for the Federation of American Scientists, has pulled some 200 pages of previously posted information from the Internet out of concern that terrorists might find them useful. They included floor plans of National Security Agency and Central Intelligence Agency facilities and images of foreign nuclear weapons plants.
- MSNBC removed from an article formerly entitled "Ashcroft Seeks Sweeping Powers" and now called "House Approves $343 Billion Defense Bill" a section about how the House Judiciary Committee's Republican staffers ordered television camera crews to leave a hearing on terrorist attacks after Ashcroft testified.
- The WhatDemocracy.com website removed content critical of "right-wing politics, including President Bush and the Republican Party, in the aftermath of the terrorist attacks "due to the potential of endangerment to our staff." It noted "we would love to address the current terrorism situation, and we should have the right to safely address our opinions, but who will step up to the plate and protect us, and how?"

Some official websites that do not bear directly on freedom of speech issues but could prove useful to watchdog groups that monitor government accountability in budgetary and regulatory matters have also left the Internet in the wake of the crisis.

Here are some instances that have come to light:

- The Agency for Toxic Substances and Disease Registry dropped a report critical of chemical plant security. And the Army Corps of Engineers site that contained information about an underground military command center near Washington was placed behind a firewall so a username and password are now required for access.
- The Department of Energy, National Transportation of Radioactive Materials site has been replaced with the note "This site temporarily unavailable."
- The Department of Transportation (DOT) has limited access to the National Pipeline Mapping System of the Office of Pipeline Safety, which lays out the network of high-pressure natural gas pipelines throughout the nation and the site of the Geographic Information Services section of the DOT's Bureau of Transportation Services. Access to these highly detailed maps of roads and utilities is now limited to federal, state, and local government officials.

- The Environmental Protection Agency has pulled from its site risk management plans, which contain detailed information about the dangers of chemical accidents—such as toxic plume maps and emergency response plans after a refinery explosion.
- The Federal Aviation Administration has pulled data from a site listing enforcement violations such as weaknesses in airport security.
- The Federal Energy Regulatory Commission has removed documents that detail specifications for energy facilities from its website.
- The International Nuclear Safety Center has removed its reactor maps and left the following message: "If you requested access to the maps of nuclear power reactor locations, these maps have been taken off-line temporarily pending the outcome of a policy review by the U.S. Department of Energy and Argonne National Laboratory." (The nuclear site locations page in National Atlas of the United States is also missing, yielding a broken link.)
- The Los Alamos National Laboratory has removed a number of reports from its laboratory publications page.
- The John Glenn Research Center of the National Aeronautics and Space Administration (NASA) noted "public access to many of our websites is temporarily limited. We apologize for any inconvenience."
- The Nuclear Regulatory Commission (NRC) displays only "select content" while "performing a review of all material" on their website, although most of the information has been there for years and "nothing top secret was on the website to begin with," according to William Beecher, the NRC spokesman.
- The U.S. Geological Survey has removed a number of pages from its registered online water-resources reports database.

IX. Online Rumors

While rumors traditionally flourish in times of crisis, the Internet offers a particularly warm soil for planting them. E-mails bearing tales of purported events on September 11 and beyond—hidden from the public and either unknown to or masked by the mass media—have traveled quickly and propagated rapidly.

Sorting through the overwhelming number of rumors and images can be daunting. But most experts believe the Internet also offers a means to find out quickly what is true and what is not. "We try on different theories, myths and we discard them pretty quickly if they don't make sense," said Steve Jones, a professor at the University of Illinois at Chicago and president of the Association of Internet Researchers.

Jones noted that while people are pretty good at discarding rumors that don't make sense, "the problem with the Internet is that we don't have the same type of conversation online that we do offline." As he put it: "The Internet continues to throw up new, possible fictions that we keep sorting through. It's too easy to rehash. People come into the debate at different times. It's almost as if the rumors recur." "Who would have imagined two weeks ago that suddenly we would look at our mail as a source of potential death?" said Gary Alan Fine, a sociology professor at Northwestern University. "In times of ambiguity, things we once thought of as normal seem frightening, and we become more open to rumor."

Aaron Lynch, a scholar in thought contagion analysis who is based at Northwestern University in Evanston, Ill., said people are drawn to pass on terrorism warnings online by the "gratifying" sense that they might be saving the life of others, who might come back to thank them someday.

One such e-mail, attributed to an acquaintance, said a woman had gone to the apartment of her Middle Eastern boyfriend, only to find he had moved out, leaving her a note not to fly on September 11.

That particular rumor received some extra veracity because the sender, Laura Katsis, had included her California phone number and this cover message: "I think you all know that I don't send out hoaxes and don't do the reactionary thing and send out anything that crosses my path. This one, however, is a friend of a friend and I've given it enough credibility in my mind that I'm writing it up and sending it out to all of you."

The information, however, is false, according to www.snopes2.com, one of several Internet sites devoted to investigating rumors and so-called urban legends. "A public information officer at the FBI's National Press Office told us that they've fielded many calls about this message, they've checked it out, and they have received no letter of warning from a girl with an Afghan boyfriend," the proprietors of the website, Barbara and David said.

Deluged with queries, Katsis's employer, Volt Information Sciences, shut down her phone extension and e-mail service. Inquiries were met either with a recorded statement or an automatic e-mail response from company officials denying any direct knowledge of the incident.

Such rumors, Barbara Mikkelson said, can be "hugely comforting in the strangest way. We're reducing terrorism—which can strike anywhere, anytime, to anybody—to 'We know the place and time, so just avoid being there.' So it restores a sense of control back into an out-of-control world."

Each of the entries in the "rumors of war" category on Mikkelson's website is color-coded: red is for false, green is for true, yellow represents an ambiguous situation and white signifies an unknown origin. A rumor that garlic cures anthrax, for example, is coded red.

On the site white bullets are the ones most commonly associated with "pure" urban legends—entries that describe plausible events so general that they could have happened to someone, somewhere, at some time, and are therefore essentially unprovable. Some legends that describe events known to have occurred in real life are also put into this category if there is no evidence that the events occurred before the origination of the legends.

Green bullets are used for two similar but distinct types of entries: claims that are demonstrably true, and urban legends that are based on real events. For the former, "demonstrably true" means that the claim has been established by a preponderance of (reliable) evidence; for the latter, a green bullet indicates that the legend described is based on an actual occurrence. (The word "based" is key here: many legends describe events that have taken place in real life, but those events did not occur until the related legend was already in circulation.)

Yellow bullets generally describe disputed claims—factual items which the available evidence is too contradictory or insufficient to establish as either true or false. This category also includes claims that have a kernel of truth to them but are not literally true as stated. (For example, an entry that read "Soupy Sales was fired for asking children to send him 'little green pieces of paper' on his TV show" would fit this classification because even though Soupy Sales did make such a request, he was not fired for doing so.) Some legends also fall into this classification when it cannot be determined whether the legends preceded similar real life events, or vice-versa.

Red bullets mark claims which cannot be established as true by a preponderance of (reliable) evidence. Some urban legends are also placed into this category because they describe events too implausible to have actually occurred, or too fantastic to have escaped mention in the media of the day.

Links send surfers to a full takeout on the rumor, the verdict on its veracity and sometimes several pages worth of information the Mikkelsons have collected.

"The first thing I do is use news databases to see what I can find out about the facts" of any rumor, Barbara Mikkelson said. "We perform various searches of a number of online databases, sometimes we call the people involved in the stories, we use what we know about related legends and stories . . . Or we go to UCLA (University of California at Los Angeles) to look into their microfilm archives."

Barbara Mikkelson is not surprised by the proliferation of rumors in the wake of the terrorist attacks. "It's a normal way for people to try and deal with times like this. What happened was horrifying, and part of the way we try to deal with something we can't comprehend is to try to fill in all the missing spots with information," she said.

"People want so badly to believe that we are not living in a world where anything can happen at any time. It's the truth, but it's too scary a truth for a lot of people," she added. "They'd much rather believe that there are prophets that can foresee everything, and that if bad stuff happens and people die, it's just because we didn't pay attention to what they said or we didn't interpret things correctly."

In the month after the September 11 attacks, the Mikkelsons' site received between 2 million and 2.5 million hits each day as Internet users sought the latest on post-attack rumors that ranged from a terrorist attack on a mall on Halloween to blue envelopes containing a deadly virus. Both proved false.

The Mikkelsons have filled a void. Created six years ago, www.snopes2.com is one of the few sites devoted exclusively to ferreting out Internet rumors, the modern-day equivalent of urban legends. The terrorist attacks have, by far, generated a greater number of falsehoods—and public interest—than any other event in the site's lifetime.

"I use it a lot myself and I send students to it," said Sabina Magliocco, an assistant professor of anthropology at California State University, Northridge, who specializes in folklore. "I think it's very reliable."

And the couple who started the website as a hobby have now become experts on the topic, regularly appearing on TV news programs such as CNN and ABC as well as newspapers across the country, including *The Dallas Morning News* and the *Seattle Post-Intelligencer*.

"We work with them all the time," said Howard Fienberg, a research analyst with the Statistical Assessment Service, a Washington-based nonprofit research organization that works to improve the public's understanding of science and social research. He said the information on the site is well-researched and credible.

The Centers for Disease Control and Prevention lists the website as a source, though it includes a disclaimer stating it does not endorse it. The U.S. Department of Energy's Hoaxbusters page also links to *www.snopes2.com.*

Urban Legends and Folklore (*urbanlegends.about.com*), which also investigates Internet rumors, defines an urban legend as something that appears mysteriously, spreads spontaneously, contains elements of horror or humor, and makes good storytelling.

"It does not have to be false, although most are," the site says. Urban legends often have a basis in fact, "but it's their life after-the-fact that gives them particular interest."

But e-mail rumors can also threaten to disrupt urban life. Thus, Massachusetts officials braced for a potential terrorist strike after an e-mail circulated widely in the region stating that "a few drunk Arab men" had warned a Boston bartender that bloodshed would occur on September 22.

Well into the fall, Harvard students circulated a rumor that their campus was No. 5 on a secret federal list of likely terrorist targets. Another e-mailed rumor, particularly widely propagated in the Middle East, held that the Israel Secret Service, known as the Mossad, was behind the September 11 attacks.

One of the first rumors circulated by e-mail and on the Internet was that the French physician and astrologer Nostradamus in 1654 had made the prediction that World War III would start with the fall of the "two brothers," supposedly a reference to the World Trade Center towers.

Lee Rainie, director of the Pew Internet & American Life Project in Washington, said the Nostradamus rumor was an example of the self-policing element of the Internet. "Within a half hour of getting the Nostradamus e-mail, I got the debunking version," Rainie said. (The Mikkelsons further noted that the lines being attributed to Nostradamus [who actually died in 1566] were written by a Canadian university student in 1997 and first appeared as a Web page essay.)

Rainie said researchers have found that Americans say they like to seek out different opinions on the Internet, although they are most comfortable with those that are consistent with theirs. "People obviously have to have their antenna out," he added. "If it seems incredible, chances are it is incredible and uncredible."

In the Middle East, the rumors, spread via the Internet and other mass media channels, took on a more sinister coloration.

Mark Siegel, a Washington communications consultant who once represented former Pakistan President Benazir Bhutto and has had extensive dealings in the Muslim world, said the intellectual elite are receptive to the message from the West because they, too, are targets of fanatics. "The problem is the masses," Siegel said. "The governments of our allied Arab friends often spread in their state-controlled media the hate that fuels the masses."

He cited the example of the televised interview with the father of Mohamed Atta, a leader of the terrorists who participated in the September 11 attacks. "Atta's father is a lawyer in Cairo, a middle-class guy," Siegel said. "He told the press that his son was innocent, that the attack on the United States was a Mossad [Israeli intelligence] operation, and that all the Jews were evacuated from the World Trade Center before the attack. That insanity was on state-controlled media all over the Arab world and on Islamic Internet sites."

X. Bioterrorism

The Internet's inherent ability to widely spread vital public health information in a crisis has been put to its first significant test on the bioterrorism front, with both doctors and consumers turning to the World Wide Web for timely answers.

"Never before in my medical career have I had a more urgent need for just-in-time, on-demand health-care information and less time to obtain it than now," Dr. William Cordell, professor of emergency medicine at Indiana University, told Laura Landro of *The Wall Street Journal.*

Cordell gave the reporter an account of an Indianapolis airport worker who came to a hospital emergency room showing classic symptoms of flu and diarrhea after anthrax was found on a mail sorting machine. Dr. Cordell consulted an anthrax response "flow chart" he had just received the day before via e-mail from a local poison center. With that as a guide, he obtained the needed cultures, prescribed antibiotic treatment and sought to calm the patient's fears. (So far, he has tested negative for the disease.)

The sheer amount of bioterrorism information on the Web is daunting: a search on Google for "anthrax" yields nearly a million results. One potential danger of the flood of bioterrorism data on the Web is that it could spur hypochondria and panic among the public. And even solid data can become quickly outdated, or hard to interpret.

In the aftermath of the anthrax attacks, health professionals sought to get the latest diagnostic and treatment data on the Web in an effort to allow doctors to easily obtain the information they need to battle bioterrorism and to give consumers practical advice on how to protect themselves.

The U.S. Centers for Disease Control and Prevention (CDC) quickly moved into the forefront of those organizations getting important information to the public. The Atlanta-based CDC set up a special site for bioterrorism data (www.bt.cdc.gov) that in the immediate aftermath of the anthrax attacks saw more more than one million hits per day.

In addition to the CDC, several other sites sought to guarantee a reliable, level-headed and clearly presented source of information. Thus, the American Medical Association stressed such issues as the need to put the risks in perspective and to understand the dangers of taking unnecessary antibiotics. "Part of our mission has to be education for calming the public's fears," said AMA Chairman Timothy Flaherty. The association, which co-sponsors the CDC webcasts, offered free access to its five recent articles on smallpox, botulism, plague, tularemia and anthrax via its www.ama-assn.org site. It also set up disaster-preparedness and medical-response Web pages. Dr. Flaherty noted that nearly 75 percent of AMA members use the Internet, thereby enabling them to quickly learn of changes in therapeutic regimens as more scientific evidence becomes available.

Even as New York University Medical Center presented a symposium on bioterrorism, emergency preparedness and chemical warfare in October 2001 for about 100 local doctors, some 8,000 more were able to watch a free Webcast of the event throughout the country. It was presented by World Medical Leaders, a for-profit site offering continuing medical-education credits for doctors who pay to hear experts lecture online. The group, which is owned by Omnicom Group, an advertising conglomorate, also has set up a bioterrorism resource center on its site, offering CDC updates and lectures from Harvard University and the National Institute of Mental Health.

The American College of Emergency Physicians sponsored a live forum on its ACEP.org website. Doctors were able to pose questions to a CDC epidemiologist online. The group has also contacted 13,000 emergency doctors by e-mail, sending them its latest morbidity and mortality weekly reports, including updated treatment protocols for biologic agents.

Other previously closed professional sites, aimed primarily at doctors, have opened their bioterrorism files to the public. For, example, Stanford University's online database for doctors, Stanford Skolar MD, allows consumers to access its new biological and chemical terrorism resources by registering for a free ten-day trial on its website at *www.skolar.com.*

Similarly, the Medical Library Association has updated its bioterrorism resources on its *mlanet.org* site to offer pertinent information to consumers who are unfamiliar with medical jargon. And the Nemours Foundation's Center for Children's Health Media is using its *KidsHealth.org* website to offer articles for parents and for different child and teenage reading levels on "what you need to know about smallpox, anthrax and coping with the uncertainties we face today."

As is usually the case, there is also a dark side to bioterrorism dealings on the Internet. Thus, some 40 operators of websites have been warned by the Federal Trade Commission (FTC) to stop making what the agency called false claims that dietary supplements can prevent, treat or cure anthrax, smallpox and other health hazards. The warnings followed an Internet surfing project by the FTC, the Food and Drug Administration and state attorneys general in some 30 states.

J. Howard Beales III, the FTC's director of consumer protection, said the online investigation uncovered more than 200 websites that were marketing bioterrorism-related products, including gas masks, protective suits, mail sterilizers, homeopathic remedies and biohazard test kits, in addition to dietary supplements.

"We started right after September 11, both monitoring complaints and organizing a surf of the Internet to look for all the different ways people might try to take advantage of the September 11 tragedy to make money," Beales said. "We found claims that a variety of dietary supplements like colloidal silver or zinc mineral water or oregano oil would be remedies for anthrax or other biological agents. So far as we know there's no scientific evidence whatsoever that even suggests those kinds of claims might be true."

Conclusion

The evidence suggests that—temporary and spotty overload problems aside—the decentralized nature of the Internet provided, and continues to provide, a coherent and novel U.S. domestic communication channel in a quasi-wartime setting. But given the clearly more intrusive role of the federal government and the perceived threats to U.S. security posed by unfettered online communications, how that powerful forum evolves from this point forward still remains a major unresolved issue.

Prepared for War, Ready for Peace?
Paramilitaries, Politics, and the Press in Northern Ireland

Tim Cooke

The reporting of sustained conflict poses particular challenges for news organizations and journalists in the search for truth, objectivity, accuracy, balance, independence and responsibility. For news media most closely linked to the arena of conflict the challenges are unique. While international or foreign media often go largely unaccountable to the society about which they report, indigenous news organizations must wrestle daily with both the short- and longer-term consequences of their judgments and actions. The very proximity of news organizations rooted in and broadcasting or publishing to a society affected by conflict, and in particular by political violence, makes them important players in the battle for hearts and minds in a war of weapons and words, of politics and pictures.

The Middle East, South Africa and Northern Ireland have all offered examples of how the news practices of indigenous journalism can be heavily conditioned by political violence. They also offer case studies of how news organizations used to reporting conflict have responded to the fresh challenge of reporting a society attempting the transition to peace. What role does the news media play in such a transition and how do news programs, newspapers and the journalists who frame our daily window on the world assess what we should see when we look through it? News organizations in Northern Ireland, in reporting on the paramilitary groups responsible for 30 years of headlines at home and abroad, have moved into the political arena. This examination of their role attempts to offer insight into this interactive process in one divided society.

Context

After decades of conflict Northern Ireland is riding the roller-coaster of constitutional change. The Good Friday Agreement of 1998 places the province firmly in the center of a political vortex that proffers the most fundamental transformation in governance since the foundation of the State in 1921—more far-reaching than the abolition of the unionist-dominated Stormont Parliament and the imposition by the British government of Direct Rule from Westminster in 1972.

One of the key reasons the conditions for such change now exist is that many of the people who have sustained and directed the political violence of the last quarter century and more have agreed, for the moment at least, to silence their guns and emphasize politics rather than paramilitarism.

Encouraged in latter years by changes in the policies of both the British and Irish governments, most of the key paramilitary groups involved in three decades of violence now have a political party that represents their thinking. On the republican side the Provisional IRA (Irish Republican Army) is represented by Sinn Fein. On the loyalist side the UDA/UFF (Ulster Defense Association/Ulster Freedom Fighters) is represented by the UDP (Ulster Democratic Party) and the Ulster Volunteer Force is represented by the PUP (Progressive Unionist Party). These three paramilitary groups, the IRA, UDA/UFF and UVF have been responsible for most of the 3,500 deaths in Northern Ireland since 1969—the IRA for some 1,600 deaths and the two loyalist groups for almost 1,000. One of the key elements of government policy aimed at encouraging a transition to politics was the devising of an election in May 1996 that helped even the smallest of these political parties (the UDP) achieve representation at the multi-party Talks sponsored by the British and Irish governments that ended on April 10, 1998, with a new cross-community agreement on future governance.

All this has had a profound effect in and on the media in Northern Ireland. After years of reporting a catalogue of horror, grief and destruction within a paradigm which condemns acts of terrorism as illegitimate and irrational, new questions have emerged as to whom government and the media view as legitimate actors in the political sphere. The transmutation of violent protagonists into politicians and brokers of peace is a process that the media has both facilitated and wrestled with. A news media proficient in reporting the paramilitaries in conflict appears less prepared for the consequences of the paramilitary role in peacemaking. Journalists are still adjusting to a changing situation that is giving the paramilitaries a new role in the press, public, and political arenas. This question was thrown into relief by an event in January 1998 that exposed the quandary—the decision by the British Secretary of State for Northern Ireland, Dr. Mo Mowlam, to visit convicted paramilitary leaders inside the high-security Maze Prison to persuade them to renew their support for the peace process at a time when it seemed on the verge of collapse. As we shall see, the event raised uncomfortable questions for the media—evident in the text and pictures that form news narrative and in the editorials of certain newspapers.

The purpose of this chapter is to examine how journalists and news organizations in Northern Ireland have been dealing with the questions of legitimacy and voice in a period of transition and to discuss the past and present influences affecting their framing and treatment of paramilitary groups inside and outside the peace process.

The role of the news media in the process of political communication has been and continues to be of particular importance in Northern Ireland. In a society with many traditional religious divisions in education, housing, employment, sport and culture and where previous attempts to build political institutions with cross-community consensus have failed, the media has been a primary arena for communication between and within the Catholic and Protestant communities. A notable factor here is that Northern Ireland does not fall victim to one of the difficulties apparent in some other divided societies—that of a media divided by language and speaking to only one side in the conflict. The mainstream news organizations in Northern Ireland are English language, and most of the population experiences exposure to more than one news source. Thus while the two morning newspapers published in Belfast cater to particular constituencies, the *Irish News* to Catholics and the *News Letter* to Protestants, the newspaper with the largest circulation, the *Belfast Telegraph* (29 percent market share) sells to Catholics and Protestants. The news services provided by BBC Northern Ireland and Ulster Television are also aimed at the whole community. This chapter draws mainly on material from the five news organizations mentioned above. Between them, the *Belfast Telegraph*, *Irish News* and *News Letter* account for some 47 percent of market share. The daily television news programs discussed here, Ulster Television's "UTV Live" at 6 P.M. and BBC Northern Ireland's "Newsline 6.30" half an hour later account for a combined share of around 70 percent.

Of course not all the paramilitary groups active in Northern Ireland are involved in the transition into the political process—and even those on ceasefire have been judged in varying degrees to have infringed upon the principles on nonviolence to which they were required to subscribe as a precondition for participation in the Talks process. Both the UDP and Sinn Fein were suspended temporarily from the Talks for varying periods during the first three months of 1998. Furthermore the IRA ceasefire, which allowed Sinn Fein to take part in the talks, is viewed by some Irish republicans as at best ill-advised and at worst a treacherous betrayal. Hence we have seen the emergence of the Continuity IRA, which bombed a number of town centers in Northern Ireland in the first months of 1998. On the loyalist side the emergence of the LVF (Loyalist Volunteer Force) is a challenge to the analysis of the established pro-British paramilitary groups the UDA and the UVF. At the beginning of 1998 the LVF carried out a series of killings of Catholics after another small republican group not on ceasefire, the INLA (Irish National Liberation Army), killed the LVF leader Billy Wright inside the Maze Prison.

Against this complex web of violence and ceasefire, infringement and observation, the emergence of groups more extreme than the established extremists, and the background of the multi-party Talks, the media has been confronted with irregular patterns and conflicting messages, reporting both paramilitaries in pursuit of peace and others in pursuit of violence. Here I examine the media's dilemma.

First, concentrating on the methods of communication between the paramilitaries and the media, I discuss the extent to which news organizations try to differentiate between propaganda and news. Key issues here are the way in which the rules about what makes news gives stories about paramilitaries and their actions a journalistic appeal while at the same time news organizations also see themselves as representatives of the wider society's anti-terrorist stance.

Second, I discuss the characteristics of a transition of actors who have been viewed from within an anti-terrorist paradigm onto the public stage and into the political sphere. In the case of Northern Ireland this has meant the same people who have been involved in specific acts of violence in what the media generally viewed as a "terrorist" campaign being accorded a public role as politicians and negotiators. The changing portrayal of individuals and movements in transition would seem to be a necessary condition for wider social and political change.

Third, focusing on one of the defining moments of the peace process (Mowlam's visit to the Maze), I examine attitudes and quandaries as violence continued to affect the framing of the paramilitary groups and their place in the peace process. With journalists, it would seem, old habits die hard and the ambivalence of paramilitary groups (including threats to return to violence and actual bombings and killings) has continued to foster suspicion and cynicism toward paramilitaries.

That does not mean, however, that change does not take place within the media. In fact there has been significant change over time in both the public role and the portrayal of paramilitary-related politicians. But as the pace of political change accelerates, news organizations can find themselves caught in a dichotomy—in the vanguard of reflecting the dynamics, consequences and potential of change while at the same time allowing the inheritance of past experience to weigh more heavily on their decisions and outlook than is apparent with some other actors. It does not follow that such a cautious approach is harmful toward positive transition. Rather, the converse may be true. It would seem the rewards offered by the news media to those embracing peace are ultimately more highly prized by the paramilitaries than the publicity benefits of violence.

1. Propaganda and News

The actions of paramilitary groups have had a dominant place in the news agenda in Northern Ireland and have frequently made headlines around the world. A town center devastated by a car bomb explosion, an indiscriminate sectarian gun attack on a public house, the killing of a prominent politician, an assault on a British Army barracks . . . events that register firmly with reporters, producers, editors, audiences, readers and government. The publicity that inevitably follows violent action is part of the paramilitary calculation, sending a message of political determination, technical ability and military will. It is a message directed toward enemies and supporters.

While the paramilitaries have, through violence, the ability to generate publicity, the character of that publicity is not in their control. Reportage of their actions routinely brings with it the condemnation of politicians and community leaders, the stories and grief of the victims, the reaction of government and of paramilitary groups on the opposing side. Within the output of the Northern Ireland media (newspapers and broadcast news programs) the negative response to paramilitary violence has been ritual and overt, reflecting the disapproval of the community (a large majority of Protestants and Catholics view the violence of the paramilitaries as politically, legally and morally wrong) and of government. That disapproval is reflected in news narrative and in the practices of newsrooms. Reportage has generally, although not exclusively,[1] characterized the activities of paramilitary groups as "terrorist," offering a negative representation of the groups and their methods.

News organizations have also been aware that they are targets of paramilitary propaganda. Against the background of societal and governmental disapproval of paramilitary activity, they have tried to avoid overt manipulation of the content of reports and of their news agendas. Apart from the broadcasting ban imposed by the British Government between October 1988 and September 1994, this effort has been self-regulated. It has also been variable, depending on the decisions of individual journalists, photographers, producers and editors, although the BBC has published its own guidelines to staff.

The paramilitaries, discontent with a pattern of coverage and condemnation which has portrayed them as evil, pyschopathic and often irrational, have taken their battle to another front, attempting to explain, justify and legitimize themselves through media under their own control and through a public relations strategy which seeks to achieve greater portrayal of their chosen image of themselves. Understanding the way in which the paramilitary organizations view themselves is crucial to understanding the image they seek to portray through the wider media. Insight into their self-perception is available through the media they have under their direct control. Here I briefly discuss five key idioms—statements, briefings, staged events, publications and murals. The first four play a pivotal role in the patterns of communication from paramilitaries to journalists while the fifth provides paramilitaries with direct communication to local communities. The way in which these idioms filter into and through the editorial and production chain and the extent to which the self-styled symbolism, imagery and terminology translate into the narrative of news are instructive as to how journalists in Northern Ireland seek to balance propaganda and news.

Statements

Statements from paramilitary groups are a well-established news source in Northern Ireland and are frequently telephoned to newsrooms in Belfast and

Dublin. They are usually accompanied by a codeword which certain journalists will recognize and that will authenticate the source. These statements are used by the paramilitaries for a variety of purposes, for example to warn of explosive devices that they have left in a particular place where they are not seeking to achieve casualties, to admit responsibility for killings or other attacks in order to achieve association in the public mind with the event, or to set out their current political analysis at a time they assess to be useful in sending a message to the government or supporters. The terminology indicates that the groups see themselves as legitimate armies with military structures and ranks. The IRA has an "Army Council," the various loyalist groups had until recently a "Combined Loyalist Military Command." The Ulster Defense Association has an "Inner Council." The statements speak of "brigades," "battalions," "companies" and "active service units." Members hold ranks and identifiable positions such as "commander," "brigadier," "quartermaster" or "volunteer." They describe members who are serving sentences in prison for violent acts as "POWs" or as "political prisoners."

Statements have been and still are a common source of information about the paramilitaries and their activities and often have an immediate news value. In the aftermath of its attacks on police or army personnel, or following a bomb attack on a town centre, it was common practice for the IRA to contact a journalist and claim responsibility. Such claims, when believed to be genuine, were regularly reported by news organizations. Information, warnings or claims judged authentic usually find their way quickly onto air or into print. While the statements often have an undeniable news value and aid understanding or interpretation of events, the terminology used in them is often rephrased or ignored by journalists, although there is no universal set of rules or guidelines adopted by news organizations.

Briefings

One-on-one briefings, sometimes at the request of journalists and other times offered by the paramilitaries, are another source of information about the groups and the historical and political context in which they see themselves.

Depending on timing and content, these briefings can result in lead story treatment by one news organization with the subject matter then being picked up by others. From the paramilitary perspective it can be an effective way of influencing news agendas or getting a message across at a chosen time, particularly when it is a message which news organizations deem to be politically significant. For example, following bomb attacks in Moira on February 20, 1998, and Portadown, February 23, 1998 the IRA briefed the BBC in Belfast with the message that it was not responsible, that its cessation of violence was intact and that there was no split in the organization. That briefing was of value to Sinn Fein in its efforts to stay involved in the Talks and turned suspicion more directly toward the Continuity IRA. The briefing resulted in a lead story on "BBC Newsline 6.30" (February 24) and was picked up and reported by all the other news organizations in Northern Ireland.

In addition, information and views gleaned in briefings—either directly from paramilitary figures or from someone considered close to their thinking—often finds its way into background analysis, explanation or context given by reporters as to the current thinking within paramilitary groups.

Staged events

On occasion paramilitary groups stage events in order to send a message to government, to the "other side" or to a faction on their own side. They may organize their own publicity, distributing photographs or video footage to the media. At other times they may specifically invite journalists and cameras to meet them at the corner of a certain street at a certain time of night. On arrival masked men with guns will emerge and parade around as if on patrol. There have also been cases of journalists being blindfolded and taken by car to a secret rendezvous where a photo opportunity had been arranged. In 1993 when the IRA was having particular success with a so-called "barrack buster" mortar device used mostly against RUC bases in rural towns, a video appeared in television newsrooms showing masked men in combat gear training with the device. The instructor featured in the video can be heard explaining that the device was similar to what had been used by the IRA in an attack on 10 Downing Street, an attack the IRA regarded as a major military and propaganda coup. Parts of the video have been used occasionally by television news programs in Northern Ireland in the context of analyzing the IRA's activity or political position.

The reporting of staged events is problematic. Journalists are not excluded from the provisions of the Prevention of Terrorism Act under which it is a criminal offense to withhold information about terrorist activities. Beyond that however there are editorial considerations with some organizations taking the view that they will not respond to invitations from illegal groups involved in violence to meet and film or record them. Others do find themselves, at times knowingly and at other times without design, at staged events and they broadcast or publish the material they gather. It is a question of judgment and practice—and both vary among journalists and news organizations.

When Billy Wright, leader of the Loyalist Volunteer Force, was shot dead by INLA inmates inside the Maze Prison in December 1997 and his body returned to his home in Portadown, a photograph was issued to the media showing him lying in an open coffin, flanked by four hooded men in uniform, three of them with handguns. What is a journalist or editor to make of this? Is it macabre bad taste to publish the photograph, is it offensive, does it glorify a dead terrorist, does it glamorize a group that murders innocent Catholics, what is the intended message of the LVF in staging the photograph? The media could choose to publish or not. Both decisions were made. The *News Letter* (December 29, 1997) published the photograph alongside a story headlined "FEAR AND FURY" with a caption "Shot dead: loyalist gunmen guard the body of LVF leader Billy Wright." The *Belfast Telegraph* on the same date also published the photograph but neither the *Irish News* nor the BBC used it.

Publications

The most sophisticated and regular publication offering insight into the affairs and analysis of the largest paramilitary group, the IRA, is *An Phoblacht/Republican News,* published as a weekly newspaper in Dublin and on the web. It carries statements from and interviews with the IRA and embraces the organization's imagery and terminology. It is designed to advance the Irish republican agenda and to communicate within the movement. It promotes Sinn Fein, giving prominence to party policy and representatives. Emphasis is given to the republican analysis, the welfare of republican prisoners, and a negative portrayal of what are termed "crown forces" (i.e., the British Army and RUC).

At times *An Phoblacht/Republican News* is a news source for journalists, particularly when it quotes directly from the IRA in relation to policy position. However, the terminology and rhetoric inherent in the editorial narrative has not normally carried over into mainstream or dominant news narrative.

Publications associated with loyalist groups—the UDA's *Defender* and the UVF's *Combat*—have limited circulation and only rarely feature as a news source.

Murals

The urban ghettoes of Northern Ireland are often awash with color—from the bunting strung between the street lights to the red, white and blue or green, white and gold painted sidewalks that mark out territory as Protestant or Catholic. Beyond this lies another more arresting landscape—the paramilitary murals that adorn the gable walls. These five- or six-meter-high brick canvases depict masked men with automatic weapons as heroes devoted to a cause that is politically, religiously and morally legitimate. They frequently invoke history, God and the use of rocket launchers or automatic rifles. Flags, emblems, armed and hooded figures acting as guardians or defenders, rolls of honor commemorating members who have been killed, celebrations of local sub-divisions within the group's structure are common. In his study of Northern Irish murals, Bill Rolston says that for both loyalists and republicans, murals are an important form of political mobilization, sending a message to the "converted" and acting as a potential source of "conversion" of others.

> . . . although also fought out at the society and international levels, it is at
> the local level that the battle for state legitimacy is waged daily. In the midst
> of that battle, murals are not just folk artifacts but a crucial factor in the

politicization of the community. Politically articulate murals simultaneously become expressions of and creators of community solidarity. Although it would be too far-fetched to argue that the propaganda war is won or lost at the local level, there can be no denying the role the murals play as crucial weapons in that war.[2]

Television, of course, demands pictures and many of the reports dealing with paramilitary groups are limited in the range of pictures available. Television journalists have embraced the paramilitary mural as an additional picture source. In the race against the clock where a television journalist is balancing concern over video of a mural which proclaims the heroism of the UVF or IRA with a demand for pictures over which to explain a development affecting a paramilitary organization, production demands can influence the result. The murals are colorful, graphic and clear and will not defame anyone. They are also part of the urban landscape and can be seen in reality by anyone daily. While judgments are made in television newsrooms about frequency of use and context, murals painted by the paramilitaries and designed to glorify their cause do find their way onto television screens in Northern Ireland regularly. Thus the murals can achieve a prominence or send a message more widely than originally intended although the growing professionalism and technical ability displayed in more recent examples suggests those who conceive them are alive to this possibility.

News Production, Judgment and Legitimacy

It is clear that while the paramilitaries are a vital news source, their access to newsprint and airwaves is not unfettered. There is at present no legislation in force that directly prevents journalists from reporting what paramilitaries say or even publishing or broadcasting interviews with them. Nevertheless news organizations in Northern Ireland rarely seek on-the-record interviews with paramilitaries for publication or broadcast, evidence of reluctance to give airtime and column space to the analysis of groups which have been killing people on a weekly and sometimes daily basis.

Yet most individual journalistic decisions are heavily influenced by judgments over news value and by production demands. The need to illustrate or visualize a story deemed important while the clock ticks toward broadcast time can be more powerful than any notion of a model for reporting on paramilitaries. This can result in different judgments at different times in balancing the overlap between news and what could be argued to be propaganda advantage for paramilitaries. Such judgments may also be affected by other factors including a current level of violence or the state of public opinion.

In an effort to achieve consistency of approach the BBC has published its own guidelines for staff on coverage of Northern Ireland. The guidelines caution against according "spurious respectability" to paramilitaries.[3] They counsel staff to "avoid anything which would glamorize the terrorist, or give an impression of legitimacy" and say statements can be "paraphrased to avoid the military titles and pomp."[4]

While news organizations see the paramilitaries as an important news source and accord their activities a major role in the news agenda, there are varying attempts to remove or dilute the most obvious propaganda and report activities in a context of disapproval. News organizations, therefore, while acknowledging the paramilitaries as a central player on the political and media stages, do not accord them the overt recognition and legitimacy the paramilities themselves believe they deserve from the public, the politicians and the press. It is to the process of how that axis of legitimacy in terms of political involvement and news coverage can change that we now turn.

2. Paramilitaries and Politics

It is evident in reading or watching reports by news organizations in Northern Ireland that political parties such as Sinn Fein, the PUP and the UDP are now woven into the tapestry of daily news. Representatives are given voice routinely, commenting with their latest analysis or calling for movement in line with their policy. In contemporary affairs, the news report in which they appear could well be about a meeting with the British Prime Minister, contact with the White House or their participation in discussing or implementing political change in Northern Ireland alongside what have been traditionally described as the "constitutional parties," i.e., against the use of violence. It is remarkable how far events and the place of Sinn Fein, the PUP and UDP in the media have moved. Five years ago the Sinn Fein President Gerry Adams was refused meetings with even the most junior British Government Minister, the United States refused to grant him an entry visa and his voice was largely banned from being heard on British and Irish airwaves. The change has come about through a complex political process in which the news media has played an important role.

Many factors have contributed to this evolutionary process, among them the emergence of Sinn Fein into the electorally successful political wing of the IRA. The Provisional IRA is an illegal organization and membership is a criminal offense in the United Kingdom and in the Republic of Ireland. For legal reasons alone it has not been possible for an identifiable individual to appear publicly as someone speaking directly for the IRA. But the "Republican Movement" is made up of both a military wing, the IRA, and a political wing, Sinn Fein. Sinn Fein is a legal political party which, since the early 1980s, has been developing an electoral strategy. In a recent election in Northern Ireland (Local Government Election May 1997) the party gained 16.9 percent of the vote, the third highest percentage of all the parties, giving it 74 of the 582 seats across the 26 local councils.

The electoral impact of political parties representing the loyalist paramilitary groups is a more recent development. The UDP was formed at the end of 1989 although it evolved from the earlier electorally unsuccessful Ulster Loyalist Democratic Party. The PUP had been active on a small scale since 1979. But both parties only emerged more recently with a cohesive public profile which translated into electoral support in the elections of 1996 and 1997. In the election to the Northern Ireland Forum in May 1996, a qualifying election for participation in the Talks on the future of Northern Ireland, the UDP and PUP between them won 5.6 percent of the vote—they had previously never managed to exceed a 1 percent share. In the Local Government Election of May 1997 they won 3.2 percent between them, yielding a total of 10 seats compared to 2 in the 1987 election. This small but significant breakthrough for the loyalist parties reflected a peace dividend and a higher media profile following the announcement of a ceasefire by the Combined Loyalist Military Command (CLMC) in October 1994, a group which represented all the loyalist paramilitary organizations. In the run-up to that announcement and in its aftermath, new articulate media-friendly voices emerged onto the public stage.

The republican and loyalist ceasefires announced in 1994 were a crucial factor in creating conditions that allowed for the beginning of a process of "normalization of relations" between parties such as Sinn Fein and the British and Irish governments. Both governments had previously refused to meet Sinn Fein representatives at a Ministerial level. Initially the Irish government under Albert Reynolds moved with greater speed and enthusiasm to embrace Sinn Fein as a legitimate player on the political stage. Under John Major's premiership, the British government was much more cautious in its response, so cautious that republicans became disillusioned and the IRA ended its ceasefire in February 1996. The election of the Labor Party under Tony Blair as the new British government in May 1997 generated new impetus, so much so that the IRA ceasefire was restored in July 1997. Before the year was out Sinn Fein was participating in the Talks at Stormont and in discussions with Prime Minister Blair at 10 Downing Street.

Crucially though, under the Major premiership, an election was organized in Northern Ireland to determine who would take part in the Talks process. The system of election all but guaranteed that the political representatives of the paramilitaries would qualify as participants. The formula was specifically designed to include the loyalist parties (the PUP and UDP), which had limited electoral support.

All this has been a lengthy and tortuous process affected by many variables, among them the level of violence, the impact of particular bomb explosions and shootings, and the broadcasting ban imposed by the Thatcher government. It has also been a process characterized by a media challenge, in interviews and opinion columns, to the ultimate commitment of parties with paramilitary connections to democratic ideals. Ed Moloney has discussed many of these variables in his essay on the broadcasting ban where he highlights some of the features of the axis between journalists and Sinn Fein in the late 1980s.

Over time though legitimate journalistic interest in the conflicts between Sinn Fein politics and the IRA's violence developed into something of a pre-occupation, not to say obsession for some. Sinn Fein interviews and press conferences became almost exclusively contests between defensive Sinn Feiners and reporters trying to get a revealing and damaging response to the latest IRA disaster . . . Some reporters began to see this essentially con-frontational approach as the only way in which the IRA could or should be covered and when the media ban was announced voices were raised com-plaining it would no longer be possible.[5]

The media's difficulty with accepting the democratic credentials of elected Sinn Fein representatives while IRA violence ran hot was a reproduction of both governmental and societal disapproval. In terms of Irish history, 1990 is not long ago but as recently as then journalist and commentator David McKittrick was writing:

From the republican point of view, Sinn Fein, the political wing of the IRA, provides a useful political and propaganda adjunct to the terrorist cam-paign. Its presence in political life is a standing embarrassment to the authorities and a continuing affront to Unionists who continue to lobby for the banning of the party. . . . The government is uncomfortable with Sinn Fein. On one level it is a legal political party, standing for elections and rep-resenting its voters. But on another it is clearly attached to the IRA and is, to most intents and purposes, subordinate to it. The government has not sought to ban Sinn Fein (which was legalized in 1974), and civil service departments routinely deal with its members. At the same time, however, ministers will not meet Sinn Fein personnel, and its representatives are, in general, banned from appearing on television and radio.[6]

The broadcasting ban, which was in effect for almost six years, was an attempt by the Thatcher government to penalize Sinn Fein particularly for its asso-ciation with the IRA. The electoral success of the party and the emergence to prominence of capable media performers caused offense to the unionist popula-tion and to the British government. In an effort to deny access to airwaves, the British Home Office introduced restrictions controlling the circumstances in which representatives of a series of organizations including the IRA, Sinn Fein, the UDA and UFF could be heard speaking on television and radio. Thatcher took the view that BBC and Independent programs were too lax, allowing groups running a dual military and political campaign to have the best of both worlds—the pub-licity impact and political leverage of bomb attacks and shootings and access to television and radio to promote their political analysis in the wake of such events. Announcing the ban in the House of Commons, the then Home Secretary Douglas Hurd said:

For some time broadcast coverage of events in Northern Ireland has included the occasional appearance of representatives of paramilitary organizations and their political wings, who have used these opportunities as an attempt to justify their criminal activities. Such appearances have caused widespread offense to viewers and listeners throughout the United Kingdom, particularly in the aftermath of a terrorist outrage. The terrorists themselves draw support and sustenance from having access to radio and television and from addressing their views more directly to the population at large than is possible through the press. The government has decided that the time has now come to deny this easy platform to those who use it to propagate terrorism.[7]

So, for example, when Gerry Adams was Member of Parliament for West Belfast while the ban was in force, he could appear on television in his capacity as MP and have his voice heard speaking about housing, roads or schools but when it came to speaking on political matters on behalf of Sinn Fein, he could be seen and his views reported but his voice could not be broadcast.

Nevertheless the fact that the broadcasting ban was introduced at all clearly suggests that news organizations were ascribing more legitimacy to Sinn Fein in particular than the British government of the time. Sinn Fein had already demonstrated significant and sustained electoral support before the ban was introduced—a fact which news organizations could scarcely ignore even if they did continue to challenge Sinn Fein on its support of "armed struggle" and its association with the IRA. Despite the British government's stated unwillingness to meet with or talk to Gerry Adams at the time, news organizations continued to give him voice as President of Sinn Fein and as MP for West Belfast between 1983 and 1992 (he lost the seat to the SDLP in 1992, regaining it in 1997).

The political landscape against which the broadcasting ban was first imposed has changed markedly (it was lifted by John Major shortly after the IRA ceasefire announcement of August 1994), as has the media landscape in which Sinn Fein, the PUP and UDP are now prominent features. Observation of this transitional process over two decades enables identification of key components that impact on a changing media relationship with the paramilitaries embarked on progressive involvement in the political process.

The key components that have influenced a changing media relationship in Northern Ireland include *politicization, electoral participation, electoral success,* the subsequent *holding of official positions,* the *emergence of celebrities* onto the media stage, the *halting of violence,* an *inclusive political initiative* and the *emergence of new extremists.*

The election of IRA prisoner Bobby Sands as an MP as he lay dying on hunger strike inside the Maze Prison in 1981 was a powerful demonstration of the republican movement's potential to harness electoral support. At Sinn Fein's *ardfheis* (annual conference) in the same year one of the party's leaders, Danny Morrison, spoke of republicans taking power "with an Armalite in one hand and a ballot paper in the other." This was the public evidence of an increasing emphasis on *politicization* and the efforts of Sinn Fein to mobilize urban and rural support behind its objectives and its strategy. Although there was nothing new in the political nature of republican objectives it did signify a broadening of the means of achieving them beyond the military arena. That politicization created dynamics of policy debate within the movement and at least offered the media potential to broaden its coverage beyond events with which republicans were connected— acts of violence, public rallies—into examination and discussion of ideology, analysis, methods and goals. It also contributed markedly to the emergence of the peace strategy within Sinn Fein.

Electoral participation in itself confers legitimacy and adds credibility to actors who receive media attention and, in the case of Northern Ireland, a legal entitlement to due and fair coverage under the Representation of the People Act, the legislation regulating election publicity. This means, for example, that parties of any background are legally entitled to make party election broadcasts as a right on BBC and Independent television. This provides a guarantee of coverage in a formal setting in which the parties themselves have control of what they say and how they present themselves within a given time frame.

Electoral success brings further rewards through public demonstration of the strength of support and the subsequent holding of official positions, the acquisition of titles (in local government, say, councillor, chairperson of committee, appointment to a health or education board, or chair of one of Northern Ireland's district councils). This results in views being quoted more widely, additional credibility via status, and at times automatic involvement in news by virtue of position.

The emergence of celebrities into the public sphere—figures who become prominent in representing a particular cause—is another feature accelerated by electoral validation. Election to public office reinforces the role of individuals as well as of parties. Another issue in the emergence of media personalities is the role of journalistic resonance, an unscientific process whereby the media repeatedly seek out and give voice to actors who bring one or more particular qualities to the news arena. These may include novelty, power of articulation, rationality, drama, charisma, and availability. This may or may not be associated with electoral success but it can certainly be intensified by voter support. Organizations can influence this process themselves by giving people titles or positions with names that translate more widely and carry overtones of authority, i.e., president, leader, chairman.

The halting of violence has been pivotal, allowing governments that had previously vowed not to talk to those engaged in violence to devise an *inclusive political initiative* in which the paramilitary groups are fully represented. Within the paramilitary organizations and the parties associated with them the inclusive nature of the process justifies the halting of their campaigns and the emphasis on politics. It also provides them with the public recognition and legitimacy they have long desired. The end of the campaigns of violence has also allowed the media more freedom to reflect and explore the analysis of the parties associated with paramilitary groups. Their involvement in a formal political dialogue sponsored by the London and Dublin administrations also makes them valid media players, right on a par with other participants. It is significant also here that the political initiative is official in nature. When the leader of the main largest nationalist party in Northern Ireland, John Hume of the SDLP (Social Democratic and Labour Party), embarked on a series of talks with Sinn Fein President Gerry Adams in 1993 in what became known as the Hume-Adams initiative, he faced widespread criticism for engaging in such dialogue in the absence of an IRA ceasefire. There can be little doubt, however, that this dialogue was a decisive factor in creating the circumstances that led to the IRA ceasefire of August 1994.

The *emergence of new extremists* is a further factor now beginning to affect the media role of Sinn Fein, the PUP and the UDP. Since the IRA, UDA and UVF announced their ceasefires, new paramilitary groups have emerged—the Continuity IRA on the republican side which has been responsible for a series of bomb attacks, and the LVF on the loyalist side which has killed ordinary members of the Catholic population in random sectarian attacks. There have also been tensions within the paramilitary groups on ceasefire and violent events involving some of their members. The result has been occasions upon which Sinn Fein, the UDP and the PUP position themselves as the moderates, expressing commitment to peaceful methods, to dialogue and to agreement. For example, in response to an attempt by the Continuity IRA to bomb a bank in Londonderry, Gerry Adams issued a statement calling for an end to all paramilitary violence. "We think this very unique opportunity for peace should be consolidated and I would call on anyone engaged in armed actions, from right across the spectrum, to cease," said Adams (*Belfast Telegraph,* March 20, 1998). Loyalists formerly involved in violence have also portrayed themselves as moderates. Following the murder of a Catholic man by the LVF in Belfast, the PUP leader David Ervine said his death had been caused by "some obscure group of head cases" (*News Letter,* January 12, 1998). As the UDP returned to the Talks after an expulsion because the paramilitary group associated with them (the UFF) had killed people, the *Irish News* (February 24, 1998) under the headline "UDP rejoins peace talks" reported: "The Ulster Democratic Party has said efforts must be redoubled inside the political talks and loyalists should not be provoked into reacting to the Portadown and Moira bombings."

Many of the elements discussed are interrelated and some are more important at particular times. They are the pivots around which media interaction has evolved with political change involving the paramilitaries in Northern Ireland over 20 years. That evolution continues.

3. Mowlam at the Maze: Media and Message

A CASE STUDY

Background Briefing

Toward the end of 1997, loyalist prisoners inside the Maze were expressing discontent with the conduct of the peace process, concern over what they saw as one-sided concessions to the IRA via the transfer of republican prisoners from England to the Republic of Ireland and the early release in the Republic of a number of IRA prisoners, and the lack of movement on resolving their own situation after a period of more than three years on ceasefire. This resulted in a vote by members of the UDA/UFF to withdraw their support for the continued presence at the Talks of the UDP, the small political party which represents their organization. In the judgment of many observers this would have been a significant and probably fatal blow to the Talks process. The sense of crisis was compounded with the killing of Billy Wright inside the prison. In retaliation the LVF, the paramilitary group which Wright led, killed a number of Catholics in gun attacks in what looked to be the beginning of a series of fatal reprisals, adding to concerns that the loyalist ceasefire as a whole could be jeopardized.

On January 6, 1998, BBC Northern Ireland reported:

> . . . further fears for the loyalist ceasefire tonight after top level meetings at the Maze Prison with UFF and UDA inmates failed to convince them to support the peace process. The UDP leader Gary McMichael said the situation was worsening and talked of the process crumbling under his feet. An Ulster Unionist delegation led by David Trimble also visited the jail in an effort to persuade loyalists to give the process another chance . . . As the week has progressed the loyalist political leadership has looked more isolated and there's a growing concern that the paramilitaries are again taking control. ("BBC Newsline 6.30," January 6, 1998)

It was after a meeting with the UDP leadership in London on January 7, 1998, that the Secretary of State for Northern Ireland Dr. Mo Mowlam announced her decision to enter the Maze Prison to try to persuade the UDA/UFF prisoners to renew their support for the Talks and allow the UDP to attend the next session on January 12.

An apparently coincidental yet important factor affecting media coverage in the following few days was the fact that the main news organizations in Northern Ireland had been invited to visit inside the Maze on January 8. The invitation to the media had been issued by Prison Service and the Northern Ireland Office. This visit was designed as a public relations exercise to offer reassurance that the prison was secure despite the escape of an IRA inmate and the killing of Wright in December 1997. So in between the announcement of Mowlam's decision to visit and her actual visit there was a unique situation in which the media were given wide access inside the jail to the very men the Secretary of State was to meet the next day, January 9. News organizations were therefore provided with dramatic and unusual visual and audio material directly related to the story which was unfolding. BBC Northern Ireland and Ulster Television, for instance, were able to take their cameras into the H-blocks and film and interview the five loyalist inmates due to meet Mowlam the next day. By the time of the media visit it had further emerged that Mowlam would also meet briefly with IRA prisoners. While this was reported and interviews with the IRA leader inside the prison were broadcast and published subsequently, the media focus stayed firmly on the loyalists.

Reportage and Reaction

The announcement of Mowlam's visit came as a surprise to the media in Northern Ireland. In their initial reports, all the mainstream news organizations described the decision as "unprecedented." Other adjectives commonplace in news narrative included "controversial" (BBC, *Belfast Telegraph*) and "dramatic" (*Irish News*). Her planned visit was characterized as "last ditch" (BBC, *Irish News*), "huge risk" (*News Letter*) and a "gamble" (BBC, *News Letter*, *Irish News*, *Belfast Telegraph*). The unusual nature of the decision and its impact on the media were noted beyond Northern Ireland. One British daily newspaper, struck by some of the wider media reaction, drew attention to the language used by the BBC's Ireland Correspondent Denis Murray in his television reports broadcast from London:

> Mo Mowlam's decision to visit the Maze Prison to talk to convicted murderers so astonished the BBC's Ireland Editor that he described it as "staggering" in a news report. This sudden intrusion of tabloid adjectival excess into the corporation's sober and careful reporting was one way, at least, of marking a historic moment. What he meant was that this was something so far outside the tramlines of Northern Ireland's assumptions that he had run out of words with which to describe it. In a region well used to the demands of extreme language to name various forms of killing and other brutality, he was rendered inarticulate by Ms. Mowlam's political quickstep. (*Independent*, January 9, 1998)

There was certainly a sense of incredulity among journalists. Mowlam's move was, as the *Independent* put it, "far outside the tramlines" of what had been the modus operandi of previous incumbents at Stormont Castle. Mowlam herself argued that she had visited the prisoners while in Opposition and that it was necessary to take risks for peace.

In their reporting of the decision, the news narrative of all the media under discussion reflected an acknowledgment that this was an effort to save a peace process that was in trouble: "It's a last ditch effort to try to save the Talks process" ("BBC Newsline 6.30," January 7, 1998), "The move is being seen as a last ditch effort to keep the loyalist parties in the Talks" (*Irish News,* January 8, 1998), "a last ditch bid to rescue the peace process" (*News Letter,* January 8, 1998), "make or break meeting" ("UTV Live," January 9, 1998),[8] "a desperate bid to rescue the talks process" (*Belfast Telegraph,* January 9, 1998).

The *News Letter* (January 8, 1998) under a front page headline "GAMBLER MO" emphasized the drama and the risk. The *Belfast Telegraph* (January 9, 1998) ran a larger than usual front page headline "MY BIGGEST GAMBLE," reporting:

> Secretary of State Mo Mowlam admitted she was taking a major politi-
> cal risk today as she came face-to-face with some of the province's most
> notorious convicted terrorists.

The front page headline in the *Irish News* (January 9, 1998) said: "Mowlam puts job on line for peace."

In a number of broadcast interviews Mowlam was asked to justify her deci-
sion and answer the charge that it looked like an act of desperation. On "BBC Newsline 6.30" (January 6, 1998) she said:

> I don't consider it desperation, I don't consider it odd. I talked to the pris-
> oners in Opposition and what I am determined to do is make sure I take
> every step possible to make sure the Talks work. I'm not negotiating . . . I will
> say that whatever they (the prisoners) are after, and I am sure they are prob-
> ably after releases, that releases will have to be addressed in an overall settle-
> ment . . . we can only get a settlement by Talks and we can only get Talks by
> parties like the UDP talking and I want them to understand that.

There was contrast between Mowlam's position as a high-ranking govern-
ment minister and the status of the prisoners, with a particular emphasis on the notoriety of the five loyalist inmates she planned to meet. The *Belfast Telegraph* (January 8, 1998) referred to the "unprecedented step by a serving cabinet member to meet terrorists in prison." The BBC ("Newsline 6.30," January 7, 1998) said "the unprecedented step by Dr. Mowlam will bring her face-to-face with convicted terrorists including UFF killer Michael Stone" and ("Newsline 6.30," January 8, 1998) highlighted the fact that "the UFF men she'll be talking to are between them serv-
ing more than 100 years for serious terrorist offenses." The *Irish News* (January 9, 1998) wrote of Mowlam placing "her political credibility in the hands of some of Northern Ireland's most feared paramilitaries . . . among those she will meet are the notorious loyalist killer Michael Stone and Johnny Adair, one of the most feared leaders of the UFF." In the same edition the newspaper wrote of Mowlam's "plan to sit down this morning with some of Northern Ireland's most notorious killers." "UTV Live" (January 9, 1998) reported: "Mo Mowlam arrived early this morning at

the Maze to meet some of Northern Ireland's most notorious terrorists—among those she talked to, triple killer Michael Stone and Johnny 'Mad Dog' Adair."

While news narrative displayed initial surprise, with focus on the dramatic and unusual nature of Mowlam's move, the opinion columns of the *Belfast Telegraph* and the *News Letter* raised ethical concerns and worries over the long-term impact on democratic ideals.

The *News Letter* described the move as "a step too far," a "breath-taking step" and a "mighty risk," using its opinion column to argue:

> . . . by giving political legitimacy to a totally unrepresentative group who have been guilty of the most heinous criminal acts, she may stand accused of dangerously by-passing the accepted standards of British democracy and justice. (*News Letter*, January 8, 1998)

The next day's opinion column, with an undertone of criticism of how the Maze is run, said:

> The visit will most certainly massage the already inflated egos of the gunmen and bombers now enjoying the freedom of the Maze but there must be no question of the Secretary of State offering more concessions to prisoners who, although they are not legally entitled to vote, have been effectively calling the shots in a process that is aimed to bring permanent peace and stability to this Province. (*News Letter*, January 9, 1998)

Similar concerns were aired in a *Belfast Telegraph* leading article:

> Behind all the honeyed words of their political representatives it is clear that the extremists in both sections of the community pose a threat which cannot be ignored. At present, the shots in the peace process are being called by people with little or no electoral mandate and both governments are having to pay heed to those who have flouted the law for years. If this society is to have any future, it must be based on the principle of democracy. A lasting solution will only be achieved if those participating in the negotiations adhere to a strictly political course in order to further their objectives. Dr. Mowlam may secure a short-term gain today, but the worry must be that she has demoted the cause of democracy in Northern Ireland. (*Belfast Telegraph*, January 9, 1998)

The *Belfast Telegraph* argued that the way in which the peace process had already been conducted meant that "terrorism has been sanitized to some extent." The opinion column continued:

> The most dangerous flaw in the peace process—and one which was identified at an early stage—is that some of those who are participating still appear

to reserve the right to return to murder and bombing. The IRA has made no promise that its campaign of terrorism will not be renewed and indeed there is speculation that it will review its ceasefire this spring. On the loyalist side the maxim has long been "Prepared for peace . . . ready for war . . ."

In a separate column a *Belfast Telegraph* commentator wrote:

Sorry Mo, the basis for agreement is not there and the more you run to and fro, imagining that your presence can bring about miracles of reconciliation, the more you are encouraging the belief that guns speak louder than words. ("Barry White's View," *Belfast Telegraph*, January 9, 1998)

In contrast, the *Irish News* opinion column (January 9, 1998) came out in support of Mowlam, praising her "exceptional courage and determination" in working toward an agreed settlement. "In pursuit of that goal," said the *Irish News*, "she is entitled to take the kind of calculated risk she is engaging in today." The same editorial attacked criticism of the decision from the DUP and sections of the Ulster Unionist Party, arguing the wider political case that the Ulster Unionist leader David Trimble was inconsistent in being willing to talk to loyalist paramilitary leaders in jail himself while refusing to engage with Sinn Fein elected representatives at Stormont.

It is noteworthy that jail visits by leaders and other representatives of political parties in Northern Ireland, including Members of Parliament such as Trimble, did not attract the kind of criticism leveled at Mowlam in and by the news media— her status as a Government Minister and Secretary of State seems to have been viewed in a different category from other politicians including other MPs.

The attitudes displayed by the three newspapers reflect divergent views in the wider population, the *Irish News* being close to majority Catholic opinion while the *News Letter* and *Belfast Telegraph* are closer to Protestant opinion. A recent survey indicates that the Catholic community is more willing than the Protestant community to accept the direct involvement of paramilitaries in the process. Asked about Mowlam's decision to meet paramilitary groups in the Maze, 78 percent of Catholics said it was the right thing to do compared to 55 percent of Protestants. Asked what should happen to paramilitary prisoners if the ceasefires hold, 28 percent of Catholics said they should be made to serve their full sentences compared to 64 percent of Protestants who held that view. Forty percent of Catholics thought paramilitary prisoners should be released early as part of a political settlement compared to 16 percent of Protestants.[9]

These indicators are consistent with the observations of one commentator in the Dublin newspaper the *Irish Times*, who wrote:

There's also a large and fairly moderate unionist constituency which will be horrified that a Northern Secretary is prepared to deal directly with people who have committed terrible acts. Psychologically, most reasonable nationalists would accept and understand Dr. Mowlam's rationale, but reasonable unionists have a different psyche and would be chary of such acts. (Gerry Moriarty, *Irish Times*, January 8, 1998)

An *Irish Times* opinion column (January 10, 1998) was also supportive of Mowlam while acknowledging the significance of her move:

> The Secretary of State's initiative represented a reversal of long-standing British policy on paramilitary prisoners. In recent years that position has gradually altered as the two governments embarked on an inclusive political process designed to involve paramilitary groups and their political supporters. The visit to the Maze represented public recognition by the British government that paramilitary prisoners constitute an important element in the Northern Ireland equation that must be addressed in any overall political settlement. (*Irish Times*, January 10, 1998)

The material available to journalists covering the story was markedly affected by the media visit on January 8 and significantly affected coverage on radio, television and in newspapers on January 8 and 9. It offered fresh pictures and interviews with the paramilitary leaders in the dramatic prison setting, giving the story a visual power it would not otherwise have had. Pictures of paramilitary leaders inside jail have always had a sense of drama. On this occasion, with Mowlam preparing for a crucial visit and the public preparing for the possibility of the collapse of the Stormont Talks, the pictures were compelling.

Both the BBC and Ulster Television nightly news programs on January 8 were dominated by the pictures inside the Maze, focusing on the loyalist leaders due to meet Mowlam the next day. Viewers were able to watch the men at the center of events walking around the prison blocks in free association,[10] watching television, giving interviews to the media, and posing for photographs in front of murals celebrating their acts of violence. "UTV Live", for instance, ran three reports, highlighting the "unprecedented access to the prison and to prisoners." Michael Stone was the prisoner given the most airtime, welcoming the meeting with Mowlam, accusing some critics of hypocrisy, dismissing reports of drink, drugs and sex in the prison as "embarrassing," and praising the bravery of the daughter of one of his victims who had spoken in support of Mowlam's decision. Among the images used in the reports were a large mural depicting four masked and armed UFF members from the "2nd Battalion C Company" with the slogan "SIMPLY THE BEST" in large letters, a photographer taking pictures of four prisoners in front of the mural, and a prisoner working out in a gym. At one stage was seen a reporter talking to a camera inside a cell saying: "This is the very cell which is occupied by Johnny Adair, the UFF leader in west Belfast. Adair's cell is decorated with the chilling celebrations of loyalist terror."

The *Belfast Telegraph* (January 9, 1998) ran a picture of Mowlam beside a separate picture of loyalist paramilitary Johnny Adair, serving 16 years for directing terrorism, posing in front of a flag showing a skull, beret and bloody knife with the slogan "Kill 'Em All . . . Let God Sort Em Out," a reference to republicans at least, and possibly to the Catholic population at large.

The *News Letter* (January 9, 1998) under a sub-headline "Face-to-face with terror chiefs" published mugshot photographs of the five leaders due to meet Mowlam, with text detailing their sentences, offenses and reputations. Under a mugshot of Johnny Adair, for example, the text ran: "Adair was jailed in 1995 for 16 years for directing terrorism. Nicknamed 'Mad Dog,' Adair directed a four-year bloody campaign during which 40 Catholics were murdered. He has survived 10 IRA and INLA assassination bids." The *Irish News* (January 9, 1998) under a headline "The men of violence who will square up to Mowlam" also detailed the biographies of the loyalists, along with similar accounts of the background of IRA prisoners also due to meet Mowlam. The *Irish News* focused on "Milltown Cemetery grenade bomber Michael Stone . . . jailed for 30 years in 1988 for a total of six murders." In its first report on Mowlam's decision, the *Irish News* (January 8, 1998) also drew attention to Stone, writing: "In a dramatic and unprecedented move, Secretary of State Mo Mowlam is to visit loyalist prisoners, including mass-murderer Michael Stone, at the Maze." The BBC ("Newsline 6.30," January 8, 1998) also gave biographies of the loyalists, detailing their convictions and sentences and showing footage of Stone's attack at Milltown in 1988 in which three people died. The same program showed archival footage of an attack by Stone in 1984 in which a Catholic milkman who was also a Sinn Fein member was killed. This report included an interview with the victim's daughter saying that while she felt contempt for Stone, Mowlam was right to talk to the prisoners in her effort to achieve peace. Both "BBC Newsline 6.30" and "UTV Live" featured politicians and members of the public speaking for and against Mowlam's visit. "UTV Live" (January 8 and 9, 1998) also included victims of violence speaking for and against.

Michael Stone's attack on republican mourners at Milltown cemetery had a huge impact in Northern Ireland at the time for three primary reasons: first because television cameras were there to capture the drama, the danger, the violence, the screams as the attack unfolded; second because his attack sat in a continuum of dramatic violence—it was preceded by the SAS shooting dead three unarmed IRA suspects in Gibraltar as they planned a bomb attack on a British Army band and succeeded by the killing of two British Army corporals at the funeral of one of Stone's victims, an event also captured by television cameras; third because three people were killed in an attack on a funeral. The combination of these factors gave him unusual notoriety among individuals who had engaged in violence in Northern Ireland, elevating him to the status of hero among loyalists and a figure of particular revulsion to republicans. It also seemed to emphasize his illegitimacy in comparison with a Secretary of State. All the news organizations drew attention to Stone in text and in pictures. "UTV Live" broadcast a television interview with him. The BBC did not. The *Irish News*, *News Letter* and *Belfast Telegraph* published quotes from Stone.

The result of Mowlam's visit was that the prisoners changed their position. Within an hour of her leaving the jail, they voted to withdraw their objection to UDP participation in the Talks. The prisoners' statement said:

> We have decided, despite our reservations, not to oppose the continued par-
> ticipation of the UDP within negotiations. This does not represent a change
> in our assessment of the Talks process but is, however, a recognition of our
> faith in the ability of the political leadership of the UDP to represent the best
> interests of the loyalist community despite the current flaws.[11]

The BBC ("Newsline 6.30," January 9, 1998) reported that "Mo Mowlam's political gamble in sitting down face-to-face with UFF terrorists has paid off . . ." and, over pictures of the UDP leaders emerging from the jail with details of the prisoners' vote, "this was the moment when it was revealed the peace process had been saved. . . ." The *News Letter* (January 10, 1998) ran a front page headline "SHE DID IT!" along with a large photograph of a smiling Mowlam. But congratulations were quickly mixed with criticism as the body of the report began: "Ministers in London and Dublin were jubilant last night claiming 'Mighty Mo' had come up trumps in the biggest gamble of her political career. They were confident she had not only saved the peace talks but prevented a bloody reaction from paramilitaries by winning support from UDA/UFF prisoners for their political leaders to stay in the process. But deep cracks immediately fractured support from elected represen-tatives both inside and outside the talks." The report went on to voice the criticisms of the Alliance Party and the UDP.

The *Belfast Telegraph* (January 10, 1998) gave prominence to praise from the British Prime Minister Tony Blair. "Mo Mowlam has achieved an enormous amount in these last few days and I think her courage and her willingness to take risks in the interests of peace have got to be warmly congratulated," said Blair. The *Irish News* (January 10, 1998) under the headline "New hope as Maze gamble pays off" included this paragraph: "The UFF inmates were said to have been impressed with Dr. Mowlam's decision to meet them and it is believed this, more than her hint at dealing with prisons issues if there was progress at Stormont, was the main fac-tor in them reversing their decision."

Mowlam did in fact enter the prison with more than just faith in her ability to change the prisoners' minds by virtue of her willingness to meet them. She pre-sented the prisoners with a 14-point plan which included a section on prisoners. It said one of the sub-committees of the Talks process, the "confidence building committee" was "prepared to work on an account of what would happen in respect of prisoner releases in the context of a settlement." Mowlam told reporters: "Let me make it clear there will be no significant changes to release arrangements in any other context, or for prisoners associated with a paramilitary organization actively engaged in terrorist activity" (*Belfast Telegraph*, January 10, 1998). Mowlam further indicated that she would personally attend the next meeting of the confidence building committee, to take place on Tuesday, January 13, at which prisoner issues would be discussed. Asked about the issue on "UTV Live" (January 9, 1998) Mowlam described the development as "a change of emphasis rather than a change of policy."

In their opinion columns the *News Letter* and *Belfast Telegraph* remained skeptical. The *News Letter* (January 10, 1998) said:

> The degree of posturing by the prisoners and their political representatives on the outside before and during and after the great visitation was breathtaking in the extreme and few democrats will have gleaned reassurance from the shenanigans . . . The Stormont talks are now on course for a Monday reconvene, but now that violence is seen to work it may be difficult to keep the moderate centre constitutional parties on board after the alarming lurch to the fringes by those supposedly in charge. A political process which is only allowed to operate at the whim of those convicted of the most heinous crimes will never succeed in bringing permanent peace and stability to this province.

The *Belfast Telegraph* (January 10, 1998) voiced similar concerns:

> With the future of the peace process hanging in the balance this weekend it is ironic that the paramilitaries should be playing such a central role. Men who have cast a dark shadow over this province are now sitting in judgment on the political negotiations and democrats anxiously await the verdict of those who have so brazenly flouted the law. The world seems to have been turned upside down . . . The paramilitaries are centre stage at present but it is vital that democrats regain the initiative.

The *Irish News* (January 10, 1998), which had supported Mowlam's initiative from the outset, offered praise and a more optimistic analysis under the heading "Full credit to Mo Mowlam":

> She placed her credibility on the line by meeting directly with both republican and loyalist inmates, and initial indications are that her decision was fully justified . . . Dr. Mowlam would undoubtedly have taken most of the blame if the talks process had suffered further defections, so she is fully entitled to be handed the credit for yesterday's positive developments. . . . Yesterday's events did not amount to any kind of historic breakthrough but

we are now at least a little closer to the goal of permanent peace. For that we should all be grateful.

While the *Irish News* was being read that morning in Belfast, Prime Minister Blair was on the telephone from Tokyo with the Irish premier Bertie Ahern, trying to regain the initiative and boost the momentum of the Talks process. The result was a "Heads of Agreement" published by the two governments the following week, an action which appeared to give the process fresh focus.

Rules, Roles and Relationships

The picture which emerges across the board in this examination of reportage and reaction is of a media seeking to convey a sense of moment, a shifting of fault lines in the rules which govern roles and relationships in Northern Ireland.

The rules, for example, of how a government behaves, who a secretary of state meets and in what circumstances. In this single action, Mowlam overturned the public precepts of her predecessors as secretary of state who had pronounced for years that they would not talk to terrorists. Here she moved beyond the policy of drawing elected representatives with paramilitary connections such as Sinn Fein or the UDP into negotiations, dealing directly with the men who had fired guns and retained the power to order others outside the jail to use their weapons. Her action appeared to convey legitimacy on those who previous governments had invested much effort in portraying as illegitimate.

In doing so, Mowlam also freed the media from some of its self-imposed restraints about interviewing convicted paramilitaries, the reasoning being that if a Cabinet Minister was prepared to talk with the prison inmates and acknowledge their role in the political process, and even arrange a media visit to see the prisoners, the latitude of the media in dealing with the paramilitary leaders would expand.

Yet while taking advantage of the facility of interviewing and photographing the paramilitary leaders, there were varying degrees of discomfort within the media. For the editorial writers of the *Belfast Telegraph* and *News Letter,* as we have seen, the discomfort was significant, expressed as clear concern that democracy had been devalued. Yet only one of the 8 political parties involved in the Talks process (the Alliance Party) objected, although divisions were aired within the Ulster Unionist Party. The other main objections came from the Democratic Unionist Party (DUP) and the smaller UK Unionists, both already refusing to participate in the Talks.

Through the use of mugshots, repetition of their crimes, references to their notoriety, and footage and photographs of flags and banners displaying macabre celebration of violent attacks that had resulted in random sectarian killings, the media portrayal was consistent with the negative view of paramilitarism discussed earlier, an example of the media applying their old rules, while taking advantage of new ones being created by Mowlam to gather and disseminate the views of the prisoners.

Yet while Mowlam herself was playing by new rules, the loyalists were still playing by old ones. Against the background of distrust and violence current at the time, the withdrawal of support for UDP participation in the Talks carried with it the implication that the ceasefire was in jeopardy. This assessment is reinforced by a comment from UDP spokesman David Adams following the vote which reversed the prisoners' original decision:

> If the vote had gone the other way and the prisoners had remained firmly opposed to the process and our participation in it, that would have necessitated a re-think by the leadership of the organization (the UFF) to the process and, I suppose, ultimately the ceasefire. (*Irish News*, January 10, 1998)

In fact, the UFF was already killing Catholics in breach of its ceasefire as part of a coordinated response with the LVF to the killing of Billy Wright. This suspicion, voiced to journalists by "security sources," was already in the public domain when Mowlam went inside the jail and was, within weeks, to become a focus of political and media attention leading to the temporary expulsion of the UDP from the Talks.

Discussion

Two weeks after Mowlam's visit to the Maze the UFF admitted involvement in the series of killings of Catholics which followed the shooting of Billy Wright. While Wright's own organization, the LVF, was responsible for most of the killings, the UFF was responsible for at least three deaths. With the RUC Chief Constable blaming the UFF and journalists and politicians asking questions about whether the UDP could remain in the Talks, the UFF issued a statement:

"The current phase of Republican aggression initiated by the INLA made a measured response unavoidable. That response has concluded . . . The UFF wishes to make it clear that it remains committed to the search for a peaceful resolution of the conflict and supports the efforts of the UDP to secure a democratically acceptable political agreement."[12]

As a result of the UFF admission the UDP withdrew from the Talks on January 26 before being formally suspended by the British and Irish Governments for a period that amounted to under a month. The UDP was back in the process on February 23.

By then the focus had turned to the IRA and Sinn Fein. The RUC Chief Constable reported that the IRA was responsible for two murders. Although the IRA denied that its ceasefire was over and Sinn Fein continued to protest that it was a separate political party, Sinn Fein was suspended from the Talks on February 20 as a penalty for the IRA killings. Sinn Fein's suspension lasted officially until March 9 but in practice the party refused to return until after a meeting with Prime Minister Blair at Downing Street later in the month. After that meeting, which brought positive comments from both sides, Adams flew to America for a White House appointment with President Clinton. UDP representatives, in common with other parties participating in the Talks, were also present at White House functions to mark St. Patrick's Day.

Imposing a political penalty for paramilitary action was a difficult balancing exercise for the British and Irish governments. Their judgment that the rules of non-violence for participation in the Talks had been broken and that there was a subsequent need to censure the UDP and Sinn Fein (the Ulster Unionists would have withdrawn if Sinn Fein had not been suspended) was weighed against the need to keep those same parties involved in the process. Hence the temporary exclusions.

In this balancing exercise and in Mowlam's visit to the Maze we witness a latitude being extended to paramilitary groups and their political associates which was only likely to be sustainable while the goal of political agreement appeared realistically achievable. The case study suggests that the transition between the arena of violence and the arena of democracy could not continue indefinitely without the disillusionment of the majority of news media in terms of narrative, framing and opinion columns coming to play a dominant role in the public sphere. While the findings of one recent survey[13] suggest the public at large takes a more utilitarian view than, say, the lead writers of the *Belfast Telegraph* and *News Letter* to the direct involvement of paramilitary groups, another survey[14] points up the priority Protestants and Catholics place on the disbandment of all paramilitary groups. Seventy percent of Protestants and 67 percent of Catholics say it is essential to disband all paramilitary groups to achieve a lasting settlement while a further 11 percent and 15 percent respectively agree disbandment is desirable. Already low tolerance levels of paramilitary activity, I suggest, are likely to decrease in the light of the recent Agreement.

From this examination we are able to discern future implications as to how the news media will deal with the issues of violence, the political process and prisoners now that agreement has been reached.

Violence: With groups such as the Continuity IRA, INLA and LVF sitting outside the peace process, there is a real possibility of further violence. There is also the possibility that some of those involved in the process will view its outcome as unsatisfactory. Northern Ireland's news organizations are unlikely to be forgiving of anyone who, having turned from violence to espouse politics, returns to violence. To those who choose to pursue violence, whether or not they have participated in the Talks, the evidence indicates that the news media will readily revert to its well-practiced anti-terrorist paradigm. While violence will achieve publicity and propaganda, news organizations will attempt to deny overt legitimacy to the groups responsible.

Political process: As and when the new political institutions—the 108-seat Assembly, the North-South Ministerial Council, the British-Irish Council and the British-Irish

Intergovernmental Conference—come into operation, the news media will accord them full legitimacy, reinforcing their role and authority through coverage. This will serve to add a further layer of legitimacy to politicians who have made the transition from paramilitarism and who are participating in the new bodies as a result of the June 1998 election. Such legitimacy may be further reinforced by the violence of the new extremists attempting to destabilize the new structures.

Prisoners: Under the Agreement, paramilitary prisoners associated with organizations maintaining ceasefires will be released within two years. In practice, according to one official source, 70 percent of serving prisoners will be released within 14 months.[15] This issue has already generated substantial public and political debate. That debate is certain to continue and will be a subject of future media focus which will display the tension between the emotive and moral issues and the realpolitik approach which, against the context of an Agreement which is working, will view the early releases as a necessary evil, the price of complicity in peace.

The question of the decommissioning of paramilitary weapons is also certain to be a focus of media interest. The Agreement sets a goal of decommissioning paramilitary arms within two years under the aegis of the already established Independent International Commission on Decommissioning. The IRA has consistently stated that it will not hand in weapons. The British Government has given the Ulster Unionists a written assurance that parties associated with paramilitary groups which have not engaged in decommissioning will be prevented from participating in government.

Aside from these practical issues arising from the Agreement, Northern Ireland will continue to offer a field of study of the way in which a news media rooted in the community and itself conditioned by conflict interacts with wider political change. No one elects journalists to their public role and yet they make decisions on behalf of society as to who gets to speak, when they get to speak and how the messenger or message is framed. Apart from legal constraints, many of those decisions are independently made against a prevailing and variable notion of a correct balance between freedom and responsibility. The notion of that responsibility clearly weighs heavily in a divided and violent society. News organizations in Northern Ireland are now faced with the question of how that responsibility is to be defined in a society that may be tentatively edging toward peace.

Endnotes

1. The *Irish News* decided in the early 1990s to specifically drop the use of the word "terrorist," taking the view that there were differences in the types of incidents happening and that overtly labeling violent acts as "terrorist" was stereotypical. In its editorials, in common with other newspapers, the *Irish News* has been overt in its denunciation of paramilitary violence.

2. Bill Rolston, *Politics and Painting: Murals and Conflict in Northern Ireland,* London, Rutherford: Fairleigh Dickinson University Press, 1991.

3. BBC Style Guide, 1993, Section 15.

4. BBC Guidelines For Factual Programs, 1989, Section 80.

5. Ed Moloney "Closing Down the Airwaves: The Story of the Broadcasting Ban" in Bill Rolston, ed., *The Media and Northern Ireland* (London: Macmillan, 1991).

6. David McKittrick, *Endgame,* Belfast: Blackstaff Press, 1994.

7. Statement by the British Home Secretary Douglas Hurd, October 19, 1988.

8. "UTV Live," Afternoon Summary, January 8, 1998.

9. Towards Referendum Day, Coopers and Lybrand for BBC "Hearts and Minds," February 1998.

10. The H-blocks of the Maze prison are largely run by the paramilitary organizations under their own command structure and prisoners have free association within the blocks. They are not locked inside cells, and they wear their own clothes and have access to gymnasium, snooker, and library facilities.

11. UDA/UFF Prisoners' Statement, January 9, 1998.

12. UFF Statement, January 23, 1998.

13. Towards Referendum Day.

14. The Search for a Settlement, Queen's University/Rowntree Survey Report, January 1998.

15. The *Belfast Telegraph* on April 16, 1998, reported details of a letter from Prime Minister Blair's Chief of Staff Jonathan Powell to Ulster Unionist MP Ken Maginnis which gave statistics relating to an early release timetable. Examples cited were 70 percent of serving prisoners released within 14 months and 80 percent by the following year, leaving 71 prisoners possibly entitled for general release after June 2000.

The Spokesperson—In the Crossfire
A Decade of Israeli Defense Crises from an Official Spokesperson's Perspective

Nachman Shai

*A*t a memorial ceremony for late Prime Minister Yitzhak Rabin on October 27, 1996, Israel Defense Forces (IDF) Chief of Staff Amnon Lipkin Shahak read an open letter to his former commander:

> Amidst the swirl of emotion and confusion in which we, Israeli society, find ourselves, the IDF you so loved, admired and believed in, the army you led to victory, has fallen from grace. It's true that there are no sacred cows, nor should there be. Yet, sharp criticism, emanating from love and the desire for improvement, has been replaced by alienation. Polarization, hedonism, factionalization, apathy, opportunism, manipulation have penetrated the nation's consciousness, and decimated consensus, transforming the IDF from one of our most hallowed institutions into the collective punching bag.[1]

In all my years covering Israel's defense issues, I had never heard such biting, calculated comments as those I heard that day from the IDF chief of staff. For the first time, Israel's highest military officer spoke openly of the alienation that exists between the IDF and the Israeli public, and between the political and the military hierarchies.

Shortly before the publication of Shahak's letter, the defense minister appointed a special committee to examine the issue of motivation among IDF recruits and reservists. The committee concluded that:

> In the past ten years, there has been a consistent drop in the motivation to serve in the IDF. . . . Political and social events since the Yom Kippur War, Operation "Peace for Galilee," the Intifada and the peace process have all had an impact on motivation.[2]

The ever-widening schism between the Israeli public and the military creates a formidable challenge for the chief military spokesperson. Ever since the Yom

Kippur War in 1973, the Israeli government and the media have typically achieved a degree of cooperation at the beginning of a given crisis, a period of rallying around the flag, so to speak. But with each subsequent crisis the duration of this period of harmony has shortened and then been followed by an even greater divide between the public and the military, between media and government.

This chapter focuses on the role of the spokesperson during a decade (1982–1991) of recurring defense crises. The cumulative effect of these events was a new, evolving reality for the chief military spokesperson in Israel. Little has been written about the role of the spokesperson, despite its increasing importance in Israeli public life.

The spokesperson is the go-between. He/she relays information from the government to the public. In ancient times, the individual who brought bad tidings was executed in the hope that the bad news would die with him. Nowadays things are not quite so hazardous for the military spokesperson, but there is still an undesirable element of danger in the job. In times of crisis he/she is sent by the military and the government to meet the media on the public relations battlefield and ends up standing in the middle ground, caught in the crossfire.

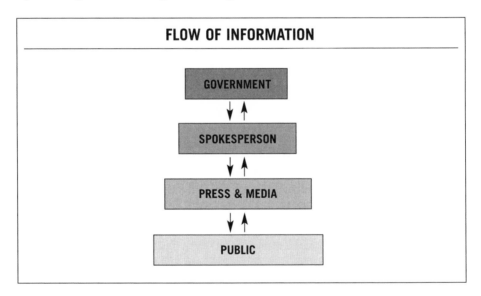

FLOW OF INFORMATION

This chapter is written from two viewpoints, those of the participant and the observer. I have included my own personal description of the events in which I played an active part as a spokesperson while also drawing upon academic research, public opinion polls, media accounts and personal interviews.

The objective of this chapter is to provide a framework for assessing the future role of the spokesperson. How will he/she survive in the new and continually changing public and media environments of the future? I will attempt to accomplish this objective by examining three defense crises: the Lebanon War (1982), the Intifada (1987) and the Gulf War (1991). In addition, I will discuss a lesser known incident called "Bus #300," which occurred during the time of the Lebanon War and which exemplified the erosion of public trust in one of Israel's most cherished defense institutions, the General Security Service.

The Media Clears Its Conscience: The Lebanon War

The Facts

The Lebanon War, officially known as Operation "Peace for Galilee," can be divided into two periods. The first period was a conventional war which began on June 6, 1982, and concluded on August 28, 1982. The second period lasted a further three years afterward, ending in 1985, at which time Israel retreated from most of the territories under its control to a twenty-kilometer-wide security zone in southern Lebanon.

In the initial phase of the war, the IDF entered southern Lebanon with the stated desire of conducting a short war. General (ret.) Yisrael Tal, at the time the most senior general in Israel's military and regarded as one of the world's foremost experts in armored warfare, described the situation on the eve of the operation: "The morale of the residents of Northern Israel was very low. . . . The situation was dire enough that people had begun to leave the area temporarily until the hostilities ended."[3]

The first part of the war was over within a week, but IDF units continued northward. This brought the IDF into contact with the Syrian army, which was deployed throughout Lebanon. The IDF surrounded Beirut. As a result of military and diplomatic pressure, PLO Chairman Yasser Arafat and his staff left Beirut on August 23, 1982.

The second phase of the war began with the massacre of civilians in the Palestinian refugee camps of Sabra and Shatila. While Israel was not directly involved in the Sabra and Shatila massacre, the incident nevertheless caused a national and international outcry and led to the establishment in Israel of a government inquiry committee known as the Kahan Commission. The result was the forced resignation of Defense Minister General (ret.) Ariel Sharon, who was replaced by the ambassador to the United States at the time, Moshe Arens.

The Media

War is the sad and inevitable reality of the history of the Middle East. Israel has fought seven wars since its establishment as a state in 1948. These wars generally fall into two categories, "no-choice wars" and "wars of choice." Initially, the Israeli government claimed that the Lebanon War was a no-choice war. Eventually, however, it was forced to admit that Israel had deliberately embarked upon a military operation in Lebanon[4] as a preventive strike against terrorist bases in southern Lebanon.[5]

Contrary to their attitude in prior wars, the media were united in their opposition to military action in Lebanon. Their criticism was a direct result of lessons learned from the Yom Kippur War. In January 1974, leading members of the media admitted to having a sense that the press had not fulfilled its obligations during the so-called good years prior to the Yom Kippur War.[6] Lulled by the government's false declarations and promises, the press had fed inaccurate information to the public. This realization led to intense soul searching by the media[7]:

> As a result of the press' changed approach to military reporting [after the Yom Kippur War], the willingness of the press to unequivocally accept the decisions of the military censor is in decline.[8]

> The Yom Kippur War was a turning point with regard to the special aura given to the term 'security' by the public and the press. Public trust was damaged and the tendency to criticize the military and to question its commanders' decisions increased.[9]

> The [Yom Kippur] War shocked the entire Israeli public and raised questions about the relationship between the media and the political and military establishments. The regulations guiding this relationship also came under scrutiny.[10]

After the Yom Kippur War, the media adopted a new style of reporting that was tough and unrelentingly critical toward the defense establishment. This new style was clearly evident during the Lebanon War. For the first time in Israeli history the press conducted a public debate about a war before it broke out, and as it drew closer the press became more vocal in its concerns:

> The Lebanon War was a turning point in the relationship between military correspondents and the defense establishment . . . . Just a few months before the war began some the journalists publicly cautioned against this war.[11]

> Since his appointment as minister of defense, some journalists have the distinct sense that [Sharon] intends to go to war in Lebanon and that he plans for it to be a large scale war.[12]

As had been the case in previous wars, the public and the media responded favorably to military action during the first week of the Lebanon War. But by the end of this week the war had expanded in scope. Criticism from the press, directed at Prime Minister Menachem Begin and Defense Minister Sharon, intensified. Sharon's stated objective of bringing about a new order in Lebanon, unprecedented in Israeli experience, shocked both the public and the press.

Military correspondents described their role in reporting the war:

Right after the fog lifted, and contrary to previous wars, we were no longer willing to comply with the wishes of the IDF or the senior echelons of the defense ministry. We reported and did what we thought was right.[13]

The public was not only not harmed by the [government's] attempt to distance the media, it actually profited from it. Why? Because the response [of the media] was such that the public received an even more complete picture of the situation [than it might have otherwise].[14]

I saw my role as military correspondent in a totally different light than I had in previous wars . . . I wanted to report on and primarily did report on the morale of the army, on the mood of our soldiers who, each day, had a cease fire in the evening, said a prayer of thanks, and in the morning were sent another thirty meters forward.[15]

This is a situation unlike any other we've seen—a war within a war. The first war is that between the people of Israel and the IDF. The other one is between the media and the political establishment.[16]

The Kahan Commission fulfilled the media's expectations. It was directly responsible for the resignation of Defense Minister Sharon and other senior military officials. Prime Minister Begin left public office and new political leadership took over. Yitzhak Shamir became prime minister.

Not surprisingly, media criticism of the government diminished with the installation of the new leadership. From that point onward there was a correlation between the pace of withdrawal from Lebanon and the intensity of the media criticism, which became particularly harsh whenever Israel suffered casualties. The slowly accumulating number of casualties throughout the lengthy war of attrition was difficult for the Israeli population to tolerate.

Public surveys, conducted from 1985 onward, indicate that approximately sixty percent of Israelis thought that the IDF should have stopped the advance into Lebanon at the forty- to forty-five-kilometer line.[17] Very few of the Israeli government's goals had been achieved and the price paid was considerable.[18]

Nurit Graetz, an Israeli researcher with expertise in the analysis of media and other public texts, summarizes: "The Lebanese war began with a consensus which weakened as the scope of the battles and its true goals ('a new order in Lebanon and in the Middle East') became known and as the number of casualties mounted. However, even this early consensus could not conceal the divisions between those opposed to and those supportive of the war."[19]

The Spokesperson

In my role as media advisor to the Israeli embassy in Washington (1981–1983) and, later, to the defense minister (1983–1985), I was able to observe the war from two different perspectives.

The role of the Israeli spokesperson in Washington is to influence the U.S. government and the American public through effective use of the media.[20] The Lebanon War, like all wars in the Middle East, endangered U.S. oil supplies and was opposed by the U.S. government. Initial reactions by both the U.S. defense department and the U.S. state department against Israel were harsh, so Moshe Arens, the Israeli ambassador to Washington during the Lebanon War, instructed the embassy to embark on a broad public relations campaign.

As his media advisor, I believed that this PR campaign was futile. The Israeli government and the media were putting out conflicting information and as Ambassador Arens—and the embassy as a whole—were highly credible in Washington I was concerned that this trust would dissipate.

When Arens later returned to Israel to become defense minister he was unscathed by the painful Lebanon episode and was able to formulate a new policy toward Lebanon. Several of my colleagues and I accompanied Arens back to Israel, to the defense ministry.

The relationship between the defense ministry and the media had been severely damaged during Ariel Sharon's tenure. My first challenge as media advisor to Arens was to restore the trust of the media, especially that of the military correspondents. I hoped to accomplish this by increasing the media's access to Minister Arens and the ministry as a whole. During the Lebanon War, new channels of communication had opened up, making it easier for both the press and the public to obtain information. Under the assumption that they would have access to any and all information, with or without our cooperation and knowledge, we chose an approach whereby we were the first to release information.

The honeymoon between Arens and the press lasted as long as he continued to withdraw Israeli troops from Lebanon. Media criticism resumed when the withdrawal was halted. It was only in 1985, during Yitzhak Rabin's term as defense minister, that troop withdrawal was completed.

When Rabin assumed office, he requested that I remain in my position as media advisor. Rabin articulated his information plan to me: "We never lie to the public. We have an obligation to tell the truth. I've done this throughout my career and will continue to do so."

The high levels of trust that Rabin enjoyed up to that point and beyond, until his assassination, were the result of this principled and practical stance, which I heartily supported. The media respected Rabin for fulfilling his promise to withdraw IDF troops from Lebanon.

Consequences and Lessons of the Lebanon War

Eleven years later, Lebanon remained a staging ground for terrorism. The IDF undertook hundreds of forays into Lebanon (the two largest occurred in 1992 and 1996), and it appears the public finds such actions acceptable if the goal is to strike a blow against terrorism.[21]

For the military:

- Media criticism dictated that the length of any action in Lebanon be short, especially if there was a chance that casualties would result.
- In the future, public opinion must be primed prior to any military engagement.
- In light of the peace process, any "by choice" military action will be difficult to justify.

For the media:

- The media regained the prestige it lost in the Yom Kippur War.
- The media proved that there are no more sacred cows or taboos with regard to defense matters.
- The media will continue to oppose wars of choice through its news coverage and editorials.

For the military spokesperson:

- The military spokesperson, trapped in the crossfire between the government and the media, sustained significant damage to his credibility.[22]
- The military spokesperson must be wary of media overexposure of the IDF, which may prove harmful to its future image.
- Effective communication can be achieved only by telling the truth, but it remains to be seen whether or not this is a realistic goal.

Another Sacred Cow: Bus #300

On Thursday, April 12, 1984, four terrorists took over a public bus that was traveling from Tel Aviv to Ashkelon. Following failed negotiations with the kidnappers, the IDF stormed the bus. Two of the terrorists were killed during the action. The remaining two terrorists, who were taken off the bus alive, were subsequently killed during interrogation. The chief of Israel's General Security Service (GSS) personally ordered the killing.[23]

The press played a pivotal role in exposing the incident and preventing a cover-up by the authorities.[24] The photographs of the terrorists coming off of the bus alive were unequivocal proof that they were killed afterward. The Israeli media, by reporting the story, keeping it alive, and demanding accountability from all parties involved[25] performed a great service to Israeli democracy. Zev Schiff describes its impact on Israel and the Israeli media:

Since [Lebanon] there is no defense matter which the press will not cover. The military censor has also become more liberal, in line with the political changes which have taken place and increased public openness . . . The strength of democracy in Israel is reflected in the military coverage and treatment of sensitive topics such as the incident of the GSS and Bus #300.[26]

During this period, I was media advisor to the defense minister. He was at the scene during the incident and was unaware of what would take place afterward. Later, when the GSS tried to place responsibility for the incident on him, Arens denied culpability. In order to dispel rumors and doubts, and despite his fears for the reputation of the GSS, he appointed an investigative committee. My job as spokesperson was to protect him from damaging innuendo. Arens emerged unscathed from the episode. The fact that he was not implicated can be attributed to his pursuit of the truth.

Coming on the heels of the scandal of the Lebanon War, the Bus #300 incident represented yet another debacle for the defense establishment; this time one of the most respected institutions in Israel, the GSS, was affected. In the eyes of the public, the integrity of the GSS had been tainted. The Israeli political, defense, judicial and parliamentary institutions endured a subsequent period of trauma.

The GSS had no formal ties to the media and no PR mechanism. This proved damaging when it came under the media spotlight,[27] particularly when its director publicly admitted to lying. The media showed no mercy to the GSS; the incident became known as the "GSS Scandal" and shattered the organization's former invulnerability.[28] GSS ex-chief Yakov Perry admitted, "The GSS is not what it was prior to the Bus #300 incident."[29]

In the past, security matters were exempt from media scrutiny. Now, any individual or organization found to be concealing the truth would be held accountable.

The Role Reversal of David and Goliath: The Intifada

The Facts

The popular uprising of the residents of Judea, Samaria and Gaza, known as the "Intifada," began on December 9, 1987, with a car accident between an Israeli and a Palestinian vehicle in which four residents of Gaza were killed. This event triggered a wave of riots and demonstrations in the territories occupied by Israel. According to General Tal, "The conditions for such a revolt had been developing for quite some time and the Palestinian pressure cooker was ripe for explosion. The socio-economic pressure among the Palestinians had been intensifying and was accompanied by deep political frustration."[30]

The extent of the uprising and the tenacity displayed by the demonstrators surprised the Israeli defense leadership. "Surprise" is a loaded word for Israelis, filled with disastrous connotations reminiscent of the Yom Kippur War. "Everyone was surprised, both the complacent Israeli officials and the leadership of the PLO . . . the Palestinians themselves were surprised."[31]

The IDF, being a conventional army, had no expertise in handling violent civilian demonstrations. The "clubbing policy" instituted by Yitzhak Rabin failed to quell the disturbances and provoked severe criticism. Special units comprised of soldiers dressed as Arabs succeeded in infiltrating terrorist cells and this, too, raised deep moral questions for the military and the public at large. The IDF, which traditionally prided itself on its ethics and humanistic values, was in danger of compromising them. "The Intifada brought about the brutalization of the IDF. This is clear proof that occupation corrupts and cannot, under any circumstances, be considered enlightened."[32]

The Intifada lasted six years. It was a war of attrition, with hundreds of casualties on the Israeli side and thousands on the Palestinian side. Israeli society is extremely sensitive to the loss of life and does not easily endure such a war.[33]

The Media

In one sense, the Intifada can be seen as the war to win over Israeli and international public opinion. The Palestinians waged this war professionally and with great expertise. The objective of their public relations efforts was to manipulate the Israeli and international press in order to incite strong opposition to Israeli policies and to bring about an immediate political solution.

The Israeli press provided objective, balanced coverage of the Intifada, unlike their coverage in previous wars. Special emphasis was placed on stories about the loss of moral values. Said Ran Edelist: ". . . I am more and more convinced that the media's reporting on the Intifada prevented the IDF from being drawn into even more bloodshed."[34]

The reaction of the IDF to the extensive coverage of the Intifada and the media's sympathetic view of the Palestinians was to limit media access to the territories. The Israeli and foreign press responded by turning to the Israeli judicial system while bypassing IDF restrictions in the field.

For the first time, the IDF was confronted with mini-cams. Scores of mini-cams were distributed to residents throughout the territories by the international press. The term "Restricted Area" no longer had any meaning.

According to Major General (ret.) Yakov Even, a former IDF spokesperson, "The press coverage of the events was broad. It fought tooth and nail against any deviations and preserved the ethical base of warfare. The press relentlessly exposed any outrageous behavior. . . ."[35]

The soldiers' frustrations with the media increased, escalating to the point of isolated street clashes between reporters and soldiers. This behavior so disturbed the IDF that it undertook a massive educational effort among the troops with the goal of reinforcing positive perceptions of a free press in a democratic society.

How much did the Intifada influence public opinion? There does not appear to be clear agreement on this issue. According to political scientist Mark Tessler, ". . . the Intifada has not fundamentally altered the political balance in Israel and it is probable that this polarization [between right and left], which in fact has been deepened by the uprising, will remain the most salient aspect of Israeli political life for some time to come."[36] On the other hand, Asher Arian asserts that "The Intifada had an impact on Israeli public opinion. Israelis said so quite clearly."[37] And General Tal argues that "Israel was forced, due, among other things, to the Intifada, to recognize the PLO as the sole representative of the Palestinian people and to agree in principle to divide the land of Israel among the two peoples."[38]

The Spokesperson

I assumed my position as chief IDF spokesperson on September 1, 1989. The IDF needed a spokesperson with a journalist's credentials in order to satisfy the demands of a modern, sophisticated press. My only request of the IDF chief of staff, Major General Dan Shomron, was that the IDF spokesperson participate in and have decision making input at the highest echelons of the IDF.

The IDF spokesperson has three different roles. He/she is spokesperson of and media advisor to the chief of staff, sole spokesperson for all members of the IDF, and commander of the IDF media unit with a staff of 250 enlisted personnel and 750 reservists.

As the chief IDF spokesperson, I looked at the Intifada as a war between Israel and the Palestinians, to be waged on the media battlefield. As in any other war, the threat had to be identified and evaluated to prepare both an offensive and a defensive posture. Strategy, tactics, goals, means and fighting forces had to be developed and deployed against the enemy.

What characterized this new battlefield?

1. A seemingly omnipresent media. My policy regarding attempts to obstruct media access was simple: it's not right, it's not worthwhile and it's not possible. It's not right because it's not democratic. It's not worthwhile because it will lead to a hostile press. It's not possible because in one way or another the media will be there.[39]

2. Fusion of local and international coverage. The Israeli public quickly learned that stories not covered by the Israeli press could easily be followed in the international media. Several factors made this phenomenon possible:
- the broad and rapid expansion of cable television in Israel;
- the accessibility and affordability of international transmission from Israel;

- the use of mini-cams;
- and the increase in foreign media coverage. The number of visiting journalists increased, adding to the approximately 300 foreign journalists already stationed in Israel on a permanent basis.

The result of the broad availability of information was that the time frame within which to shape and react to events was greatly compressed. The foreign media, with its need for immediate information and its lack of patience, left the Israeli government no choice but to respond. If it had not, the world—and more importantly, the Israeli public—might have received unbalanced and inaccurate information.

3. Ascendancy of the electronic media. Despite the importance of print media in shaping public opinion, the electronic media—particularly television—was clearly dominant in setting the world and Israeli agenda.

4. Military censorship. The authority of the military censor was diminished by the Israeli Supreme Court's Shnitzer decision.[40] The ruling stated that the censor is authorized to act only when the information presents a clear and present danger to Israel's security. The dilution of the censor's authority came at a time when the media had deliberately violated the censor's regulations.

5. The new, aggressive Israeli press. Increasing commercialization, accompanied by fierce competition, characterized the new era of the Israeli media.[41] There was no sacred ground in this competition. Everything was fair game, including defense and security matters.

The Palestinians were quick to recognize and capitalize on these changes. They established an effective mechanism for providing information to the foreign press. As for their message, they were clever in reversing the classic David and Goliath roles, becoming David and portraying the Israelis as Goliath. Mortimer B. Zuckerman said at the time that "The images of the Intifada have transformed the perception of Israel and of reality because the Arabs have succeeded brilliantly in shifting the ground of debate."[42]

The Palestinian-Israeli public relations struggle highlighted the issue of speed versus credibility. The Israeli system was built on a labor-intensive, time-consuming process of checking and re-checking information. Said Brigadier General (ret.) Efraim Lapid, ex-chief IDF spokesperson (and my immediate predecessor), "The key to our success with regard to information lies in the matter of credibility. At the present time when tensions in the territories are so high, it is more important than ever to feel that the spokesperson's reports have been thoroughly checked and are credible."[43]

The need for meticulous verification and the damaging results of a breakdown in the process are described by Major General Even: "Our field reports contain both errors and deliberately misleading statements, even outright lies. As a result the cred-ibility of the IDF spokesperson has been damaged . . . in addition his moral credi-bility has been decimated."[44]

During the course of the Intifada, Israel's prestigious state comptroller com-pleted an audit of the IDF spokesperson's unit. The comptroller's report stated that "the IDF spokesperson's unit had difficulty reporting on the events of the uprising in Judea, Samaria and Gaza in a timely fashion. This was due to the fact that the reports from the field arrived late thereby delaying the relay of information to the media. At times this led to a decline in IDF credibility in the eyes of both the Israeli and foreign press."[45] Simultaneously, General (ret.) Shlomo Gazit prepared an in-depth internal IDF report on the spokesperson's performance during the Intifada. In it, he suggested three operating principles for the unit: openness, independence and apoliticism.

These two reports served as the basis for the implementation of conceptual and organizational changes in the unit. During internal discussions, I expressed my concern about the shortsightedness of our operation and the lack of resources for future confrontations. "The IDF should see itself as moving into a new and differ-ent period. I envision direct broadcasts from the battlefield in an attempt to bypass the censor. This possibility is a direct corollary of the signs we are currently seeing in the massive opening up of the electronic media. . . ."[46]

It was evident that total news management was no longer possible. The gov-ernment and the army had to recognize the necessity of presenting a full, truthful picture of events to the public in order to preserve IDF credibility. This credibility was vital in order to maintain public morale and national consensus.

I chose to address this issue by making two policy changes. First, there was to be immediate accountability for mistaken IDF reports or announcements. By pub-licly admitting mistakes, we would strengthen the credibility of all other informa-tion issued by the spokesman's unit. Second, information released by the spokesperson's office was to be attributed to "official military sources" rather than the IDF spokesperson. I wanted to utilize the voice and authority of the IDF spokesperson during emergencies only. Little did I know how close we were to a national emergency.

Consequences and Lessons from the Intifada

The Intifada was Israel's longest war. The IDF and Israeli society were in a contin-uous violent struggle with the Palestinians. It occurred during a period of contin-ued terrorism that began with the Lebanon War and ended with the Gulf War, a time of crisis upon crisis. The IDF was unable to exercise the full extent of its power against the Intifada because the core of the matter was political in nature. The Intifada ended in September 1993 with the signing of a peace accord between Israel and the Palestinians.

For the military:
- The Intifada led to a weakening in the primary values of Israel's defense institutions.
- The trauma of yet another intelligence failure reverberated throughout the IDF and Israeli society.

For the media:
- The media fanned the flames of public debate over the Intifada. They were equally critical of the civilian and military leaderships. The Intifada proved that support is no longer guaranteed even for a war of no choice.
- The media will continue its critical stance toward the government and defense establishments.

For the military spokesperson:
- The IDF spokesperson failed to bridge the gap between the media and the government.
- He was caught in the crossfire without the support of his superiors. As a result, his best tool for survival was the truth.

Credibility: The Gulf War

The Gulf War, from Israel's perspective, occurred over two distinct periods. The first period began on August 2, 1990, with the Iraqi invasion of Kuwait, and ended with the first "Scud" missile attacks on Israel on January 17, 1991. The second period was characterized by additional attacks and ended on February 28, 1991, with a cease-fire agreement.

Period One: The Facts

Israel kept a low profile during the initial invasion of Kuwait. But Israelis had taken note earlier that year, in April 1990, when Saddam Hussein, in a large military demonstration, threatened to destroy half of Israel with missiles. On May 28, 1990, at a meeting of Arab heads of state, Hussein repeated his threat.[47]

By as early as August 1990, there were high-level discussions in the Israeli government about distributing gas masks to civilians. The IDF chief of staff favored immediate distribution. Defense Minister Arens disagreed, arguing that the probability of Saddam Hussein's using chemical weapons was low: "The best scenario for us is to prepare for future danger and to maintain a low profile so that Saddam Hussein will not be aided in his attempts to portray the conflict as part of the ongoing Israeli-Arab conflict."[48]

The IDF prepared to confront the Iraqi threat using both defensive and offensive tactics.[49] In accordance with the cabinet's decision, the distribution of gas masks began on October 15, 1990. Israel was the only country in the world whose entire population possessed gas masks, which were kept on hand at all times. As President Bush's deadline of January 15, 1991, for the withdrawal of Iraqi troops approached, Israeli contact with the U.S. defense establishment intensified. The primary U.S. objective was to cement its alliance with Israel and provide assurances that it would defend Israel against Iraqi missile attacks.[50]

The Media

The media was low key in its coverage of the preparations for war. It focused on the debate within the government and the military concerning the distribution of gas masks. The media's coverage reflected the Israeli public's deep concern about the possibility of yet another military confrontation in addition to the ongoing Intifada: engagement in two military confrontations at once would be difficult, even for Israeli's well-trained military.

At such times, the Israeli press instinctively assumes a patriotic manner. Yakov Erez: "An Israeli journalist is first and foremost an Israeli and a journalist second."[51] Defense Minister Arens met with the Editors' Committee, which consisted of the chief editors of the Israeli news media. Arens enlisted and received their help in maintaining public calm, telling them that "[A panic] could weaken us."[52] The IDF chief of staff made similar requests of the military correspondents in a meeting on January 15, 1991. "The public is relatively calm. The gas mask distribution was successful," said the chief of staff, "Israel is ready for war."[53]

The Spokesperson

As the Gulf War began, the IDF spokesperson's office had just completed its restructuring (see next page). This, along with other considerations, led to the decision of the chief of staff to charge the IDF spokesperson with the task of overseeing all IDF information matters, including defense guidance for the civilian population.

To accomplish this objective, the IDF spokesperson set up three teams: a unit think tank comprising an array of experts, the IDF Information Team, and the Civilian Information Team. The IDF Information Team comprised senior officers representing relevant IDF branches, while the Civilian Information Team was made up of officials representing government ministries responsible for public relations.

The major task during this period was the campaign associated with the distribution of gas masks. The information plan prepared by the IDF spokesperson consisted of six principles: prevent public panic while at the same time spreading messages of defiance against Iraq; take initiative; be open; be credible; create and maintain national consensus; and coordinate efforts so as to speak to the public in a unified voice.

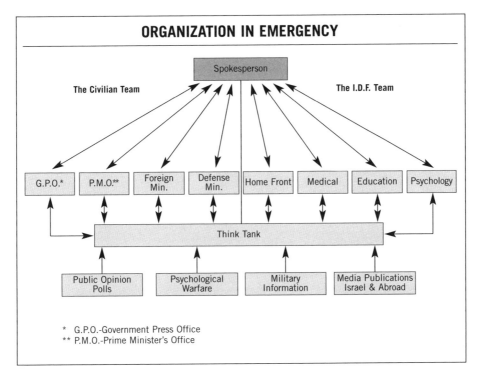

ORGANIZATION IN EMERGENCY

Spokesperson

The Civilian Team   The I.D.F. Team

G.P.O.* | P.M.O.** | Foreign Min. | Defense Min. | Home Front | Medical | Education | Psychology

Think Tank

Public Opinion Polls | Psychological Warfare | Military Information | Media Publications Israel & Abroad

*   G.P.O.-Government Press Office
** P.M.O.-Prime Minister's Office

It was imperative that we hold to these principles if we wanted to distribute the gas masks without creating undue panic. We also did not want to give the impression that Israel was initiating the war.

The public information campaign consisted of three phases: preparation for distribution, distribution, and aftermath. The test of the plan's success was public reaction. The response was surprising: people went to the distribution stations, took their gas masks in an orderly and quiet fashion, and went home.

Two issues were still outstanding as we approached war: the "voice of the nation" and the integration of radio and television broadcasts. The voice of the nation is an Israeli concept that refers to an individual who assumes the task of explaining wartime events to the general population. This unofficial role was instituted on the eve of the 1967 war and continued in subsequent wars. There was no one in place to assume this role at the time of the Gulf War.

On January 15, 1991, I was a guest on a television talk show. At the end of the interview, the host, Dan Shilon, one of Israel's prominent television personalities, requested that I look straight into the camera and explain to the public why there was no need to worry. I was taken by surprise. Nevertheless, I turned to the viewers and, drawing on my knowledge and experience, explained at length and in my own words that the army was prepared. "Everyone in Israel can rest assured," I said. "Of course there are threats out there, but we have a strong army. We must remember this."

It was at that moment that I unwittingly assumed the role of the voice of the nation. The difference between my predecessors and me was that while they had been civilians who were chosen for that role, I was in uniform.

The second unresolved issue, the integration of radio and television broadcasts, was more complex than it had been in previous wars. In the past it was customary for the two public radio stations to combine their broadcasts: it was patriotic, it prevented competition, and it allowed for the pooling of resources.[54] Now there were new TV stations, both cable and Channel 2.[55] The competition among the media engendered opposition to integrated broadcasts. Personally, I was not sure if the old model would work in the new marketplace. The matter was resolved on January 13, 1991. The ministers of defense, education and communication, along with upper management of the electronic media and the IDF spokesperson, decided that the radio broadcasts would be combined and that the television stations would consult with one another but maintain separate broadcasts. The IDF spokesperson was charged with determining the date of integration. On January 16, 1991, joint radio broadcasts commenced.

As the IDF spokesperson, I gave the broadcasters assurances that the IDF would not interfere with content. The joint broadcasts were free of military influence and were composed on the basis of professional considerations only (except for occasional restrictions placed by the military censor which, of course, was still functioning).

The groundwork was now set for our campaign over the next forty days. There were two key informational elements: developing public consensus with regard to a defensive war in which Israel would not respond with force, and reinforcing the impression that Israel had not been taken by surprise.

The stance of non-responsiveness was unusual in light of Israel's history, in which wars either were initiated by its army or were a reaction to enemy attacks. In the case of the Gulf War, however, the Israeli public was reluctant from the outset to embark on a new war and pleased that the Allies were willing to fight in Israel's stead.

Period Two: The Facts

A total of forty missiles hit Israel during the course of seventeen missile attacks. Most of the missiles were aimed at the central and northern areas of the country; a few missiles fell in the south and in the east and landed in Arab-populated areas. One death was caused by a direct missile hit and several other deaths resulted from heart attacks and/or misuse of gas masks. There were several hundred injured, suffering mostly minor injuries. Property damage was valued at approximately US$250 million.[56]

All of the missiles were fired from Iraq. The United States informed Israel that it was taking steps to destroy the missiles but the attacks continued. Israel did not retaliate. Said General Tal: "These missiles bring tidings of the modern strategic threat which will make its mark on Israel's national security and on the type of deterrence used in the future. . . . Despite the fact that it did not respond to the missile attacks, Israel did not lose its deterrence capabilities during the Gulf War."[57]

The Media

The previously low-key media coverage changed the moment the war broke out.[58] Each daily newspaper followed the war according to its own particular style and editorial slant.[59] Ha'aretz was moderate and balanced; Hadashot sensationalist; *Yediot Aharonot* (an evening paper) had huge, bold headlines and *Ma'ariv* had a style similar to that of *Yediot*.

The IDF chief of staff, in a meeting on January 24, 1991, informed the Editors' Committee that he found the accounts in their coverage to be highly exaggerated. He reminded them that Saddam Hussein was closely following their coverage in order to judge Israel's response and determinine his future course of action accordingly.

Public debate over the wisdom of restraint ensued. At the same time, a number of articles appeared in the press supporting the government's policy that Israel not interfere in the war.[60] Other public controversies—where to hide during attacks (in sealed rooms or in bomb shelters), the effectiveness of the gas masks, whether to leave urban centers for the suburbs—were all discussed at length and received extensive media coverage. The open debate showed that freedom of the press in Israel was alive and well. It helped to maintain national consensus.

The electronic media captured the public's attention during the war. Radio was devoted solely to broadcasting a siren at the time of an attack; at all other times it was silent. This unique Israeli phenomenon is known as "silent radio." According to Uri Paz, "The silent radio was a lifeline for many Israelis as they sat in their sealed rooms, trembling with fear and waiting for the missiles to fall and, afterwards, to hear the outcome of the attacks."[61] Television broadcasts carried reports, commentary and guidelines for the public while at the same time providing entertainment and respite.

The integrated radio broadcasts were controversial throughout the war. Dan Shilon described them as a "violation of the public interest."[62] On the other hand, Arieh Mekel, director general of the Israel Broadcasting Authority, said, "It is preferable to speak to the public in a unified, patriotic voice."[63]

My primary concern regarding integrated radio broadcasts was the potential for government interference with content. But the broadcasts remained totally independent. Chava Tidhar and Dafna Lamish found in their research that public controversies in Israel during the war were fully reflected in the broadcasts.[64] As far as the public was concerned, "[they] loved the joint radio broadcasts. In an audience survey done by Israel Radio, ninety-two percent of the public advocated continuing joint broadcasts, only eight percent wanted to return to the separate broadcasts."[65] This, in my estimation, was proof of their success.

The Spokesperson

The following charts are designed to illustrate the information flows to and from the IDF spokesperson during the Gulf War. One chart represents the flow of input to the spokesperson, the second represents output.

Input

Input consists of all information, evaluations, advice and guidelines received by the spokesperson's unit, which assisted in decision making.

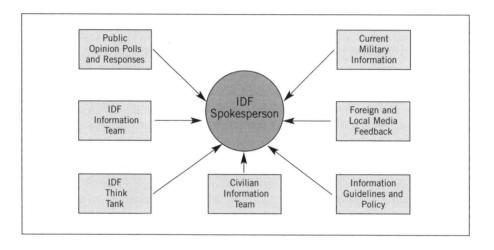

Output

Output includes guidelines and information for formulating public statements sent to public constituents and official organizations.

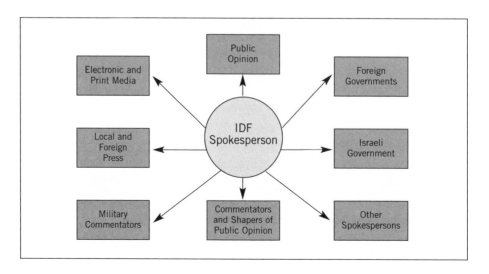

In the early morning hours of January 18, 1991, the first Iraqi missiles fell on Israel. On the way to the IDF underground command center in Tel Aviv, I made a request to go on the air. Up to that moment the media were confused about how to react to the attack. The fact that the broadcasters were unnerved was reflected on the air. Using my cellular phone, I spoke on the air for several minutes. I did not have many details and was not able to relay much information. I said, "This is the chief IDF spokesperson. The IDF is handling the situation. In the meantime, please follow the defense guidelines which you have been given. I will know more in a little while and when I do, I will pass the information on to you." In this manner I was able to make direct contact with the public at home in their sealed rooms. This mode of communication continued throughout the missile attacks.

The moment a missile was fired, and immediately following the sirens, I would go on the air, on both radio and television, with instructions on what to do during the next several minutes and, later, during the long hours of waiting for the all clear. According to Tamar Gross, "The soothing tone of the spokesperson, his empathy and his understanding of the difficulties involved in being in a sealed room (for example, his suggestion to drink water in order to calm down), made him resoundingly popular, to the extent that he was almost forgiven for his unit's oversights earlier in the war."[66]

My broadcasts were carried by television and radio simultaneously. The television stations used slides and voice-overs. My preference was to remain close to the information source, in the IDF underground command center, and to give instructions to the public from there. This was to enable people to remove the annoying and frightening gas masks in the quickest possible amount of time. The diagram below illustrates communication procedures during the war.

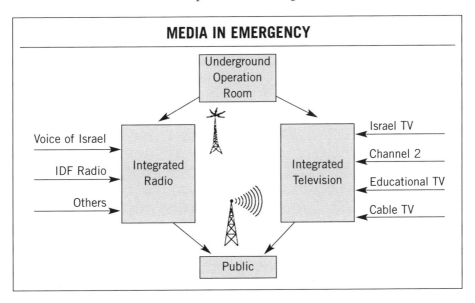

The newscasters were extremely cooperative with us in our efforts to maintain public calm. According to Colonel (ret.) Moshe Even Chen, chief of the IDF department of behavioral science: "The best of the Israeli press was on display during the war. These individuals are part of this country, they live here and fear for Israel. They acted and spoke accordingly."[67] But they were to have their regrets after the war was over.

I attempted to focus on the sole objective of guiding the public and maintaining calm. Every so often I would make an exception with a political statement such as: "Israel has a right to self defense and will act when appropriate," or "We cannot sit quietly by as these attacks occur."[68] Overall, however, the tone remained one of understatement.

There were a number of crises. For example, Yitzhak Rabin announced that he did not use his sealed room but instead went into his bomb shelter. This revelation was quite damaging. There was considerable public pressure to hear from government leaders. Where is the prime minister? the media asked. Where is the minister of defense? Our answer was that, at that stage, policy statements were not required. What was necessary was a dialogue with the public in the time between the siren and the all clear, when people were most frightened and burdened. Said Nurit Graetz: "The fact that the government leaders did not appear very often and the person who was there was Nachman Shai did not contribute to the power and authority base of the leadership. Nachman Shai, not Yitzhak Shamir, was the hero of the Gulf War. He was the one who conducted a personal dialogue with the public. [Shai], with his intellectual, anti-macho image, clear policy, and demands for public cooperation, provided the only leadership."[69]

The centrality of the IDF spokesperson's role during the Gulf War drew some critical comment, but the public response was overwhelmingly positive. Evidence of this comes from a poll conducted by the Gutman Institute for Social Research: sixty-seven percent of the public felt that the IDF spokesperson was completely trustworthy; twenty-six percent found him to be mostly trustworthy.[70] Additional research carried out by the ministry of defense[71] determined that:

- the level of public trust in the IDF officers and in their decision-making ability was very high (a ninety-two percent approval rating, higher than the normal eighty-one percent);
- the level of trust placed in the IDF spokesperson was extremely high during the entire period of the war;
- eighty percent of those polled found the media reports to be highly credible, while fifteen percent found the reports to be credible some of the time.

A wealth of research also appears in the publication *Psychology*.[72] The findings confirm that the public was in distress during the initial stages of the war but was calm later on. This is a crucial measure of the effectiveness of the spokesperson.

Consequences and Lessons of the Gulf War

Israel did not actually fight in the Gulf War. The greatest concern was for the war's effect on Israel's self-image and perceived ability to deter enemies. General Tal claims that there was no such negative effect,[73] but this remains to be seen. Memories of the Gulf War surface whenever tensions rise in the region.

For the military:
• This was the first war that took place exclusively on the home front.
• It was a long-range war. There was no ground contact between fighting forces.
• Above all, for the first time there had been imminent threat of the use of non-conventional weapons against Israel.

For the media:
• The Israeli media supported the policy of restraint until the end of the war, at which time the legitimacy of this policy was questioned.
• The electronic media provided the government with the means to inform and soothe an anxious public.

For the spokesperson:
• The Gulf War, from the Israeli perspective, was one of words and declarations; therefore, the spokesperson naturally became one of the central figures of the war.
• The direct, unfiltered communication between the spokesperson and the general public proved to be highly effective.

Credibility Again: The Gas Masks

In real-life dramas, the occasional happy ending may ultimately be followed by a jolting epilogue. This was true in the case of the Gulf War. Two and a half weeks after the end of the war, Zev Schiff reported that thousands of gas masks distributed by the IDF to the public were defective.[74] In essence, the article stated that hundreds of thousands of gas masks supplied to the adult Israeli population provided inadequate protection. The article also included the revelation that approximately 170,000 of the gas masks that had been purchased by Israel were old and had been previously sold.

During the war, the state comptroller had questioned the defense minister regarding the effectiveness of the gas masks. At the time the minister denied the allegations, expressing confidence in the quality of the masks. The release of the damaging information just after the war had an explosive impact. Zev Schiff acknowledged that he had been aware of the situation much earlier but had refrained from publicizing it in order to prevent a panic.[75]

The press was outraged. Among the headlines that appeared in March 1991 were "The Public Deserves to Know the Truth" (*HaTzofeh*), "Inadequate Credibility" (*Ha'aretz*), "The Public Has the Sense That It Is Not Getting the Truth About This Matter" (*Ma'ariv*), "Was There an Oversight? Was the Report Wrong?" (*Yediot Aharonot*), "Was It a Lie?" (*Hadashot*), "Protection, Financing and Credibility" (*Davar*), and "We've Been Deceived and Taken for a Ride" (*Al HaMishmar*).

A few of these articles also mentioned the role of the IDF spokesperson. "Something is rotten in the gas mask fiasco. The primary verification for this was provided by none other than the IDF spokesperson, Brigadier General Nachman Shai."[76] Yoel Marcus wrote: "In hindsight I feel like I was taken for a fool. During the entire war I sat in my sealed room with my gas mask on my face listening to the soothing voice of Nachman Shai advising me to be calm and to drink water."[77] Yehuda Meltzer added, "The situation of the IDF spokesperson is a parable about what happens when credibility comes face to face with conflicting values. His soothing tone isn't enough. There must be some clarification. If I am asked to lie, do I? . . . And if I am to believe [Nachman Shai], he must say: If I am pressured to provide false information, I will refuse. It comes as no surprise that he was loyal to his 'client,' to his superiors. Now that he's in trouble we know it's back to business as usual."[78]

I attached these articles and others to a letter addressed to IDF chief of staff Major General Shomron on March 22, 1991. In it, I wrote:

> I had no inkling about what was happening, not even when the state comptroller's report was under scrutiny. I hope the report is wrong. If not, it will be difficult for me to accept that I addressed the public as a representative of the defense establishment, in which I believe, when the effectiveness of the protection device provided to the citizens of Israel was under suspicion.
>
> This is diametrically opposed to my understanding of the role of the spokesperson, who is to be integrated into and knowledgeable about the decision making process. The damage done to the spokesperson's credibility is significant and will only worsen with time. I can see no other alternative but to go public with the appropriate correspondence and information. We must tell the truth, however difficult that may be, if we want to preserve and restore the public's faith in the IDF.

The chief of staff invited me to meet with him. At that time he made it clear that he had not misled me, nor had he caused me to mislead the public.[79] In his judgment, the gas masks provided adequate protection and the state comptroller's assessment was incorrect. This was to be the IDF position in the upcoming public debates, which turned out to be open war between defense and military officials and the state comptroller's office.

Orit Galili wrote, "IDF Spokesperson Nachman Shai played a pivotal role in these discussions, particularly regarding outgoing Chief of Staff Dan Shomron's response. In his briefings, Shai was able to polish Shomron's message and thereby win empathy for the IDF."[80]

The stance of both the defense minister and chief of staff seemed plausible and made it possible for me to engage in the new information campaign. Nevertheless, IDF credibility had been damaged. It is now clear that the IDF did have information regarding the quality of the masks and that there was correspondence with the state comptroller asserting that the masks worked. I was unaware of this at the time.

My information was verified time and again during the war. I did not knowingly release any inaccurate information. The quality of the gas masks was verified as well. My superiors supported me throughout the incident, and in so doing protected themselves. We were all affected, but I felt personally responsible since it had been my role to inform and reassure the public.

The gas mask scandal precipitated a credibility crisis for the IDF and its spokesperson. Prior to the Gulf War, the media had doubted IDF credibility. During the Gulf War, these doubts were almost completely put to rest. The gas mask incident proved that the doubt and skepticism were justified.

Conclusions: The Bulletproof Vest

Each war is different from the previous ones. Unfortunately, preparation for future wars is often based on past wars. One can only hope that there will be no more wars in the Middle East. However, Israel takes the threat of a non-conventional war very seriously. In the event of another war, Israel, both as a state and as a society, will be different than it is today; the processes described in this chapter will continue as the circumstances change.

What will the next war look like? From a military perspective it will be a horrific war in which non-conventional weapons will be deployed from afar. A current opinion is, "This war did not ensure the eradication of the [missile] threat. [Israel's] ability to protect itself from more precise nuclear weapons, conventional or unconventional, is uncertain."[81] Zev Schiff examines Israel's ability to deter the Arabs and is disturbed by the implications for the future.[82]

The media will also be different. We are moving in the new world of information technology. Arnon Zuckerman describes a future scenario in which international networks will engage in fierce competition, leaving no story or piece of information unreported.[83] Professor Elihu Katz is pessimistic about the press of the future: "In a word, the combination of information management, instant news, empty analysis and the best of intentions threatens the future of critical journalism."[84]

Barrie Dunsmore predicts that the next war will be broadcast live.[85] Marvin Kalb agrees: "Will there be 'live' coverage of the next war? Absolutely."[86]

I had the opportunity to address these issues in the spring of 1991. In an article written at that time, I suggested that ". . . [t]he Israeli model of quick, brief wars does not lend itself to keeping the media away from the action. . . . The realities of the country prevent the obscuring of details. Preventing access to and movement in areas of warfare is not possible."[87]

Based on this assumption, and contrary to the experience of the Gulf War, I recommended the attachment of media teams to military units: "[Such a policy] will have a definite impact on local and world opinion and, in the long run, will be to our benefit."[88] This would be official IDF policy during wartime.

The past twenty years have taught us that, above all, Israel should never again be surprised by a war. The IDF is continuously monitoring the enemy—its troop movements, preparedness, equipment and intentions. Now the IDF must monitor the media in precisely the same manner. The operating assumption is that the media will endeavor to expose the facts in any future conflict; the IDF must be equipped to meet this challenge head-on. Any attempt to hide the truth is doomed to failure. In order to survive the crossfire, the IDF spokesperson must adhere to the truth. The truth is his bulletproof vest.

Endnotes

1. Amnon Shahak, "Speech at Memorial for Yitzhak Rabin," *Ha'aretz*, October 31, 1996, B2.

2. *Ha'aretz*, November 19, 1996.

3. See Yisrael Tal, *National Security: The Few Opposite the Many* (Tel Aviv: Zmora Beitan Press, 1996); and Efraim Inbar, "The No-Choice War," in Ian Lustick, ed., *Arab-Israeli Relations: Contending Perspectives After the War* (New York: Garland Publishing, 1994), p. 192.

4. See Tal, *National Security: The Few Opposite the Many*; and Inbar, "The No-Choice War."

5. See Inbar, "The No-Choice War."

6. *Journalists Yearbook* (Tel Aviv: The Journalists Association of Israel, 1974), "The Media in the War," Discussion in the Press Council, p. 109–26.

7. See Moshe Negbi, *Paper Tiger* (Tel Aviv: Sifriat HaPoalim, 1985).

8. Dina Goren, *Defence Secrecy and Freedom of the Press* (Jerusalem: Magnes Press, 1974), p. 220.

9. Menahem Hofnung, *Israel: State Security vs. The Rule of Law, 1948–1991* (Jerusalem: Nevo Press, 1991), p. 189.

10. Dan Caspi and Yehiel Limor, *The Brokers: The Media in Israel, 1948–1990* (Tel Aviv: Sifriat Eshkolot, 1992), p. 247.

11. Ze'ev Schiff, "Information Trapped By Defense," in Tali Zelinger, ed., *From Our Military Correspondent* (Tel Aviv: Israel Defense Ministry Press: 1990), p. 15.

12. Yakov Erez, "The Military Correspondent," *From Our Military Correspondent*, p. 48.

13. Eitan Haber, "A War Without Consensus" in *Journalist Yearbook* (Tel Aviv: The Journalists Association of Israel, 1938), p. 9.

14. Ze'ev Schiff, "A War Without Consensus" in *Journalist Yearbook* (Tel Aviv: The Journalists Association of Israel, 1938), p. 11.

15. Hirsh Goodman, *Jerusalem Post*. It should be noted that in previous wars, the reporting activities of military correspondents were in line with IDF policy. In *Journalist Yearbook* (Tel Aviv: The Journalists Association of Israel, 1938), p. 13.

16. Amiram Nir, op. cit, p. 13.

17. Asher Arian, *Security Threatened: Surveying Israeli Opinion on Peace and War*, Jaffe Center for Strategic Studies at Tel Aviv University (Tel Aviv: *Yediot Aharonot*, 1995).

18. Ibid.

19. Nurit Graetz, *Lingers in Her Dream: Myths of Israeli Freedom* (Tel Aviv: Sifriat Ofakim, 1995), p. 99.

20. A formidable obstacle is the tendency among the media to side with their own government in matters of foreign affairs; this applies to both the domestic press corps and to correspondents stationed abroad. For an excellent analysis of this phenomenon see Dina Goren, *Communication and Reality*, (Keter Publishing House Jerusalem, 1986), p. 131. Foreign correspondents, it should be noted, can also identify strongly with the country in which they serve. See Thomas L. Friedman, *From Beirut to Jerusalem* (New York: Farrar, Straus, Giroux, 1989).

21. See Arian, *Security Threatened*.

22. This was a further worsening of the military spokesperson's position, following a forced resignation in the aftermath of the Yom Kippur War because of the failure of the IDF to adequately manage military information. See Eviatar Ben Tsedef, "Did the Israeli Media Provide Sufficient Warning Before the Yom Kippur War?" *Patuah 3* (March 1996), p. 48.

23. The Israeli General Security Service (also known as the Shin Bet) is one of the intelligence arms of Israel's defense establishment. It is directly accountable to the prime minister's office and not to the defense ministry.

24. See Yehiel Gutman, *Scandal in the GSS* (Tel Aviv: *Yediot Aharonot*, 1995).

25. Despite extensive media coverage and wide public attention, the whole story of the Bus #300 incident is still not known. See "7 Days," *Yediot Aharonot*, July 26, 1996.

26. Ze'ev Schiff. *Information Trapped by Defense*, p. 58.

27. See Hofnung, *State Security vs. The Rule of Law.*

28. In the years since the Bus #300 incident, the GSS has attempted to rebuild its relationship with the press. It was fairly successful until Prime Minister Rabin's assassination, which led to the resignation of yet another GSS director.

29. Yehiel Gutman, *Scandal in the GSS* (Tel Aviv: *Yediot Arahonot*, 1995), p. 5.

30. Tal, *National Security*, p. 194.

31. Ze'ev Schiff and Ehud Ya'ari, *Intifada* (Jerusalem: Schoken Books, 1990), p. 7.

32. Ibid., p. 149.

33. It is worth noting, however, that during this period the desire of young soldiers to serve in the army, even in elite combat units, remained high and even increased. A unpublished survey conducted by the IDF department of behavioral science showed that while motivation decreased during the Lebanon War, during the Intifada it returned to the high levels that were typical during the Yom Kippur War. This can perhaps be attributed to the fact that there was greater national consensus of opinion concerning the Intifada than the Lebanon War, hence the morale of enlisted soldiers was higher during the Intifada.

34. Ran Edelist, "With an Iron Fist" *From Our Military Correspondent*, 15, p. 17.

35. Yakov Even, "Lessons of the Dialogue Between the Media and the Military," *From Our Military Correspondent*, p. 25.

36. Mark Tessler, "The Intifada and Political Discourse," *Arab-Israeli Relations*, p. 364–65.

37. Arian, *Security Threatened*, p. 79.

38. Tal, *National Security*, p. 195.

39. Interview with Yakov Even, "The Media Show," ITV Channel 4, Great Britain. December 3, 1989.

40. Ze'ev Segal, *Freedom of the Press: Between Myth and Reality* (Tel Aviv: Papyrus, Tel Aviv University Press, 1996), p. 70.

41. See Caspi and Limor, *The Brokers*, p. 125.

42. Mortimer B. Zuckerman, *U.S. News & World Report*, January 20, 1990, p. 78.

43. Efraim Lapid, "Credibility Is the Key," *From Our Military Correspondent*, p. 31.

44. Even, *From Our Military Correspondent*, 25.

45. *State Comptroller's Annual Report*, 1989 (The Government Printer), Jerusalem, p. 7.

46. Nachman Shai, "The Electronic Aspect of Military Coverage," *From Our Military Correspondent*, p. 22–23.

47. Emanuel Hasidov, *The Gulf War* (Tel Aviv: Saar Press, 1993), p. 226.

48. Moshe Arens, *War and Peace in the Middle East: 1988–1992* (Tel Aviv: *Yediot Aharonot*, 1995), p. 162.

49. Ibid., p. 181.

50. Ibid., p. 160.

51. Shalom Rosenfeld and Mordechai Naor, *Viper: The Gulf War Through Four Israeli Dailies* (Tel Aviv: Tel Aviv University Press, 1990), p. 170.

52. A meeting between Defense Minister, M. Arens, and Editors Committee January 14, 1991.

53. A meeting between the IDF chief of general staff, Major General Dan Shomron, and military correspondents January 15, 1991.

54. Caspi and Limor, *The Brokers*, p. 111.

55. See Orit Galili, "I Saw and Heard," *Ha'aretz*, January 16, 1991.

56. As widely reported.

57. Tal, *National Security*, p. 195.

58. For an interesting study on how the Israeli media satisfies the public's needs in times of emergency, see Ziona Peled and Elihu Katz, "Media Functions in Wartime: The Israel Home Front in October, 1973," in J. Blumer and E. Katz, eds., *The Uses of Mass Communication: Current Perspectives on Gratification Research* (Beverly Hills: Sage, 1974), p. 49–69.

59. Rosenfeld and Naor, *Viper*, p. 44.

60. It is worth noting that each newspaper took this position independently. See *Ma'ariv*, 21 January 1991; and *Ha'aretz*, 23 January 1991.

61. Uri Paz, "Radio Conscripted as an Instrument of War," *The Journalists Yearbook* (Tel Aviv: The Journalists Association of Israel, 1992), p. 146.

62. An Interview with Dan Shilon, *Hadashot*, February 2, 1991.

63. From "Tonight," Israel Television, March 5, 1991.

64. See Chava Tidhar and Dafna Lamish, "Israeli Broadcasting Facing the Scud Missile Attacks," in T.A. McLain and L. Shyless, eds., *The 1000 Hour War* (London: Greenwood Press, 1993).

65. Listeners Poll, Israeli Radio, January 23–24, 1991.

66. Tamar Gross, "The IDF Spokesperson Is Sleeping," in Reno Tzror, ed., *People Died of Fear* (Tel Aviv: Peratim Publishers, 1991), p. 96.

67. Col. Even Chen made these comments to me in a personal interview in October 1996.

68. I made these particular statements on January 23, 1991.

69. Graetz, *Lingers in Her Dream: Myth of Israeli Freedom*, p. 149.

70. Shlomit Levi, "Government Support as in Six Day War," *Ma'ariv*, February 1, 1991.

71. This research has not been published.

72. *Psychology: An Israeli Scientific Journal of Study and Research*, special issue on research about the Gulf War, Volume 4, no. 1–2, 1994, Published by Israel Psychological Association.

73. Tal, *National Security*, p. 196.
74. Ze'ev Schiff, *Ha'aretz*, March 17, 1991.
75. Mr. Schiff said this to me in a personal interview on August 8, 1996.
76. Ze'ev Schiff, *Ha'aretz*, March 1991.
77. Yoel Marcus, *Ha'aretz*, March 17, 1991.
78. Yehuda Meltzer, *Hadashot*, March 1991.
79. The public was smart. According to a defense ministry report, the public's confidence in the gas masks was relatively low before the war. It went up during the war and fell again following the war. It is possible that this ebb in confidence was attributable to the state comptroller's annual report.
80. Orit Galili, "I Saw and Heard," *Ha'aretz*, April 11, 1991.
81. Noah Milgrom, *Psychology: An Israel Scientific Journal of Study and Research*, Volume 4, 1994. p. 7–19.
82. Ze'ev Schiff, "Israel After the War," in Lustick, Ian (ed.), *Arab-Israeli Relations: Contending Perspectives after the War*, p. 211.
83. Arnon Zuckerman, *The Seventh Eye: A Bimonthly Journal* (July–August 1996), (Jerusalem: The Israel Democracy Institute).
84. Elihu Katz, "The End of Journalism: Notes on Watching the War" (unpublished).
85. Barrie Dunsmore, *The Next War: Live?* (Cambridge, MA: The Joan Shorenstein Center on the Press, Politics and Public Policy, Harvard University, 1996).
86. Ibid.
87. Shai, "We Are All C.N.N." in Shaham, Nathan and Ra'anan, Zvi (eds.), *The Gulf War*, (Tel Aviv: Sifriat HaPoalim, 1991), p. 151.
88. Oded Ben Meir, "The Media In Wartime," *Davar*, March 31, 1991.

Real-Time Television Coverage of Armed Conflicts and Diplomatic Crises
Does It Pressure or Distort Foreign Policy Decisions?

Nik Gowing

*I*nstant, real-time television coverage of the latest generation of armed conflicts is the curse of policy-makers. The relationship between such coverage and foreign policy is profound but fickle. Conventional wisdom is that real-time television coverage creates a demand that "something must be done" and drives the making of foreign policy.

This chapter challenges that belief.

Frequently the relationship is not as profound as conventional wisdom assumes. Ministers and officials resist the pressure with an iron will. TV's ability to provide rapid, raw, real-time images as a "video ticker-tape" service should not be mistaken for a power to sway policy-makers.

Television journalists must not delude themselves about the impact of their images on foreign policy. On a few occasions it can be great, especially when it comes to responding with humanitarian aid. Routinely, however, there is little or no policy impact when the TV pictures cry out for a determined, pro-active foreign policy response to end a conflict.

Introduction

Whenever I approached ministers, policy-makers, officials or military officers and told them of my attempt to unravel the precise impact of real-time television on their work, without exception their reactions were amusingly predictable. First came a knowing smirk, then a grin, finally the raised eyebrows and a chuckle.

No politician or official is immune from the new power of real-time TV coverage out of a crisis zone to influence the making of foreign policy. The relationship of real-time television to policy-making frequently goes to the heart of governance. "Diplomats . . ." one senior British official reflected, "We are used to working methodically, slowly, systematically and reflectively."[1]

But *real-time* images no longer allow such leisurely reflection. They compress transmission and policy response times. In turn this puts pressure on *choice* and *priorities* in crisis management. Such images distort and skew the work of diplomats, military planners and politicians.

In an analogy to nuclear physics, it can be said that real-time television has dramatically shortened the "half-life" of both a story and its impact.[2] No president or prime minister will ever again enjoy the six-day "cocoon of time and privacy afforded by the absence of television scrutiny"[3] that President Kennedy enjoyed in 1962 as he wrestled with the Cuban Missile Crisis. No foreign or defense minister can expect to repeat the experience of US Secretary of Defense Robert McNamara who did not switch on a television set "during the whole two weeks of that [Cuban] crisis."[4]

There has always been tension between the media and the policy-makers. Many in government continue to view the media with contempt. They resent deeply the erosion of their power to control the real-time information flow to journalists. Most still expect to manipulate the media with the three C's—"control, confidentiality and coolness."[5]

To this end they would prefer that real-time television went away. It will not. It has created new challenges for governments who would prefer to deflect pressures or delay responses.

Real-time television is thus having to be understood, accepted and factored into policy-making. Sir David Hannay, former British ambassador to the United Nations, has expressed publicly what many ministers and diplomats confirm in private. "It is no good trying to abolish this factor: it is with us for the foreseeable future. It is no good deploring it in a rather elitist way."[6]

This study is an attempt to draw together the experiences of both policy-makers and journalists in order to clarify a relationship that is profound, complex, uncomfortable, often contradictory and still evolving in an uncertain fashion.

At times the chapter tilts toward historical analysis of a few crisis points which since 1990 have destroyed all the naive, premature post-Cold War hopes of a New World Order: Bosnia, Croatia, Somalia, the former Soviet Union. It makes no claim to an exhaustive contemporary history of any of these crises or the two dozen others in the world. Rather, it draws upon various specific events to illustrate and test the relationship under examination. In doing so it uncovers new and hitherto unreported perspectives, sometimes created by the very presence of journalists and/or a television camera. Inevitably Bosnia dominates the study.

I have drawn upon more than one hundred interviews with senior officials and politicians at the heart of policy-making in several countries. I urged all political appointees—past and present—to be non-partisan in their responses.

Some interviews were on the record and are openly sourced in the footnotes.

Many were on background. Most interviewees agreed to meet me, sometimes for several hours of discussion, on condition that I respected their anonymity. This I have done out of a sense of gratitude for both their time and willingness to talk frankly at a time when many issues were still raw, controversial and subject to political scrutiny or dispute.

Consequently I have left many points sourced anonymously, identified in the endnotes as "background interview," with a date where appropriate. A handful of strictly off-the-record conversations are not even sourced by date. I do, however, appreciate the inevitable unease of any readers who in principle disapprove of anonymous sourcing.

Given the multilateral complexity of the events being studied it is both possible and probable that some perspectives have been omitted. Further contributions to clarify the record or correct facts will be much appreciated.

Real-time Television: A Definition

The 1990s were the "Decade of the Dish."[7] While the military arsenal contains the latest stealth and smart technology, the television journalist's arsenal contains a laptop computer, a Marisat telephone, and a portable "up-link" satellite the size of a large umbrella.

Real-time images are those television pictures beamed back live by satellite from a location. Alternatively they may have been taped a few minutes earlier, or perhaps an hour or two beforehand—but little more.

The presence of a satellite dish has created a new grammar and editorial agenda for TV news coverage. It is beamed out of a war zone virtually instantly without the dangerous challenge of dispatching video cassettes by road, air or sea—often through road blocks and fighting—to a distant TV station. As the experience of covering Lebanon in the 1980s showed, such logistics create both a crude editorial filtering effect and a vital time delay which means the pictures are out of date (though still relevant or newsworthy) by the time they are transmitted.

The absence of a satellite dish usually means significantly less TV coverage of a crisis. Often no dish means no coverage. On the other hand, the presence of a dish creates news coverage because of a TV news manager's corporate obligation to justify its costly deployment. Sometimes live "two-way" interviews on location with correspondents or key news figures help to generate news or keep up the profile and/or momentum of a story, even though there is no particular news development to warrant them. Without real-time satellite up-links such an editorial momentum cannot be maintained.

The very presence of a satellite dish in a conflict zone thus creates new dynamics and pressures in television journalism. In the words of Ted Koppel of ABC News, who reported from Vietnam: "You write differently when you know your piece won't make air for another day or two. You function differently. . . . You have time to think. You have some time to report. . . .The capacity to go live creates its own terrible dynamic. . . . Putting someone on the air while an event is unfolding is clearly a technological *tour de force*, but it is an impediment, not an aid, to good journalism."[8]

It is an impediment that is now understood by the policy-makers, which is why they have little trust in TV reporting. As one senior US official put it: "Television is often wrong. *We* have to make sure we are right."[9] Another official said: "Television is a joke, and it is scary to think that this is the way many Americans get their news."[10] A senior Downing Street insider added: "Something must be done, [but] TV means we can do the wrong thing."[11]

In Britain, Edward Bickham, former Special Adviser to the British Foreign Secretary, has expressed publicly what many former Foreign Office colleagues told this author privately. "The power of television in foreign policy is a mixed blessing. As a medium it plays too much to the heart, and too little to the head. It presents powerful, emotive images which conjure strong reactions. . . . Anecdotes about individual suffering make compelling television, but they rarely form a good basis to make policy. . . . Foreign policy should be made by democratic governments, accountable to Parliament, not in reaction to which trouble spots the news gathering organizations can afford to cover from time to time. . . . Reactions to the priorities of the news room are unlikely to yield a coherent or a sustainable foreign policy."[12]

Such official distrust of the skewed, incomplete picture provided by TV coverage is one key reason why in general, real-time television has less impact on foreign policy formulation than many assume. But on many occasions television is right and reports events before the policy-makers even know about them. That is the moment when the impact of real-time television can be profound.

Television and Foreign Policy: The Conundrum

"In the country of the blind, the one eyed man is king."[13]

In the new generation of armed conflicts, the great Western political and military powers have often found themselves unsighted. For long periods—especially in the early stages—they have been blind, knowing little of what was happening. They have also misread much of whatever limited information came their way.

The lens of a single television camera—the "one-eyed man"—has often provided images that leave enduring impressions which no diplomatic cable or military signal can ever convey. The television image frequently speaks where words or government telegrams and reporting do not.

Real-time television has sharpened that impact.

The presence in a war zone of TV cameras and accompanying satellite dish reduces the time span of the news cycle to a point where there is virtually no time lag. Where once there were delays of days or hours in getting news video out of a conflict zone and onto the air, now it is often merely a matter of minutes. Frequently there is no delay at all. That is why coverage is *real-time*.

In turn, the ability to transmit in real-time increases the frequency of updated news stories. *In extremis* it allows indefinite live and worldwide coverage of a developing conflict like the storming of the Russian White House in October 1993. Officials confirm that information often comes to them first from television or text news services well before official diplomatic and military communications channels can provide data, precision, clarification and context.

Real-time television coverage from any zone of conflict is thus an irreversible fact of political life. For TV news operations only three factors stand in the way of routine real-time transmission from any crisis location. They are coverage costs, changing editorial priorities and the occasional bureaucratic obstruction of some governments to the installation of portable satellite dishes. Distance and remoteness are no longer an obstacle. Government efforts to censor or control television reporting are usually (though not always) bypassed as a matter of routine.

The impact of what many call the "CNN factor" or "CNN curve" cannot be disputed. The now legendary reputation that CNN has built for itself in real-time coverage of crises is an important marketing tool for the corporation.

Prod a little deeper, however, and many in government say the "CNN factor" is in reality more of a catch-all term for a much broader phenomenon. Other international broadcasters like Sky, Superchannel and BBC World Service TV have similar impact on governments, especially outside the USA. More services will soon join them, like CBC News World International. The worldwide provision of news video and satellite services by Reuters, WTN and Associated Press Television multiplies the scope of real-time television, as do the growing number of German, Hispanic and other language services under development.

By receiving live transmissions of press conferences, speeches, interviews and sometimes unfolding horrors, the government machines experience no delay in receiving raw information. As such, real-time television provides a "video ticker-tape" service.

The conventional wisdom is that such vivid immediacy regularly forces some kind of change in policy—especially after horrific events in conflicts like Bosnia. This chapter will detail examples of this cause-and-effect relationship, including the role of TV news in prompting humanitarian aid operations.

But such a connection is not the norm.

A clutch of important examples do not in themselves confirm an *automatic* cause-and-effect paradigm. As the number of cases of "territorial disputes, armed

ethnic conflicts, civil wars and the collapse of governmental authority"[14] prolifer-
ates, the chances that horrific images of war will stir governments to take action is
diminishing fast.[15] The answer to the question *Ethnic Conflicts: Who Cares?* can be
summarized as "Some people do. Most don't. Many more people should."[16]

As will be shown, instant coverage of the Sarajevo market massacre in
February 1994 contributed in some part—but not as much as many assume—to
bringing peace and a prolonged ceasefire to that city[17]; TV coverage of a dead
American serviceman being dragged through Mogadishu in October 1993 created
public pressure on the Clinton administration to confirm a US intention to withdraw from Somalia; TV pictures of suffering in the besieged Moslem town of
Srebrenica forced the United Nations Security Council to create Safe Areas in April
1993.

But real-time television coverage did not, for example, force policies to save
the besieged UN Safe Area of Gorazde from Bosnian Serb bombardment in April
1994. Neither did it force policies to relieve the horrors of the Central African state
of Rwanda and save 200,000 people from death in the same month[18] or policies to
save Burundi from similar mass, inter-tribal slaughter in October 1993 on a scale of
bloodletting far more extensive and horrifying than what was being witnessed in
Bosnia or Croatia at the same time.[19] Vivid reporting of the Burundi carnage from
the BBC's George Alagiah created virtually no significant diplomatic resonance.

Most important, television coverage in 1991 did not force Western governments to adopt policies aimed at preventing armed conflict in the former
Yugoslavia which Western intelligence agencies had warned was inevitable. First in
Croatia, then in Bosnia in 1992, television encouraged only limited crisis management at the lowest common denominator of agreement by governments who had
no decisive political will to pre-empt war.[20] On the other hand, television played
virtually no part in the international decision to deploy a UN force in Macedonia
designed to prevent war spilling over from Bosnia.

In general, television merely highlighted the West's impotence and failure to
find enough of a diplomatic consensus to prevent or pre-empt war. Its coverage
became a catalyst for humanitarian operations but did not force crisis prevention.[21]
Governments worked to apply diplomatic bandages while the warring parties
deceived them. "Bosnia was not a diplomat's dream," observed UN Assistant
Secretary-General Alvaro de Soto in a masterly diplomatic understatement. "It was
like diving into an empty swimming pool."[22]

As Professor Lawrence Freedman has concluded: "The basic failure was to
watch passively as the Yugoslav crisis brewed, so that once it bubbled over and alarm
bells began to ring, the possibilities for constructive action had already been narrowed. . . . The lesson here is that emerging crises such as this need to be monitored
and acted upon long before they go critical."[23]

The 1991 war in Slovenia was brief and cost only eight Slovenian lives. "A pleasant war to watch . . ." one European diplomat remarked in retrospect, ". . . and relatively unbloody." But TV suggested much worse. It showed aerial attacks, convoys of military hardware on the motorways and the mobilization of the Yugoslav People's Army. The international community made diplomatic *demarches,* but found its efforts neutralized by the determination of the belligerents to fight and their ability to deceive Western governments. Television coverage made no difference.

Meanwhile the Serb siege and bombardment of Vukovar had begun in August 1991. For many weeks it produced heartrending TV images of destroyed buildings and columns of refugees reminiscent of World War II. Then in October came the sights and sounds of medieval Dubrovnik being shelled from land and sea and apparently being destroyed.[24]

Slovenia, Vukovar and Dubrovnik are three important examples of how television's powerful role as a video tip-sheet must not be confused with a power to influence or drive policy decisions—a power that is often significantly less than many believe. Indeed, closer questioning of officials, politicians and journalists for this chapter confirms a fickle relationship that is the opposite of conventional wisdom.

Some senior officials describe how regularly they and their ministers at the highest levels have been moved, shocked, humbled and emotionally troubled by the horrors they have seen on TV. They "saw images of people who could have been themselves. Yugoslavia kept officials awake at night," said one British source.[25] "People were genuinely upset by the substance of what TV showed. [At times] John Major was upset," confirmed a former senior Downing Street official.[26] "Universal guilt has begun to haunt policy-makers and military strategists in recent years, as media demands have become ever more incessant for interventions in disputes and disasters," wrote David Fisher, Under-Secretary of State in the British Ministry of Defence.[27]

Following the Gulf War in February 1991, such emotions were translated into a firm policy response. Television images motivated John Major to defy diplomatic advice and press for Safe Havens to protect the Kurds in northern Iraq. It was a rare example of governments bowing to the power of real-time television on a foreign policy issue.[28] That power is also partly confirmed by the reluctance of Western governments to protect the Shia Marsh Arabs in southern Iraq, where there was virtually no TV coverage of their plight.[29] Officials involved in considering policies to protect the Shias later claimed, however, that it was insurmountable practical difficulties—not the lack of TV coverage—that weighed most heavily against any UN operation to protect the Shias.

"If TV was the only bedrock of policy it would have changed policy, but it wasn't," said the senior Downing Street official. "TV is a major source, but not the primary source."

This official and many others confirmed that television is merely one part of a much broader mosaic of government intelligence and reporting channels on which the world's most powerful nations base their decisions.

Governments want to resist the impact of television images, yet ministers and officials know they have to be *seen* to respond.

In the years before the arrival of the mobile satellite dish governments could get away with policy responses that took advantage of slower public awareness within a longer time frame. Now ministers and officials have learned to adapt by making instant responses that make the most limited commitments possible.[30] The impression when a prime minister speaks in a rushed doorstep interview, or the US president makes a soundbite comment on the White House lawn, is often of governments being prompted to respond to TV images. "We have to look active and concerned without giving away positions before having made a considered decision," one Downing Street insider confirmed.[31]

But TV sound-bites and official declarations of horror, outrage or condemnation must not be mistaken for action or changes in policy. They are what one senior British official labeled "pseudo decisions for pseudo action."[32] As one former senior US official put it: "Reacting can be anything from a UN resolution to sending a press spokesman out."[33]

At times most government officials have talked of their "iron will" to maintain a policy line and not be deflected by the power of television images.[34] On Bosnia, under a headline *Keeping our Heads in a Nightmare*, the British Foreign Secretary Douglas Hurd wrote a detailed justification that concluded: "What we are doing in Bosnia is not abdication, but sense."[35]

The challenge for TV news crews is to cover crises as rapidly, as comprehensively and as accurately as possible. The challenge for governments is to appear to react while quietly adhering to the continuum of a "cold and rational" policy line[36] drafted at the start of a crisis. "A government is there to decide what to do and what not to do. Television only distorts decision making when a government allows it to distort," said Sir Robin Renwick, former British ambassador to the United States.[37]

Yet in the confidential surroundings of EU, NATO and WEU councils—unmonitored by journalists—foreign ministers have been heard regularly asking aloud whether they have to be seen to respond, or whether they could ride the impact of TV pictures until it faded.[38]

"Governments have to be prepared to cope and have bloody sticky moments," said one official. "They must be willing to sustain the policy line during [TV coverage], then after TV has gone away."[39] A senior Downing Street official at the heart of the political process on Bosnia confirmed: "Politicians were prepared to withstand images. The Prime Minister and Foreign Secretary will always take a long view. We were driven by TV pressure, but it was never overwhelming."[40] A senior military officer added: "TV plays a key role, however TV has not changed my view. But the way it [Bosnia] has been presented [on television] then affected the way I presented it [the policy] politically."[41]

In other words, there can be considerable cause, but much less effect. Such a conclusion challenges Kinder and Iyengar's broad belief that "TV news is news that matters."[42] On the other hand TV's real-time coverage of foreign armed conflicts does still make it a "serious and relentless player"[43] in the political process.

The official downplaying of the role of real-time television helps explain how mounting humanitarian operations became a convenient cover for limited political action—which is how the Bosnian government viewed international policy toward them. In the view of their UN ambassador, Mohamed Sacirbey: "Whenever there was a movement towards greater action, it was not based on any systematic approach to the problem. It was based upon what one saw on the television screens. . . . If you look at how humanitarian relief is delivered in Bosnia you see that those areas where the TV cameras are most present are the ones that are the best fed; the ones that receive the most medicines. While on the other hand, many of our people have starved and died of disease and shelling where there are no TV cameras."[44]

In a rare moment of candor, one British official even went so far as to describe the London Conference on the former Yugoslavia in August 1992 as a high-profile "stalling machinery" created for public relations purposes, where "the UK and US agreed to smother Bosnia Herzegovina with cotton wool in order to subdue the fighting." Throughout the Croatia and Bosnia crises, governments succeeded by and large in keeping to that line unpressured by television coverage.

But non-governmental organizations like the International Committee of the Red Cross say that such political responses have often been disastrous for their humanitarian activities. "Political leaders were pushed to make immediate responses because of what they saw on television screens," one official told this author. "But [often] they were not the most appropriate."

Thus, fundamental changes or reversals of policy in the wake of shocking TV news footage from a war zone are rarer than many assume. Indeed, governments frequently go out of their way to *appear* to modify policy when little or nothing of substance has changed. And then any change is justified on the basis of the often vaguely defined but frequently cited concepts of either "public opinion" or "national interest."

This study will show that such justifications are often spurious conveniences. As one senior Downing Street official at the heart of post-Cold War policy-making expressed it: "Public Opinion and National Interest are two cant phrases that have been around for two hundred years. Over Yugoslavia it is not sure what the public opinion wanted."[45] Mark Gearan, President Clinton's communications director, characterized the citing of public opinion to justify foreign policy decisions as "an additive to bolster an argument. Public opinion is not that important."[46]

Yet, the role of television in policy-making cannot legitimately be described as "a sideshow about a footnote."[47] Where they are deployed, TV news cameras do have a role in prioritizing crisis management both *within* a specific crisis and *between* different crises. They highlight the new fault lines in what has been described variously as the developing "Clash *of* Civilizations,"[48] the "Clash *within* Civilizations,"[49] "the Coming Anarchy"[50] or some other variant of the ethnic instability fast developing across the globe.[51]

Former British Foreign Secretary Douglas Hurd has admitted that for a distant but strategically important conflict like the war in Tajikistan the usual flow of Foreign Office telegrams failed to create the same impact on him as a couple of minutes of news video he saw one Sunday night on ITN.[52]

"What is new is that a selection of these tragedies is now visible to people around the world," Mr. Hurd has concluded. "Before the days of [lightweight] video cameras . . . people might have heard about atrocities, but accounts were often old and disputed. The cameras are not everywhere. But where the cameras operate, the facts are brutally clear."[53]

In other words, where TV news cameras and satellite dishes are assigned they highlight the "clashes" and "flash points for crisis and bloodshed"[54] that Western governments have yet to comprehend fully or come to terms with.

For such conflicts Western policy-makers have a choice. Either they can choose to respond preemptively as the "clashes" intensify, or they must accept passively a trend toward "important and bloody conflicts"[55] that is inevitable and will not be prevented by either diplomatic or military means—or television.[56]

Thus real-time television coverage serves to highlight the policy dilemma but does not resolve it. Indeed, the likelihood is that where real-time TV coverage occurs it draws attention to armed crises in which the world's leading powers have no political will to get involved and no ability to broker or impose a peace. As the eminent war historian Professor Sir Michael Howard has put it with reference to war in the former Yugoslavia: "Television brings it closer to us, but provides us with no new means to resolve it."[57]

No television news executives, correspondents, producers or camera personnel should try to convince themselves otherwise.

The Gulf War: No Longer Relevant?

I have resisted all temptation to return in detail to the Gulf War of 1991 to discuss censorship, news management and the so-called "CNN factor." That path of controversy is now well worn.

In journalistic and policy terms the Gulf War was a heavily controlled, well-choreographed affair fought to a relatively precise battle plan in a near-perfect environment for war and the restriction of TV images. In his book *Second Front*,

John MacArthur labeled the bitter media/military relationship in the Gulf as "Operation Desert Muzzle" which for the press involved what he called a "stunning loss of prerogative" because of their forced adherence to government manipulation on coverage.[58]

In the Gulf, live television pictures did not dictate policy or force policy changes. They distorted public impressions and confirmed the war strategy being carried out.[59] CNN's live pictures of the bombing of Baghdad allowed allied commanders to assess at first hand the success of their air strikes. Even catastrophes did not change policy. Images of the carnage after the allied bombing of the Al Amariya bunker shocked TV audiences. But they did not significantly undermine public support for the war. However, in Somalia and Bosnia gruesome images did—on occasions—weaken the political consensus for military involvement.

Apart from the few enterprising "unilateral" TV teams who defied military controls in the Gulf, the vast majority of TV correspondents (but not all) submitted to traditional propaganda techniques designed to mobilize consent.[60] Both willingly and reluctantly they conformed to Walter Lippmann's celebrated principles of journalism[61] under which "the public is seen as stupid, volatile and best kept in the dark, with policy left in the hands of a superior elite who can better judge the national interest."[62]

Only in the final moments of the Gulf land war did TV images influence policy. President Bush saw TV pictures of the apparent carnage after allied warplanes attacked retreating Iraqis in the Mutla Gap on the road north from Kuwait City to Iraq. The word *apparent* is used because the eventual estimated death toll in what became known as the "turkey shoot" was eventually found to be significantly lower than what the first gruesome images of charred bodies had suggested.[63] Yet those pictures did play a major part in Bush's decision to halt the ground war at a moment which coincided conveniently with 100 hours of battle.[64] It was not the *horror* of the pictures that swayed the President, but the realization that the war was effectively over and TV should not be allowed to show needless further casualties.[65]

Compared to the battle to liberate Kuwait, the armed conflicts in this new post-Gulf War period are of a wholly unpredictable and unmanageable dimension. The nature of international involvement is of a new, uncharted kind. UN troops are not assigned as combatants but as part of a non-combatant force of interposition. As a result the core issues have now progressed well beyond the kind of recriminations between the military, the politicians and some journalists seen during and after the Gulf War.[66]

In these new wars ministers and officials cannot control journalists as they did in the Gulf. They can no longer assume that the media is willing "to rely excessively on the government as a news source and defer to its positions."[67] Of course many journalists—though not all—will still have to defer to the White House, Downing

Street, the Elysee Palace or the Matignon for policy announcements.[68] But governments can no longer impose censorship and news management of the kind they enjoyed in the Gulf, and which in theory the military continue to advocate.[69]

In the Gulf War, policy-makers controlled the uneasy partnership between television and the military in line with the established principle that governments coerce society in order to build and preserve consensus about defense and security policy. But in Bosnia, Somalia, Russia and the growing number of regional conflicts, television and the military have traveled alongside each other on a steep learning curve. There is a new, mutually complementary partnership where policy-makers have virtually no control over TV coverage, where "no previous rules apply,"[70] and where it is virtually impossible for governments to "coerce society" on what is taking place in the war zone. In the midst of Bosnia's political and military anarchy, for example, TV crews and reporters can take risks as they see fit. In many of these new conflicts a significant number have paid with their lives, unlike in the Gulf War.

This is an important new development in crisis management.

Many policy-makers say that the instant power of real-time television and the loss of government control of information from a war zone will now be a more significant factor in a government's decision on whether or not to become engaged in a conflict. "It will be a definite factor in decision making," said Col. Bill Smullen, who from 1988 until 1993 was special adviser on public affairs to General Colin Powell, former chairman of the US Joint Chiefs of Staff.[71] "It could now be a factor in *not* going to war."

Having criticized the press and TV news organizations for their "stunning loss of prerogative" in the Gulf War, MacArthur concludes (as does this chapter's author) that in the former Yugoslavia there has been no such loss of prerogative. Instead, MacArthur says that "the press has shown enormous prerogative. Hooray for the media—especially the British correspondents."[72]

Such plaudits are not, however, without irony. By late 1992 TV coverage of Bosnia began to orient itself to locations involving United Nations troop deployments. The journalistic drive to report unfolding horrors had not lessened. The chances of being killed had—significantly.[73]

Unlike during the Gulf War, the escalating viciousness and banditry of Bosnia pressured TV teams to seek the unspoken but vital protection of being "tactical bound" to the armed umbrella of UN military operations.[74] UNPROFOR bases became like a mother ship to journalists, even helping to supply food, fuel, spares and a few home comforts.[75] Only occasionally did journalists go "unilateral" and defy warnings of significant danger from UN forces who themselves would not even travel in their armored vehicles because of the perceived military danger.[76]

After all the principled complaints by journalists of pool arrangements and news management during the Gulf War, in February 1994 after the Sarajevo market massacre, journalists, camera crews and photographers even willingly submitted to a UN pool system as the safest and most productive way to secure pictures and report facts. Unlike in the Gulf War, most of the 250 media personnel accepted that pooling on primary news coverage is preferable to some kind of uncontrolled media anarchy in a war zone.

These, then, are the realities of the new generation of war and real-time television coverage.

Television and Policy-making: The Paradox

Frequently ministers and officials talk resentfully of this "profound" relationship between television and policy-making because it creates a clamor that "something must be done."[77]

"I tell my staff: real-time reporting has changed the name of the game," said one senior British official. "It skews the details and the realities of what is happening in a war."[78]

The United Nations/European Union negotiating team for the former Yugoslavia in Geneva told how they often quipped that "television and CNN have become the sixth permanent member of the UN Security Council."[79]

Yet probe further and this author found evidence of a determination to keep to a policy line and to resist the immediately profound and emotive impact of real-time coverage of a conflict on television. "It is not that great and it is always easy to resist," said Marlin Fitzwater, who was press secretary to Presidents Reagan and Bush, and who worked in White House press relations for a total of ten years.[80]

This is a paradox because TV often creates a clamor for action which policy-makers would prefer not to be drawn into.

At times it is difficult to unravel the contradiction. On the one hand the impact of real time television remains great. In the view of former UN Secretary General Boutros Boutros-Ghali: "Today the media do not simply report the news. Television has become part of the event it covers. It has changed the way the world reacts to crises. Public emotion becomes so intense that United Nations work is undermined. On television, the problem may become simplified and exaggerated."[81]

On the other hand, as will be shown in detail later, television coverage of a conflict like Bosnia is superficial and flawed. Journalists know the shortcomings. So do governments and the military. Lt. Colonel Alastair Duncan, a former British UNPROFOR commander, described the paradox in relation to the former Yugoslavia thus: "It is very difficult to know what is happening in Bosnia [yet] it suffers from news-hype. It is a very vicious and nasty civil war, and it is largely ignored."[82]

Yet real-time television has served to highlight events which do not otherwise appear on a policy-maker's radar screen. Douglas Hurd has described correctly "the searchlight of media coverage [which] is not the even and regular sweep of a light-house." The result is "patchy" coverage and "unlit tragedies" which create "a steadily growing extra dimension to the business of government, and in particular to the business of diplomacy." [83]

"The TV camera puts an issue on the agenda when it might otherwise not have been there," one of Mr. Hurd's senior officials confirmed.[84] According to former US Secretary of State Lawrence Eagleburger: "The television sets a great deal of the agenda, and then the president and his secretary of state have to deal with it. There's just no argument."[85]

This appears to support the conventional wisdom of a cause-and-effect relationship which the veteran American television and radio broadcaster Daniel Schorr has described as "an interactive system of formulating policy and the instantaneity of modern television [which] makes it necessary to formulate policy on the run."[86]

The ultimate test of this argument is to examine the converse. The virtual absence of images from conflicts in Nagorno-Karabakh, Moldova, Tajikistan, Afghanistan, Abkhazia, Angola, Liberia, Burundi, Kashmir, Sudan or the southern marshes of Iraq has consistently led to little or no pressure for action by Western governments or the United Nations. Yet the conflicts listed above are just as awful as Bosnia and in many cases much worse.[87]

For example, as noted earlier, while the world focused on Sarajevo and Bosnia in March 1994, it is estimated one thousand people died in one violent two-day period in Burundi.[88] At the same time a US diplomat was describing Sudan as "Somalia without CNN,"[89] with a humanitarian situation worse than in Somalia. In 1994 new names were being added monthly to the list of conflicts, like Algeria and Yemen.[90]

But television news operations can only cover one or two crises or disasters at once. They cannot and do not cover every armed crisis in the world.[91] They have been severely tested trying to cover parts of Bosnia adequately, let alone comprehensively,[92] and the cost pressures on TV news in an increasingly aggressive commercial environment are becoming greater.[93] Television editors have to make choices according to costs, logistics, personal safety of staff and their estimate of audience interest. However, these editorial choices have an important influence on the priorities in government crisis management.

"We are under no pressure to do something about crises that are not on TV," one senior Downing Street official confirmed.[94] "It is television that put Bosnia on the agenda for the last two years, and did not in Angola," said Lawrence Eagleburger.[95]

Television coverage is thus a powerful influence in problem recognition, which in turn helps to *shape* the foreign policy agenda. But television does not necessarily *dictate* policy responses.[96]

In Whitehall, one British official defined the limit. "Television is a big influence on a daily basis, but the key is keeping a balanced, even keel over the long term."[97] On Bosnia another British official conceded that "TV almost derailed policy on several occasions, but the spine held. It had to. The secret was to respond to limit the damage, and be seen to react without undermining the specific [policy] focus."[98] Britain's UN ambassador Sir David Hannay concluded: "We are a pretty stubborn lot. When it comes to an earth shattering event we will not be swept off our feet."[99]

Washington is little different. "Television does not have much day-to-day impact. [It] is never called up as collateral to make decisions," said Charles Kupchan, director of the European Affairs desk at the National Security Council from 1993 to 1994.[100] "As a source of information for the National Security Council [television] is not that important. Gross pictures of suffering [in Bosnia] were not going to force intervention because the policy-makers have decided these fights are not worth picking."

"When something dreadful happened on TV it did not open up new policy options or change them," according to Marshall Harris, who worked as Special Assistant to Secretary of State James Baker in 1992, then Bosnian Desk officer at the State Department until he resigned in August 1993.[101] "The effect of television is not as much as people have suggested. Clinton would have preferred no coverage. The fact that people are seeing horrors does not necessarily force them [the administration] to do something they do not want to do. . . . The resources, assets, power and control at the disposal of an administration far outweigh the ability of television material to manipulate or drive foreign policy."

Warren Zimmerman, US ambassador to Belgrade from 1989 to 1992, then Head of the US Office of Refugees until he retired prematurely, is skeptical about the power of TV. "If we had had no CNN or ITN, I do not see how it [policy on the former Yugoslavia] would have been any different."[102]

After five years in the US State Department followed by two years on the US National Security Council, which included high level involvement in Gulf War policy, Philip Zelikow concluded: "Television is influential on problem recognition, but has very little influence on foreign policy content. Television presents problems, insists problems are addressed, but has no effect on the way policy is constructed. . . . No television does it [crisis coverage] well enough to have an influence on policy."[103]

Hence the broad conclusion of Stewart Purvis, Editor-in-Chief of ITN, on television's overall role in the West's policy toward the former Yugoslavia: "We influenced events, but not the outcome."[104]

Yet as Bosnia, Somalia and other regional conflicts have shown, the unforeseen often takes place. That can be the moment of policy weakness when there is a degree of policy panic on tactical issues. Diplomats have confirmed it is at such moments that TV coverage has tested and challenged the kind of overall minimalist strategy seen in Bosnia. Governments came under fire from journalists and politicians for failing to take sufficient action to prevent or pre-empt deeper crises.[105] Television images pressed governments sharply and suddenly in a direction at odds with policy. They either filled an apparent vacuum or created a new one, thereby testing to the limit a government's determination to manage a flurry of emotions without modifying policy.

"When governments have a clear policy, they have anticipated a situation and they know what they want to do and where they want to go, then television has little impact. In fact they ride it," according to Kofi Annan, Secretary-General of the United Nations.[106] "When there is a problem, and the policy has not been thought, there is a knee-jerk reaction. They have to do something or face a public relations disaster."

Ministers and officials have confirmed how in such situations they found themselves fighting the tide of a "fantastically powerful medium [television], which is often crude, and where the words that go with it are often trite."[107] At this point institutional resistance has sometimes weakened. "We are not impervious to events and human emotions. We can be angry and upset like everyone else, and if the policies are shown not to be working then we must react," said Sir David Hannay, then British ambassador to the UN.[108]

Such occasions have been rare, but they help explain this author's description of a fickle and unpredictable relationship between real-time television and policy-makers—a relationship whose precise influence continues to be disputed by colleagues at the highest levels of government.

For example, in the view of Madeleine Albright, former US ambassador to the UN: "Television's ability to bring graphic images of pain and outrage into our living rooms has heightened the pressure both for immediate engagement in areas of international crisis, and immediate disengagement when events do not go according to plan."[109] But three weeks after Ms. Albright spoke, the then US Secretary of State, Warren Christopher, cautioned against over-emphasizing any cause-and-effect relationship. He told the US Senate Foreign Relations Committee that "television is a wonderful phenomenon and sometimes even an instrument of freedom. But television images cannot be the North Star of America's foreign policy."[110]

Rick Inderfurth, former Alternate US Representative to the United Nations, provided what is arguably the most vivid illumination of this fickle dichotomy. "There are many times when there are horrific images and there is no policy impact. It is very difficult to work out and anticipate how the CNN factor will come into play. It is like waking up with a big bruise, and you don't know where it came from and what hit you."[111]

Television Coverage of Foreign Crises: How Much Do Ministers and Officials Watch It?

A further important paradox has undermined the belief that television influences those who make foreign policy. Few ministers and senior officials have either the wish or the time to watch television, including news.[112]

In Britain most ministers have a television in their office, but almost none of them ever watches it.[113] During the Gulf War, the British Foreign Secretary's private office installed two televisions, and senior officials monitored the output. But the arrangement was not permanent. Similarly only a tiny number of officials have TV's in their offices. "When I arrived here, one of the first things I did was put that in," said one newly appointed aide as he pointed towards the TV in his office.[114]

So on almost every occasion when ministers or officials feel pressured to respond to an outrage there is a high chance none of them will have actually seen the TV coverage in question.[115] There are many reasons: from official engagements and pressures on the diary, to traveling or the grueling need to process ministerial paperwork. As one senior British official expressed it: "Ministers have better uses for their time than watching television."[116]

In contrast, US officials at all levels have televisions in their offices, as this author discovered. Some—but not many—are news "junkies" and have a TV switched on permanently to CNN, usually with the sound muted. They want both to know instantly how the media are spinning policy issues and to have access to what one official called the "shorthand intelligence" provided by round-the-clock news.[117]

According to White House sources, President Bush watched TV newscasts a significant amount, but President Clinton less so. "He does not really watch anything," said George Stephanopoulos, former Special Advisor to President Clinton on Policy and Strategy, but "television does have an influence on him."[118]

However, by and large, television's influence on presidents has not outweighed policy considerations. "That [TV] is not where the pressure comes from. It comes from other sources," said Marlin Fitzwater.

While Clinton's National Security Adviser Anthony Lake rarely watched television news coverage, if ever, his predecessor Brent Scowcroft did—though not to be influenced. Scowcroft considered TV an invaluable policy tool, but not a primary information source. "Scowcroft religiously looked at TV, but only to validate the intelligence that he was receiving," said one former aide.[119] Another described how the general usually urged caution in the wake of emotive TV pictures. "He would always remind us it is awful. But if we start on a slippery slope, we will never fix it."[120]

Most others, however, did not feel they needed the CNN "tip sheet" as a permanent accompaniment to their duties. During his time in office CIA Director

Robert Gates ordered that his TV be removed. "Gates did not rely on TV, just intelligence . . . TV does not focus for long enough and it is often too sensational."[121] Similarly, many of those officials interviewed for this chapter said they virtually never switched on their TV sets. They also confirmed they rarely saw sets on in the offices of bosses or colleagues. For example, according to Charles Kupchan, "TV was never on in [National Security Adviser] Lake's office, or [Deputy National Security Adviser] Sandy Berger's, or [Staff Director] Nancy Soderberg's."[122]

When TV coverage has been brought to an administration's attention it has therefore usually been via the monitoring operations in the various government public affairs offices or watch centers. The White House Situation Room contains seven TV sets tuned to news coverage and monitored 24 hours a day. Urgent information or an alert is transmitted immediately by phone to the relevant desk. In the White House, news video from any US network can be replayed directly to any office at any time on demand.

It must be said, however, that some fellow politicians and policy-makers have not accepted the claims of ministers and officials that they don't watch television and therefore are not influenced by it. For example, Barbara McDougall, Canadian External Affairs Minister during much of the Yugoslav crisis from 1991 to 1993, made a point of watching television coverage and believes that despite what most of her opposite numbers claimed, they did too.

"Television is every bit as valuable as the academic cables you get from diplomats. It does have an influence," said Ms. McDougall. "I took notice. At Foreign Ministers' meetings I heard them talk about what they had seen on CNN or the BBC."[123]

In Britain, ministers and officials have described how it is often their wives, children, families, office drivers, colleagues or friends who see appalling images then express to them their horror with words like "Did you see that . . .? You've got to do something"[124] or "Where is Douglas? [the Foreign Secretary] He must see this!"[125] It has been a combination of private buzz at home or in government corridors, plus the newspaper follow-ups to the TV image, which has often created the momentum that no minister or senior official can resist. "There is a fair determination to resist and limit the power of television," said Sir Robin Renwick, Britain's former ambassador to the US. Then he recalled pressure on Bosnia from his own teenage daughter at home. "But we are susceptible, and we hate horrors too."[126]

As one British official described it: "It is not the politicians or ministers who see the images. It is the staff. The whips. The messengers. Even their wives. They say: 'crikey! perhaps we should review policy.' TV is so powerful and has such impact on the public and back benches [in the British House of Commons]. We cannot take an Olympian approach. Suddenly there is all that doubt. We have to take account. We cannot say 'no comment.'"[127]

Barbara McDougall had no doubt that "there is an ambivalent attitude towards television. It is fickle." But she still believed that she—like many ministers—did modify foreign policy because of TV coverage. "But how? I am not sure. It is hard to know how our brains reacted."[128]

Instinct about the likely political impact has been one factor. "The camera does not lie," said one senior British official.[129] "You cannot fight against it, because inevitably the truth comes out. TV creates resonances and political sonic ripples that cannot be ignored."

And it seems that in these "political sonic ripples" lies the clue to whatever cause-and-effect relationship does exist between real-time TV coverage and policy-making.

"Political Sonic Ripples": The Catalyst for Policy-Making

The number of people who watch news channels and who are motivated by the impact of real-time television pictures is far smaller than most assume. The well-publicized "reach" of TV news channels like CNN[130] is far greater than the less-publicized number who actually watch.

In the US, the regular viewing figure for CNN is on average six-tenths of one rating point—some 500,000 "households"—and getting smaller. Viewing figures for the international service are only guestimates, but overall they are believed to be "tiny, tiny."[131] Most important, the vast majority of those who do watch tend to be passive news addicts who are not involved in the business of policy-making, especially on foreign affairs.[132]

For the purposes of this analysis, the TV viewing audience can be sub-divided into *elites* and mass public opinion. Interviews for this chapter suggest that the elite of policy-making ministers and government officials tends to be "ambivalent"[133] to the power of TV images, even though real-time news coverage does help prioritize crisis management.

As already seen, the second tiny elite of families, close friends and working colleagues does have some limited influence on policy-makers in a random, *ad hoc* way.

The largest group is mass public opinion. The vast majority of these viewers tend to be indifferent to news, except the 5–10 percent classified as "attentive public" who regularly watch bulletins and updates. Except at times of national crisis mass public opinion watches at fixed times and does not tune in to rolling news.

It is estimated that in the US some 30 million households watch what can be described as the filtered, intensively edited, 22-minute summaries on the early evening network newscasts. In Britain some 16 to 18 million viewers watch the main half-hour nine- and ten-o'clock main evening bulletins. Occasionally this mass of viewers is moved emotionally by what it sees. But on issues like air strikes for Bosnia they are not affected in a way that is informed enough to be considered seriously by the foreign policy-makers who take both the policy decisions and ultimate responsibility.

The third elite are the journalists and lawmaker politicians who make the greatest effort to stay actively tuned in to round-the-clock (and therefore real-time) news broadcasts. The small number of what one British official has called *political sonic ripples* which affect foreign policy are found in this elite. Occasionally this elite includes some, if not all, of the 5–10 percent "attentive public."

This elite group comprises editors, leader writers, Op-Ed columnists and motivated politicians who frequently have no responsibility for policy-making but are affected (often emotionally) by the vivid horrors real-time television brings to them. There are not many of them, and like ministers and officials "most of the politicians miss most things on television," according to Stephen Hess,[134] who has analyzed the relationship between TV and members of the US Congress.[135] But when they see television, or public pressure brings it to their attention, then it is these lawmaker politicians and journalists who have significant impact on the policy-makers.

Without exception, the ministers and foreign policy officials who played down the impact of real-time television images on themselves pointed to this numerically tiny but politically powerful elite as the group which *does influence foreign policy-making based on what it sees on television*. Marlin Fitzwater, White House Press Secretary to President George H. W. Bush, confirmed that "the pressure of television on decision making by the President is always indirect."[136]

The views of this influential elite play back to the policy-makers through both newspaper opinion columns and broadcast interviews with ranking politicians responding to what they have seen on television. Having read the daily newspaper cuttings, President Clinton paid "real attention to the op-eds to see what people are saying," the president's special advisor George Stephanopoulos confirmed.[137]

Thus the power of columnists like William Safire, Anthony Lewis, Mary McGrory, David Broder, Jim Hoagland and George Will in the US, or Simon Jenkins, Andrew Marr, Edward Mortimer and others in the UK, is great. "Events take on a momentum of their own according to how they are picked up by the newspapers, especially the Op-Eds," Charles Kupchan confirmed after his time at the National Security Council.[138]

The true impact of real-time television on forcing policy-makers is therefore not because a minister or official sees for himself graphic real-time television coverage and says: "My God, we must stop this!" The impact is indirect and via the newspaper cuttings and/or the political process. "Editorial policies of major newspapers have consequences among the elites and the policy-makers," confirmed Mark Gearan, former White House Communications Director.[139]

"There is no primary pressure from TV images," Marshall Harris confirmed as a result of his State Department experience. "It depends on journalistic pick up and the grapevine of who is watching it."[140] One European analyst added that "since they [the Clinton Administration] did not have a policy [on Bosnia] they worried more about the *New York Times!*" In Canada, ministers have also felt beholden to pressure from non-governmental organizations (NGOs) and constituents.[141]

It is important to note, however, that the dominant role of newspapers over television at critical moments in government foreign policy-making is not new. On May 9, 1969 Marvin Kalb of CBS and William Beecher of *The New York Times* together broke the news that on the orders of President Nixon the US Air Force had begun a secret bombing campaign of Vietcong supply lines through Cambodia. The reports enraged Nixon. By his own admission, Kalb's own TV and radio reports had far less political impact than Beecher's front page revelations in *The New York Times.*[142]

In Britain, unlike in the US, ministers and officials take more note of breakfast radio than overall TV coverage. They also spend time reading and analyzing summaries of newspaper coverage because they can digest quickly a daily government cuttings service instead of watching a TV news broadcast in real time. "Papers have more clout than TV," said one former British official.[143] "There are no summaries of broadcast news, so there has to be a fuss in the papers first."

Finally there is the role of public opinion.

If politicians are to be believed, public opinion plays a more defining role than TV. Ministers claim they rely more on their instinctive sense of the likely public and political reaction to the TV images than the impact of the images both on themselves and close officials. If the ministerial explanation is accepted, then TV images drive public opinion just as they drive the newspaper columnists. In turn, public opinion (or lack of) drives (or neutralizes) policy decisions.

But in the United States, on foreign policy the Clinton administration appeared to have only a passing anxiety for public opinion, unless it turned dramatically against the government, which rarely happens on foreign issues. "We [the White House] do not poll on foreign policy as a matter of policy—principle," according to George Stephanopoulos.[144]

There is, however, one clear example of how the force of public opinion *did* break a government's determination that TV images should not sway policy—particularly on a military mission, where casualties have to be expected as inevitable.

In October 1993, the macabre images of the naked body of one dead US Special Forces crewman being dragged through the streets of Mogadishu, plus video of the battered face and faltering words of Chief Warrant Officer Michael Durant,[145] led to thousands of phone calls to Capitol Hill demanding that America withdraw its troops from Somalia. This in turn led to intense Congressional pressure on President Clinton to announce a withdrawal, which reluctantly he did shortly afterwards.[146]

Even though the CNN factor "worked in spades," administration sources have confirmed to this author that it was political pressure from Congress, more than the President's personal response to the pictures, which forced a withdrawal decision. "If that event had happened and it was not on TV, it would have been far less dramatic for policy—[although] it still might have had an effect," said then Alternate US Representative to the UN, Rick Inderfurth.[147]

Former National Security Adviser Anthony Lake confirmed that the TV pictures forced a decision which was already being contemplated on the future of US troops in Somalia. "In all candor we could have done that much earlier," he admitted.[148] But having made such an analysis, six months later Mr. Lake confirmed in private conversations that he himself had never seen the video of either the dead US Ranger or Durant. He only saw the still pictures in newspapers.

In general, however, the frequent government citings of "public opinion" can be considered as political froth for most foreign policy issues. Governments pay lip service to the vagaries of public views which during crises like Bosnia they know are usually ill-informed, inexpert, uncritical and therefore unreliable.[149] Administrations invoke public opinion when it suits them, and they know full well the limits. "Public opinion is really a narrow band. [Only] a small section is influenced," said Barbara McDougall after her time as Canadian External Affairs Minister.[150]

For example, a week after the Sarajevo mortar attack on February 5, 1994, Madeleine Albright, then US ambassador to the United Nations, explained an apparent hardening of US policy by saying that "pictures on television have helped to educate the American people about the horrors of people dying . . . the polls are showing increasing public support."[151]

Ambassador Albright's statement appears to have been somewhat disingenuous, however. Within the administration there was no particular interest in what opinion polls were saying on Bosnia. Rather, the citing of opinion polls was a political device designed to give political justification to President Clinton's decision to "put some steel" into US policy on Bosnia and "appear strong" in the eyes of the American people.[152] "Policies in the garbage can were dusted off" by the Clinton administration "and rushed forward" in the hope of removing Bosnia from the headlines, said Philip Zelikow.[153]

Indeed a Gallup poll following the Sarajevo market massacre showed only a tiny margin of 48 percent to 43 percent in favor of air strikes, but with conditions attached.[154] It was hardly the kind of resounding political justification for modifying the policy rhetoric on Bosnia which Ambassador Albright had implied.

"We can't always take the spoken claims about public support as real," said Marlin Fitzwater. "Albright claimed public support was changing when it was not.

She was invoking a public view when it was not there. There was no avalanche of letters to Congress. There was no strong public opinion."[155]

Similarly, extended public polling during the whole Bosnia crisis signaled how little the TV coverage of specific outrages had changed the profile of public opinion. As one senior Red Cross official told this author: "On one side there are pictures on television, but on the other hand people are bored by it. They are not motivated."

In other words, it can be argued that any government's citing of opinion poll pressure as the reason for an apparent policy change has often been bogus.

"Polling information is virtually completely useless," in Philip Zelikow's government experience. "Foreign policy is not dictated by polls, except when there is a traumatic event. Public opinion may not care about Bosnia. The government worries more about the future of policy and the way government is *seen* to respond."[156]

Edward Bickham, former Special Adviser to the British Foreign Secretary, has detailed how the British government weighed the options. He said that on Bosnia, television images created an instant sense of revulsion and an urge for "something to be done." But on the basis of regular opinion polls and the light post bags relating to the former Yugoslavia, ministers decided that public pressure was not really significant. "Although surveys show at times over half the British public would have supported armed involvement in the Bosnian conflict, the strange thing is how shallow the demand for such action proved to be."[157]

Yet senior ministers have remained vigilant and fearful of the effect of television images on public opinion. As one regular observer of European Union meetings on Bosnia remarked about the behavior of Foreign Ministers: "They were afraid of the public. The main issue in policy-making is the press and public opinion. They always asked themselves 'what am I going to say?'"[158]

Yet statements after such meetings tended to be palliatives. Hence the bitterness and frustration felt by many journalists over the West's minimalist policy responses to the Bosnia bloodletting. Instead of more pro-active policies of intervention or pre-emption there was lowest-common-denominator policy-making dictated by the need to achieve consensus in the United Nations, NATO, the European Union, etc. It is an explanation, but no consolation to journalists who have taken risks to witness a war like Bosnia.

"This will be recorded as the first genocide in history where journalists were reporting it as it was actually happening, and governments didn't stop it," claimed the Pulitzer Prize–winning correspondent Roy Gutman. "It's outrageous and hypocritical."[159]

Ultimately, journalistic voices of anger on Bosnia did not weigh as heavily on government thinking as many have assumed. Neither did public opinion. By and large the aim of governments was to maintain within limits a well-defined, low-risk, low-cost policy line.

"The Last Thing We Want Is Pictures From Gorazde—We Can Only Just Cope With Sarajevo"

So far this chapter has gone a long way toward questioning the conventional belief in a powerful, *automatic* direct relationship between television news images and foreign policy. There are, however, important examples where television has had a significant impact and distorted policy-making.

The quotation above from a senior British official in the spring of 1992 illustrates both the impact and the resentment which real-time television coverage can create.

The official had just been told that a BBC TV team had entered the town of Gorazde three months into the siege by Bosnian Serb forces. Pictures to be aired that night would portray a harrowing picture of starvation, desperation and death. Instantly they would widen the perception of the Bosnia conflict beyond the hills around Sarajevo into an area of terror and conflict so far little seen by a television or newspaper correspondent. Western governments would no longer be able to claim ignorance about ethnic horrors being perpetrated in vast areas of Bosnia which were unmonitored by the UN and European Community Monitor Missions (ECMM).

The immediate impact of such images was to draw up policies for increased humanitarian aid which many argue became palliatives for more pro-active diplomatic and military action designed to end the war. The role of TV pictures was critical.

Sylvana Foa, former United Nations High Commissioner for Refugees, confirmed that "television is our lifeline to the politicians who want nothing to do with us or hope that the problem will go away from public consciousness."[160] Or as Ms. Foa put it when asked about the importance of television coverage to the sustaining of UNHCR operations in Bosnia: "Without you, we have no weapon at all."[161]

The exasperated words from the British official thus go a long way to highlighting one important role of television in educating and informing Western governments during the first year of war in the former Yugoslavia.[162] "We drew the map as we went," one UN commander confided.[163] From 1991 until the autumn of 1992 Western intelligence-gathering was negligible.[164] "We were grasping for ways to fill the void and television filled that," said one senior military officer. "Reporters have filled in gaps."[165]

In 1992 General Lewis Mackenzie, the Canadian commander of 1,200 UNPROFOR troops, could barely discover what was happening in and around his base in Sarajevo, let alone the rest of Bosnia Herzegovina.[166] He had no international phone system or satellite dish and listened to the BBC World Service in the hope of discovering what was happening elsewhere in his "patch."[167]

The limited UN operation had poor communications which were nonsecure and could be monitored by the warring factions.[168] UN civilian officials and military officers had to book phone calls through the local operator to contact their head-quarters operation in Sarajevo, Zagreb or New York.[169]

One senior UN officer described General Morillon's efforts to contact the Bosnian Serb military headquarters from the besieged Moslem town of Srebrenica. "Morillon was broadcasting in French on a Canadian radio network to a French Canadian in Visoko, who transmitted it in English on a Motorola [handset] to Kiseljak [UN headquarters]. Kiseljak then re-transmitted it to [UN] Sector Sarajevo, where it was picked up by a Ukrainian who passed it to a Frenchman, who then spoke to the Chief of Staff [British]."[170] Eventually the message reached the Bosnian Serbs.

Television, with its random "searchlight," was thus a primary if erratic source of raw information,[171] reinforced by equally brave newspaper reporting. It provided detailed information on specific incidents where cameras were present, but was "no good on the general picture." In the second half of 1992, intelligence resources were eventually switched "very quickly" to cover Bosnia.[172] By 1993 the level of UN intelligence was far higher, though still well short of the optimum, despite the hundreds of NATO sorties flown each month in the No-Fly Zone and the UN forces on the ground.[173]

The implications for the partiality and safety of journalists were immense. Unwittingly TV cameras and reporters had become collectors of intelligence for UN operations. (It should be noted that in order to preserve its image of neutrality, the UN insists on the term "military information" instead of intelligence).[174]

Even in late spring of 1993, almost six months after the deployment of the first British UNPROFOR battalion, a British intelligence briefing on Bosnia in London was punctuated with phrases like: "based on what we saw on television last night, we have concluded that . . ." and "we have a lot of your reporting to tell us about that."[175] The phrase was probably a half-truth. Yet it did signal the limited ability of UN forces, reconnaissance patrols, overflights and AWACS missions to chart with full precision the swirl of the ethnic conflict around them in the early months of the UNPROFOR mission.[176]

All sides benefited and used the "tip-sheet" nature of real-time television.

The UNPROFOR Chief of Staff Brigadier Vere Hayes first heard from CNN that he would be monitoring a Bosnian Serb withdrawal from Mount Igman in August 1993. After two hours he had received no confirmation so he phoned Geneva to see if the CNN report was correct. Even in early 1994 a senior British source was confirming: "TV is often well ahead of the military. I learn from television."[177]

UN negotiators in Geneva have described how one or other of the warring parties would see a television report of, say, an attack. Without checking the details a Bosnian, Croat or Serb official then rushed into the room, issued a *demarche* and sometimes threatened to abandon the talks with words like "it is no longer possible for me to stay at the negotiations while my people are being killed."[178]

Often TV coverage was used as a convenient excuse to stall or break off talks, without having to take the blame. "It was an irritation because it distracted our attention and eyes from the main focus, and we became sidetracked into something that mattered less," said one member of the UN negotiating team.[179]

Similarly a senior US diplomat based in Belgrade explained how staff had to "modify" their reporting because they knew the State Department in Washington had seen pictures via CNN. "We often got questions from the seventh floor [from the most senior officials at State]. Is it true what CNN are reporting? Is it really like we are seeing on CNN?"[180]

That goes some way to explaining why government insiders talk of the "profound" effect of television while also rejecting its power to influence policy-making.

Senior UN military officers in Bosnia complained that governments like Britain received information first via often emotive TV news packages instead of via more considered military reports sometime later. "It is very difficult to compete with electronic news gathering," said Lt. Colonel Alastair Duncan, commander of the Prince of Wales section of the British UNPROFOR battalion in Bosnia.[181] He highlighted the "pressure of commanding officers" because of the intense scrutiny by television seen in London. "TV puts additional pressures on the hard-pressed people on the ground," said one senior Whitehall-based official.[182]

Another senior UN military officer in Bosnia reinforced the point. "The power of news and Ceefax [text news] was reaching ministers before we could get a factual, coordinated story transmitted from HQ. We got urgent cables from London to ask what so-and-so was doing. The ability of TV to transmit selective evidence creates problems for ministers. . . . Questions would always be coming to us. If TV crews had not been in places then we would not get these questions."[183]

In London, officials accepted that television slanted their impressions of Bosnia. "TV skewed the way London saw things," one senior British-based officer confirmed. "It distorted the view of the theater [of operations], even with military reporting. The random agenda of the media itself created priorities in the minds of officials and ministers."[184]

At times dramatic TV news footage has therefore had a critical impact on how the politicians—many of whom did not fully understand the intricacies of a war like Bosnia—viewed the conflict. "In the summer [of 1993] there was wobble [political doubt] in the House of Commons. But the reality was that Colonel Duncan had things very much under control, and things were not as bad as portrayed," said one senior officer.[185] He added that UNPROFOR had reported that "we are very relaxed," but it was "very difficult" to convince headquarters in Britain.

As another officer expressed it: "It annoyed me intensely on one occasion. We had said that all was going well, then someone [in London] saw something on the news saying all was not well. I was then questioned very closely. They believed TV but not me. They said: 'are you sure you have the right idea?'"[186]

For the United States, of course, this pressure was not an issue as the US had no troops in Bosnia or Croatia.

Television Coverage of War: Random, Fickle and Incomplete

The word "fickle" describes not only the relationship between real-time television coverage and the foreign policy-makers but also the way television has reported war in the former Yugoslavia.

Television reporting and journalism in general will always be a dreadfully imperfect way to portray or understand any conflict. Bosnia proves the point. That war has provided prime examples both of the impact of television and the massive difficulties in uncovering the extent of what really took place.

Some incidents have been etched indelibly on memories: the bread queue massacre in Sarajevo in May 1992[187]; the food market massacre in August 1992[188]; revelations of the Bosnian Serb detention camps in August 1992[189]; the Croat massacre of Muslims in the central Bosnian village of Ahmici in April 1993[190]; the water queue massacre in July 1993[191]; the mortaring of the Sarajevo market in February 1994.[192] The outside world knew about these horrors because a television camera arrived shortly afterward to witness the aftermath, and a satellite dish was conveniently nearby to transmit the video almost instantly.

But no list will ever reflect accurately the scale of carnage in Bosnia and what TV in particular never saw. "The very worst is always out of sight," wrote Ed Vulliamy of *The Guardian*. "The horrors we have seen are only the tip of the iceberg."[193] If it could ever be collated, the true list of horrors in Bosnia would be endless, as highlighted by the grim tally of 9,900 people killed in Sarajevo alone during the 22 months to February 1994.[194]

Television also failed to portray accurately the reality of the peace negotiations. "Many stories were so wide of what was happening," said EU peace negotiator Lord Owen. For example: "The Moslems denied at the microphone [in the United Nations building in Geneva] that they were in negotiations over Sarajevo, but they had been in negotiations for months."[195]

In many respects television reporting and journalism excelled in Bosnia, especially for risk taking, revelations and the vivid firsthand portrayal of the horrors human beings were inflicting on each other.[196] One UN official wrote: "The appearance of a camera crew has on several occasions halted, or at least postponed, atrocities which the perpetrators would prefer to be conducted in private. More than one British commander on the ground has remarked that the press is the only truly effective weapon."[197]

But in many crucial respects the international press have been humbled by their inability to represent even a modest percentage of the ghastliness taking place. After the mortaring of the Sarajevo market on February 5, the editor of the city's remarkable newspaper *Oslobodenje* asked: "Why is there all this fuss in the West about one incident?" After all, death by mortar was a daily event throughout Bosnia.[198]

Bloody events in Bosnia and elsewhere had a terrifying, unpredictable momentum of their own. Television put some incidents on the political map, but far from all.[199] "What appears on television is true and immediate and influences opinion and policy. What fails to appear effectively never happens," wrote the pseudonymous UN official "Kenneth Roberts."[200] The chances of comprehensive journalistic coverage diminished sharply as the war progressed and the dangers for journalists intensified.

The mortaring of a Sarajevo market could be covered by crews and journalists billeted less than a mile away.[201] A similar horror in another part of Bosnia would only receive coverage if there happened to be a camera in the vicinity.[202]

Why the international focus on the Serb siege of Sarajevo, but very little on the "unmitigated horror"[203] of the virtually unreported Croat siege of the western Bosnian city of Mostar?[204] "To talk of Croats is muddling the issue," one senior British official confirmed. "It is only the Serbs for the United States."[205]

Until UN officials entered Mostar in March 1994, the city's plight was even more ghastly than the Serb stranglehold on Sarajevo.[206] There was exceptional and occasional TV reporting by a handful of brave correspondents like the BBC's Jeremy Bowen.[207] Others tried but were killed—like three members of an Italian TV crew who tried to reach Mostar in February 1994, and two more, a photographer and interpreter, killed in May two months *after* the Croat/Moslem political agreement was signed in March.

But when they emerged, television reports did occasionally create great impact on the ground.

On November 15, 1993 senior UN officers and civilian staff were sitting in the mess at UNPROFOR's Bosnia HQ in Kiseljak watching a tape of Bowen's extended Mostar report. Everyone was moved by what the video showed them.

The UN Chief of Staff, Brigadier Angus Ramsay, turned to Larry Stachewicz, a senior UN Field Service Officer. "What we have seen in Mostar is pitiful and horrifying," said the Brigadier. "Could we review the film and see what can be done about Mostar?"[208] Stachewicz says the BBC tape stirred consciences in a way no order from the UN could have done. "It said we have to get into Mostar. How can we do it?"

Eight days after viewing the BBC report Stachewicz led a small UN team into Mostar "at great risk." The Croat stranglehold on the city was so dangerous that the Spanish UN battalion enjoyed no control and had taken high casualties. Yet somehow, a month later, Ramsay, Stachewicz and their teams moved into Mostar with a mobile field hospital donated by South Africa. It was burned down not long after, but those involved in getting it there say that Bowen's TV pictures played a vital part in providing the motivation.[209]

That hospital success was a rare, if brief, success in a prolonged period of ghastliness relating to Mostar. "TV spurred us to make a policy, but we could not implement it," said Stachewicz.[210] "TV [coverage of the city] would have changed the whole balance on Mostar. It would have given us [the United Nations] strong leverage."

But because of the logistics nightmare, coverage of Mostar was minimal and the city's predicament never grabbed world attention like that of Sarajevo. Conditions were too dangerous for TV crews to work. Broadcasters would not risk deploying their satellite dishes. Consequently there was never the same drip feed of emotive real-time siege stories to catch international sympathy, as happened with Sarajevo. One senior UN officer confirmed the ignorance about Mostar. "No one knows what is going on in Mostar. There is a very low level of information."[211] And Larry Stachewicz confirms why not highlighting Mostar's plight like Sarajevo's was such a journalistic failing—albeit understandable. "The Croats have been by far the worst aggressors in this conflict," he said.

Mostar also showed how for every horror witnessed by a journalist there could be ten, a hundred or perhaps even a thousand more.[212] For example the *Guardian* journalist Ed Vulliamy has described how he drove down a road where shortly afterwards some 250 Muslims were executed.[213] Larry Stachewicz described how in March 1994 he drove through a village near Vares where he said he saw some five hundred Muslim men, women and children hanging.[214] Neither incident—like an unknown number in Bosnia—was witnessed by a TV camera. Therefore neither created any public revulsion or international political outrage.

Aid workers regularly witnessed horrors, but routinely they did not carry cameras. Had they done so, the worldwide distribution of any horrific pictures would have instantly compromised their delicate neutrality. Imagine the international fury if by chance cameras had recorded the kind of incidents which UN or Red Cross workers saw.

In its own imperfect, random way, TV's limited coverage exposed both its own fallibility and the fallibility of diplomatic crisis management and policy planning. As one British official described the process: "Policy planning has always been a suspect science. Television's impact on policy has always meant that it [policy planning] has been for the birds."[215] It also complicated the work of the peace negotiators. "[The] random TV image may not be representative of the situation on the ground, but it has a weight of its own to be used by the protagonists," said one staff member.[216]

Yet for all the humanitarian operations, television coverage remained their most vital ally. As Sylvana Foa of the UNHCR put it: "Without TV coverage we are nothing. Our operations and their impact would die without TV."[217]

How TV Images Did Change Foreign Policy: Some Examples

Despite the overall resistance of governments to real-time television images, several case studies show how on a limited number of critical occasions such pictures did force changes in policy during moments of policy weakness.

February 1991: The Gulf War Refugees Saved by Television

The new impact of TV images on foreign policy was first identified after the Gulf War in February 1991.[218] Tens of thousands of Kurds sought refuge from Iraqi forces in the freezing mountains of southeast Turkey. In a unique departure from its normal harsh policy banning journalists from entering such regions, the Turkish government allowed TV cameras into the area, along with their portable satellite dishes. Harrowing live TV images of the squalor, dying babies and malnourished Kurds had a profound impact on Western policy-making.

Electronic images had presented viewers with not only live SCUD missile attacks on Tel Aviv or Dhahran, or the victorious allied advance into Kuwait. Now there was also the horror and squalor of the war's tragic consequences. After all the vigorous controls during the Gulf War, television's new, highly mobile satellite technology had overcome the power of politicians and legislators to control it.[219]

The images personally moved then British Prime Minister John Major "as he was putting on his socks in his flat" one Sunday morning.[220] In a vivid example of "belt and braces" policy-making he defied diplomatic advice. He made policy "on the back of an envelope" flying to the EC summit in Luxembourg.[221] Within days Mr. Major persuaded first his EC partners and then President George H. W. Bush to create "humanitarian enclaves" in Iraq, which quickly became "safe havens" protected by UN air and ground forces under "Operation Provide Comfort." President Bush said at the time: "No one can see the pictures . . . and not be deeply moved."[222]

It can be argued that the power of TV images during the Kurdish crisis is confirmed by the West's simultaneous reluctance to take action to protect the Shias in southern Iraq. Access to the southern marshes by TV reporters and crews was impossible.[223] As a result there were no TV images and there was no pressure for Western action.[224]

Some diplomats, however, say that the Shia crisis developed more slowly. They say they did have reliable information on what Iraqi forces were doing to the Shias. However, even if there had been powerful television images, it is unlikely another "Safe Haven" operation could have been organized. There were insurmountable military and political problems—not least the unwillingness of Gulf states to host the kind of military operation Turkey was willing to support for the Kurds.

Nevertheless, Shia resentment remained long after the end of the Gulf War.[225] More than two years after Kuwait was liberated, organizations like Amnesty International who monitor the Shias and the continuing abuse of human rights declared bitterly: "You've probably never heard of the Marsh Arabs before. You probably never will again."[226]

August 1992: The Horrors of the Bosnian Prison Camps Revealed

"The sunken eyes stare with a mixture of bewilderment and beseeching inquiry from behind strands of barbed wire."[227]

The case of what some labeled the Bosnian "concentration camps" illustrates the great power of television to catapult an issue onto the diplomatic agenda. Above a full front-page color picture the London *Daily Mail* labeled the first television pictures shot by ITN as "*The Proof.*"[228]

The horrors of the Bosnian Serb prisoner camps are now well known. The TV images will not easily be forgotten. "Haunting images of emaciated prisoners tore at our consciences," was how twenty months later President Clinton's National Security Adviser Anthony Lake chose to describe his memory of the TV pictures.[229]

Roy Gutman won a Pulitzer Prize for reporting which led to his revelations in *Newsday* on August 2, 1992.[230] Four days later ITN broadcast television images of emaciated figures behind barbed wire in Omarksa and Trnopolje camps. They confirmed Roy Gutman's report and left the profound, unforgettable impression of Dachau or Auschwitz revisited. The TV pictures highlighted not only a policy vacuum, but government suppression of information.

For their reporting, ITN's correspondents, Ian Williams and Penny Marshall, received several awards, including "Best News and Actuality Coverage" from BAFTA. Ed Vulliamy of *The Guardian*, who accompanied the ITN team, was named as Granada TV's "Foreign Correspondent of the Year, 1992."[231] Vulliamy believes his newspaper story would never have made the same impact had it not been reenforced by the simultaneous transmission of the vivid and emotive ITN pictures.[232]

Within minutes of transmission, there was outrage in Europe and America. Government ministers and congressmen condemned such barbaric treatment in what some willingly labeled "concentration camps."

In Britain, the Overseas Aid Minister Baroness Chalker appeared visibly shaken as she watched the film live in the Channel Four News studio. She pledged that Britain would do all it could to end "the appalling atrocities." Soon afterwards President George H. W. Bush called a press conference and labeled the scenes a "humanitarian nightmare." He pledged that America "will not rest until the international community has gained access to all detention camps." Bush demanded action by the United Nations to restore human rights in Bosnia and guarantee the passage of humanitarian aid.

The impression given by governments was one of great shock and surprise at what Gutman's article had revealed and ITN's TV images confirmed. The following day, British Foreign Secretary Douglas Hurd said: "The abuses which have been brought to light are intolerable and must be stopped."[233]

But had the abuses in the camps really been "brought to light"? Or had they been known about by governments for some time? Was such surprise credible?

There is clear evidence that the UN, the US government and to a lesser extent the International Red Cross had known for more than two months. They had in their possession significant but incomplete detail of the inhuman treatment in the detention camps. Gutman and ITN's pictures smoked out a truth which many leading Western governments (but maybe not all) already knew about. It was, though, information on which they had felt neither compelled nor willing to take political action. Indeed they actively resisted any behind-the-scenes pressure for action.

According to John Fox, who was then East European specialist in the US State Department's policy planning staff: "The US government had in its possession credible and verified reports of the existence of the camps—Serbian-run camps—in Bosnia and elsewhere as of June, certainly July 1992, well ahead of the media revelations."[234]

According to middle-ranking officials there was a heated internal debate in the State Department with those at the highest level who had political responsibility. "You can't have concentration camps in this day and age and not have a public outcry," said George Kenney, a former official on the Yugoslav desk. "We had to say what we thought. Instead the State Department's position was: 'Let's pretend it isn't happening. Let's—let's try to push it out of our consciousness.'"[235]

On June 24, 1992, a front report from Dan Stets of the *Philadelphia Inquirer* in Sarajevo, had already revealed *prima facie* evidence that Bosnian Moslems were being held in "concentration camps."[236] The claims and details came from Zlatko Hurtic, a Bosnian lawyer who had 120 statements from witnesses and represented a coalition of human rights groups called "Save Humanity." A procession of journalists visited Hurtic and received the same information but the details never created any political or diplomatic resonance. There was no impact internationally, and no follow-up. A similar Bosnian document prepared on May 9 was also passed to the UN and the US government. It detailed mass executions in Brcko and alleged "concentration camps" in the Bosnian Krajina.[237]

Stets had seen the list, but he could not verify personally Hurtic's claim that "40,000 have been murdered along the Drina River and that another 70,000 are still in concentration camps." Yet documentation prepared by "Save Humanity" and seen by Stets was detailed enough to confirm at least the existence of camps and what the *Inquirer* was willing to headline as "a systematic extermination campaign." Hurtic appealed for international human rights organizations to investigate further, but to little effect.

Roy Gutman's investigations had begun in Banja Luka in early July when he discovered that Moslems were being removed from their home towns on railway wagons. On July 14 he visited Manjaca "prisoner-of-war camp" where a German photographer traveling with him was able to snap three sneak still pictures of prisoners with shaven heads.[238] Gutman's revelation of torture and appalling conditions was printed on July 19. He recorded the fact that officials from the International Red Cross (ICRC) were present during his visit.

On July 29, beneath the same picture of cowed Moslem prisoners with shaven heads, Maggie O'Kane's splash front page report in *The Guardian* revealed further details of the "concentration camps" and executions in Trnopolje, Omarska and Bratunac.[239] O'Kane's report stirred ITN's interest in establishing the precise nature of the camps. The Bosnian Serb leader Radovan Karadzic happened to be in London at the time. That day he denied the existence of the camps. At the same time it was this author who decided to challenge Karadzic face-to-face and demand that ITN have access to the camps to check the allegations. After a heated exchange Karadzic agreed.

By late July Roy Gutman had met a handful of eye-witnesses to the "routine daily slaughter" in Omarska which *Newsday* would soon headline as "Death Camps."[240] He and his foreign editor tried to alert the US foreign policy establishment, while wondering why US intelligence and/or the UN had not alerted the world. "I began to develop a theory," Gutman wrote, "that the Western governments had written off Bosnia and had not bothered to tell the public. Media reports such as mine represented so much inconvenience."[241]

Eighteen months later Gutman said: "From the moment I heard about Omarska I did everything I could to ring the alarm bell. I called the White House. I called the House Foreign Affairs Committee—seven or eight or maybe ten different efforts to alert the US government to the fact that there was possibly a death camp; that they should look into it and that they should come up with the truth of it. And nothing happened. Absolutely nothing happened."[242]

On August 3, the day after Gutman's first article (and three days before ITN's reports), the State Department spokesman Richard Boucher confirmed that "Serbian forces are maintaining what they call detention centers for Croatians and Moslems, and we do have our own reports similar to the reports that you have seen in the press."

On August 4, however, Assistant Secretary of State Tom Niles tried to roll back on Boucher's statement. "We don't have, thus far, substantiated information that would confirm the existence of these camps," Niles told an incredulous congressional committee.

Despite a categorical denial later by the then-Acting Secretary of State Lawrence Eagleburger, John Fox from the policy planning staff claims the seventh floor [the highest political level at the State Department] gave instructions "deliberately not to tell the truth" about the camps.[243]

Until, that is, the ITN pictures on August 6 confirmed their existence, beyond any doubt.

That evening the British Foreign Office played down the significance of the camp revelations. A spokesman responded that "reports of death camps are exaggerated" and that there was "no systematic execution of prisoners by the Serbs." But he accepted that it was "not a pretty picture."[244]

Simultaneously in New York, Albert Peters, spokesman for the United Nations High Commissioner for Refugees, told a heated press briefing that one month earlier on July 3 the UNHCR had circulated to the ICRC, UNPROFOR and the EC Monitoring Missions a memorandum. It contained "information on alleged abuses collected by UNHCR field officers from various credible sources" relating to four camps.[245] Hurtic was one of the sources.

Peters said the UN believed the ICRC had used the document as a basis for interviewing 4,000 people since July 7, but access to many areas had been denied. In addition, on July 27 the UNHCR had circulated to "more than 4,300 journalists, diplomats and humanitarian organizations around the world"[246] a document containing details "of one of the worst alleged prison camps"—Omarska.

To this day the Red Cross say they were never able to undertake the interviews as the UNHCR claimed. Key officials in the British Foreign Office deny they ever received, heard of or saw the UNHCR memorandum.[247]

On hearing of the revelations about Omarska and Trnopolje camps and the UNHCR claim to have circulated a document, one key British official "called back to the UN to find out where their [the British government's] copy was."[248] The official added: "Only after the TV [coverage] did we act. We did not know the UN had already reported what was happening in these camps."

On Friday, August 7, after transmission of ITN's reports and the appearance of newspaper front pages filled with the now unforgettable picture of an emaciated prisoner, the British Foreign Secretary postponed his departure for holiday in Italy to chair an emergency meeting of some fifteen officials. "There was a perceived need to respond, but not a crusading zeal," said one senior official who attended.[249] He confirmed that Mr. Hurd's private office "did not know what was going on." Up to that point they had received "no reports from any [humanitarian] agency." Such was the political pressure to take action that the UN department of the Foreign Office urgently employed extra staff to handle the new workload of records, registration, communications and logistics.

As for the International Committee of the Red Cross, they did not know about the camps. "I can be very clear about this," Thierry Germond, ICRC Delegate General for Europe, confirmed. "Probably the UN had some kind of allegations. We had never been approached on it by the UNHCR."[250]

In any case, the ICRC had been in no position to carry out the interviews and investigation. In mid-May 1992 the chief ICRC delegate in Sarajevo had been murdered. Subsequently all ICRC staff in Bosnia were withdrawn pending a political agreement from all three warring factions to allow them to work safely.

Therefore, until the end of June there were no ICRC staff in Bosnia to follow up whatever information the UN and/or US government might have passed to their headquarters in Geneva. The ICRC confirms that, like Roy Gutman, it heard rumors of large numbers of people detained in Omarska, but they "did not have a full picture."

And the UNHCR memorandum? "If such a document existed and was circulated to governments, I never knew about it," said Monsieur Germond. "I would find it very strange that governments would have the information and not call us about it."

By early August what Monsieur Germond calls the "Sherlock Holmes" efforts by the ICRC, ITN and Roy Gutman to discover the accuracy of the rumors were converging independently of each other. Whether they knew beforehand or not, governments were galvanized immediately by the TV images.

"Governments have been compelled through those pictures to put the issue of prisoners at the top of the agenda, at least for several weeks," Monsieur Germond confirmed. "Without them [the TV images], the governments would not have been prepared to put this at the top of the agenda, even if it is not possible to establish the extent of the influence."

The ICRC further believes that without the international pressure created by the TV pictures, the "big shock" of so many prisoners would never have been discovered. The camps became a central issue at the EC/UN Yugoslav Conference in London in late August. The Bosnian Serb leader Radovan Karadzic made commitments to close them down, and the Omarska camp was quickly shut, but not without further indiscriminate executions of detainees.[251]

Having created an obscene showcase closure at Trnopolje camp for TV cameras,[252] Karadzic then prevaricated. He harnessed the camp issue as a political bargaining chip at the same time as more camps were found to exist in towns and villages across Bosnia.[253]

Eventually most camps were emptied, albeit slowly. Over subsequent months many prisoners who survived were moved to refugee camps outside Bosnia under ICRC supervision. For that reason the ICRC believes that instead of contributing to the freedom of the camp prisoners, the ITN/*Newsday* revelations inadvertently helped the Bosnian Serbs in their aim of ethnic cleansing. "We got people out of hell," one official told this author, "but without the international pressure to get people out we could have kept open the possibility of keeping them [the Bosnian Moslems] in the area."

Thus, as with the Srebrenica "Safe Area" concept (see later in the chapter), television coverage forced policy decisions which were deemed a correct, understandable response at the time. Yet they also helped contribute to the war aims of the main guilty party—the Bosnian Serbs.

Ultimately, whether there was a conspiracy at either international or national levels to suppress emerging information on the camps remains open to debate.

In the US there is clear evidence that the horrors of the camps were known to the Bush administration but suppressed at some level to avoid creating a political issue which might demand a more assertive US response. Deputy Secretary of State at the time, Lawrence Eagleburger, denies emphatically that there was any cover-up. He called such claims "baloney."[254]

Meanwhile there does not appear to have been a cover-up in Europe, although why the US knew and other governments in the anti-Serb alliance like Britain and France were not informed remains a strange, unanswered question.

For his part, Roy Gutman believes the US failure to follow up what it knew of the camps in June and July 1992 was a significant lost opportunity to throw the Serb aggressors off balance.[255]

As for the distribution of the UNHCR memorandum, the claims and counter claims will probably never be resolved. For the moment the failure to know or act can probably be explained by a mix of bureaucratic bungling, incompetence, overstretch in undermanned staffs, and failures in both inter-institutional and inter-governmental communications when outsiders would expect much better.

April 1993: Srebrenica: The "Safe Area" Created From Nothing

In April 1993, television images were instrumental in saving the mainly Bosnian Moslem town of Srebrenica from Bosnian Serb forces. No television camera was inside Gorazde one year later when the threat was identical.

It was TV images filmed by a freelance reporter/cameraman,[256] plus the defiance of the UN commander General Morillon, which helped to save the town of Srebrenica from being overrun and the swollen Moslem refugee population from being slaughtered.[257] Inside the United Nations and the broader international community the TV images created political chaos and diplomatic resentment. They forced the creation of Safe Areas in defiance of the wishes of the main Western powers.

In the spring of 1993 Bosnian Serb forces were pursuing relentlessly their year-long policy of ethnic cleansing in eastern Bosnia. By mid-March much of the area had already fallen. Srebrenica, Gorazde and Zepa were the last significant obstacles to the Serb takeover of the area, and Bosnian forces were holding out.[258]

Tens of thousands of Bosnian Moslems had sought refuge in Srebrenica, which remained under Serb artillery attack. There was virtually no food. The conditions were appalling. For months the UN had tried to take food convoys into the town, but with little success. The intolerable conditions were known to humanitarian agencies. But in the face of Serb obstruction of all aid convoys the UN found themselves powerless to help.

General Morillon made a "Damascene conversion"[259] and decided to make a stand over Srebrenica "by force of personality and bravery."[260] In Morillon's own words: "The Serbs had decided, despite their promises, to finish off the cleansing of Moslems in the areas. . . . Any attack on the town would take the form of a catastrophe."[261]

Defying UN headquarters in New York, General Morillon and a small team of UN soldiers and aid agencies headed through the mountains for Srebrenica on a snowbound logging track.[262]

"He was appalled by what he heard and wanted to stop the Serbs. He got no order. He did something himself and brought the whole thing to a head. That whole area would have been cleansed of Moslems."[263]

When Morillon's team finally entered Srebrenica they were surrounded by desperate Moslem women and children who refused to let him leave. The scale of the potential catastrophe was clear. Morillon tried to slip out of the town, but was overwhelmed emotionally by the numbers of Moslems trying to find sanctuary from the Serbs.[264] He addressed the Moslems from his jeep, and declared he would not desert them or their plight. Later his life would be threatened by the "murderous furor" of a "spontaneous demonstration" organized by the Bosnia Serb army's chief of staff.[265]

One senior UN official said: "The UN ideal is to have a commander who does what New York orders him to do and does not dispute it. More important he should not embarrass New York by showing up things and events which New York does not want highlighted or does not know about."[266]

On the international diplomatic front Morillon was creating enough problems. An amateur video camera would soon compound them.

Until Morillon's personal commitment the West had heard skimpy reports of the ghastliness inside Srebrenica, but seen nothing first hand. The best television could do was a few brief seconds of scripted copy describing conditions based on reports from Medecins sans Frontières, accompanied by a dot on a map to represent the town. Nothing else.

By this time TV journalist Tony Birtley had spent three weeks trying to enter Srebrenica. He tried trekking by donkey. He tried walking.[267] Finally he conned his way onto a Bosnian Mi-8 helicopter that was shipping a tiny amount of ammunition to the beleaguered troops.[268] Flying at treetop height above the Serb artillery positions, he secured access to Srebrenica without the comfort of staff benefits, pension and life assurance if it all went wrong.[269]

Tony Birtley's smuggled video images created the impression of a death camp. They showed squalor, desperation, hunger and humiliation. They confirmed the reason for General Morillon's defiance and had a profound impact worldwide. As a result, it is argued that Birtley's enterprise and bravery saved Srebrenica, along with the unilateral, controversial and unorthodox pressures and guarantees of General Morillon. Together they provided governments with the stark reality that they had to do something or be accused of being accomplices to the slaughter of many thousands of Moslems. Together Birtley and Morillon defied Western indifference.

At the time the international mood was one of concern, but disengagement from the horror of Srebrenica. The British Foreign Office minister Douglas Hogg said on the radio one morning: "If you are asking me if we have a policy that will certainly save Srebrenica in a few hours, the answer I regret to say is 'No.'"[270]

Around the world Birtley's images made politicians realize the horror of the town in a way that the dribble of official reports from humanitarian operations and the speculations had failed to.

UN headquarters in New York was furious. "Morillon was cursed by the 37th floor because of what he showed in Srebrenica," said one senior official.[271] "It forced the [former] Secretary-General [Boutros Boutros-Ghali] to take action. It made the UN Peacekeeping Department look to be fools and incompetent. But TV did it for Morillon."

The UN's target was Morillon. The Bosnian Serb target was Tony Birtley and his video camera. As UN trucks began transporting Moslem women and children out of the town, Serb forces targeted Birtley for thwarting their military intentions. They hit him with a mortar and shattered his leg in four places. He was lucky to survive. A covert UN evacuation saved his leg from instant amputation.[272]

By now, the horror of Srebrenica had a new international political momentum of its own. Politicians in Western capitals wrung their hands and steered firmly away from intervention that might save the town. The idea of creating Safe Areas was rejected, even though in London at least there was what one official called "a certain admiration of General Morillon for kicking away orthodoxy and defying instructions."[273] "There was a political feeling that if he could save Srebrenica then it would prevent the Moslems losing Eastern Bosnia." The stated British position at the time was the opposite. In public the Foreign Office dismissed the Safe Area idea as both a bad precedent to set and a bad principle to adopt.

But at UN headquarters in New York the TV images had already stirred the majority non-aligned nations on the Security Council. Their number included several Islamic states sympathetic to the Bosnian Moslems.[274] These nations had long complained of being repeatedly steamrollered by the Permanent Five (the US, Russia, China, France and the United Kingdom). Unusually they wanted to flex their political muscles within the Security Council and embarrass the big powers. Srebrenica was their chance.

Venezuela held the rotating chair of the Security Council. Led by the outspoken and flamboyant Venezuelan ambassador Dr. Diego Arria, the non-aligned defied first the Permanent Five, then the firm advice of the UN Secretariat, quoting the UN force commander General Wahlgren.[275] All of them had warned that a Safe Area was a vague concept with no political or military foundation.[276] It would become an enclave with the same overwhelming humanitarian and security problems as the Gaza strip and all permanent refugee camps around the world.

"The major powers were resenting the media's involvement," Dr. Arria confirmed. "Ours was a cry of impotence. It was the knowledge [from TV images] that drove me because they gave me information."

Dr. Arria claims the Permanent Five tried to block the distribution of information about Srebrenica in order to justify not taking action. They also accepted the UN Secretariat's advice against Safe Areas, because (as one ambassador is reported to have said) "we cannot base UN resolutions on press releases."

There was bitter internal wrangling. Dr. Arria believes he "terrified" the big powers because based on Birtley's TV pictures "I told the truth." He believes that in return the permanent UN secretariat tried to hoodwink him. "The only ally we [the non-aligned] had during the whole period was the media—especially TV. Otherwise we would not have known. I used to tell Hannay [the British UN ambassador] that one day public opinion will catch up with you."

"TV images were fundamental," one senior UN official agreed.[277] "The non-aligned relied on television rather than the UN. If TV had not existed then the non-aligned would not have had the basis to pressure. Dr. Arria took on an extraordinary role as a one-man ginger group. He demanded daily meetings [over the weekend] with the P5 ambassadors, then hustled and hustled. He kept asking: what is happening in Srebrenica? What is the UN doing? What does the UN know?"

Late in the evening of April 16, 1993, the non-aligned nations achieved their aim of thwarting the big powers. Security Council Resolution 819 authorized the establishment of Safe Areas in Srebrenica and Zepa, even though no one knew precisely what a Safe Area meant in legal and military terms, or how to police and defend it. How big would the area be? Would it be demilitarized? To the non-aligned nations such details did not matter. What did matter was the principle of responding to the humanitarian disaster being portrayed on television.[278] A later follow-up resolution would create another four Safe Areas.[279]

Sir David Hannay has confirmed the strong objections to creating Safe Areas within the closed Security Council session. But in the end the TV pictures "tipped the resistance."[280] One of the reasons TV played such a role is important. The big Western governments have large, well-oiled mechanisms to gather and assess information from a variety of sources—the diplomatic service, the military and the intelligence communities. Smaller nations like those who stood their ground on Srebrenica have limited and sometimes virtually non-existent government reporting machineries. "So they rely on the mass-media and their opinions are formed by that. That is why [TV] pictures are very influential [to them]," said Sir David Hannay.[281]

Under orders from the Security Council, the overall UN commander in the former Yugoslavia, General Wahlgren, was left to draw a blue line on the map and decide how best to defend a few square kilometers which senior military officers advised could not be defended. "A Balkan Lesotho," was the grim and accurate prediction by one Serb leader for the Moslem enclave which was about to be created.[282]

The subsequent squalid status and conditions of Srebrenica are hardly surprising given what can now be revealed about the nature of the negotiations.

The Security Council did not realize that while they were wrangling over Resolution 819, negotiations to end hostilities around Srebrenica were already underway. At the very moment the ink was drying on 819 in New York, the Serb and Bosnian commanders were preparing to meet at Sarajevo airport under UN auspices. The text of 819 arrived during the meeting, but it was a declaration of intent, impossible for UNPROFOR to implement and at odds with the thrust of the agreement being worked out between the Serbs and Bosnians. Events had moved on. In Sarajevo, 819 was seen as no longer relevant, so the UN officers ignored it.

At 2 A.M. on April 18, after fourteen hours, Generals Mladic and Halilovic agreed on the principle of a Serb/Bosnian ceasefire. Details would be decided later. It was this agreement between the warring parties, not Resolution 819, which froze the war around Srebrenica.

General Wahlgren ordered Morillon's Chief of Staff Brigadier Vere Hayes to chair negotiations on the detail. He wanted Hayes to secure a larger ceasefire area, not just the town of Srebrenica. But by his own admission Brigadier Hayes had no training or expertise in techniques of mediation and negotiation. Such was the lack of preparation for UN duties.

"I was left there with the deputy Serb commander and the deputy Bosnian commander. The first set of talks to establish principle lasted eighteen hours. Then I had 72 hours to negotiate detail and implement the agreement on the ground. I did not have a clue what to do," the Brigadier recalled.[283]

They negotiated "hammer and tongs" for another 24 hours. "The Canadians [UN troops] were on their way, but they did not know what to do because we had not agreed it!"

Discussions became protracted and debilitating. The Bosnian and Serb commanders eventually agreed that Srebrenica would be demilitarized and that

Bosnian troops would either hand in their weapons or leave the area. But they could not agree on the size of the area to be affected.

Such were the pressures and uncertainties about what he was being asked to do that at 3 A.M. on April 20 Brigadier Hayes felt the need to get on his knees and pray for inspiration. With no one to consult he took it upon himself to insist that the Srebrenica Safe Area embrace both the town and the hills around. But the Bosnian Serbs flatly rejected Hayes's proposal. Mladic insisted that only the town itself was covered.

Without referring upwards, Hayes took it upon himself to write out the operational order. Srebrenica *would* include the surrounding hills. "Because neither side would agree I told them what I was going to do," said Hayes. "I said 'Oy! Time Out! Sign up!' And they stopped."

That was how Srebrenica came to be demilitarized. Full implementation of the UN Safe Area principle itself took many months, and despite what is commonly believed, in many respects it never took place properly because of Serb objections.

Senior UN officials—on both the political and military sides—quickly feared that the creation of such "safe" areas had done the Bosnian Serb commander General Mladic an enormous military favor. First it assisted the process of ethnic cleansing and corralled Moslems into a deep valley from which they could not leave without risk. Second it released Mladic's forces from outside Srebrenica, Zepa and Gorazde for other military operations against the Bosnians.

In hindsight it is now believed that General Mladic probably never intended to capture Srebrenica. He just wanted to kill or terrorize as many Moslems as possible while his policy of ethnic cleansing continued elsewhere unchallenged. It was a policy repeated in Gorazde a year later with terrifying success—virtually unchallenged by the UN until too late.

It can be argued that by forcing the creation of the Safe Areas, TV images facilitated the Bosnian Serb war aims at the time. They hastened the "cleansing" of Eastern Bosnia.

The deep disquiet over the Safe Areas was further compounded by furious arguments surrounding the activities and demands of the Security Council delegation which later visited Srebrenica to examine what they had created. "They came out as a busload of school boys wanting to have their photographs taken. They almost caused a riot," said one senior UN source. The source complained about the cavalier way the delegation taunted Serb forces with a video camera, with the result that "the Serbs went mad and cocked their weapons." The delegation also handed out cigarettes and demanded the press accompany them at all times, ignoring opposition from the warring factions and the fact that their insistence jeopardized the very objective of their visit—namely to visit Srebrenica.

Dr. Arria rejects such complaints. Rather, he says UN forces "behaved like a servant to the Serbs," were "prejudiced," and "conspired with the Serbs not to allow journalists into Srebrenica [with us]."

One month after their creation, conditions in the Safe Areas were bad enough. Optimistically European Union foreign ministers called the UN-protected enclaves "temporary."[284] "A death camp with a peaceful air about it," was how Srebrenica's Deputy Mayor described each of the areas.[285] Three months on, the Safe Areas remained miraculously intact despite accusations they were a "sham,"[286] the constant fears about their viability,[287] the degrading conditions,[288] the continuing sporadic artillery barrages on the Moslems, and the incursions by Serb forces. One year later, the terrible conditions remained with the Moslems "effectively imprisoned by the Serbs."[289]

The systematic Serb bombardment of Gorazde and its Bosnian population in the spring of 1994 showed how fragile the concept of virtually undefended Safe Areas had always been. For a year their survival had hung by a thread, but with none of the world TV attention being accorded to Sarajevo.[290] Enclaves like Srebrenica were forgotten "even though their plight is much worse [than Sarajevo]."[291] Some 44,000 Moslems lived without work or schooling in an "eerie, netherworld existence between war and peace" in the most appalling conditions.[292] Even the UN protection force of 150 Canadian troops said they felt "like refugees."[293]

Tony Birtley's pictures and General Morillon's lone stand forced creation of a Safe Area in Srebrenica which undoubtedly saved lives. The impact of Birtley's images was recognized by the Royal Television Society in Britain who named him Television Journalist of the Year.[294]

But the Areas developed all the worst characteristics which the original opponents had feared. Each became a rest, recuperation and "divisional supply dump"[295] for Bosnian forces. While preparing for renewed fighting the Moslem forces could live off UN food handouts under the UN's protective umbrella and prepare attacks against the Bosnian Serbs.

In January 1994 the departing UNPROFOR commander Lt. General Francis Briquemont wrote in a confidential report: "Taking the benefit of UNPROFOR protection and supplied by the humanitarian aid convoys, the BiH forces have been reorganized, resupplied and trained. Their morale is now very high. The BiH army attacks the Serbs from a Safe Area, the Serbs retaliate, mainly on the confrontation line, and the Bosnian Presidency accuses UNPROFOR for not protecting them against the Serb aggression and appeal for Air Strikes against the Serb gun positions."[296]

Arguably the biggest disaster was that in defining the boundaries of Safe Areas, the UN had frozen the military situation on the ground.[297] The UN delimited small packets of land to be left under nominal Moslem control monitored by the UN, but with no form of defense. Thereby it recognized Serb territorial gains.

The creation of Safe Areas in a fit of exasperation that Friday night in April 1993 saved many thousands of lives. But it has been argued that the Areas complicated whatever chances there might once have been for peace negotiations.[298] Hence the unrelenting Bosnian Serb fury about the Safe Area principle,[299] and the determination of their military commander General Mladic to remove them as an obstacle to his overall war aims. Only after the virtual annihilation of Gorazde in April 1994 and the subsequent creation by the United Nations and NATO of a 20-kilometer exclusion zone did each Safe Area finally have any prospect of being "safe."

"It is a sheer miracle that we have not had a disaster," one senior UN official said in the weeks before Gorazde happened.[300] "The Safe Area is an irresponsible concept. It is totally unviable and undefendable, with no chance of normal economic activity. It could have gone wrong so easily. Conditions have not been close to disaster because the Serbs held their fire."

As Gorazde showed in the spring of 1994, when the Bosnian-Serbs no longer held their fire, and they set themselves a military goal of neutralizing an enclave, they had the power and gall to do it. Finally one Safe Area *did* become a disaster. It highlighted the impotence of both Western minimalist policies and all the theological talk of prevention and pre-emption in conflict resolution.

In retrospect did Dr. Arria believe both his dependence on TV pictures and the Security Council's defiance of diplomatic advice had been right? "I did not know that what we were creating was a trap," he now concludes.[301]

April 1993: The Ahmici Massacre

The Croat/Muslim War We Almost Never Heard Of

Throughout the first year of war in Bosnia the international community's efforts were aimed preeminently at heaping responsibility on the Bosnian Serbs for their policy of "cleansing" territory by force. By and large the media took their cue from the regular declarations by Western ministers. The Serbs were the main guilty party. All Western diplomatic efforts by the UN and EU focused on tightening the economic and political noose around Serb interests.

This political focusing of guilt meant that the surge in fighting between Croats and Moslems in central Bosnia during the spring of 1993 received virtually no coverage, although it was just as vicious and known to Western governments. The tension between Serbs and Croats in the Krajina region of Croatia was barely covered. This was due to both overload on the journalists in the war zone, plus an inevitable reluctance of their editors to perceive more than one evil party in the war.

The *apparent* diplomatic perception in Western capitals—in public at least—was no different either. Kennedy School Professor Graham Allison, formerly Assistant US Defense Secretary in the Clinton Administration, reflects a widely held view. "We [the US] have to have a black hat and a white hat. The possibility that there are three black hats is too confusing for most Americans and has been very hard for this administration."[302]

Emotive TV coverage of the discovery on April 22 of the Croat massacre of Moslems in Ahmici created the kind of diplomatic vacuum referred to earlier. It challenged dramatically the convenient and simplistic journalistic and political perception that only the Serbs were guilty.

A small group of British military vehicles had been on a UN patrol in the hills near their base in Vitez. By chance they heard from Moslems in one village about large numbers of people killed in a neighboring village. Accompanied by a pool cameraman and two correspondents from ITN and the BBC the British patrol entered Ahmici. They found Croat houses untouched and Moslem houses burned. Worse was to come. Inside the Moslem houses they discovered the charred remains of Moslems who had been rounded up and burned alive.[303]

In the words of the commander, Lt. Colonel Bob Stewart of the British Cheshire regiment: "Here and there the outline of a body was recognizable. Two small bodies appeared to be lying on their stomachs, but their heads were bent backwards over their arched backs at an impossible angle. In one the eyes were completely burnt. At first I was too shocked to notice the smell, but then it hit me. God, I felt sick."[304]

The TV camera recorded on video the British soldiers searching the village and turning up further horrors. It also recorded the emotions of soldiers confronting scenes they had never faced before, along with a burst of rage by Colonel Stewart when asked by a Croat soldier if the UN troops had permission to be in the village. It was gruesome but compelling news television.

Within a couple of hours the images of charred flesh and bones were broadcast by ITN and the BBC from their fly-away satellite dish in the British base a few miles away. Their dreadful nature meant some pictures had to be edited out. As the BBC's Martin Bell said in what some called an insensitive "stand-up" delivered in the charred basement of a house: "What happened here can frankly not be shown in detail. But the room is full of the charred remains of bodies and they died in the greatest agony."[305]

Later Bell wrote: "There are images of massacres and mutilations too terrible to be seen which we cannot transmit . . . What you see leaves you simply speechless with grief. I actually couldn't get the words out, for, I suppose, the first time in my life."[306]

Western policy-makers had long known of Croat aggression. "For a long time we knew they were equally evil," said one senior British source.[307] "The UK government knew; but the public did not. The media had not concentrated on it."

The impact of the Ahmici images on both diplomats and politicians was profound. Suddenly those who—either out of ignorance or convenience—labeled the Serbs as the sole evil party were forced to draw breath. The full complexities of the

Bosnian war were finally exposed. The Croats were shown to be equally evil. While cabinet ministers had known, politicians with only a superficial understanding of the Bosnian conflict quickly had second thoughts about backing possible military action against only the Serbs. At the time a new head of political steam seemed to be building to force such action.

The British government had known the realities in Central Bosnia for months. But to avoid undermining the diplomatic offensive against the Serbs they never made a point of fingering the Croats in public. One British source told this author that on January 19, 1993, a report to a meeting of senior cabinet ministers, officials and military officers described how "Croats are by far the biggest culprits" in central Bosnia. This source said that the information was "roundly sat on" by one senior minister. "It was information they did not want to hear. There was a belief that the Croats were OK and can do no wrong. Our reports on the Croats were being dismissed."[308]

In the spring of 1993, before the Ahmici incident, there was anger in UNPRO-FOR that the Croats had blocked roads and were torching Moslem villages south of Gornij Vakuf. "The Croats were doing what the Serbs were doing," said one senior UN officer.[309] But Western capitals still took no notice. "We were punching cloud. We were reporting, but nothing was being done about it. There was a lot of horror on the ground, but no international pressure on the Croats."

Such was their exasperation that senior UN officers tried to harness the power of television to get the message over. "We had to show that the Croats were as bad as the Serbs." UNPROFOR officers encouraged TV crews to go to the area, but failed. "Why do you not go down there to show what is happening?" senior officers reportedly prompted the journalists. "But the UK press were only interested in UK forces."[310]

It must be said, though, that not all senior UN officers were so keen to use "the avenue" of TV coverage to reenforce a political point which was not being acknowledged in Western capitals. "I knew it was open to me," said one command-ing officer,[311] "but I did not use it. If the camera was there, then so be it, but I did not want to manipulate it. It would be very dangerous."

Then, in April, unplanned by Western governments and therefore unwel-come, came the TV pictures from Ahmici. At a stroke they forced the Croat/Moslem conflict onto the diplomatic map when governments had not planned for it. "It showed there were no angels in Bosnia," said a member of the UN negotiating team.[312] At that time the negotiators were trying to get Croats and Moslems to cooperate. "Those images were not helpful."

In Britain at least, the coverage instantly forced a rapid diluting of the politi-cal consensus against the Serbs. The British government openly rejected air strikes and privately welcomed the coverage of the Ahmici massacre. As one senior

Downing Street official put it much later: "Images [like Ahmici] that complicated the Bosnia-Herzegovina story made it easier for us [to reject air strikes]."[313]

TV news coverage of the Ahmici massacre thus changed the diplomatic landscape, despite the British Foreign Secretary's later claim that Central Bosnia had gone "virtually unreported."[314] But the impact of Ahmici in highlighting the Croat/Moslem war had a relatively short half-life. It was soon forgotten, and the Serbs quickly regained their position as sole evil party in the war.

It also led to a distorted perception of what developed subsequently during early summer in central Bosnia. After the Croats were fingered as murderers of Moslems, UN forces witnessed a "huge land grab" by mainly Moslem Bosnian government forces throughout the Lasva river valley toward Gornij Vakuf. But the press showed virtually no interest in Moslem atrocities. International media attention returned to focusing on the plight of Sarajevo. As one senior UN officer put it: "While the world was seeing the hard pressed Moslems in Sarajevo, the [Bosnian] Third Corps was pushing the Croats back relentlessly. In my area the air strikes would have to be against the Moslems, but that was not politically correct."[315]

Television coverage of the Moslem push was token and sporadic at best. "Central Bosnia was ignored because murder became normal—a daily occurrence. There was 'total normality.' As soon as a level of fighting becomes a certain level it is no longer news and therefore not newsworthy."[316] As another senior officer put it: "There was an anaesthetizing effect of regular coverage."[317]

On the basis of audience research, the editorial justification to shift away from Central Bosnia at such a moment was understandable. As Stewart Purvis, editor-in-chief of ITN, put it: "Viewers do not like stories that come up time and again when there is nothing new to say. [But] we have fallen into the trap of listening more to the fear of boredom."[318]

Thus it could be said that chance coverage of the Ahmici massacre revealed both the profound impact and the consequent inadequacy of TV coverage. The true diplomatic agenda briefly stood unmasked. But soon both the agenda and TV coverage returned to most of their preconceptions.

July–August 1993

Sarajevo: The Partial Myth of Shells and Mortars

Questions must be raised about the reporting of some elements of the prolonged Sarajevo crisis. The picture seen by the outside world did not always conform to reality.

At critical moments the accuracy of real-time television coverage—and therefore its impact—was skewed by the absence of crucial facts in the reporting. UN officials bitterly labeled some journalists and their reporting as "glamour without responsibility."[319]

There is, of course, no doubt that during 1992 and 1993 Bosnian Serb forces surrounded Sarajevo. They deployed heavy artillery nicknamed "Top-Guns" in the hills, and snipers within the city. Their aim was to inflict terror on the mainly Moslem population and force its eventual evacuation or annihilation. "There is nothing quite like the Sarajevo feeling," wrote Ed Vulliamy.[320] "In Sarajevo, you are never out of range." Because of the presence of satellite transmission dishes in Sarajevo the city's ordeal became a matter of deep and constant international concern.

There was much brave reporting of the daily horrors and deaths. But was the reality the same as the picture portrayed on TV?

"The fact is that no one is starving in Sarajevo, or ever has been," wrote the anonymous UN official 'Kenneth Roberts.' One look at the quantity of goods on sale in the markets, or one encounter with a besuited Sarajevo government delegation visiting central Bosnia is enough to disprove the much peddled image of a city totally besieged and isolated."[321]

In late July 1993 Sarajevo's predicament came to a head. Bosnian Serb forces moved to tighten the noose around the city. Their commander General Mladic was seen on television gloating at the sight of burning Moslem houses and farms around Mound Igman outside the city. He toured the area arrogantly in his army helicopter, defying the UN No-Fly zone and a UN attempt to shoot him down which failed because the UN commander could not communicate with UN headquarters.

Sarajevo's plight seemed to have taken a new and ominous turn. This was reflected in a sudden mass influx of reporters and camera crews who expected allied air strikes and sensed what one correspondent called "more than a whiff of Baghdad Mark II." UN officials noted what one described as a "blood lust" among journalists.[322] One leading correspondent asked a colleague over breakfast: "What is it going to take us to get the US and their allies to intervene here?"[323]

An emotive wave of TV reporting and alarmist newspaper headlines followed. They demanded both explicitly and implicitly that the international community take measures to save Sarajevo.

The London *Independent*, for example, launched a campaign which some analysts linked cynically to the newspaper's dropping circulation numbers. On August 2, under the headline "*Sarajevo: Action Now!*" it covered its front page with the names of more than 2,000 people who they said shared the paper's "sense of outrage that our leaders are vacillating while Sarajevo dies."

The emotional pressures for the first determined Western military response to the Bosnian Serbs were intense. At the start of the August holiday season in Western capitals vivid on-the-spot reporting seemed to play a crucial role in stirring up an unstoppable diplomatic momentum. NATO representatives met and produced two strongly worded declarations which authorized a significant military build-up in preparation for air strikes. But there was no final commitment to take action.

One high ranking military officer confirmed the crucial role of TV coverage in prompting the NATO decision. "Air strikes has been wound up by TV," he said.[324] However, one British official described *The Independent*'s "heart on the sleeve campaigning" at that moment as "counter productive for politicians" because it "subverts the ability of newspapers to have an impact."[325]

While the situation in Sarajevo seemed to be on the point of degenerating into a humanitarian catastrophe, there remain legitimate questions as to whether the reality in and around the city was as television and others portrayed it. "The Serbs on Igman was one of the worst examples of bad reporting," according to EU peace negotiator Lord Owen. "[Peace] negotiations were held up by [the issue of] the Serbs on Igman when it was not an issue. But the Press was saying that this was a big strategic change. Izetbegovic [the Bosnian President] sat in his hotel and would not come to the negotiations."[326]

The pressures on journalistic neutrality and impartiality are an age-old problem, especially in war.[327] Given the declared partiality and emotional sympathies of many journalists toward the beleaguered people of Sarajevo,[328] it is professionally perilous to raise such questions. They challenge the integrity of some colleagues who were prepared ultimately to risk their lives in Bosnia and the news organizations that sent them there.

Yet interviewing, debriefing and cross-checking for this chapter confirms that the questions must be raised and the challenge made. They bear out the complaint of UN official "Kenneth Roberts" and another (or the same) anonymous "senior UN official" who wrote to *Foreign Policy* magazine. "The press corps there [in Sarajevo] developed its own momentum and esprit. Much of it set out to invoke international military intervention against the Serb aggressors—a principal strategy of the Bosnian government. That induced in some a personal commitment—indeed crusade—that lay uneasily with the maintenance of true professional standards, Publication, in turn, helped to create an appetite back home for more of the same."[329]

Whether by design or by default, a significant part of the reporting of Sarajevo was skewed and driven by the inevitable personal emotion of correspondents who, like the Sarajevans, endured the daily fear of relentless Serb bombardment. As Roy Gutman described the work of some reporters, they "didn't take the time to get their compasses straight."[330]

Not unnaturally, reporters became embroiled in the intense emotions of a frightened, war-weary population who expected that the presence of foreign journalists (and the United Nations) would herald a decisive Western intervention to end the horror.[331] By their own admission, correspondents often found that their passions and commitment on the issue of Sarajevo's plight became intense.

Frequently, however, there was selective omission of certain critical facts in the reporting which could often provide balance and context to the headlines, and therefore dilute their emotive and political impact. One example was the barely reported refusal of the Bosnian government—not the Serbs—to reconnect Sarajevo's gas and electricity supplies in the summer of 1993.[332] Another was the Bosnian government's obstruction of international efforts to restore water.[333]

When asked for their view, not all colleagues accepted this criticism. Indeed they were affronted by the suggestion. Yet some conceded there are good grounds for such complaints of distortion by selective omission, whether knowingly by a correspondent on the ground or later during the editing and sub-editing process over which he/she had no control.

In a rare and belated public acknowledgement of the problem an editorial in the *Daily Telegraph* questioned "the credulity of some sections of the media." It concluded: "The media do no service to the international community by oversimplifying the issues. Finding the right balance is all the more essential because outside intervention in the conflict has so often been spurred by the latest emotional media report of the bloodshed. If journalists are to be the catalyst for foreign policy initiatives they must retain a measure of detachment."[334]

In the US in particular some correspondents say their newspapers or TV stations rarely accepted reporting that undermined the beleaguered image of the Bosnian Moslems. America in particular could only cope with "one black hat." By May 1994 the Clinton administration was quietly realizing the culpability and duplicity of some Bosnian tactics. But it refused to acknowledge the fact publicly for fear of antagonizing the sizeable committed and diehard pro-Moslem lobby in Congress.[335]

"Led by *The New York Times*, the US position was that the Bosnians are the victims," one UN source confirmed. "The basic view is that the Serbs are vicious and the others are OK."

More seriously, stories which were critical of the Bosnians or implicated them were often spiked. "Editors did not want to believe it," one American reporter told this author. "Anyone who defies the conventional wisdom will find themselves in deep trouble," said another.

David Binder of *The New York Times* has covered Central Europe and the Balkans intermittently for 31 years. He said that work putting into context the universal demonology of the Serbs and casting the Bosnians in a less-than-favorable light has not been printed. Binder described for the record what some other journalists will only say privately. There is what he labeled a "tyranny of victimology" which is prompted by the reporter's "herd instinct" and the age-old journalistic lust for "a hot story on the front page."

"Balanced journalism has gone out of the window," said Binder. "One of the reasons is that it is not entertaining. For the masses to be entertained we have to take sides. It is considered politically correct in New York and Washington to bash the Serbs on any and all occasions to the point where it becomes almost racist. Serbs are evilized virtually to the exclusion of any reporting that might balance that."[336]

One key example was the brinkmanship over the apparent "siege of Sarajevo" in late July 1993. UN sources say that during this critical period of tension Sarajevo was *not* totally cut off as the reporting and the unseemly public row over the city's "siege" status suggested.[337] "Sarajevo was not strangled. That's an emotive phrase," one senior British official complained.[338]

UN sources say President Izetbegovic stoked world headlines by claiming that Serb forces had blocked their convoy routes and "stepped on our windpipe." But at the time UN officials knew that technically two supply routes remained open. In order to stop Sarajevo becoming a ghost city Bosnian forces were also stopping the population from leaving. The reported belief that Sarajevo was being "encircled" was wrong and was undermining peace talks taking place in Geneva.[339] UN officers reported that because of the impact of the Sarajevo crisis "Stoltenberg [the UN peace negotiator in Geneva] would call and ask what is going on. I told him: I have no idea."[340]

Senior UN officials became especially concerned that the skewed press reporting of Sarajevo was distorting impressions within the UN organization itself and among members of the Security Council. This in turn distorted UN policy-making on the Security Council. Officials in Zagreb and New York ordered their colleagues in Sarajevo to brief the press and correct the record. They did, but they claim it failed to correct the imbalance in reporting.

"The media had a blank spot. The media turned a blind eye," one UN official in Sarajevo complained. "It did not fit their preconceptions of what was happening—of the encirclement."[341] The UN Chief of Staff, Brigadier Vere Hayes, was interviewed on American TV. "On US television I explained it, but the State Department did not like that."

One equally emotive issue was the way reporters and news organizations portrayed the Serb shelling of Sarajevo. No one who was inside the city during mortar or artillery salvos can overstate the horrifying sensation of apparently being targeted by the heavy guns in the surrounding hills. Such experiences have affected the partiality of some journalists, by their own admission. But UN officials who monitored the armed exchanges between Bosnians and Serbs say the impression given by the media with a headline like "Serbs shell Sarajevo, killing XX" was frequently misleading. "There has been too much limp reporting of 'Serb shelling,'" according to EU peace negotiator Lord Owen. "It is an instinctive feeling of being on the side of the oppressed."[342]

As one senior UN military officer based in Sarajevo expressed it: "I would be surprised by what I heard on the news compared to what I saw." He said that Serb shelling of the Bosnian army "would be reported as Sarajevo under heavy shelling. Reports would say the Serbs fired 500 shells in Sarajevo, without saying that 480 were aimed at the Bosnian army, and maybe twenty at the city."[343]

The distinction being examined here is a fine one. The offensive and deadly nature of Serb deployments was not questioned, nor the ruthlessness of the snipers. But in the UN's view a medium as powerful as television should have given an accurate, balanced view. In Sarajevo the picture portrayed by reporting was of Serb forces as the only guilty party when often (though not always) they had been provoked by a Bosnian offensive.[344] "TV portrays only Moslem weakness and Serb strength, but not Moslem strength," said one senior UN officer at the heart of the UN operation.[345]

And this officer explained how the Bosnian army frequently tested Serb lines in a location which they knew meant that Serb artillery would have to fire shells over the main hotel for the press. "Moslems around Zuc would shell Serb villages with a number of mortars. The Serbs responded from artillery in their barracks at Lukavica [on the other side of the city]. Shells were fired over the Holiday Inn, and over the press's head. This was very loud."[346]

The fact that the Serbs had only artillery and mortars and relatively little infantry around Sarajevo, while the Bosnian forces were predominantly infantry with a few mobile mortar launchers, went a long way to furthering the international image of the Bosnian side as the disadvantaged underdogs. But as UN officials kept repeating, and a confidential report by the outgoing UNPROFOR commander Lt. General Francis Briquemont confirmed in January 1994, the Bosnians attacked the Serb positions with infantry and the Serbs could only respond with artillery.

On January 9 General Briquemont wrote: "In Sarajevo the BiH army [Bosnian government] provoke the BSA [Bosnian Serb Army] on a daily basis. This is very easy for us to notice as the BiH mortars are generally located near UNPROFOR units and Headquarters."[347] The General added: "Since the middle of December, the BiH army jumped another step by launching heavy infantry attacks from Sarajevo to the Serb held suburbs of the city."

"A significant proportion of Serb shelling is brought on by Moslem attacks," one high-ranking British officer confirmed.[348] To an outsider the shelling and mortaring was always disproportionate: an infantry attack did not have to be repelled with heavy artillery shells. But like it or not, such were the dispositions, capabilities and viciousness in the Bosnian war.

Ambassador Herbert Okun, Deputy to Cyrus Vance, the Special UN Envoy for the former Yugoslavia from 1991 to 1993, confirmed how—despite the impression from press reporting—the Serb shelling was usually not random. "The Bosnian government forces were constantly probing Serb lines and occasionally launching major offensives to break the siege of Sarajevo. But the constant impression given by the US press was that the Serbs were overwhelmingly powerful and sitting back in the hills taking pot shots at the city. They should have reported clashes between opposing forces. Instead they told of the horrors of the siege—which were real enough—but they also ignored the Moslem attempts to break out. Ironically, they thereby helped create the image that the Bosnian Serbs were omnipotent."[349]

"The shelling is due to an imbalance in the Serb and Moslem military forces," said one senior officer who frequently tried to change the media's perception in Sarajevo. "[But] telling the press that was like taking a pork chop into a synagogue!"[350]

October 1993

Somalia: The TV Images That Sent Home US Troops

As already discussed, the gruesome images of the naked body of one dead US Special Forces crewman being dragged through the streets of Mogadishu, plus video of the shaken Chief Warrant Officer Michael Durant,[351] forced—via Congressional pressure—President Clinton's announcement of a phased US withdrawal from the Somalia UN operation. However, the precise impact of television coverage is not quite as great as it was widely assumed to be.

The images of the dead US Ranger did not fit the strict definition of real-time because they were many hours old by the time of transmission. They were, however, real time in the sense that they were transmitted from the television dish in Mogadishu virtually as soon as they were received and the necessary editorial approval had been given on grounds of both taste and common decency.

The decision to broadcast the pictures and the freelance source of the images (a driver associated with General Aideed) caused some self-examination among TV executives, especially in the US.[352] The driver once worked for Reuters and was associated with the man the US identified as its enemy. As ITN's Stewart Purvis put it: "The Somali driver shows how fine the line is between information and manipulation; between exposure and titillation."[353]

Senior UN sources told this author that if the US government had taken a clear position on Somalia and begun preparing the US public for an eventual winding down of its commitment, then the images of the dead serviceman would never have had quite the same powerful impact on the public as they did.

According to the White House, for President Clinton the sight of the dead US Ranger on TV "was the worst day of my life." After the pictures were transmitted, US National Adviser Anthony Lake then made an extraordinary confession about the influence of real-time TV reporting on an administration which should have had access to the most sophisticated means of collecting and processing data from any crisis zone. Not only did Mr. Lake never see the video of either the dead soldier or Durant, he said that to those in the White House who did: "the [TV] pictures helped make us recognize that the military situation in Mogadishu had deteriorated in a way that we had not frankly recognized."[354] As a result the images made President Clinton "very angry" and lent a "new urgency" for the White House to clarify policy.[355]

It must be noted, however, that until that failed Special Forces raid took place, the US Somalia involvement had been a success, despite casualties and the fact that for months the administration had dithered on whether or not to end the operation. On the plus side, the UN was assuring deliveries of food aid. On the minus side, US forces seemed to have sleepwalked into war with an enemy "war lord"— General Aideed—and there was no military or political decision on when withdrawal would take place.

It is important to appreciate the random nature of the gruesome pictures that emerged.

On October 3 more than a dozen US soldiers had been killed in Mogadishu. But there were no TV images of either the military operations or the bodies, so America scarcely reacted. Similarly, before that date the Pentagon had rejected hearsay reports in Mogadishu that the bodies of some other dead US soldiers had been put on show and their charred flesh displayed "like trophies."[356] The deaths of 25 Pakistani UN troops in June had also generated virtually no international outrage, except in Pakistan.

Yet the pictures of the failed US mission forced President Clinton's hand because of the intense public pressure via Congress. The decision to withdraw was made even though at the start of the mission the Pentagon had made no clear prediction or assessment of a likely casualty rate, and the number of those who died was less than occasionally died in routine training accidents.[357] But the pictures struck a raw political nerve at a time when the administration was uncertain as to whether US troops were still making a valuable contribution to the UN aid mission. Clinton and his advisers were split on whether to keep troops in Somalia or withdraw them.

Broadly, the well-worn phrase "television got the US into Somalia [under Bush] and got the US out [under Clinton]" stands up to examination. But according to sources in the former administration, in reality the original decision by President George H. W. Bush to commit forces in November 1992 came after several months of preparation based on an alarming diplomatic warning from the US ambassador to Kenya Smith Hempstone in May that starvation and a humanitarian catastrophe loomed.[358] TV's pressure on politicians, newspaper columnists and the public four months later was the climax to a long period of planning and consultations with the United Nations in which TV coverage played only a marginal role.

"It took months of TV coverage of Somalia, and then the administration decided to go over there," said Col. Bill Smullen, who worked at the time in the office of the Chairman of the Joint Chiefs of Staff. After the US presidential election in November, US television news found it had the time and resources to focus on Somalia. This coincided with a dramatic worsening of the famine.

"After the election, the media had free time and that was when the pressure started building up," said former White House Press Secretary Marlin Fitzwater.[359] "We heard it from every corner, that something must be done. Finally the pressure was too great. The President said 'I just can't live with this for two months' [until he left office in January 1993]. TV tipped us over the top at a time when the death rate [from starvation] was over one hundred a day." Fitzwater himself could not look at the images any more. "I could not stand to eat my dinner watching TV at night. It made me sick," he said.[360]

Similarly, Clinton's decision to withdraw was not as clear cut as most people think they remember. The President did not just buckle to congressional pressure. He rejected demands for an early January 1994 withdrawal deadline. He decided instead on March 31. "He withstood the pressure for an early pull-out," said White House Communications Director Mark Gearan.[361]

However, it must be noted that if Clinton had wanted to keep US troops in Somalia he could have mounted an effective public "spin" presentation to justify continuation of the policy. On April 14, 1994, the President was able to mount quickly just such a presentation after the disastrous "friendly-fire" shoot-down of two US helicopters by two US jet fighters in the UN No-Fly zone over northern Iraq. Within hours of the accident Clinton was in the White House briefing room saying of the twenty-four officers who died: "They lost their lives while trying to save the lives of others. The important work they are doing must and will continue."

The US policy against Saddam Hussein in Iraq demanded such a policy "spin." The campaign against "war lord" Mohamed Aideed in Somalia did not. Neither Marlin Fitzwater nor his White House successor Mark Gearan believe that any amount of policy "spinning" could have counteracted the power of the image of the dead US Ranger. Neither could pressure have been brought to bear on broadcast organizations to prevent the image being broadcast, however profound and inevitable the effect on policy. "The charge of hiding deaths is almost worse than showing it," said Fitzwater.

5 February 1994

Sarajevo Market: The Mortar That Shocked The World[362]

Conventional wisdom has it that the determined international response to the carnage of the Sarajevo marketplace in February 1994 was a direct result of the horrific TV images.[363] The reality was different.

Subsequent evidence suggests the pictures were an important catalyst to galvanize urgent action, but their overall effect was not as profound as many have assumed.[364] Other equally critical diplomatic and military factors had already quietly been at work for several weeks.

"It did not take just the TV coverage of the Sarajevo massacre to push things forward. Things were moving," confirmed White House Communications Director Mark Gearan. "The fact of the incident weighed with us most. It would not have triggered action if people were not already thinking about action," said Sir Robin Renwick, British ambassador in Washington.[365]

Before the market massacre the Clinton administration had wavered publicly for months on whether to "do something" on Bosnia. Coincidentally, in the hours before the massacre the administration had authorized publication of the latest draft of its new policy on "The Limits of Peacekeeping." They were clearly defined limits beyond which neither politicians nor television images would push the policy-makers.[366]

US involvement in peacekeeping would be "more selective and more effective." Peacekeeping was "not at the center of our foreign and defense policy" because "our armed forces primary mission is not to conduct peace operations but to win wars." The key test for the administration would be "vital national interest." In one of those quirks of coincidence the mortaring of Sarajevo's market suddenly tested the new US principles to the limit.

First reports of the Sarajevo market massacre "incensed" President Clinton. They pushed him and some (though not all) of his advisers into the Oval Office on a Saturday afternoon. The carnage did not require a journalist to say explicitly "something must be done." The horrific TV pictures made their own silent, non-political plea. No viewer, whether politician or not, could fail to be appalled by the unsanitized images of shredded limbs, headless bodies, the puddles of blood and the torsos being shipped on trucks like animal carcasses.

The President was said to be "outraged" by what he saw on television, even though the White House had "become so inured to violence that the early reports . . . created only a small stir."[367] Initially Clinton's reaction was described officially as "tentative." He did not want to be seen to react to TV images.[368] Even though the Secretary of State Warren Christopher was said to be "traumatized" by the incident, the first White House emergency meeting was brief and inconclusive.[369] To many administration officials the TV coverage "made it very clear that things can't go on." As so often on Bosnia the instinct of those at the top was "to tread water." In other words, in the immediate aftermath TV images were not all powerful among those who authorized policy.

Following the massacre, the President's political conflict was between exercising "caution," and as National Security Adviser Anthony Lake put it, a realization that "we've got to do something."[370] Indeed the President went out of his way not to appear to be responding too hastily to TV images. He made a point of discussing health care strategy, playing golf and giving the impression of "business as usual," even to the point of not inviting the Chairman of the Joint Chiefs of Staff to a Sunday meeting for fear of raising expectations with the press over air strikes.

The pressure came not from television images but on the phone from the French government. France had been furious with the Serb leadership for two weeks. At a meeting with European Union foreign ministers in Brussels in mid-January President Milosevic and the Bosnia Serb leader Radovan Karadzic had reneged on assurances relating to the peace process given to the French. The French government felt betrayed. Under growing domestic political pressure Paris was determined to take political revenge against the Serbs.

Even before Christmas, on December 22, France had been mobilizing other EU governments relatively successfully. In Paris, Foreign Minister Alain Juppe had given US Secretary of State Warren Christopher a firm message that either the US must do more to become engaged or the EU would take tougher action alone. "Juppe tore Christopher off a strip," one diplomatic source told this author.

Despite public declarations of intent at the NATO summit on January 10, the Clinton administration had resisted,[371] while beginning to come round to the idea of giving more US political clout to UN peace efforts. British Foreign Secretary Douglas Hurd then traveled to Washington in the week before the massacre to reinforce the European pressure. By February 5 "the US was already beginning to stiffen their position."[372]

Then came the market massacre. "It helped the [French] argument," confirmed White House Communications Director Mark Gearan.[373] Taking its cue from the incident (not the TV pictures), France led the way in demanding that the West threaten air strikes against the Bosnian Serbs, who were immediately presumed responsible for firing the mortar. The French used intense diplomatic activity in person and by telephone to force US agreement and involvement.

Graham Allison, Assistant US Defense Secretary at the time, confirmed that: "France was pressing for action. The Sarajevo market massacre crystallized for the Clinton administration that it had to do something; that we could not do nothing. Those who wanted to do something seized on it."[374]

Within two days, US caution dissipated. According to Hans Binnendijk, Acting Director of Policy Planning in the State Department at the time, in the end: "TV did turn things around. The US was only being supportive in negotiations. Redman [the US special envoy] was supportive but not taking an active role. If the outrages continued, then vital US interests *would* be at stake."[375]

Four days later Clinton backed NATO in issuing an unprecedented ultimatum to the Bosnian Serbs: withdraw your weapons or they will be the target of air strikes.[376]

Despite the impression Clinton wanted to give, TV pictures had played a part, but more because of their claimed impact on the public rather than the US administration. Sources told this author that a sense of the "public relations" needs was moving policy more than strategic thinking.

A further factor eased the US government's dilemmas. Their ability to threaten air strikes so rapidly was strengthened because unlike during the previous three years NATO had already prepared an operational plan. It had been authorized during the brinkmanship over the Sarajevo siege in July and August 1993. During the intervening six months aircraft and military equipment had already been pre-positioned in Italy and the Adriatic.

As US Secretary of State Warren Christopher reflected some time later: "Television images moved forward a policy we had clearly started on."[377] But he added: "Television should not be the sole determinant of policy."

But the question must be asked: how determined would the West's response have been if there had been no real-time television pictures of the massacre? Graham Allison said: "If a shell had fallen in Sarajevo and 68 people had been killed, and there would have been no pictures of it, would the US policy have changed? I do not think it would have."[378]

In retrospect, however, there may be a convenient rewriting of history on diplomatic activity following the mortar attack. Three days after the carnage, the Clinton administration seemed to be having second thoughts. By this time TV coverage of Bosnia in the US was virtually nil, having been relegated by the Harding/Kerrigan skating drama and the East Coast's enormous snow storms. Despite the contention of US Ambassador to the UN Madeleine Albright that "the polls are showing increasing public support,"[379] public opinion quickly became indifferent once again. The impact of the Sarajevo market pictures had reached its natural half-life. For a time there were signals that the administration's intent no longer matched the rhetoric.

On the record, administration officials discreetly signaled that the US would permit the tough NATO ultimatum[380] to be moderated to a "looser interpretation."[381] The Bosnian Serbs therefore believed they could keep their artillery loaded and targeted because of "wariness on the part of President Clinton . . . to commit the US, NATO or the United Nations to goals they fear cannot be carried out."[382]

The mistake of sending such conciliatory signals undermined fatally the high-stakes NATO/UN bluff and/or ultimatum on air strikes if the Bosnian Serbs did not withdraw their heavy weapons. The damage from the remarks reported on February 16 was done. Within hours, the Clinton administration realized its error. They quickly denied that "the US was willing to give Serbian forces extra latitude in meeting NATO's ultimatum."[383] Two days later the President made a nationwide broadcast openly backing the West's determination to use air strikes. For perhaps the first time in three years of war, the Serbs could be in no doubt.

The contrast with the British reaction to the mortar attack was stark. Although the atrocity took place on a Saturday when ministers and officials were involved in private weekend domestic activities, the British Foreign Secretary and a single official moved rapidly to condemn the mortar attack. However, neither had seen the horrific pictures aired on the lunchtime TV bulletins.

"It [the bomb] triggered an immediate response diplomatically," said one of the senior officials concerned. "None of us had seen the pictures when we did what we did. I knew what it would be like. I knew that it was going to be shocking, ghastly scenes. Some things you cannot ride."[384]

Mr. Hurd and his officials based their decision to act on radio and agency reports of the incident when the death toll was thirty. "Those who fired the shell carry a fearful responsibility for murder," the Foreign Secretary declared in a written statement. His official conceded, however, that if the incident had been of an equal level of carnage yet away from Sarajevo in an area not readily accessible to TV cameras then probably the response would not have been as swift and emphatic. He added, however, that at the EU foreign ministers meeting two days later, the ghastly TV images were an important factor in making ministers feel they should do more than just issue a routine statement of condemnation.[385]

So, once again, the fickle nature of the relationship of real-time television to policy-making was highlighted. In April 1993 Serb shelling of the Srebrenica Safe Area had killed 56 Moslems and injured 90 more. But there were no television pictures, and the slaughter led to no dramatic international response. At that time Larry Hollingworth, the senior UNHCR official, had said of the Serb commander who ordered the bombardment: "I personally hope he burns in the hottest corner of hell. I hope that their [Serb] sleep is punctuated by the screams of the children and the cries of their mothers."[386] But as there were no TV images of the carnage, there was no enduring international outrage.

While in people's minds the pictures of the market massacre seemed to mark a turning point and watershed for Sarajevo's plight, it was the *incident itself* more than the TV coverage as such that began to give a momentum toward a fragile peace for the city. The market bombing was part of a convergence of disconnected events and political forces, some of which were already underway.

The UN's new, robust commander Lt. General Sir Michael Rose—who was formerly a British Special Forces commander—had just arrived. Rose carried no political baggage with any side to the conflict. He had the self confidence and determination to "tell the Bosnian Serbs that if they continued to behave in a savage way they would themselves suffer savagely—and to mean it."[387] Rose stood up to Bosnian and Serb leaders where others might have recoiled.

Also, after three years of war, all the institutional instruments in the diplomatic orchestra were playing the same tune: the United Nations, the European

Union, NATO and the United States. This enabled a unique diplomatic window of opportunity to be seized. The United States, through its special ambassador Charles Redman, became engaged and assumed a leading role as a peace negotiator. Then, upset by what they perceived as the inconsiderate elitism of the big Western powers at the United Nations, Russia took umbrage. Moscow unilaterally deployed its own Russian peacekeeping troops and dispatched its envoy Vitali Churkin to counterbalance and at times upstage Redman's efforts.

The NATO ultimatum against the Bosnian Serbs worked. Using a masterly mix of ultimatum, bluff, brinkmanship and half-truths General Rose forced them to withdraw their artillery from the mountains around Sarajevo and corral some of it under UN supervision.[388] Using the same tactics Rose, and later others, also forced the Bosnians to the negotiating table. Six weeks after the market massacre, the Bosnian government and the Croats surprised most observers by signing in Washington an agreement to ally themselves in an unlikely Croat-Moslem federation.

However, the full story of the Sarajevo market massacre has yet to be told. All the indications are that in some important respects the story is different from what many assume. For the UN, the immediate international outrage and leveling of blame at the Bosnian Serbs served an important purpose. It gave General Rose vital negotiating leverage to force the Bosnian Serb artillery and mortars off the hilltops around Sarajevo, and later to impose a wider exclusion zone. It was leverage that Rose used brilliantly.

Yet who fired the mortar? Was it indeed a Serb emplacement, or was it a mobile Bosnian mortar? The question remains unanswered. Following a series of independent crater analyses and investigations by military experts, UN officials no longer say categorically that a Serb mortar killed the 68 people. They say their verdict is "neutral." That is a significant word for any UN official to use. While being non-committal in one sense in that "neutral" does not identify the Bosnians as responsible for the mortar, in another sense "neutral" sends a clear signal. The UN is no longer convinced that the mortar was fired from a Serb position.

It is an ambiguity which poses a vital and awkward question in relation to the power of real-time TV coverage. The immediate assumption on February 5 was that the mortar was planned, authorized and fired by the Serbs. The later evidence questions that. But what if world leaders like Clinton, Major and Balladur had felt themselves forced by public anger over the TV images to launch air strikes against the Serbs, when later investigations questioned the Serb culpability for the market massacre?

This is the ultimate fear of ministers, diplomats and the military. It is the fear that emotive pictures provided by real-time TV coverage forces them into an impulsive policy response when the reality on the ground is different.

Rarely does television portray the complete story.

April 1994

Gorazde: The Bombardment and the Provocations

In April 1994 Western intelligence intercepts confirmed that the Serb leaders, President Milosevic, Dr. Karadzic and General Mladic had set themselves the objective of seizing all but the center of the Gorazde Safe Area. The Serb plan was motivated in part as revenge for the Bosnian success in capturing territory near Maglaj in central Bosnia.

However, Bosnian Serb intentions became blurred by the efforts of the Bosnian forces in the town to provoke the Serbs into attacking Gorazde. UN military sources confirm that despite widely held impressions to the contrary this is what the Bosnian Moslem army did. The Bosnian forces "orchestrated their defeat" in the hope of forcing NATO air strikes that finally would bring the involvement of the outside world into the war.[389] Until the Serbs withdrew, Western governments had been taken in by the Bosnian tactics. There was a "massive overreaction" by the West which could have led to disaster for the whole UN operation in Bosnia.[390]

On television the twenty-day Serb offensive was widely reported at a distance from Sarajevo using secondhand information from UN aid workers and emotional ham radio reports which claimed a dreadful amount of bloodletting. TV and newspaper reporting stoked pressure on the West to act decisively with the military might it had long threatened. The role of Bosnian provocations in starting the Gorazde crisis went virtually unreported, even after the Bosnian Serbs withdrew.

During the bombardment one senior UN official believed that had there been Birtley-style real-time TV images from inside Gorazde while the town was being shelled they would have prompted a more defiant UN military response, as happened with Srebrenica. But had those same TV images existed, they would also have confirmed the reality. Conditions in Gorazde were terrifying but—as happened with the exaggerated radio appeals from Zepa a year earlier—they were not as awful as the emotive radio reports suggested.

Subsequent reporting confirmed that the level of destruction and casualties in Gorazde was "a fraction" of the high levels claimed during the panic.[391] UN officials later told visiting US congressmen that Bosnian casualties in Gorazde "were closer to 200 than 2,000" and that "the extent of the . . . fighting around the east Bosnian town was exaggerated by UN officials there."[392]

With the benefit of hindsight, the extent of that exaggeration is now clear. Yet the claims at the time and the emotion being stirred daily by TV and press reporting went a long way to forcing the UN and NATO perilously close to military action. It is now known that such action could in no way be justified by the reality in Gorazde.

The Power . . . and the Resentment

While the work of TV crews, journalists and UN operations in Bosnia increasingly became mutually complementary, at times the relationship was marked by resentment. There was not only friction over interpretations of events.[393] There were also moments when both the UN military and humanitarian operations cursed activities that any self-respecting TV team must always consider legitimate journalistic activity and enterprise.

Often the military were positively delighted when cameras accompanied them[394] and witnessed the events unfolding, like the Serb shelling of Konjevic Polje in March 1993.[395] On occasions they actively encouraged TV coverage to achieve their own tactical goals.[396]

One example was the 400-vehicle humanitarian operation known as the "Convoy of Joy." It was halted by Croat forces in an enclave they controlled near Novi Travnik in the summer of 1993 and UN forces could not negotiate its release.

In the hope of putting pressure on the Croats the UNPROFOR chief of staff, Brigadier Hayes, encouraged British UN troops to take a TV crew to the location. In the midst of chaos, and at great personal risk, they filmed several Moslem truck drivers being hauled from their cabs and shot or pitch-forked to death. The images were transmitted worldwide and led to the Croat leadership ordering the HVO Vice President Dario Kordich (a former journalist) to release the convoy forthwith. "Kordich realized the world was watching," said one senior UN officer present at the time.[397]

"Because of the media attention and the reaction to people being pulled out and killed, Kordich was ordered to get the convoy together," Brigadier Hayes confirmed. "TV had exactly the effect we hoped it would have. It gave the convoy an insurance policy."[398] There was a belief among UN officers that Kordich had been encouraged by Croat leaders to seize a portion of the Moslem food on the convoy. The original Croat permission for the convoy to pass through their enclave had thus been a ruse to grab food supplies which they could get in no other way. The Croats had never expected a TV crew to be present.[399]

On other occasions, however, the military were resentful when—in their view—TV teams inadvertently created incidents that left an impression of conflict or desperation where the reality was less dramatic. They claim the resulting coverage not only gave a false impression in Western capitals. More significantly it caused costly and time-consuming diversions of hard-pressed troops and aid officials from planned humanitarian operations, thereby disrupting schedules.

They cite three examples to illustrate the complaint.

In late autumn 1992 a BBC TV team filmed and broadcast a harrowing news story about a mental hospital in the town of Tarcin. Conditions for patients were miserable. According to a senior military officer,[400] the BBC correspondent Kate Adie tried to persuade Lt. Col Bob Stewart, commander of the British Cheshire regiment, "of the critical importance that he should do something about that."

The Danish UNHCR representative Anders Levinson was also pressed to respond. "Anders rushed into the Cheshire's mess. Bob Stewart and the officers were having tea. Anders said that Kate Adie has discovered a mental hospital near Tarcin and I have to go to deliver aid and blankets."[401] The British force commander for Bosnia and Croatia, Brigadier Andrew Cumming, was in their Vitez base at the time. He asked Anders Levinson whether he already knew about this hospital and the conditions. Levinson said he had known about it for some time. Brigadier Cumming asked: so why do something now? Levinson is said to have replied: "Because Kate Adie has been there."[402]

According to one officer, Colonel Stewart and the Cheshire Regiment "had to drop everything and do something about it." The resulting aid mission to Tarcin was considered both good profile and TV exposure for the recently arrived British forces. But it irritated UNPROFOR and the UNHCR, not least because a British convoy was having to enter an area assigned to Spanish UN forces.

"It deflected UK forces off their main job of escorting food to warehouses," said one senior British officer.[403] "It was a one-day wonder; a pain in the arse. London asked what we were doing up there. We got our fingers rapped on that because our reconnaissance squadron [diverted to Tarcin] was doing a lot of important work. It took away UK forces from Zenica and Vitez. [Planned] UNHCR operations were delayed for 48 hours."

Any journalist's view, on the other hand, will be that TV coverage brought a modest degree of comfort and aid to the mental patients which otherwise might have taken weeks.

A second incident took place in the Central Bosnian town of Gornij Vakuf in January 1993. UNPROFOR forces claimed the arrival of a BBC TV crew unintentionally started a battle.

At the time the peace was delicate and the town in a state of high tension. Following recent publication of the Vance-Owen Plan both Croat and Moslem forces were determined to control Gornij Vakuf. "It was a town where nothing was moving except the dust and tumbleweed. Eyes were looking at each other in the dark."[404]

In the military view, the BBC crew precipitated fighting which probably would have happened eventually but not necessarily at that moment. British UNPROFOR troops believed they knew what was going to happen because they had contacts with both warring parties. The Croat/Moslem tension was high. "It could have been anything that set off fighting."[405] For that reason they had warned journalists to keep out.

Yet it is the prospect of confrontation that attracts a TV team. According to one British officer, Kate Adie and her crew "drove into this in their two BBC Land Rovers and fighting erupted. Kate was caught [by the fighting] and bundled into a cellar, then rescued in a Warrior [armored personnel carrier] after six hours. It endangered our guys. Kate shattered our efforts to broker peace."[406]

A third example is the well-documented case of five-year-old Irma Hadzimuratovic. Irma was severely injured by what could be classified as a routine mortar attack in Sarajevo on July 30, 1993, which received just three lines of coverage in a Reuters wire story. Shrapnel was lodged in the girl's spine. For eight days she had fought for her life in hospital. Despite the many other casualties in his care, on a Saturday evening one Bosnian doctor took it upon himself to try to save Irma and bring her condition to the world's attention.

Touched by the doctor's unannounced visit to the BBC office on the evening of August 7, correspondent Alan Little delayed closing up the office. He and a Reuters cameraman visited the Kosevo hospital and prepared what he assumed would be a routine report of the suffering of one Sarajevo victim for a weekend evening bulletin. He could never have expected the response. News desks in London were moved deeply by the story. Within hours Irma became the focus of extraordinary media attention as a symbol of Sarajevo's apparent hell.[407]

At the time Western capitals were on holiday. There was no domestic political activity. There was, therefore, the usual seasonal shortage of news stories. Thousands of Bosnians faced a similar medical misery that Saturday night. Yet suddenly Irma's case was generating a remarkable news-making momentum of its own. It was momentum no correspondent in the field could ever plan for.

Fueled by the obvious possibilities to boost both summer circulation and TV viewing figures, Irma's case became issue of the week. The media could blame everyone for Irma's plight—governments, the United Nations, doctors, the Red Cross—along with the apparent failure of the system to evacuate patients like her to the safety of European hospitals.

Irma's name quickly became a cynical acronym for **I**nstant **R**esponse to **M**edia **A**ttention. The switchboard at 10 Downing Street was inundated on Sunday night by callers asking how the government planned to help Irma. On Monday a UNHCR official accused the BBC of cheap journalism as some newspapers vied with each other to provide an evacuation aircraft.

The British Prime Minister John Major had already been sufficiently moved (or politically motivated, say the skeptics[408]) to organize a military airlift for Irma and 40 other cases. Western governments offered hospital beds they had refused to offer until the reporting of Irma's case. Within 48 hours a lone initiative from a single doctor in Sarajevo had exploded out of political and journalistic control.[409] As Maggie O'Kane expressed it: "Irma's story was a newspaper classic. She had it all:

children, foreigners not doing anything, a hero PM, bureaucracy and mercy flights."[410]

Simultaneously a heated inter-agency and inter-governmental row ignited over accusations of inaction and failures in UN evacuation procedures. Angry UN officials and medical staff accused Britain of choosing evacuees according to its political priorities, not assessed medical needs. They resented the fact that one girl's plight had grabbed world attention, distorted the real medical problems in Sarajevo[411] and by-passed an evacuation list of another 400 deserving cases.[412] They rejected British claims that Whitehall had been unaware of the medical crisis until television showed pictures of Irma.[413]

"Because you can't help everybody doesn't mean you shouldn't help some-body," was how the British Foreign Secretary Douglas Hurd justified what the cyn-ics decried as blatant political exploitation of the Bosnian misery for quick headlines. The UNHCR spokesperson Sylvana Foa responded bitterly: "Sarajevo is not a supermarket, where you can say 'I will have that one and this one.' What are the criteria here? Why not just children with blond hair and blue eyes?"[414]

Irma's case and the media response exploded spontaneously from a unique convergence of circumstances and one journalist's chance response to them accom-panied by a TV camera. The resulting British evacuation mission probably pre-vented several deaths.[415] Yet it alienated many who continued to risk their lives to remain in the heart of the Sarajevo misery through further periods of shelling and sniping.

It also appalled many journalists who have risked their lives and distinguished themselves covering Bosnia. The BBC's Martin Bell encapsulated the feelings. "Never mind the thousands of others who suffered unheeded. I happened to be in central Bosnia at the time—a time of unusually heavy fighting with casualties to match. And the flight of 10,000 Croats in desperate circumstances from their homes around Bugojno. From our base in Vitez we were actually able to see some BBC programmes. That the BBC on that Tuesday night should devote more than half of its main news programme to the plight of a single five-year-old girl struck me as daft. I felt like a humble foot soldier in an army whose high command had taken leave of its collective senses—and I told them so."[416]

However, it must be said that journalistically a personalized human-interest drama like Irma's did more to highlight the misery of Sarajevo than the usual round of news stories covering atrocities in a depersonalized way. Martin Bell accepts that. But like many colleagues he points to the ephemeral nature of the government response, which fades once the media agenda changes.

"If it takes Irma to connect the government to the feelings of ordinary peo-ple; to alert them to what is happening in Bosnia; and to conclude that if you can't help everybody that doesn't mean you can't help anybody, then clearly there is no harm done—provided that there is a follow-up; that it isn't just a conscience-clearing exercise done for publicity."[417]

The coverage of Irma's case underlined once again both the fickle power of TV and the resulting institutional resentments. Many more Bosnians were maimed in the same way as Irma. Apart from the brave, effective but controversial single-handed mercy missions of the British nurse Sally Becker,[418] they received virtually no media attention and no special treatment. Once Irma had arrived in Britain with other evacuees, media concern for those left in Sarajevo faded rapidly. As one British official reflected: "The UK has a wounded heart for a very short period of time."[419] The observation was both correct and a useful insight into the kind of calculation governments make when for just a few days TV coverage creates an issue like Irma.

On the humanitarian side the publicizing of Irma's plight did, however, bring one significant bonus which delighted the agencies. As Sylvana Foa, spokesperson of the UNHCR, put it three months later: "Little Irma gave us [the UNHCR] the boost we needed. It got us offers of 1,800 beds around the world."[420]

And while Sally Becker's missions infuriated the UN military for the risks she took in cities like Mostar and the way she expected them to help her, they did succeed in evacuating sick children. In Sylvana Foa's words: "Sally Becker turns up in Bosnia with a TV crew, and sixteen sick children get promises of admission to the UK in three days, including visas for relatives. It usually takes at least three weeks, and usually the Health Secretary does not get involved personally!"[421]

The chance presence of a camera has also saved lives. One example was Spanish coverage of a column of Moslem prisoners being marched up a hill out of Mostar by Croat forces on May 11, 1993. The crew from TVE had been tipped off about the forced exodus by Spanish UNPROFOR troops. They feared the scores of men would be executed but had no power to intervene under the UN mandate. The column was only seen at a distance in long shot, and the total footage was minimal. Worldwide transmission, however, shamed the Croat leadership. They had believed the forced expulsion was taking place in secret. In an attempt to save face internationally they ordered the immediate release of the Moslem prisoners. Some time later the wife of a man who was in the column told an ITN producer that had it not been for the Spanish coverage her husband "would surely be dead."[422]

And then there was the exasperation. The British government—like the US in Somalia—became frustrated that "saving lives by UN convoys made less headlines than dead bodies," as one official put it.[423] "UNHCR successes have been very under sung," said another.[424] "We had great difficulty getting TV coverage on convoys. Endless meetings concluded with instructions to the ODA [Overseas Development Administration] press officers to get positive coverage of convoys. We could not get a more positive picture of UK policy."[425]

Another official said: "A convoy getting through is not a good story. Steady good news is always outweighed by startling images of a catastrophe."[426] Lt. Colonel Alistair Duncan, commander of Britain's Prince of Wales regiment in UNPROFOR, said his troops successfully escorted more than nine hundred convoys during their six-month duty. "Convoys were happening unreported and unsung every day over huge distances. All convoys during my period got to their destination."[427]

However, television coverage suggested otherwise.

Hence both the power of TV . . . and the official resentment.

Conclusion

This chapter has challenged the conventional assumption of a profound, *automatic* cause-and-effect relationship between real-time TV coverage and foreign policy-making. In doing so, the conclusion might seem to endorse the views of cynics that little has changed since dispatches from the Crimea or the Spanish-American war. That is not the case.

Those dispatches took days or even weeks to reach their newspapers, by which time war had moved on. TV coverage of Vietnam was not "real time" either. It was constrained by the need to develop film or ship video to limited satellite feeding facilities—often a plane ride away in Bangkok, Hong Kong or further afield.

Similarly, coverage of the Falklands war was sanitized as much by time delays as the tiny number of journalists accompanying the British forces. Because of logistics and a degree of official "obstruction," the most gruesome images of British guardsmen being brought ashore after their troop ship was bombed in Bluff Cove were not transmitted until ten days after the Argentine surrender.[428] The only unexpurgated images from the Gulf War which showed the destruction of two Iraqi tanks and US soldiers killed by Iraqi fire were filmed by a freelance "unilateral" and were not transmitted until well after the event.[429]

Hence the crucial new role of real-time TV coverage transmitted from a conflict zone by "fly-away" satellite dish.

While this chapter has challenged the conventional wisdom, there is no doubt that for *some* policy-makers real-time TV coverage does have a defining role in policy. As former US Secretary of State Lawrence Eagleburger put it: "If you're on the receiving end; if you're trying to figure out what the policy ought to be, let me tell you: I would love to have had the period of time it took to decide we were going to war with Spain. When you have something like the Sarajevo event, and the President is in the office fifteen minutes later: come on! The time frame and the amount of time you're permitted to think through the consequences of what you're going to do is much reduced."[430]

But such a candid insight leaves unanswered the fundamental question of television's role in the immense, looming foreign policy challenges in the growing global instability.

It is estimated there is a potential for 2,000 ethnic conflicts in Africa[431] and 260 conflicts in the Russian "Near-Abroad."[432] If the "battle lines of the future" are being already drawn and the "bloody conflicts"[433] have already begun, is real-time television merely highlighting conflicts which Western governments ultimately have no ability to prevent, or political will to solve?

The evidence is not encouraging. The answer is probably yes.

As British Foreign Secretary Douglas Hurd repeatedly made clear on Bosnia: "We have not been and are not willing to begin some form of military intervention which we judge useless or worse, simply because of day-by-day pressures from the media—pressures which I repeat are understandable, perhaps inevitable.[434]

For many reasons history is likely to show that the war in Bosnia was a watershed. It has defined starkly the limits to any moral imperative for foreign intervention in the new generation of regional conflicts.[435] It has highlighted the high price of international multilateralism in institutions like the UN, EU and NATO—a price which in Europe will become higher as more nations join the EU.

Without a determined international commitment, the chances for effective diplomacy are small, if not negligible. As Ambassador Herbert Okun put it after being involved in two years of UN shuttle diplomacy in the former Yugoslavia: "Diplomacy without force is like baseball without a bat."[436]

In the international community (and therefore at the UN) there is a new realism. More than ever, leading governments fear committing themselves to any peace *keeping* or peace *enforcing* operations which ultimately seem doomed to fail. A resolution passed in the UN Security Council does not necessarily signal a political will to take action.

In May 1994 the United States grouped together the whole range of options under the rubric *peace operations*.[437] In defining her new criteria and "even stricter standards"[438] for approving any future peace operations, the US seems to have further narrowed the chances of any being launched. The minimal international "fig leaf" response to the Rwanda carnage illustrated the new pragmatism and reluctance. It underlined the unwillingness of any nation—large or small—to back policies which might commit them to a military quagmire and political humiliation in a distant land of which their electorate know either little or nothing.

Real-time TV coverage of armed conflicts like Bosnia or Rwanda helps those people know a little more, but not enough to persuade governments to show greater political will. It also generates a new factor which must be considered when drawing up a policy: the fear of a steady rate of casualties being seen regularly on

TV before all political and military goals have been achieved. In Somalia the video of one dead US soldier in humiliating circumstances was enough to force a policy change. By their nature, military "peace operations" in the new generation of conflicts can never be of the short, sharp, overwhelming kind that politicians and military planners now believe is vital to sustain a public consensus for involvement.

When he announced US Presidential Decision Directive 25 on US Involvement in Peace Operations, the US National Security Adviser Anthony Lake said: "When I wake up every morning and look at the headlines and the stories and the images on television of these conflicts, I want to work to end every conflict, I want to work to save every child out there, and I know the President does, and I know the American people do. But neither we nor the international community have the resources nor the mandate to do so."[439]

On another earlier occasion Mr. Lake had made clear one key defining limit in the new world disorder. "Effective diplomacy is linked to practical calculations of power."[440] His view reflects that of many leading governments, although some may not be as willing to be so candid.

The ultimate validity of this view seems to be confirmed by the war historian Sir Michael Howard. "As in all cases of civil conflict, outsiders, however powerful and well-intentioned, can only limit the damage and do what they can to bind up the wounds. . . . We cannot solve the problems of the world, even if CNN brings them every night into our sitting rooms."[441]

In other words, inherent in the cause-and-effect relationship between TV images and foreign policy are sharply defined limits—just like the limits to the ultimate ability of ministers and diplomats to end a war.

Future real-time television coverage of the proliferation of regional conflicts will create emotions but ultimately make no difference to the fundamental calculations in foreign policy-making. No journalist should believe otherwise, however ghastly the horrors he witnesses and reports on.

It is likely something will be done, but not much.

Endnotes

1. Background interview, January 21, 1994.

2. A comparison with the concept of radiation "half-life" in physics. "The time required for half of something to undergo a specific process, especially for half the nuclei in a sample of radioactive material to undergo decay." In *Webster's II New Riverside Dictionary.*

3. "The Video Vise," by Michael Beschloss in *The Washington Post*, May 2, 1993. Later expanded into *Presidents, Television and Foreign Crises*, by Michael Beschloss. Washington: The Annenberg Washington Program (1993).

4. Quoted in Beschloss (1993) *Ibid.*

5. A lexicon used by the US State Department.

6. "The United Nations in the post Cold War era." Speech by Sir David Hannay to the German-UN Association in Bonn on April 11, 1994.

7. "Bosnia: Television's War," by Martin Bell. Presentation to Wilton Park conference on February 28, 1994.

8. Speech by Ted Koppel of ABC News after receiving the Goldsmith Career Award for Excellence in Journalism at the Joan Shorenstein Center, Harvard University, on March 10, 1994.

9. Background interview, April 22, 1994.

10. US official quoted in "Low Marks for the Hack Pack," by Tom Rosenstiel of the *Los Angeles Times*, reprinted in *The Guardian* on February 3, 1994.

11. Background interview, April 13, 1994.

12. "Playing to the Heart of the Nation," by Edward Bickham, Special Adviser to the British Foreign Secretary 1991–93. Published in *Spectrum*, autumn 1993, p. 3.

13. Desiderus Erasmus, *Adagia*, 1508.

14. The definition of "these current threats to peace" is taken from President Clinton's *Presidential Decision Directive (PDD) No. 25* on *"Multilateral Peace Operations"* published on May 5, 1994.

15. For greater precision on the explosion of conflicts and their genesis see "Causes and Implications of Ethnic Conflict," by Michael E. Brown in *Ethnic Conflict and International Security,* edited by Michael E. Brown (1993), p. 3–27.

16. Quoted with the permission of Michael Brown, Senior Fellow at the Center for Science and International Affairs, from his presentation on "Ethnic Conflicts, Who Cares?" at the Kennedy School of Government, Harvard University, on April 19, 1994.

17. Confirmed by senior government officials from several countries in background interviews for this chapter.

18. Human rights organizations estimate 100,000 Rwandans were killed in the first two weeks of carnage following the shooting down of a plane carrying the country's president on April 6. The UN secretary general later announced that an estimated 200,000 people had died in the first three weeks of violence. See "UN Council Urged to Weigh Action on Saving Rwanda," by Paul Lewis in *The New York Times*, April 30, 1994.

19. Human Rights Watch/Africa estimates that between 30,000 and 50,000 people were killed in Burundi in one week in October 1993. Data quoted in "Two Nations Joined by Common History," by Jerry Gray in *The New York Times,* April 9, 1994.

20. "Diplomacy and Deceit," presented by the author. An ITN production for Channel Four TV, broadcast on August 2, 1993.

21. *Op cit.* "The Video Vise," by Michael Beschloss in *The Washington Post,* May 2, 1993.

22. Meeting at the Kennedy School, Harvard University, May 3, 1994.

23. See p. 16 in *External Intervention in the Yugoslav Wars,* by Professor Lawrence Freedman of the War Studies Department at Kings College, London. This paper was prepared for the Humanitas conference on the Former Yugoslavia from February 25 to 27, 1994. Reproduced with the author's permission.

24. Award-winning images shot by ITN cameraman Nigel Thompson suggested the systematic destruction of Dubrovnik. Detailed examination of the city long after the siege was lifted showed that damage was less than the dramatic pictures indicated.

25. Background interview, December 23, 1993.

26. *Op cit.* Background interview, April 13, 1994.

27. "The Ethics of Intervention," by David Fisher in *Survival* vol. 36, no. 1, spring 1994, p. 51–59.

28. "Dictating the Global Agenda," by Nik Gowing in *Spectrum*, summer 1991, reproduced by the Royal Institute for International Affairs in *The World Today,* June 1991, p. 111.

29. More than two years after Kuwait was liberated, organizations like Amnesty International declared bitterly: *You've probably never heard of the Marsh Arabs before. You probably never will again.* A full page newspaper campaign to alert the world to the continuing plight of the Shias. See *The Guardian*, April 14, 1993, p. 11.

30. Quoted from personal interview with Michael Brown (*op cit.*) at Harvard University on April 19, 1994.

31. *Op cit.* Background interview, April 13, 1994.

32. *Op cit.* Background interview, April 13, 1994.

33. Background interview, April 14, 1994.

34. Based on background interviews with many politicians, officials and military officers who requested anonymity.

35. "Keeping our Heads in a Nightmare," by Douglas Hurd in *The Guardian*, July 1, 1993.

36. Background interview, July 19, 1993.

37. Interview with author, May 6, 1994.

38. Background interview, March 23, 1994.

39. *Op cit.* Background interview, January 21, 1994.

40. Background interview, January 6, 1994.

41. Background interview, January 26, 1994.

42. *News that Matters,* by Shanto Iyengar and Donald Kinder. Chicago: University of Chicago Press (1987), p. 2.

43. *Ibid.* p. 5.

44. Untransmitted part of on-the-record taped interview with Mohamed Sacirbey for *Diplomacy and Deceit (op cit.).*

45. *Op cit.* Background interview, April 13, 1994.

46. Interview with the author, May 6, 1994.

47. *Op cit.* "Bosnia—Television's War," by Martin Bell. Presentation on February 28, 1994, p. 12.

48. "The Clash of Civilizations," by Samuel Huntington in *Foreign Affairs*, vol. 72, no. 3, summer 1993, p. 22–49.

49. Professor Stanley Hoffman, presentation at Harvard University, March 15, 1994.

50. "The Coming Anarchy," by Robert Kaplan in *Atlantic Monthly*, February 1994.

51. *Op cit.* Michael Brown (1993).

52. "The New World Disorder." Speech by Douglas Hurd to the Royal Institute for International Affairs, London, on January 27, 1993.

53. *Ibid.*

54. *Op cit.* Huntington (1993), p. 29.

55. *Ibid.*

56. When this conclusion was put to many of those interviewed for this chapter there were no voices of dissent.

57. Professor Sir Michael Howard, Lovett Professor of Military and Naval History at Yale University. "Cold War, Chill Peace" was delivered as the Ditchley Foundation Annual Lecture on July 9, 1993.

58. See *Second Front: Censorship and Propaganda in the Gulf War,* by John R. MacArthur. Berkeley: University of California Press (1993), p. 146 and p. 199.

59. See transcript of former US Secretary of State (1992) Lawrence Eagleburger during debate on *Reliable Sources*, broadcast by CNN on February 13, 1993, p. 3.

60. See *op cit.* MacArthur (1993), p. 138. Also "The Media's Role in US Foreign Policy," by Edward S. Herman. *Journal of International Affairs*, summer 1993, vol. 47, no. 1, p. 37–43.

61. *Public Opinion*, by Walter Lippmann. New York: MacMillan (1961), p. 31–2.

62. *Op cit.* Herman (1993), p. 29.

63. Confirmed by Philip Zelikow, member of National Security Council and adviser to the president during the Gulf War (1990–91). Interviewed by author on March 24, 1994.

64. Author's interview with an official who was in the Oval Office at the moment it was realized the 100th hour of land battle was imminent. Confirmed by Philip Zelikow, *op cit.*

65. Author's interview with Marlin Fitzwater, Press Secretary to President Bush, on May 6, 1994.

66. See MacArthur (1993) *op cit.* for full discussion of Gulf War controversy.

67. *Op cit.* Herman (1993), p. 25.

68. See, for example, "Follow the Leader—When Covering the Third World, Major Newspapers Take Their Cues from the White House," by Ken Silverstein in *American Journalism Review*, November 1993.

69. See, for example, "Awash with War Correspondents," by Commodore Christopher Craig, and "The Media in Modern Warfare—Friend or Foe?" by Wing Commander Hugh Piper, in *Despatches* published by TAPIO at the Ministry of Defence. No. 4. autumn 1993, p. 34–44.

70. For a vivid description of the new relationship see: "You against us. The Army, Television and the Real World," by Martin Bell. Presentation to the Army Staff College Higher Command and Staff course in February 1994.

71. Interview with author, May 5, 1994.

72. Interview with author, April 21, 1994.

73. "Testament of an Interventionist," by Martin Bell. *British Journalism Review* vol. 4, no. 4, 1993, p. 8.

74. *Broken Lives,* by Lt. Col. Bob Stewart. London: Harper Collins (1993), p. 103.

75. Background interview B, January 17, 1994. For color, see "White Warriors Lost in the Ether," by Maggie O'Kane in *The Guardian*, June 19, 1993.

76. Background interview, March 16, 1994.

77. For a detailed exposition of government attitudes to the "Something must be done" pressures, see "The Power of Comment," a speech by Douglas Hurd to The Travellers Club, London, on September 9, 1993.

78. Background interview, January 21, 1994.

79. John Mills, spokesman for the peace talks, in an interview with the author, January 17, 1994.

80. Interview with the author, May 6, 1994. Mr. Fitzwater's posts in the White House were: 1989–93: Press Secretary to George Bush; 1987–89: Press Relations Assistant to President Reagan; 1985–87: Press Secretary to Vice President Dan Quayle; 1983–87: Deputy Press Secretary for Domestic Policy.

81. Speech to CNN's 4th *World Report* Contributors Conference in Atlanta, May 5, 1993.

82. "Operating in Bosnia." Presentation by Colonel Alastair Duncan to Royal United Services Institute, London, on February 23, 1994.

83. *Op cit.* Douglas Hurd speech on September 9, 1993.

84. Background interview A, January 13, 1994.

85. *Op cit.* Transcript of CNN's *Reliable Sources*, February 13, 1994, p. 1.

86. Theodore H. White Lecture by Daniel Schorr, November 18, 1993.

87. Various conversations by the author with non-governmental humanitarian organizations.

88. "1,000 Estimated Dead in Burundi." Reuters report from Bujumbura quoted in *The Boston Globe* on March 24, 1994.

89. "Follow the Leader," by Ken Silverstein. *American Journalism Review*, November 1993, p. 35.

90. "Algeria is said to be Moving Towards Break Up" in *The New York Times*, April 4, 1994.

91. In January 1994, ITN's operation in Bosnia, based in only one location, was costed at £23,000 for a ten-day period. (Stewart Purvis, Editor-in-Chief, ITN)

92. *A Witness to Genocide,* by Roy Gutman. Shaftesbury: Element Books (1993), p. vii.

93. "Parting of the Ways?" by Tony Hall, Director of BBC News and Current Affairs, in *British Journalism Review* vol. 4, no. 1, 1993, p. 28.

94. Background interview, January 6, 1994.

95. *Op cit.* Transcript of CNN's *Reliable Sources*, February 13, 1994, p. 1.

96. *Op cit.* Interview with Philip Zelikow. The point is explained further in "Foreign Policy Engineering: From Theory to Practice and Back Again" in *International Security*, vol. 18, no. 4, spring 1994.

97. Background interview, November 23, 1993.

98. Background interview A, November 30, 1993.

99. Interview with author, April 22, 1994.

100. Interview with author, April 21, 1994.

101. Interview with author, April 15, 1994.

102. Interview with author, April 14, 1994.

103. *Op cit.* Interview with the author, March 24, 1994.

104. Interview with the author, January 13, 1994.

105. Background interview, April 15, 1994.

106. Interview with author, April 21, 1994.

107. *Op cit.* Interview with Sir David Hannay, British ambassador to the UN, on April 22, 1994.

108. *Ibid.*

109. Testimony to US Senate Foreign Relations Committee, October 20, 1993.

110. US Senate Foreign Relations Committee, November 4, 1993.

111. Interview with author, April 22, 1994.

112. *Op cit.* Background interview, January 13, 1994.

113. Background interview, May 9, 1994.

114. *Op cit.* Background interview, November 23, 1993.

115. Background interview, February 11, 1994.

116. Background interview B, November 30, 1993.

117. Confirmed by John Shattuck, former US Assistant Secretary of State for Human Rights and Humanitarian Affairs, in an interview with the author on April 13, 1994.

118. Meeting at Harvard University, May 10, 1994.

119. Author's interview with Larry Stachewicz, former assistant to Brent Scowcroft, on April 16, 1994.

120. Background interview, May 4, 1994.

121. *Ibid.*

122. *Op cit.* Interview with author, April 21, 1994.

123. Interview with author, April 29, 1994.

124. *Op cit.* Background interview A, January 13, 1994.

125. The words of a senior British figure overheard by the author after watching TV images of the Omarska and Trnopolje camps, August 2, 1992.

126. *Op cit.* Interview with author, May 6, 1994.

127. *Op cit.* Background interview A, January 13, 1994.

128. *Op cit.* Interview with author, April 29, 1994.

129. *Op cit.* Background interview, November 30, 1993.

130. According to CNN's 1993 data, the National news service was received by 63 million households and the International service by 66 million.

131. Peter Vesey, Vice-President CNN International, interviewed by Richard Parker of the Kennedy School, Harvard University, on February 18, 1994.

132. *Common Knowledge: News and the Construction of Political Meaning,* by W.R. Neuman, Marion Just and Ann Crigler (1992), Chicago: University of Chicago Press, p. 111.

133. Ambivalent is a word frequently used by those in government who were interviewed for this chapter.

134. Interview with author, May 5, 1994.

135. See *Live from Capitol Hill*, by Stephen Hess. Washington, DC: Brookings Institution (1991). Also *The Ultimate Insiders: US Senators in the National Media*, by Stephen Hess. Washington, DC: Brookings Institution (1986).

136. *Op cit.* Interview with author, May 6, 1994.

137. *Op cit.* Meeting at Harvard University, May 10, 1994.

138. *Op cit.* Interview with author, April 21, 1994.

139. *Op cit.* Interview with author, May 7, 1994.

140. *Op cit.* Interview with author, April 15, 1994.

141. Interviews by the author with former Prime Minister Kim Campbell (on April 26, 1994) and *op cit.* Barbara McDougall.

142. See Epilogue in *The Nixon Memo,* by Marvin Kalb (1994). Chicago: University of Chicago Press.

143. Background interview, December 23, 1993.

144. *Op cit.* Meeting at Harvard University, May 10, 1994.

145. October 4 and 5, 1993.

146. "The Roof Falls in on Clinton's Pioneers," by R.W. Apple of *The New York Times*, reprinted in *The Guardian* on October 14, 1993.

147. *Op cit.* Interview with author, April 22, 1994.

148. "Bosnia: America's Interests and America's Role." A speech by Anthony Lake at Johns Hopkins University, Baltimore, on April 7, 1994.

149. See *The Nature and Origins of Mass Opinion,* by John R. Zaller (1992), Cambridge, England: The University of Cambridge Press, p. 311.

150. *Op cit.* Interview with author, April 29, 1994.

151. Madeleine Albright on NBC's "Meet the Press," February 13, 1994.

152. *Op cit.* David Gergen quoted in "As US Sought a Bosnia Policy, the French Offered a Good Idea." *The New York Times*, February 14, 1994.

153. *Op cit.* Interview with author, March 24, 1994.

154. For more details of the poll data, with analysis, see: "TV War Images Pump Up the Pundits more than the Public," by Mark Jurkowitz in *The Boston Phoenix*, March 4, 1994.

155. *Op cit.* Interview with author, May 6, 1994.

156. *Op cit.* Interview with author, March 24, 1994.

157. *Op cit.* Bickham (1993).

158. *Op cit.* Background interview, March 23, 1994.

159. "Exposing Genocide." Interview with Roy Gutman in *American Journalism Review,* June 1993, p. 34.

160. Interview with author, December 18, 1993.

161. Presentation by Ms. Foa to the Diplomatic and Commonwealth Writers Association in London on November 17, 1993.

162. Background interview, February 6, 1993.

163. *Op cit.* Background interview A, January 17, 1994.

164. *Op cit.* Stewart (1993), p. 111.

165. *Op cit.* Background interview, January 26, 1994.

166. *Peacekeeper,* by General Lewis Mackenzie. Vancouver: Douglas and McIntyre (1993), p. 284.

167. Interview with author, February 26, 1994.

168. *Op cit.* Mackenzie (1993), p. 319 and 324.

169. *Op cit.* Stewart (1993), p. 109 and p. 138.

170. Background interview B, January 13, 1994.

171. Background interview A, January 17, 1994.

172. *Op cit.* Background interview, April 13, 1994.

173. *Op cit.* Background interview, January 26, 1994.

174. *Op cit.* Mackenzie (1993), p. 282.

175. Background briefing, May 20, 1993.

176. Background interviews A and B, January 17, 1994.

177. *Op cit.* Background interview, January 26, 1994.

178. Background interview, January 19, 1994.

179. *Ibid.*

180. Background interview, February 16, 1994.

181. *Op cit.* Colonel Alastair Duncan, February 23, 1994.

182. *Op cit.* Background interview, January 21, 1994.

183. *Op cit.* Background interview A, January 17, 1994.

184. *Op cit.* Background interview B, January 17, 1994.

185. *Op cit.* Background interview A, January 17, 1994.

186. *Op cit.* Background interview, March 16, 1994.

187. May 27, 1992. A Bosnian Serb mortar hit a queue outside a bakery leaving 16 people dead and more than 100 injured.

188. August 30, 1992. A shell hit a crowded food market in western Sarajevo, killing 15 and injuring more than 100.

189. Channel 4 News/News at Ten (ITN), August 6, 1993.

190. Discovered April 22, 1993, described in *op cit. Broken Lives,* by Lt. Col. Bob Stewart (1993), p. 294–9.

191. July 12, 1993. A mortar shell hit a queue of people waiting for fresh water, killing 12 people and injuring 15.

192. February 5, 1994. A mortar attack on Sarajevo's central market killed 68 and injured more than 200.

193. "This War has Changed My Life," by Ed Vulliamy. *British Journalism Review* vol. 4, no. 2, 1993, p. 10.

194. "Blood Washes the Streets of Sarajevo," by John Mullin in *The Guardian*, February 7, 1994.

195. Interview with author, January 25, 1994.

196. For a graphic sample read *Seasons in Hell,* by Ed Vulliamy. London: Simon and Schuster (1994), p. 126–136.

197. "Glamour without Responsibility," by "Kenneth Roberts," the pseudonym for a UN official. *The Spectator*, March 5, 1994.

198. Interview with Zlatko Dizdarevic, editor of *Oslobodenje*, on ABC News "Good Morning America," February 10, 1994.

199. "From Bosnia, a Curse for Policy-makers," by Nik Gowing, *Boston Globe*, February 9, 1994.

200. *Op cit.* "Glamour without Responsibility," by "Kenneth Roberts."

201. February 5, 1994.

202. *Op cit.* Gowing in *The Boston Globe*, February 9, 1994.

203. Background interview with British official, January 21, 1994.

204. *The Washington Post*, January 29, 1994.

205. *Op cit.* Background interview, January 21, 1994.

206. In "Wide River Still Divides Mostar's Bitter Neighbors," Yigal Chazan confirmed in a report from Mostar that Moslems in the east of the city had been subject to "perhaps the cruellest siege of the war." *The Guardian*, March 14, 1994, p. 4.

207. "Assignment" on "BBC 2," November 2, 1993.

208. Described by Larry Stachewicz in an interview with the author on April 16, 1994.

209. Background interview with former UN military officer, May 6, 1994.

210. *Op cit.* Interview with author, April 16, 1994.

211. *Op cit.* Background interview A, January 17, 1994.

212. European Union mediator Lord Owen quoting humanitarian agencies in an address to Diplomatic and Commonwealth Writers Association, November 3, 1992.

213. *Op cit.* Vulliamy (1993), p. 7.

214. *Op cit.* Interview with author, April 16, 1994.

215. *Op cit.* Background interview A, January 13, 1994.

216. *Op cit.* Background interview, January 19, 1994.

217. Interview with author, December 18, 1993.

218. *Op cit.* "Dictating the Global Agenda," by Nik Gowing, June 1991.

219. *Ibid.* Gowing (1991).

220. *Op cit.* Background interview, January 6, 1994.

221. *Ibid.*

222. President Bush quoted in the Theodore H. White Lecture by Daniel Schorr, November 18, 1993.

223. *Distant Voices,* by John Pilger. London: Vintage (1992), p. 126.

224. *Op cit.* Background interview, January 6, 1994.

225. "Iraq Shiites Smoldering Anger," by Trevor Rowe. *International Herald Tribune*, November 23, 1992.

226. *Op cit.* A full page newspaper ad campaign. *The Guardian*, April 14, 1993, p. 11.

227. "The Proof" on the front page of the *Daily Mail*, August 7, 1992.

228. *Ibid.*

229. *Op cit.* Speech at Johns Hopkins University on April 7, 1994.

230. Reprinted in *A Witness to Genocide,* by Roy Gutman (1993) *op cit.*

231. For "Shame of Camp Omarska," by Ed Vulliamy in *The Guardian*, August 7, 1993; then "Macabre Trade in Weary Hostages of Misfortune," on August 8, 1992, followed by reporting from other camps during subsequent months.

232. Interview with author, April 14, 1994.

233. "Bosnia: US and UK at Odds," by Simon Tisdall et al. in *The Guardian*, August 8, 1992.

234. Remarks made in a taped interview with Peter Jennings of ABC News during "While America Watched: The Bosnia Tragedy." Transmitted on March 17, 1994.

235. Remarks made in a taped interview with Peter Jennings of ABC News *op cit.* March 17, 1994.

236. "Muslim Survivors Tell of Torture, Slaughter at Hands of the Serbs," by Dan Stets in *The Philadelphia Inquirer*, June 24, 1992.

237. *Op cit. Seasons in Hell*, by Ed Vulliamy (1994), p. 97.

238. *Op cit.* Gutman (1993), p. ix–xi.

239. "Moslems Nightmare under the Long Hot Yugoslav Sun," by Maggie O'Kane in *The Guardian*, July 29, 1992.

240. August 2, 1992 in *op cit.* Gutman (1993), p. 44.

241. *Ibid.* Gutman (1993), p. xiii.

242. Remarks made in a taped interview with Peter Jennings of ABC News *op cit.* March 17, 1994.

243. Remarks made in taped interviews with Fox and Eagleburger by Peter Jennings of ABC News *op cit.* March 17, 1994.

244. Author's telephone interview with Foreign Office official on August 6, 1992.

245. Quoted from text of UNHCR Press Briefing on August 6, 1992. *UN document 3771B.*

246. *Ibid.*

247. *Op cit.* Background interview, January 21, 1994.

248. *Op cit.* Background interview, January 21, 1994.

249. *Op cit.* Background interview, December 23, 1994.

250. Interviewed by the author, March 16, 1994.

251. *Op cit. Seasons in Hell*, by Ed Vulliamy (1994), p. 107–109.

252. *Ibid.* p. 113.

253. *Ibid.* p. 115 and p. 158.

254. See p. 3 of transcript for *op cit.* "While America Watched: The Bosnia Tragedy," ABC News, March 17, 1994.

255. *Op cit.* Gutman (1993), p. xxxii.

256. Tony Birtley, on contract to ABC News and later ITN.

257. UNHCR coordinator Larry Hollingworth speaking on Channel 4 News, London, August 30, 1993.

258. "Enclave that Finally Ran Out of Luck," by Yigal Chazan and Haris Nezirovic. *The Guardian*, April 17, 1993.

259. "UN's Generals Who Were Unable to Call the Shots," by Ian Traynor. *The Guardian*, January 20, 1994.

260. *Op cit.* Mackenzie (1993), p. 104.

261. *Croire et Oser*, by General Philippe Morillon. Paris: Grasset (1993), p. 166–7.
262. March 12, 1994.
263. *Op cit.* Background interview, January 13, 1994.
264. *Op cit.* Morillon, p. 171–4.
265. *Op cit.* Morillon, p. 180.
266. Background interview, December 20, 1993.
267. *Op cit.* Morillon, p. 171.
268. For more detail see unpublished speech by the author "The New World Disorder: The Media, Politics and Defence" delivered to the British Army Staff College, Camberley, on May 13, 1993.
269. For more details of Tony Birtley's freelance status see "Recognition for the Freelance," by Stewart Purvis, Editor-in-Chief of ITN, in the letters column of *The Guardian*, February 25, 1994.
270. Speaking on the "Today" programme, BBC Radio 4. Quoted in "Siege of Srebrenica," *The Guardian*, April 17, 1993.
271. Background interview, December 20, 1994.
272. *Op cit.* Author's meeting with Tony Birtley on April 28, 1993.
273. *Op cit.* Background interview, December 23, 1993.
274. *Op cit.* Background interview, December 20, 1993.
275. Dr. Arria clarified the circumstances surrounding the creation of the Safe Areas under his Security Council Presidency in an interview with the author on April 21, 1994.
276. According to Dr. Arria, General Wahlgren later denied to him that he had ever recommended to the UN Peacekeeping Department against the idea of Safe Areas. Dr. Arria said that General Wahlgren told him he had never expressed such a view, and that he was misrepresented.
277. *Op cit.* Background interview, December 20, 1993.
278. *Op cit.* Background interview, December 20, 1993.
279. Security Council Resolution 824 on May 6, 1993 declared further Safe Areas in Sarajevo, Tuzla, Zepa, Gorazde and Bihac.
280. *Op cit.* Interview with the author on April 22, 1994.
281. *Ibid.*
282. "Dark Shadows over Bosnia 'Safe Areas,'" by Marcus Tanner. *The Independent*, May 26, 1993.
283. Interview with the author, January 13, 1994.
284. British Foreign Secretary Douglas Hurd at EU Foreign Affairs Council in Luxembourg, May 8, 1993.
285. "Sleepwalkers Lost in the Nightmare of Srebrenica," by Robert Block. *The Independent*, May 26, 1993.
286. "Time to Put a Stop to the 'Safe Areas' sham." Editorial in *The Independent*, June 8, 1993.
287. "UN Fears Bosnian 'Safe Areas' Face Disaster," by Ian Traynor. *The Guardian*, July 17, 1993.
288. "Leaving Them to Starve." Editorial in *The Guardian*, July 1, 1993.

289. "Trapped by a New Enemy in the Enclave of Despair," by Yigal Chazan. *The Guardian*, January 20, 1994.

290. "Whatever Happened to Bosnia?" by Robert Block in *The Independent*, October 20, 1993.

291. UNHCR spokeswoman Lyndall Sachs quoted in Yigal Chazan, January 20, 1994, *op cit.*

292. "Bosnians Live Trapped in UN Zone—Srebrenica Survives Cut Off From the World," by John Pomfret. *The Washington Post*, January 30, 1994.

293. "For Canadian Troops in Bosnia, UN Role Is Mission Impossible," by John Pomfret in *The Washington Post*, January 31, 1994.

294. February 22, 1994.

295. *Op cit.* Background interview B, January 13, 1994.

296. Letter from Lt. General Francis Briquemont to Mr. Akashi, Special Representative to the Secretary General, dated Sarajevo, January 9, 1994.

297. "West Sets the Stage for a Human Tragedy," by Tony Barber, Robert Block and Marcus Tanner. *The Independent*, June 8, 1993.

298. "Patching a Tattered Policy," by Robert Mauthner. *The Financial Times*, June 12, 1993.

299. Confirmed in an interview by the author with General Ratko Mladic, military commander of the Bosnian Serb forces in Zvornik, on June 29, 1993.

300. *Op cit.* Background interview, December 20, 1993.

301. *Op cit.* Background interview with author, April 21, 1994.

302. Interview with author, May 3, 1994.

303. For full and detailed description of the scenes discovered, see *op cit.* Stewart (1993), p. 294–9.

304. *Op cit.* Stewart (1993), p. 296.

305. Martin Bell's script quoted in "The Stand-Up Syndrome," by Steve Taylor in *American Journalism Review* July/August 1993, p. 37.

306. *Op cit.* "Testament of an Interventionist," by Martin Bell.

307. *Op cit.* Background interview, January 26, 1994.

308. Background interview, date known to author.

309. *Op cit.* Background interview A, January 17, 1994.

310. *Op cit.* Background interview A, January 17, 1994.

311. *Op cit.* Background interview, March 16, 1994.

312. *Op cit.* Background interview, January 19, 1994.

313. *Op cit.* Background interview, January 6, 1994.

314. *Op cit.* Speech by Douglas Hurd, September 9, 1993.

315. *Op cit.* Background interview, March 16, 1994.

316. *Op cit.* Background interview, March 16, 1994.

317. *Op cit.* Background interview B, January 17, 1994.

318. Interview with author, January 13, 1994.

319. *Op cit.* "Glamour Without Responsibility," by "Kenneth Roberts," *The Spectator*, March 5, 1994, p. 14.

320. For a vivid portrayal of life in Sarajevo, see *Seasons in Hell,* by Ed Vulliamy (1994), p. 76–79.

321. *Op cit.* "Kenneth Roberts."

322. *Op cit.* Background interview B, January 13, 1994.

323. Heard by Dan Stets of the *Philadelphia Inquirer.* Quoted during interview with this author on March 15, 1994.

324. *Op cit.* Background interview, January 26, 1994.

325. *Op cit.* Background interview A, January 13, 1994.

326. *Op cit.* Interview with author, January 25, 1994.

327. For a fuller analysis of the ethical dilemmas and shortcomings of journalists see, for example, *The News at Any Cost—How Journalists Compromise Their Ethics to Shape the News,* by Tom Goldstein. New York: Simon and Schuster (1985).

328. See "Back to Baghdad?" by John Simpson in *The Spectator,* February 19, 1994, p. 13.

329. Letter from a "senior UN official with significant responsibility in the former Yugoslavia" printed in *Foreign Policy* no. 94, spring 1994, p. 161–3.

330. *Op cit.* "Exposing Genocide." Interview with Roy Gutman in *American Journalism Review,* June 1993, p. 35.

331. See the emotions expressed in "700 Days," by Zlatko Dizdarevic in *The New York Times Magazine* on April 10, 1994, taken from his book *Sarajevo: A War Journal.*

> Here in Sarajevo, hundreds of TV crews parade before our very eyes; dozens of foreign journalists, reporters, writers. Everything is known here, right down to the minutest details, and yet nothing.
>
> What's even worse is that almost since the beginning of the war, this "army of liberation" has been here with its white tanks, its armored personnel carriers showing off all over town, the fingers of its soldiers ready on the trigger, and still—nothing. As a human being, I am stunned by all of this and ashamed.

332. *Op cit.* John Simpson, February 19, 1994.

333. *Op cit.* "Kenneth Roberts."

334. "Rose's Welcome Candour" in *The Daily Telegraph,* April 28, 1994.

335. *Op cit.* Background interview, May 9, 1994.

336. Interview with author, May 5, 1994.

337. *Op cit.* Background interview A, January 17, 1994.

338. *Op cit.* Background interview, January 21, 1994.

339. *Op cit.* Background interview B, January 13, 1994.

340. *Op cit.* Background interview B, January 13, 1994

341. *Op cit.* Background interview B, January 13, 1994.

342. *Op cit.* Interview with author, January 25, 1994.

343. *Op cit.* Background interview, May 6, 1994.

344. *Op cit.* Background interview A, January 17, 1994.

345. *Op cit.* Background interview, May 6, 1994.

346. *Ibid.*

347. *Op cit.* General Briquemont's letter to Mr. Akashi.

348. *Op cit.* Background interview, January 26, 1994.

349. Interview with the author, April 20, 1994.

350. *Op cit.* Background interview B, January 13, 1994.

351. October 4 and 5, 1993.

352. For fuller discussion of arguments see "When Pictures Drive Foreign Policy," by Jacqueline Sharkey. *American Journalism Review*, December 1993, p. 16–18.

353. Analysis by Stewart Purvis on *Medium Wave*, BBC Radio 4 on January 2, 1994.

354. *Op cit.* quoted in Daniel Schorr lecture, November 18, 1993.

355. *Ibid.* p. 14.

356. Interview with Paul Watson of the *Toronto Star* in "Determined to Get the Evidence," *American Journalism Review*, December 1993, p. 16.

357. *Op cit.* Interview with Col. Bill Smullen, May 5, 1994.

358. Background interview, May 4, 1994.

359. *Op cit.* Interview with author, May 6, 1994.

360. *Op cit.* Interview with author, May 6, 1994.

361. *Op cit.* Interview with author, May 7, 1994.

362. February 5, 1994.

363. See, for example, "An Opportunity to Reshape Policy—Graphic Bosnia Images May Shift Public View," by R.W. Apple in *The New York Times*, February 8, 1994.

364. *Op cit.* Ed Siegel, February 6, 1994; Walter Goodman, February 14, 1994; Martin Bell, February 28, 1994.

365. *Op cit.* Interview with author, May 6, 1994.

366. The authorized statement, "The Limits to Peacekeeping," by National Security Adviser Anthony Lake, was published in *The New York Times* on February 6, 1994—the day after the market massacre. The detail and context were later updated and expanded, then published as *Presidential Decision Directive (PDD) 25 on Peace Operations*, on May 5, 1994.

367. "As US Sought a Bosnia Policy, the French Offered a Good Idea," by Elaine Sciolino with Douglas Jehl. *The New York Times*, February 14, 1994.

368. *Ibid.*

369. "Blood Bath" in *Newsweek*, February 14, 1994, p. 20.

370. *Ibid.*

371. Background interview, May 3, 1994.

372. *Op cit.* Background interview, May 9, 1994.

373. *Op cit.* Interview with author, May 7, 1994.

374. *Op cit.* Interview with author, May 3, 1994.

375. Interview with author on April 14, 1994.

376. *The New York Times*, February 10, 1994.

377. Interview on NBC's "Today" on March 6, 1994.

378. *Op cit.* Interview with author, May 3, 1994.

379. *Op cit.* NBC News "Meet the Press," February 13, 1994.

380. February 10, 1994.

381. "US Says Serbs Can Unload Big Guns or Re-Aim Them," by Douglas Jehl in *The New York Times*, February 16, 1994.

382. *Ibid.*

383. "US Denies Bending on Deadline" in *The New York Times*, February 17, 1994.

384. Background interview, February 11, 1994.

385. *Op cit.* Background interview, February 11, 1994.

386. "NATO Enforces No-Fly Zone; Serb Shells Kill 56 in Srebrenica," by John Daniszewski, *The Associated Press*, April 13, 1993.

387. For an on-the-record synthesis of what many diplomats, politicians and UN officials were saying privately see "Literature from the Ashes," by John Simpson in *The Spectator*, February 16, 1994, p. 11–12.

388. Confirmed in background interview with senior UN military officer, May 6, 1994 *op cit.*

389. A UN general and UN civilian quoted anonymously in "Two UN Officials Accuse US of Prolonging War in Bosnia," by John Pomfret in *The Washington Post*, April 30, 1994.

390. *Ibid.*

391. See "UN Military Aide Says Plight of Gorazde Is Exaggerated," by Roger Cohen in *The New York Times*, April 30, 1994.

392. US Rep. John P. Murtha (D-Pa) quoted in Pomfret *op cit.*

393. See, for example, *Broken Lives,* by Colonel Bob Stewart (1993) *op cit.* p. 200–1.

394. See, for example, *Ibid.* p. 180.

395. *Ibid.* p. 267–8.

396. *Op cit.* "Glamour Without Responsibility," by "Kenneth Roberts," in *The Spectator*, March 5, 1994.

397. *Op cit.* Background interview, March 16, 1994.

398. Interview with author, January 5, 1994.

399. *Op cit.* Background interview, March 16, 1994.

400. *Op cit.* Background interview A, January 17, 1994.

401. *Ibid.*

402. *Ibid.*

403. *Op cit.* Background interview A, January 17, 1994.

404. *Ibid.*

405. *Ibid.*

406. *Ibid.*

407. For fuller details of the chronology see "Fighting for Irma," by Maggie O'Kane and Robi Dutta in *The Guardian*, August 13, 1993.

408. See, for example: "Leadership Based on What the Papers Say," by Mark Lawson in *The Independent* on August 17, 1993.

409. The mood was summarized in "Random Compassion," by Nick Cohen and Marcus Tanner in *The Independent on Sunday*, August 15, 1993.

410. *Ibid.*

411. "No Food, No Water, No Health," by Sir Donald Acheson, former government Chief Medical Officer who wrote as Special Representative of the World Health Organization in Sarajevo. His article appeared in *The Guardian* on August 18, 1993.

412. Dr. Patrick Peillod, head of the UN's evacuation committee, quoted in "Airlift Slows Despite 400 In Need," by Patrick Wintour et al. in *The Guardian*, August 16, 1993.

413. Foreign Minister Douglas Hogg quoted in "An Airlift With Odious Elements." *The Guardian*, August 16, 1993.

414. Quoted in "Leadership Based on What the Papers Say," by Mark Lawson, *The Independent* on August 17, 1993 *op cit.*

415. For a follow-up to the evacuees' conditions see "Courage and Pain of Bosnia Child Evacuees," by Paul Myers, *The Guardian*, December 20, 1993.

416. *Op cit.* "Bosnia: Television's War," by Martin Bell, p. 5.

417. *Op cit.* "Testament of an Interventionist," by Martin Bell. *British Journalism Review* vol. 4, no. 4, 1993, p. 10.

418. For more details of evacuations and Sally Becker's missions see, for example: "Magnificent Bosnia Airlift Criticized," by John Ezard in *The Guardian*, December 18, 1993; "Circuses Take Priority Over Bread in Devastated Bosnia," by Colin Smith in *The Sunday Times*, December 19, 1993; "Operation Angel Flies Bosnians Out for Treatment," by Angella Johnson in *The Guardian*, December 20, 1993.

419. *Op cit.* Background interview, January 21, 1994.

420. *Op cit.* Briefing by Sylvana Foa, November 17, 1993.

421. *Ibid.*

422. Encounter with Peter Morgan, Channel Four News producer in mid-June, 1993.

423. *Op cit.* Background interview, December 23, 1993.

424. *Op cit.* Background interview, January 21, 1994.

425. *Op cit.* Background interview, December 23, 1993.

426. *Op cit.* Background interview, January 6, 1994.

427. *Op cit.* Lt. Colonel Alistair Duncan, February 1994.

428. The Argentine air strike on the HMS Sir Galahad at anchor in Bluff Cove took place on June 8, 1982. The burning ship and casualties being brought ashore were filmed on videotape by the BBC pool cameraman Bernard Hesketh. The Argentine surrender in Port Stanley was six days later on June 14. Taped coverage was transmitted a day later having been flown off the islands by jet. The footage of the Bluff Cove disaster—including badly maimed Welsh Guardsmen and ships' crew—was transported from the Falklands by ship. It was not transmitted until June 24—sixteen days after the event and ten days after the Argentine surrender.

429. Cited in *From The House of War,* by John Simpson. London: Hutchinson (1991).

430. *Op cit.* On CNN's *Reliable Sources*, February 13, 1994, p. 4.

431. Background interview with senior Red Cross official, December 16, 1993.

432. Cited by Professor Nikolai Petrov, Geography Department, University of Moscow, during presentation at Tufts University on March 6, 1994.

433. *Op cit.* Huntington (1993).

434. *Op cit.* Douglas Hurd's speech, September 9, 1993.

435. See, for example, "The Lessons of Yugoslavia," a presentation given by Cedric Thornberry, Head of Civil Affairs, for the UN Protection Force in Yugoslavia. Delivered to the Center for Defence Studies, Kings College, London on December 7, 1993.

436. Interview in *The New York Times*, July 11, 1993.

437. *Op cit.* Presidential Decision Directive No. 25, May 5, 1994.
438. *Ibid.* p. 5.
439. Briefing at the White House attended by the author on May 5, 1994.
440. *Op cit.* Speech at Johns Hopkins University, April 7, 1994.
441. *Op cit.* Howard (1993).

The Role of the News Media in Unequal Political Conflicts
From the 1987 *Intifada* to the 1991 Gulf War and Back Again

Gadi Wolfsfeld

*T*he role of the news media in political conflicts is a topic that has received more public attention than academic study. Discussions of this issue have themselves become a routine part of news stories and public discussions about such conflicts. The discourse often centers on such issues as the need for security versus the public's right to know or whether or not the news media reports the news or creates it. Examples of this phenomenon can be found by noting the amount of public debate that surrounded media coverage of the Falklands, Grenada, the Tiananmen Square student uprising in China, the massive protests throughout the Soviet Union and Eastern Europe, the Palestinian *intifada* (uprising) in 1987, and the 1991 Gulf War.

Social scientists have generated very little theory on this issue. This scarcity can be attributed, at least in part, to artificial distinctions that have been created by studying different forms of conflict. The role of the media has been looked at in reference to protest (Gamson, 1990; Gitlin, 1980; Goldenberg, 1975; Lipsky 1970; Olien, Tichenor, and Donohue 1989; Wolfsfeld, 1984a, 1984b), terrorism (for reviews see: Alexander, 1990; Paletz, 1991; Picard and Sheets, 1987a, 1987b), and war (Gannett, 1991; Gervasi, 1982; Glasgow University Media Group 1985; Hallin, 1987, 1986, 1984; Knightly, 1975; Mandelbaum, 1982; Patterson, 1984; Twentieth Century Fund, 1985) but there has been no serious attempt to develop a theory that could offer a more general view of the issue.

There are at least two necessary conditions for achieving a broader perspective on the role of the news media in political conflicts. The first is the development of a theoretical model that explains how the role of the media varies among and within different types of conflict. Second, we need a growing list of case studies that allows us to offer comparative evidence about the strengths and weaknesses of that model.

The goal of this chapter is to show how the role of the news media changes over time and circumstances. The major research question that will guide the discussion is as follows: Under what conditions are the news media most likely to play an independent role in political conflicts? This question, it will be argued, is best answered by employing a transactional model (Wolfsfeld, 1991) which focuses on changes in the interactions between antagonists and the news media.

The theoretical discussion in this chapter will focus more specifically on unequal political conflicts, which are defined as those public confrontations between a government and at least one other antagonist and in which the state (or one of the states) has a significantly superior amount of coercive resources at its disposal. A great many conflicts fall under this category, including protests, terrorist acts, riots, revolutions (both successful and attempted), and all-out war between a powerful country and a weaker one.

The first part of our discussion will attempt to outline the basic principles of the model. The transactional model will then be used in three case studies to explain the changing role of the press in three conflicts in the Middle East. This part of the argument will start by considering the role of the news media in the *intifada*, and then move on to look at the role of the press in two facets of the Gulf War: the major conflict between the United States and Iraq and the less conspicuous but nonetheless revealing confrontation between the Israelis and the Palestinians. The plan is to use these three cases to illustrate the advantages of employing a transactional model as a means of explaining how the role of the press changes over time and circumstance.

Some Initial Principles

The role of the news media in unequal conflicts can be better understood if we begin by considering the strategic needs of the two sides. The weaker side in the conflict—the challenger—must find a means of bringing third parties into the conflict on its side in order to create a more equal balance of power. "If a fight starts, watch the crowd," Schattschneider (1960) advised us more than 30 years ago. The scope of the conflict, he observed, frequently changes during its course and the introduction and subtraction of players alters the power relations among the contestants. Where the scope is narrow, the weaker party has much to gain and little to lose by broadening the scope, drawing third parties into the conflict as mediators or partisans.

The news media, especially in recent years, often play a critical role in this process; they are often the only means for bringing the case of the weaker side to other parties. In order to accomplish this, the challenger must successfully promote its frames of the conflict to the news media (Gamson and Stuart, 1992; Ryan, 1991). Once the issue is on the pubic agenda, it puts pressure on third parties to respond.

The more powerful side in such conflicts approaches the news media from a somewhat different strategic perspective. Powerful governments often attempt to dominate the informational environment in order to either neutralize the role of the news media by keeping the conflict off the public agenda or in more serious challenges to ensure that the official voice drowns out all others. In these cases, which may be the rule rather than the exception, the conflict usually takes its natural course, with the powerful defeating the weak.

Thus, when the news media, by choice or by compulsion, adopt the frame being promoted by the more powerful antagonist, they are less likely to play a central role in unequal political conflicts. As an analogy one can consider a conflict between a rich landlord and a group of poor tenants. If a large sum of money were given by an interested party to the wealthy landlord it would be unlikely to have much of an effect on either the behavior of the parties or the course of the conflict. If, on the other hand, that same amount of money were given to the poor tenants it could have a dramatic impact on the behavior of the antagonists and on the course of the conflict. The tenants would be able to carry out a much more sophisticated mobilization effort and hire professionals such as lawyers and public relations people to aid their cause.

The same principle holds for the distribution of favorable media coverage: the more positive attention that is given to resource-poor antagonists, the more dramatic its effects. Even a balanced type of coverage will offer the weaker antagonist important opportunities to challenge the dominant frames. Resources given equally to both parties will still be a more significant development for the weak than for the powerful.

A great deal has been written by scholars about the institutional advantages enjoyed by the powerful in gaining access to the news media (see especially: Bennett, 1990; Gans, 1979; Herman and Chomsky, 1988; Paletz and Entman, 1981; Tichenor, Donohue, and Olien, 1980; Wolfsfeld, 1991). Governments do have significant advantages over weaker challengers in such critical areas as organization, resources, and their ability to selectively reward and punish journalists. Perhaps the most important advantage is that the powerful are given automatic standing while weaker antagonists often have to prove their newsworthiness in order to achieve public standing.

There is, however, another side to this story, one that has been virtually ignored in the literature. The fact is that the ability of the powerful to manage news stories tends to *vary over time and circumstance* and the key to understanding these differences can be best explained by their ability to *take control of the informational environment*. The greater the powerful's monopoly on information, the greater its value as a news source, and the less likely the news media is to turn to alternative sources of information. This, we shall argue, is the key situational variable that determines whether or not the news media will play an independent role in any particular conflict.

It can be said that the ability of the more powerful antagonist to control the informational environment in a political conflict will depend on three factors. The first factor is the *powerful antagonist's relative ability to initiate and control events.* When the situation is under control, so is the story. Governments are in a much better position to coordinate their press relations when they can anticipate the events that will be covered. When, on the other hand, the powerful are forced to *react* to events, it suggests that others are setting and framing the media's agenda. Consider, for example how much easier it was for the Reagan administration to control the informational environment during the invasion of Grenada in 1983 (Sharkey, 1991), when compared with the very difficult situation they faced when the Marines were forced to deal with Shi'ite guerrillas in Lebanon.

A second variable that determines the extent of dominance over the informational environment is the willingness and ability of the more powerful antagonist to *regulate the flow of information* to the press. Governments, both democratic and non-democratic, often find compelling reasons to employ censorship during political conflicts and this increases the value of official sources of information by eliminating competition. Powerful antagonists also have other means of controlling the flow of information such as denying access or accreditation to journalists (or specific journalists), expelling them, shutting down press agencies working for the other antagonist, or even placing rival news sources or journalists under arrest.

The ability of the powerful to regulate the flow of information to the press is also affected by the nature of the *logistic and geographic* environment. Powerful governments prefer to operate under conditions in which they can isolate the areas of actual conflict and regulate the entry and exit of journalists. But the powerful are not always in a position to choose the sites of conflict and this can have a critical effect on their ability to control the informational environment. While the physical circumstances of certain locales tend to facilitate government control, others are more porous and offer easier access for reporters and this increases the level of journalistic independence. An illustration of this point can be made by comparing the ability of the British to control the press during the Falklands/Malvinas campaign (Glasgow University Media Group, 1985; Morrison & Tumber, 1988) with the difficulties they faced attempting to regulate information about their conflict with the I.R.A. in both London and Northern Ireland.

The third and final factor that determines the powerful's level of control over the informational environment is *the degree of political dispute among elites about the conflict.* When the various factions within a government are promoting different frames about a conflict it is more difficult to control the informational environment because journalists are able to choose among a variety of sources. When, on the other hand, the official frame is the only frame available among the elites, journalists will have little choice but to also adopt that frame.

In this case, rather than offering an illustration of how this varies among conflicts, we shall point to an example that shows how the informational environment can also change in the course of a conflict. Hallin's (1986) work on the Vietnam War offers an excellent case study of how media coverage is affected by the amount of consensus among the elite. In the early years of the Vietnam War there was very little disagreement within Washington about either the goals of the war or the methods being used to achieve those aims. The Cold War frame that dominated media discourse in those years of the war was never really replaced by competing frames, but as the consensus among the political elite began to break down, other less positive frames of the war also began to emerge. As Hallin points out, it was not that the press stopped relying on elite sources for guidance and information, but rather that the anti-war movement had made serious inroads within that elite.

The ability of the underdog to compete successfully with more powerful antagonists will depend to a large extent on their ability to exploit these opportunities. Some measure of success in this area will come to those challengers who are able to initiate and control events that are considered newsworthy, to find innovative ways to circumvent the powerful's control over the flow of information, and to make serious inroads among political elites.

There is, however, another catch. There are basically two doors for gaining access to the news media (Gamson and Wolfsfeld, 1993; Wolfsfeld, 1991). The front door is reserved for the powerful who are considered to be *inherently* newsworthy and are not required to carry out any overly sensational behavior to gain admittance. The weak must enter through the back door, a gateway especially designed for deviants. To gain public standing, the weak are often forced to create some form of drama, and this often entails what might best be called the "dues of disorder." While challengers can increase their level of news value through such acts, they often pay an extremely heavy price in the cultural domain by being framed as either deviant and/or dangerous (Alinsky, 1971; Bennett, 1990; Gans, 1979; Goldenberg, 1975; Paletz and Entman, 1981; Shoemaker 1982, 1984; Wolfsfeld, 1984a, 1988).

The most successful challengers are those who overcome this dilemma by creating newsworthy events that are dramatic yet positive. A strategy of civil disobedience, such as that employed by Gandhi (Ahluwallia, 1960; Barrier, 1976; Brown, 1977) and Martin Luther King (see especially: Garrow, 1978) is a good example of this type of tactic, for such actions are seen as newsworthy but not aggressive. This method is especially effective when the more powerful antagonist responds violently because the ensuing stories and images frame the weak as victims.[1] This, however, brings us to a separate discussion about the struggle over symbols and meaning, a topic that goes beyond the scope of the present chapter.

The Independence of the News Media

As stated earlier, the goal of this piece is to ask about the circumstances under which the news media will play an independent role in political conflicts. The question of independence refers to the extent to which the press becomes an active agent in a given conflict rather than a passive conveyer of political information. The central issue is the extent to which the press is *willing* and *able* to use professional discretion in making genuine *choices* about how to collect and publicize news. This notion of independence implies that press freedom can just as easily be surrendered as taken away.

It is possible to examine the course of a conflict and establish whether the news media takes an independent role by asking about such factors as: 1) the extent to which the news media use exclusively official sources for information; 2) the extent to which journalists appear to be *initiating* stories rather than simply transmitting stories that were planted by the authorities; and 3) the extent to which the antagonists appear to be unprepared or surprised by the coverage they are receiving. The degree of press independence is seen as a variable that changes over time and circumstances, including those discussed earlier.

It is important to make a distinction between *independent* media effects, where the news media play an active role in the conflict, and *transmissional effects*, in which the press serves as a mere conduit for messages being sent by the antagonists. As an example, let us assume that a political leader decides to use the news media in order to announce to the world that (s)he intends to escalate a particular conflict, say by sending more troops. Let us further assume that the opposing leader, as a direct result of this message, decides to also mobilize troops. The news media clearly did not have an independent influence on this conflict.

If, on the other hand, the first leader had intended to keep the escalation a secret, and certain journalists managed to discover that information and to publicize it, any subsequent outcomes could legitimately be classified as an independent effect of the news media. The question centers on whether the news media took an *active* role either in obtaining the information or in framing it in a particular manner. While such a distinction may be much easier to make in theory than in practice, researchers must attempt to trace the flow of influence between the antagonists and the news media.

The Significance of Media Effects

It is helpful to make a distinction between three possible scenarios for media effects. One would cover those cases in which the news media had virtually no effect on either the major players or the conflict itself. The second would deal with those cases when the media do seem to be having an important effect on the conflict, but mostly in a passive, transmissional manner where one or both of the antagonists have successfully taken control of the press and used it as a tool of influence. The final scenario is the most interesting one: where the role of the news media is both independent and significant.

It is important, therefore, to consider both the significance of the news media's role as well as their level of independence. Even when the media do achieve a certain amount of autonomy in a conflict one still has to ask whether or not they had an important influence on the behavior of the antagonists and/or the course of the conflict. There are certainly instances in which the press covers political strife in a relatively independent manner, but has no real impact on the conflict.

To decide whether or not the media played a significant role, the researcher needs to ask two basic questions: 1) To what extent do the antagonists appear to be adapting their behavior as a result of either the presence of the media or the manner in which the press is covering the conflict? 2) To what extent does the conflict appear to be taking a certain course for reasons that can at least partially be attributed to media presence or coverage?

In this particular piece we are focusing more specifically on those occasions in which the news media offer a significant amount of time or space to the weaker side of an unequal conflict and thus increase the probability of third-party intervention. Knightly (1975) offers an excellent example of such a case that occurred in the nineteenth century in which news began to reach Constantinople of atrocities committed by the Turkish army against the Christian population in Southern Bulgaria. Reports suggested that over 12,000 men, women and children had been killed, and the *London Daily News* sent a reporter by the name of Janaurius Aloysius MacGahan. He reported:

> I think I came in a fair and impartial frame of mind . . . I fear I am no longer impartial, and I am certainly no longer cool . . . There are things too horrible to allow anything like calm inquiry; things the vileness of which the eye refuses to look upon, and which the mind refuses to contemplate . . . (p. 50).

According to Knightly, MacGahan's stories caused such worldwide indignation against the Turks that: "Russia decided that his disclosures justified a war and on April 29, 1877, began hostilities against Turkey" (p. 51).

Knightly also writes about the case of Haile Selassie, who used a similar strategy when Mussolini invaded Ethiopia in 1935. Selassie hoped that news of civilian casualties would arouse world opinion and the League of Nations to stop the Italian invasion of Ethiopia.

It is important to remember that the question of whether or not the news media plays an important role in such conflicts should always be examined from a comparative perspective. The questions being raised in this chapter ask about the *degree* of press independence and the *extent* of actual effects. The best strategy therefore is to always attempt to answer these questions by contrasting conflicts and attempting to ascertain how the role of the news media varies.

Researchers should also bear in mind that the news media are not monolithic. The extent to which each news medium will depend on or influence each antagonist will vary as will the degree of influence it will have on the conflict. This particular essay will leave aside this issue in the interest of brevity, but a fuller discussion must also consider variations among the news media (for some initial ideas in this direction see: Wolfsfeld, 1991).

In sum, the role of the news media in unequal political conflicts is often determined by the ability of the more powerful antagonist to control the informational environment. This control, it is argued, is related to three variables: the powerful's ability to initiate and control conflict events, the ability to regulate the flow of information, and the extent of consensus among elites. The news media are more likely to play an independent role when the powerful lose control because it allows the weaker side a better platform for the promotion of its frame of the conflict and increases the probability for third parties to intervene. The discussion turns then to the three case studies.

Methodology

As stated, we will be attempting to apply the model to the *intifada* and two different aspects of the Gulf War: the major conflict between the Allies and Iraq and the less prominent conflict between the Israelis and the Palestinians. The use of such different conflicts should offer some useful insights into both the strengths and weaknesses of the theory.

The major methodology for collecting empirical data on these issues is through in-depth interviews with journalists and official sources who interacted during each of these conflicts. It is important to bear in mind, however, that these interviews often serve to illustrate and detail what is already publicly known about these conflicts. The news media themselves have offered hundreds of articles and broadcasts on the role of the press in each of these conflicts. The educated public generally knows, for example, about the differences in the intensity of the two clashes and the very different levels of consensus surrounding the two conflicts.

The interviewees should be seen as expert informants who can shed a significant amount of light on: 1) how the four central variables affected their own behavior and the behavior of others during the conflict; 2) the nature of their interactions with the other actors; and 3) some of the outcomes of this process of interactions. We do not, on the other hand, consider these professionals to be reliable authorities on more general questions such as the role of the media in the mobilization of public opinion. These case studies will focus therefore more specifically on the interactions between the antagonists and the news media and possible outcomes of this process for each of the parties.

Twenty interviews were carried out with informants about their experiences in the *intifada*. Interviews were conducted with reporters from a variety of newspapers and television stations (both foreign and local), with the first and second army spokesmen to deal with the *intifada* and representatives of their office, with the political advisor to the Minister of Defense, and with a number of Palestinian leaders who had ongoing contacts with the press.[2] Most of these interviews were carried out during the first year of violence (1988), although some were carried out in the following years. The time frame being studied is this first year of the *intifada* in which the conflict received the most amount of media attention. The role of the news media no doubt declined after that point, but we do not consider that issue within the present discussion.

Fifteen interviews were conducted with military press officers and journalists about their role in the Gulf War. Interviews were carried out with American print and television journalists who were based in Saudi Arabia during the war as well as several who covered the war from the Pentagon. Most of the Public Information Officers who were interviewed also served in Saudi Arabia during the war, although one was based in Washington. The officers represented the Army, Navy, and Marines and two held senior positions on General Shwarzkopf's staff. Interviews about the Gulf War were conducted in Jerusalem in the spring of 1991 and in the Pentagon in the summer of that same year.

Twelve interviews were carried out with people who had something to say about the Israeli-Palestinian conflict during the Gulf War. The sources included Israeli government officials, foreign and local journalists, and several Palestinians. It is also worth noting that some of the foreign correspondents who were interviewed because they spent time in the Gulf also spent some time covering the Israeli side of this story. These interviews were carried out in Israel in the fall of 1991 and during the first half of 1992.[3]

All of the interviews used a flexible format with discussions centering on the same core issues: the influence of media presence and coverage on the antagonists, antagonist strategies for controlling, manipulating, or accommodating the news media, the logistical and normative environment that characterized the two conflicts, the centrality of the media in antagonist strategy, the ways in which the role of the media changed during the course of the conflict, the nature of the relationship between the actors and journalists, attempts at punishment and rewards of actors and reporters, how "fair" and "representative" was the coverage antagonists were given, and what lessons can be learned from their own experience about the role of the news media in such conflicts. Each of the interviews lasted about an hour.

The researcher also carried out a number of direct observations about the *intifada* by traveling in the territories with reporters as they were covering these events. We shall also refer to some content analyses of media coverage about the conflicts that were either published by other researchers or carried out for the purposes of this study.

The *Intifada*

The Palestinian *intifada* began in December of 1987. The role of the news media in this conflict quickly became a major controversy both in Israel and abroad. At the beginning of the uprising many Israelis felt that the presence of the media was the major cause of violence and called for banning the press from the territories. A great deal of the initial debate within the Israeli government centered on what should be "done" about the media (Lederman, 1992).

The argument here is that the news media did play an independent role in the *intifada* due to the particular nature of the conflict. It is critical to emphasize, however, that this does not mean that the news media "caused" the *intifada*. The central reasons for the uprising are best found by examining the social and political history of the Arab-Israeli conflict; Palestinian violence came from a genuine sense of anger and frustration. Nevertheless, the nature, direction, and intensity of this particular stage of this conflict were certainly affected by the presence of the news media, the reports that were filed, and the international reactions to that coverage.

The *intifada* offers an almost textbook case of how a seemingly weaker challenger can successfully promote its frames to the news media. The Israeli army was totally incapable of controlling the informational environment and found it virtually impossible to promote its "law and order" frame of the conflict to the international news media.[4] The scenes of armed Israeli soldiers battling stone-throwing youths produced a very vivid image of injustice that resonated around the world. These images, we shall argue, had significant effects on the behavior of both Israelis and Palestinians and the course of the conflict.

A Complete Lack of Control

The model discussed earlier pointed to three factors determining the ability of the powerful antagonist to control the informational environment: the ability to initiate and control conflict events, the ability to regulate the flow of information, and the degree of consensus among political elites. All three of these factors worked against the Israeli government and thus the press played an especially independent and significant role in this conflict. The events that defined the news story in the initial months of the *intifada* were massive protests of unarmed Palestinians defying the occupying army. Protests were breaking out all over the West Bank and Gaza and the spokesperson's office was attempting to offer the army's perspective on what was happening in the field. The incidents themselves were controlled by the protesters and the spokesperson's office found themselves trying to keep up with the pace of events. As they described it, their basic media strategy was one of "damage control," as best illustrated in the following comments by a very senior officer in the Army spokesperson's office.

Whereas the Palestinians' main objective is to attract media attention, our main objective is to PLAY IT DOWN [said in English]. We have no interest in getting attention. People come to me all the time and say "why don't you initiate something?" "Initiate—what exactly should I initiate." The ideal story from my point of view is to be able to say: "Today nothing happened in the field."

The major news stories centered on incidents in which Israeli soldiers were accused of brutality in dealing with Palestinian rioters. The story that came out in later trials was one of general confusion, in which field soldiers were never sure about how much force to use in suppressing the riots, and this contributed to the government's lack of control over developments. In addition, while responding to charges of brutality is never an agreeable task, it is made especially difficult because of the military's need to investigate each story before issuing a response. These investigations usually take days, and the news media are not in the business of waiting.

The Israeli military also found it extremely difficult to regulate the flow of information to the news media for both political and geographic reasons. The army initiated a number of policies that were designed to gain control over the flow of information about the *intifada*. The press were often prohibited from entering certain areas, which made it more difficult for them to film the violence.[5] The Israeli government also shut down the Palestinian Press Service, which was providing journalists with beepers that kept them informed of any protests breaking out in the territories. The effects of these policies, however, were probably minimal.

Israel is a basically open society, and any attempts to limit the flow of information from the territories is both politically and geographically impossible. It is especially difficult to shut off physical access to the West Bank. Journalists can normally take an Arab taxi from East Jerusalem to anywhere in the West Bank, cover a story, and be back within a few hours to send the reports overseas. Another reason the Israelis were reluctant to completely seal off the territories was their fear that Palestinians would be supplied with video cameras and produce footage that not only would be more damaging to Israel but would also get more attention because it was smuggled out in secret.[6]

The army spokesperson talked about the development of military policy on how to handle the news media during the *intifada*:

It was a process, perhaps an evolution . . . . There was no decision by the senior staff which said that on this day of the riots we will act this way and on another day differently. I must say that when the issue of the media came up in the first days of the discussion, I insisted that the areas will stay open, and that's for three reasons: first, because of the principle, and I believe in that principle that we must have freedom of the press in a democratic country,

and one has to pay a price for that . . . . Secondly, if we close the area we are
only making it worse for ourselves, because as it is there is very unsymmet-
rical reporting. This would give complete advantage to the Palestinian side
and they [the media] wouldn't be willing to hear our side if we closed the
area. The third reason is practical, we have no way to hermetically seal the
area, and we'd have to use a great deal of forces to close it.

The Israeli army was unable, then, to control either the events themselves or
the flow of information about them. It found itself "running after the story" and
thus unable to have almost any effect on media frames of the conflict which were
being broadcast around the world. This lack of control led to a more active and
independent news media.

A Lack of Political Consensus Among Elites

There is little need to dwell on the lack of national or international consensus surrounding Israel's occupation in the territories. The issue over what to do about the
territories has been the major political issue dividing the Israeli polity since the
early 1970s, and the major source of friction between Israel and the rest of the
world for an equally long period of time.

On the face of it, however, the period when the *intifada* broke out should have
been a time of political consensus among Israeli elites, for the country was being
ruled by a "national unity government." The two major political parties, Labour
and Likud, had decided to join together in a single government and therefore the
Minister of Defense (Yitzhak Rabin) was from the Labour party while the Prime
Minister (Yitzhak Shamir) was from Likud. Nevertheless, Israel has a multi-party
political system, and the smaller parties from the left and the right formed a very
vocal opposition to government policy in the territories.[7] While the right wing
Knesset members were demanding a much tougher stand toward Palestinian rioters, the left was talking about the corruption of the Israeli army and the need to end
the occupation.

The fact that many Israeli opinion leaders were themselves condemning the
actions of the military created an ideological environment that was as open as the
geographic one. News sources of varying political views were all pressing to be
heard, holding press conferences and staging demonstrations. When the issue
became an international one it allowed for an even greater diversity of news sources
as leaders from around the world and the United Nations were all expressing their
views on Israeli behavior. Naturally, these positions were given extensive coverage
in the Israeli press and the controversy became more intense.

In sum, three factors led to Israel's inability to control the informational environment: its inability to control or initiate events in the field, its inability to regu-

late the flow of information to the news media, and the lack of consensus about the conflict among the elite in Israel. These are the major reasons the news media was able to play an independent role in the *intifada*. The discussion turns then to the question of whether the news media's role was also significant.

Behavioral and Political Outcomes

To assess whether the news media played an important role in changing the course of an unequal political conflict, it is useful to focus on two classes of outcomes: those associated with changes in the behavior of the antagonists, and those better categorized as changes in the overall balance of power.

When looking at changes in behavior, one attempts to determine the extent to which antagonist actions can be attributed either to the presence of the news media or to the ways in which the conflict was covered. This relationship can be demonstrated with evidence suggesting that antagonist actions were based on either a *reaction* to the news media or in *anticipation* of how the news media might deal with certain behaviors. Media power need not be *overtly* exercised in order to have an effect. When political leaders plant intentional sound bites into their speeches it is a sign of their dependency on the news media and thus can legitimately be considered an effect of the news media on political behavior. The central question is whether either or both of the antagonists adapted their behavior because of the news media.

Although there is some controversy about this point, the conclusion of this study is that both the Palestinians and the Israeli army were very sensitive to both the presence of the news media and the coverage the *intifada* received. The majority of interviews point to the fact that the presence of the news media tended to increase the level of Palestinian militancy and decrease the amount of force used by Israeli soldiers. The two antagonists were attempting to send very different messages to the world and because these confrontations were being played out in public each adapted their behavior accordingly.

There can be little doubt that both antagonists were very aware of the importance of the news media in the conflict. One of the people who participated in many of the general planning sessions of the Israeli army was asked how often the subject of the news media came up:

> Very often, very often. People talk about what is being said in the media, and everyone talks about what happened before and after what was shown. And whenever there is a decision to carry out some type of operation there is a decision whether to close it to the media or not. The major reason for closing the area is that the media causes a great deal of problems.

It is more difficult to obtain a similar assessment about the importance of media considerations in Palestinian planning, but there is a good deal of evidence about the degree of media awareness among Palestinian residents. One of the reporters offered a particularly telling example:

> I was in a very remote village not so long ago and I can't even remember the name. According to what the villagers say, it seems that the soldiers carried out a bit of vandalism there. There was one house where they had been conducting a search and had wrecked the place pretty badly. Anyway, we came to the place about two days after this happened, and they hadn't touched anything—the house was totally upside down and there must be at least twenty people living in that house. People live there and it is clear that the mess really bothered them—even the refrigerator in the kitchen was upside down. We asked them: "Why didn't you straighten things up after it happened." They said: "We were waiting for the televisions to come, we were waiting for somebody to take a picture of it."

One of the most controversial issues during the early months of the *intifada* was whether the presence of news cameras had a significant effect on the extent of violence in Palestinian demonstrations. This study cannot offer a definitive answer to that question, but it can offer some perspective. In general, the Israeli army claimed that the presence of the news media had a clear and direct effect on the level of violence while Palestinians maintained that press influence was minimal. Clearly each side has a political stake in their position: the Palestinians wanted to emphasize the authenticity of their struggle while the Israelis would have liked to dismiss the *intifada* as a mere show for the media.[8]

The deciding vote is best cast by the journalists who covered the events. They also have an interest in minimizing the influence of the cameras ("we cover the news—we don't create it"), yet most of those interviewed admitted that the cameras did have an escalatory influence on the events themselves.[9] As many pointed out, there are very few people, whether they be protesters, politicians, or ordinary citizens, who are not affected by the presence of television cameras. One reporter claimed that if he wanted he could start a demonstration in five minutes simply by taking his camera out.[10]

It is important to reemphasize, however, that asserting the existence of such a relationship says absolutely nothing about the authenticity of the protests. Protesters who change their behavior when the media arrives do so because they are attempting to send a political message to the public. The media's influence on the level of political violence is *self-imposed* by the actors in order to achieve political goals. It is also useful to remember that political violence exists without the presence of the news media; it may, however, take on a somewhat different shape and direction.

The extent of media influence on the behavior of Israeli soldiers is a much less controversial issue. Military officials, journalists, and Palestinians who were interviewed all agreed that the presence of cameras had an *inhibitory* influence on the use of force by soldiers. The officers and the enlisted men were all very aware of the international implications when "beating scenes" were broadcast around the world. Indeed, the influence of the news media on Israeli behavior is perhaps best illustrated by the fact that many training sessions for soldiers going into the territories soon included clips of these news broadcasts as a vivid reminder of the risks of such behavior.

These indicators suggest then that both of the antagonists considered the news media to be an important element in the *intifada*. It was taken into account in planning and there is solid evidence that points to the fact that the presence and coverage of the news media also had an effect on their behavior.

Gauging *political* changes attributable to the news media is a much trickier business. The clearest way for the news media to have a political effect on an unequal conflict is to adopt the frame being promoted by the weaker party which increases the level of political legitimacy attributed to that challenger. An increase in political legitimacy will usually lead to an increase in political support and increases the likelihood of third-party intervention. It is difficult to measure political legitimacy and even more problematic to ascertain whether or not any changes should be attributed to news coverage. We can rely in part, however, on the testimonies of some of those who were involved in the conflict.

It is only fair to point out that some of the Palestinians who were interviewed tended to discount the importance of the news media in their struggle. Some felt that putting too much emphasis on the news media somehow cheapened the genuine sacrifices they had made in standing up to the Israeli army. All agreed, however, that the media had helped place them on a more equal footing with Israel. The words of one of these skeptics is fairly typical.

> What it [the press] mainly did was to expose Israel. Something that Israel is not used to. Israel got used to getting away with everything here. Now, even the Israeli reporters cover what is happening in those towns . . . You expose them. The mass media is an advantage to you; the important thing is that you are equal to them [the Israelis]. And secondly when we talk about public opinion, do you know that it took us twenty-one years to convince the world that we are under occupation. And after twenty-one years Mr. Shultz comes here to speak of improving the plight of the occupied.

If one believes that the struggle over the public agenda is a competitive one, then the choices made by the news media have important effects on the political process. Another Palestinian talked about the feeling among the leadership after the first year of the *intifada*.

> They [the Palestinians] feel they have gained what they deserve, this is the
> normal way of thinking. At least the world is willing to listen to what the
> Palestinians have to say and not only to what the Israelis have to say. So now
> the balance is more even. In this respect, of course, we have succeeded.

There is also good reason to suspect that the news media's focus on the
intifada had at least something to do with mobilizing a number of third parties into
the conflict. This is again a difficult point to prove because it is never easy to separate the effects of the incidents themselves—say, Israeli soldiers beating Palestinian
protesters—from the effects that can be attributed to the way the incidents were
covered. U.S. officials who were interviewed about these issues do suggest that
media coverage of the *intifada* played a "key contributing factor" to Secretary of
State Shultz's decision to intervene in the dispute (Makovsky, 1989). The point is
that it is virtually impossible for political leaders to ignore any political conflict that
is being placed so high on the public agenda.

In sum, the bulk of evidence suggests that the news media did play an independent and significant role in the early stages of the *intifada*. Their independence is
demonstrated by the inability of the Israelis to control their presence or the coverage
and by the decision of the international press to offer an unusually large amount of
sympathetic coverage to the Palestinian story. The centrality of the news media is
illustrated by the way in which the behavior of both Israelis and the Palestinians was
altered by the news media and the evidence that suggests that the amount of press
attention altered the political balance of power between the two sides.

The Gulf War

The Gulf War offers a stark contrast to the *intifada* in terms of the ability of the
more powerful antagonist to control the informational environment. The lack of
independence experienced by the press is already well documented (Fialka, 1991;
Gannett Foundation, 1991). The purpose of this essay is to argue that the lack of
independence can be better understood by examining the three factors that have
been emphasized throughout this work. In addition, we also want to point to some
exceptions in which the allied domination over the news media faltered, because
such variations offer critical insights about how the role of the news media can
change over the course of a conflict.

The Initiation and Control of Events

In direct contrast to the situation that characterized the *intifada*, the United States
and its allies had a great deal of control over the Gulf War. It was the allies who
decided when the air war would begin, when the ground war would start, and when
the war would end. With the possible exception of the battle of Khafji, the Iraqis
spent most of the war buried in their bunkers. The ability to control the battlefield

offers antagonists an important advantage in planning information campaigns because all of the press releases and briefings can be prepared in advance. Jack Nelson, the Washington bureau chief of the *Los Angeles Times*, made a similar point in a round-table discussion about the media held soon after the end of the war.

> . . . I think the priorities about what to cover were clearly laid down in the briefing sessions. One day you had to focus on particular kinds of air-raids, another day you had to focus on polluting the Gulf or the burning of Kuwait, another day you had to focus on the prisoners of war. The initiative came from the government itself, or from the military (Gannett Foundation, 1991, p. 73).

In the case of the Gulf War it was the Iraqis who were reacting, or, more accurately, not reacting to the actions of the allies. One of the senior officers who dealt with the news media during the Gulf War was able to actually plan months in advance the types of news stories that the press would cover during different phases of the campaign. Thus, he had his staff prepare personal interest stories about the troops during the buildup stage and to find the proper Air Force films highlighting the latest technology during the air war. The allies were rarely surprised by the events in the Gulf War, and this ensured that they were also seldom surprised by media coverage of the war.

Regulating the Flow of Information

The level of informational control applied by the allies and the Iraqis is well known. Indeed, these press restrictions were the major "media story" of the war. The news media complained bitterly and publicly about the constraints being placed on their coverage. This story appeared, for example, in *Time* magazine on January 21, 1991, and is typical of the genre:

> As soon as the Pentagon rules for dealing with the news media were made final, the presidents of the four major U.S. television news networks sent a letter of protest to Secretary of Defense Dick Cheney. So did editors of *The Washington Post*, the *Chicago Tribune*, the *Philadelphia Inquirer*, *Time* and the Associated Press, while *The New York Times* issued a similar statement. The network presidents charged that the rules "go far beyond what is required to protect troop safety and mission security . . . and raise the specter of government censorship of a free press."

The methods of information control were both direct and effective. All contacts with the reporters were centralized through "JIBs": Journalist Information Bureaus. Pools were organized to ensure that the flow of information could be strictly regulated and all stories had to be submitted to the military censor for approval. Reporters were forced to sign secrecy agreements in which they agreed, among other things, not to send any pictures of American casualties without censor approval.[11] The vast majority of the information was provided in briefing sessions in Dhahran and Riyadh, where the military supplied not only all of the information, but also many of the films that would be shown around the world.

The journalists were extremely frustrated by their lack of independence but there was little they could do about it. One journalist said he'd never known reporters under such pressure to explain to their editors why they couldn't get to the story. It was impossible to check the accuracy of the facts that they were being given. The journalists' anger was hardly diminished after the war was over, when many discovered how many stories they had gotten wrong. One reporter was asked whether he felt that their stories were influenced by the need to side with the allies:

> No, I really think the information was simply not available. In a lot of the stories I was writing at the last day or two of the ground war and the week afterward, every single one of those stories is wrong with regard to every single fact. I reported, for example, that the war stopped because the Americans ran out of targets, and it simply wasn't true. If I was told there were a hundred facts, maybe ninety of them have proven false.

The exact statistics are less important than the sense of frustration that lies behind them. The evidence suggests that conventional wisdom is quite accurate: the allies in the Gulf War were able to exercise a remarkable amount of informational control. As Lawrence Grossman, a former president of NBC News and PBS, put it, "the press was held captive" (Gannett Foundation, 1991).

As suggested earlier, a good deal of the journalists' problems were related to the geography of the area, which made it almost impossible for them to leave the briefing sessions. They needed military vehicles to get to the scenes of battles; a number of reporters who went out on their own got lost, and Bob Simon was captured by the Iraqis. One of the senior press officers compared the situation in the Gulf with his experience in Vietnam.

> For those reporters who I had escorted as a young lieutenant in Vietnam it was a very nostalgic trip for both of us. They realized that this was not Vietnam, the size of California where you could run out and get a quick fire fight, come back to the Hotel Rex, file your story and that was the end of it.

The difficulty in obtaining information was not just a matter of geography, however, for the situation in Washington was not much better. One of the correspondents describes the effects of the war on the flow of information in the Pentagon.

This building tightened up like a ship at war. It went to general quarters. You just couldn't talk to people. Nobody returned phone calls. People wouldn't go for walks with you like they sometimes do to give a sense of what was going on, because they just didn't know what was happening, because the information was so tightly controlled and funnelled from the Central Command right to the war room, that I don't know what else we could have done . . . . I think that as long as there is an environment like the one this war occurred in, with the short, very rigid, chain of command and with a powerful press spokesman, we are just going to have to accept the facts as the Pentagon tells us here at the briefing.

A Few Cracks in the Wall

While the ability of the allies to regulate the flow of information was extraordinary, there were several points during the war in which the news media did achieve some degree of independence. An examination of these exceptions offers important lessons about how situational variables can alter the role of the news media. One of the most revealing of these examples is the change in the media's ability to collect information as the allies moved from the air war to a ground war. In an air war, the inability of journalists to accompany the military into battle severely limits their independence and enhances the capability of the government to control the informational environment. Knightly (1975) reports a similar set of circumstances during the latter stages of the Vietnam War in which the bombing of North Vietnam, Laos, and Cambodia was given much less publicity than the ground war despite the enormous difference in the amount of devastation carried out in the two arenas.

The ground war in the Gulf conflict was extremely brief. Nevertheless, all of the journalists and military people who were interviewed agreed that the control over correspondents began to break down when the army and the marines began to move into Kuwait and Iraq (see also Fialka, 1991; Young, 1991). The military was especially concerned with the increasing number of "unilaterals" who were breaking away from the pools and independently collecting information. One of the officers in charge of dealing with the media talked about this change.

The only breakdown I felt occurred was once the ground war started; you had unilaterals out there on their own and actually providing some pretty decent coverage in cases. What we had anticipated that never occurred was that once the ground war started, the entire country would be a kind of garrison. That is to say, that there would not be unrestricted travel on the roads of Saudi Arabia, that news media who were trying to get into the battlefield would essentially be stopped on the road. Well, that didn't happen . . . Our great fear was that pool reporters seeing that would say, why do I have to put up with these pool restrictions which most of them hated.

The journalists were well aware of the opportunities that the ground war offered even before it began. Consider the following comments by one of the television reporters who covered the war:

> I was one who did not feel that it was worth all the risks before the ground war started . . . in terms of breaking the pool rules because I thought the time to break them would be the time when you'd actually get something out of breaking them, which would be during the ground war. I thought the ground war would go on for some weeks and this would be the time to go out . . . So I felt the time to break them was when the ground war started and then just say "fuck you" to the Army and do whatever you wanted to do. And by then things would be too chaotic to really deal with it.

In the final analysis this had very little impact on the role of the media because the ground war was so short. It is a critical reminder, however, that the informational environment is subject to change, and with it the level of antagonist control and media dependence.

There were also three other incidents in which the allies lost control over the flow of information, and one of them may have played an important role in the war ending when it did. The three events which we would include in this category would be: the bombing of what the Iraqis claimed was a baby milk factory, the destruction of the bunker in Baghdad, and at the very end of the war, the "Highway of Death" in which about a thousand Iraqi army vehicles were trapped and destroyed by allied aircraft.

In each of these cases the pictures of destruction and devastation offered a very different frame of the war from that promoted by the allies. The Iraqis were providing a certain amount of information to the press throughout the war, especially through Peter Arnett, the CNN correspondent in Baghdad. Nevertheless, the images coming out of these three incidents were far more vivid and powerful and the United States found itself very much on the defensive in its attempt to discount Iraqi claims about the brutality of the American attack. One reporter was asked whether in his opinion these pictures had any effect on American policy:

> Oh yeah. I think the military and the administration realized right away that they couldn't stand to make more of these. That the public was so gungho on the war that they'd overlook the first couple, but it became clear that if there were a lot of images of civilians killed, that wasn't going to work. I think they were hypersensitive about that. I think it may have affected what Bush did when he ended the war, brought it to a close and saved the Iraqi

army from a massacre. He knew the media images of a massacre wouldn't be helpful.

The fact that reporters and photographers were able to reach Highway Six near the end of the war certainly had an effect on the tone of war coverage. The pictures of charred bodies strewn over a wide space of land and the decision by the news media to label the roadway the "Highway of Death" certainly had an important effect on media frames of the war. There is at least one serious piece of investigative reporting (*Newsweek*, January 20, 1992) which offers convincing evidence that the images which were being shown from the "Highway of Death" did indeed have an important effect on the recommendation of Joint Chiefs Chairman Colin Powell to stop the allied attack. The decisions leaders must make in these situations must be based not only on the objective question of whether more bloodshed is militarily justified, but also the effects such pictures could have on public opinion.

More than anything else, these exceptions illustrate how quickly the role of the news media can change. The Iraqis depended on the news media to mobilize international opinion against the American attack. As the far weaker antagonist, it was their only way of defending themselves against a far superior war machine. Although there were brief moments of success in this area, the Americans' overall control over the informational environment precluded any independent and significant role for the news media. The conflict, for the most part, ran its expected course with the far more powerful allied forces defeating the Iraqis.

The Extent of Consensus Among the Elite

It is extremely revealing to examine the changing level of political consensus among elites in the United States about the Gulf War and its effects on news coverage. An important key to understanding media coverage of this conflict can be found by examining the changing amount of congressional opposition to the war. The great debate about whether or not to allow the president to go to war was a fairly close one, and the news media offered a great deal of coverage of that controversy. The final vote in the Senate took place on January 13, 1991, when the president was given the green light, by a vote of 52 to 47, to use military force. The Congress was mostly silent, however, after the outbreak of the war, apart from expressing support for the troops.

This change in political consensus is reflected directly in the way the news media covered the conflict. A *Tyndall Report* published by ADT research (Gannett Foundation, 1991) conducted a content analysis of television news stories that appeared before and after the outbreak of war. They found that in the three weeks prior to the war, "controversy stories" outnumbered "yellow ribbon" stories (in support of the troops) by 45 to 8, but in the following six weeks "ribbon" stories dominated 36 to 19.

One of the journalists who was based in Washington talked about the difference between covering the story during "Desert Shield" (the buildup period) and "Desert Storm." When asked whether or not it was easier to get information before the war broke out, he replied:

> Yes, because more people had opinions. There were more critics, critics in the Congress, critics in the think tanks. But once there was a declaration of war, basically because Congress voted and the U.S. committed its young men and women to fight, the critics were no longer critical. They immediately turned to support the Commander in Chief. In some ways it was a nice thing to see and feel but if the war would have lasted longer, I think people would have raised more questions about what we were doing.

It is important to bear in mind that even when there was a good deal of dispute among the American elite, there was never any disagreement about the need to stop Saddam Hussein. The injustice frame that was being promoted by Iraq never even competed with the American claims about Iraqi aggression. The debate within the United States centered on the most effective means of carrying out that goal: economic sanctions or military intervention. These were the competing frames that appeared in the Western news media and neither could offer much help to Iraq in its attempt to mobilize support from third parties.

Behavioral and Political Outcomes

It is not clear which is the more difficult task: to demonstrate that the media did have an influence on a conflict or to prove that they did not. The notion of a significant media influence, it will be recalled, is based on whether or not the political condition or the behavior of the antagonists appears to have been altered by the presence of the news media or the coverage that was given to the conflict. The basic question is whether or not the news media had any effect on American behavior, Iraqi behavior, or on the course of conflict.

None of the interviewees could point to incidents in which either the presence of the news media or press coverage had an effect on the allied military operations in the Gulf. The direction of influence seems to have been one sided: the allies seem to have had a great deal of impact on the news media, but the media does not seem to have had any influence on either of the antagonists. While it is difficult to be certain as to whether the allied war plan was changed due to any media coverage, there is no logical reason why it should have. As discussed, Western press coverage was generally supportive of the allies and the discussion of "collateral" damage was limited.

The cases of the bunker and the "Highway of Death" may again stand as exceptions to this rule because, as discussed, there were several reports in the news media that suggested that the military command had carried out some changes in policy (e.g., less bombing of bunkers) because of these incidents. In general, however, it appears that the allies carried out their basic war plan without interruption from either the news media or Iraq.

Another piece of evidence that supports the claim of minimal effects is that Iraq was unable to use the news media to mobilize third parties into the conflict. Western public opinion remained highly supportive of the war effort throughout the war.[12] Although the Arab press may have been much less enthusiastic about the war, none of the Arab coalition partners abandoned the cause, and no new antagonists joined the battle after it had begun. There were protests in several Arab capitals that may have been accelerated through extensive coverage of Iraqi casualties in some of the Arab press. Even here, however, there is no reason to believe that any of these events had any effect on the course of the war.

In short, the Gulf War took its predictable course with the powerful allied forces defeating the weak Iraqis. The specific conditions of the Gulf War provided the allies with almost total control over the informational environment, and this precluded an autonomous role for the news media. The press may have served as a useful tool for defeating the Iraqis but had no independent effect on either the course of the war or its outcome.

Israelis and Palestinians During the Gulf War

The discussion now returns to the role of the news media in the Israeli-Palestinian conflict, but moves forward in time to the period of the Gulf War. The reason for choosing this case is to show once again how the role of the news media can change over time and circumstance. The central players in this conflict remained the same but the political context changed dramatically and with it the ability of Israel to control the informational environment. The role of the news media changed accordingly; the American and Israeli press who had been so independent and active during the early stages of the *intifada* became mere electronic bulletin boards for the promotion of Israeli frames of the conflict.

It is helpful to begin by placing these events in historic and political context. In the years following the early stages of the *intifada*, the story was no longer considered newsworthy. The Palestinian protests and the Israeli reaction had all but disappeared from the American press and had been driven off the front pages of the Israeli newspapers as well. As with all such conflicts, the *intifada* had become routine and the international news media had moved on to cover other parts of the world.

The Iraqi invasion of Kuwait in August of 1990 brought the Palestinian issue back to international attention but within a very different political context. Saddam Hussein attempted to link the solution of the Gulf crisis to a resolution of the

Israeli-Palestinian conflict, implying that he would withdraw from Kuwait if the Israelis would also withdraw from the West Bank and Gaza. The P.L.O.'s decision to support Iraq's stand against the Western world helped complete the frame in which the Iraqis and the Palestinians were the enemies of the West while Israel found itself firmly in the Western camp.

The Palestinian issue no longer had an independent media frame. The Palestinian story had become a secondary subplot within the major story of the Gulf crisis. This, as well as the three factors we have been stressing throughout this chapter, all had an important impact on the ability of the Israelis to take control of the informational environment.

The Control Over Events and the Flow of Information

The Israelis took complete control over the territories during the Gulf War in order to ensure that there would be no Palestinian actions. The Israeli authorities had several reasons for concern in this area. A few months before the outbreak of the war the Palestinians had carried out a large protest on the Temple Mount in Jerusalem which had resulted in the deaths of twenty-two Palestinians and a storm of protests from the outside world. In addition, several Palestinian spokespeople had also suggested that they would be carrying out terrorist actions against Israel and the United States if war were to break out with Iraq.

The Israeli government initiated a curfew lasting for most of the war. The Palestinians remained in their homes with occasional respites for getting food and water. Although the curfew was mainly intended as a means of preventing any Palestinian sabotage, it also created an extremely effective means of regulating the flow of information about the Palestinian issue. As a closed military area, reporters were not allowed to travel without military escorts.

There was, however, another important factor that allowed the Israelis to take control of the flow of information during the Gulf War. The major Israeli story of the war was the Iraqi SCUDs falling on the cities of Israel. In anticipation of the war, the Israelis had spent months setting up large press centers in both Tel Aviv and Jerusalem which were designed to serve as the exclusive sources of information for all arriving journalists. The centers were staffed on a twenty-four-hour basis with official spokespeople and contained a large variety of technological hardware designed to allow the international press to receive and distribute the Israeli perspective on the war in the most efficient way possible.

The contrast from the days of the *intifada* was a striking one. The journalists had all moved from the occupied territories to the official press centers in Tel Aviv and Jerusalem. The Israelis, instead of reacting to negative stories, were now in full command of the press who were eagerly awaiting every briefing. The number of reporters covering Israel went from three hundred to over a thousand; the new arrivals were especially dependent on official sources of information owing to their lack of contacts in the area. One of the reporters who covered both the *intifada* and the present stage of the conflict commented on the change.

> . . . During the *intifada* things had become strained, but always cordial and professional. During the war, Israel had a story that it was happy to tell the world. They also had a lot of fresh journalists here to sort of sell the story to. They made a big effort to keep journalists busy with half-way decent briefings all the time. They always had events for them. They would have these briefings, sometimes two a day. And if they had it in Tel Aviv they would simulcast it back to Jerusalem. I could see they were fairly well attended. It was a good vehicle to get the message out, to get the right spin on the story.

The Israelis had understandably become a much more valued source of information than the Palestinians. Thus, not only were journalists less *able* to gather information about the Palestinian perspective, they were also less *willing* to do so. This had an important effect on the quantity and quality of their interactions with the Palestinians. The territories had become one of the minor stories of the war and those few foreign reporters who were assigned to the territories considered it a bad break for their careers.

The fact that the territories had such low news value may also explain why there was so little protest from the international press about their inability to independently travel in the territories and collect information. Again this is in direct contrast to the days of the *intifada* in which any restrictions on press movements brought scores of protest from around the word. There are of course other explanations for this lack of concern over the closing of the territories, but judgments about the relative unimportance of Palestinian sources certainly played a part in this process.[13]

The Extent of Consensus Among the Elite

The level of consensus among the political elite within Israel and the international community was also very different than that which characterized the *intifada*. The left and right in Israel were not only in agreement with the government's decision to exercise restraint against Iraq, there was also a wide consensus of antagonism against the Palestinians for their support of Iraq. The most well-known example of this phenomenon was when Knesset member Yosi Sarid, an established member of the left wing opposition, came out with a public statement saying that the Palestinians would have to "look for him" when the war was over.

The Palestinians were attempting to promote two major frames during the war. The first was the linkage frame which they hoped would be adopted as part of the final peace agreement between Iraq and the Allies. The second frame might be best labelled "the curfew as oppression" frame; it was a plea for help to ease the burden of the curfew which had, for all intents and purposes, placed the Palestinian population under house arrest for the duration of the war. Neither of these frames had any domestic sponsors in Israel and there were also very few international sponsors outside of the country.

The third frame is perhaps best called the "dancing on the roofs" frame, which calls attention to the joy Palestinians felt at the sight of SCUDs raining down on Israeli cities. One of the ironic twists of this war is that the Palestinians seemed no less enthusiastic about this frame than the Israelis (although they might not agree with the frame's title). Palestinian sources frequently called up Israeli and foreign reporters to cheer the SCUD attacks on Israel and sent in photographs and video tapes of such actions as the building of large cardboard SCUDs in honor of Saddam Hussein. Although some Palestinian leaders did express some reservations about the pro-Iraqi position, their voices were drowned out by the overwhelming majority of sources.

All of this served to increase the consensus among the Israeli elite and the news media against the Palestinians. Some of the more revealing interviews took place with the Israeli correspondents who cover the Palestinian beat. These journalists, all of whom speak fluent Arabic, are normally quite sympathetic to the Palestinian case. Consider, however, the words of one of the leading reporters in this field.

> I think something happened to all the journalists during the war. We all became part of the Israeli consensus. Everyone had their own political views and everyone received a slap in the face. We suddenly felt ourselves part of the consensus of the whole country. It was war, with SCUDs falling all over the place. Suddenly we began to look at them differently, as people, and as sources. Suddenly, these people who we talk to day in and day out seemed different and we were no longer buying the images they were selling.

A Lack of Outcomes

It can be stated then that the Gulf War offered the Israelis an almost unprecedented control over the informational environment. The news value of Israeli officials had risen to a much greater extent than their Palestinian counterparts, and it was the Israeli story of destruction—not Palestinian suffering—that dominated press reports coming out of Tel Aviv and Jerusalem. In carrying out a curfew, the Israelis ensured that the Palestinians could not divert the world's attention from the story of the SCUDs.

It is important to stress, however, that the Palestinian angle could have developed differently if the Israelis had not been able to take control of the territories.

Massive protests in the occupied territories followed by Israeli reprisals could have led to many more incidents such as the Temple Mount, and the calls for linkage might have multiplied. Questions of morality aside, when one controls the territory one also controls the story.

To assess the relative success of the antagonists in promoting their frames to the news media, it is important to consider the strategic goals of each side. The Palestinians and the Iraqis both hoped to make the Israeli occupation a major issue of the Gulf conflict, while the allies and the Israelis wanted to keep the world focused on the invasion of Kuwait. The Iraqis hoped to use the Palestinian issue as a wedge to divide the coalition, and the international news media were an important element of this strategy. While the chances of such a strategy succeeding were never great, Israel's ability to keep the Palestinians off the news agenda made it even more difficult.[14]

The results of this struggle can be better assessed by looking at how Palestinians were covered during the war. *The New York Times* will serve as an example for this exercise.[15] An examination of the news and editorials about Palestinians that were published in that paper during the actual war shows that by far the most important frame was the strategic one in which some type of reference was made to the Palestinian support of Iraq. There are over two hundred and fifty stories in which this link was made (albeit often as an aside) and this serves as an important reminder of how specific frames are shaped by the more general political context.

The Israeli-Palestinian conflict received relatively little attention during the war, despite the attempts of Iraq and the P.L.O. The news items and editorials that dealt with this issue can be classified under three major categories. There were fifteen articles that dealt with the hardships Palestinians were enduring under the curfew and about an equal number that talked about Palestinians cheering the SCUD attacks on Israel. Finally, there were only seventeen articles that talked about whether or not to link the Palestinian problem to Iraq's withdrawal from Kuwait. Revealingly, the vast majority of these pieces were devoted to reporting about a variety of Western leaders who had rejected such a linkage.

This distribution of coverage highlights the American perspective on the Gulf War: The major question for the United States concerned the array of forces who were allied with each side. *The New York Times* was clearly reflecting this perspective and thus the Palestinians were only newsworthy within the more general political context. The Palestinian story was certainly linked to the Gulf conflict, but not in a particularly sympathetic frame. This line of argument could lead us to conclude that the major reason for the lack of sympathy for the Palestinians in the American press at this time was that—in direct contrast to the *intifada*—the Americans and the Israelis were on the same side. Whereas the Americans had good control over the press at this time, any successes in this area should be attributed to American power rather than anything that was going on in Israel or the occupied territories.

There is much truth to this claim but it does not negate the more central argument that has been made throughout this piece. The high level of international consensus was indeed one of the factors which made it much more difficult for both the Iraqis and the Palestinians to promote their frames to the Western news media. The Israelis' control over the informational environment in their part of the world was simply one more element in the more general process of emasculating the press that took place during the Gulf War. The Americans and the Israelis worked together on a number of fronts during this period and the news front was an important one.

The point of all this is to show how the role of the news media changes along with political circumstance. Palestinian hardships, and the evils of occupation, which under different circumstances could have been a major news story, became a relatively marginal item in the Western coverage of the war. The news media did not play an important role in this stage of the Israeli-Palestinian conflict. There was no international pressure on Israel to ease the Palestinian burden, the Palestinians remained under curfew for the duration of the war, and the possibility of linkage remained off of the international agenda.

What lessons can we draw from this case when compared to the others which have been discussed? We would suggest two. First, the situational variables we have been emphasizing throughout this chapter are directly related to the more general political process. The ability of the challenger to initiate events, the flow of information from the antagonists to the news media, and the extent of consensus among elites all depend on the nature of the political climate at the time of the transactions. The differences between the role of the news media in the *intifada* and in this later stage of the Israeli-Palestinian conflict are best understood by looking at the effects of the political process on the informational environment. The transactions among the Israelis, the Palestinians, and the news media were completely altered by Iraq's invasion of Kuwait, and the international crisis that followed.

The second lesson comes from the fact that the Israeli-Palestinian conflict was framed by the Western press as a minor story during the Gulf War. Indeed, as alluded to earlier, the question of whether or not to include this issue as a central part of the Gulf conflict was a major bone of contention between the allies and Iraq. This teaches us that those who look at the role of the media in such conflicts should be just as conscious of what is left out as what is included. Many challengers are simply ignored by the news media and in these cases the powerful are under no pressure to even rebut the arguments of their rival. The agenda-setting function of the news media not only tells us what to think about, but also what to ignore.

While the allies were able to mobilize the news media in the war against Iraq, the Israelis managed to neutralize the news media by turning the Palestinian question into a nonissue.[17] This was especially easy during this period, for the world was clearly focused on the Gulf.[18] It will be remembered that during the *intifada*, some Israeli officials suggested that the best they could hope for was no news at all. In the case of the Gulf War, they finally got their wish.

Conclusion

In any unequal conflict the weaker side's only chance of victory is to mobilize third parties to intervene on its behalf. Protesters hope to find others to support them, terrorists hope to shock the world into reacting, and weaker countries seek international support against the strong. The struggle over the news media is a critical element in this process and it is perhaps ironic that those who need the news media the most also find it the hardest to enlist.

The point of this chapter has been to move beyond this truism and ask about the conditions under which the news media play an independent and significant role in such conflicts. The ability of the powerful to frame the story, it has been argued, is directly related to its ability to take control of the informational environment. This control, in turn, depends on three factors: the ability to initiate and control conflict events, the ability to regulate the flow of information, and the degree of consensus among elites.

The case studies illustrated how the role of the news media varies: whereas they played an independent and significant role in the *intifada*, their role in the two facets of the Gulf War was much more marginal. As a final teaser, let us consider one more unequal conflict in which the news media seems to have played a significant role. In the aftermath of the Gulf War, a serious conflict emerged between the Kurds and the Iraqis in Northern Iraq. The Kurds, assumedly with American encouragement, were carrying out a rebellion against Saddam Hussein. Hussein responded in force and the Kurds were being routed by the Iraqi army.

At this point of the strife the George H.W. Bush administration had no intention of intervening in the conflict. The important point to bear in mind is that neither Iraq nor the United States was able to take control of the informational environment. The news media that had been shackled during the war was now covering the Kurdish story with almost complete independence. The reporters were free to roam around the area, talk to whomever they pleased, and the TV cameras were brought out in force. Here, as in the case of the *intifada*, the news media placed a major emphasis on the Kurds as victims, and Bush was being blamed for the Kurdish plight. *Newsweek* (April 15, 1991), for example, featured a destitute Kurdish child on their cover with the caption "Why won't he help us?"

The tragic pictures that were being sent around the world may very well have had something to do with Bush's change of heart when he reluctantly decided to intervene in that conflict. Daniel Schorr puts it very directly, based on his own observations of the process:

> Score one for the power of the media, especially television, as a policy-making force. Coverage of the massacre and exodus of the Kurds generated public pressures that were instrumental in slowing the hasty American military withdrawal from Iraq and forcing a return to help guard and care for the victims of Saddam Hussein's vengeance (Schorr, 1991, p. 21).

If these assertions are accurate, the media played an important equalizing role in that conflict by serving as a catalyst for the mobilization of third parties. In order to add one more twist to this story it is useful to think back to the Kurdish rebellion in 1988, when even more Kurds were killed. The news media were not able to cover those events and the conflict took its expected course, with the Iraqis defeating the Kurds.

The point of these final musings is to illustrate the complexity of the problem. The role of the news media tends to vary over time and circumstance, and theory must deal with these changes. Hopefully the ideas that were presented in this piece will contribute to a more systematic approach to the issue.

Afterword

This monograph was written in the fall of 1992, while I was a Fellow at the Joan Shorenstein Center on the Press, Politics and Public Policy. I wish to thank the entire staff of the Center for the warm and gracious support they provided during my stay there. I want to especially thank Marvin Kalb, the director of the Center, for all of his guidance, Fred Schauer, who provided a detailed critique of this piece, and Edith Holway, who was willing and able to leap over every conceivable administrative hurdle to help.

I also want to single out Bill Gamson who worked very closely with me on this project. He was a constant source of ideas and criticism and contributed countless hours going over earlier drafts of this piece. This study was also presented at a seminar of the Boston College Media Research and Action Project, which is directed by Bill together with Charlotte Ryan. I want to thank the members of the seminar, especially David Ryan, for all of their comments which proved helpful in writing the final version of the paper.

Endnotes

1. This statement is not meant to imply that leaders who carry out civil disobedience aspire to be beaten, but that those with experience in this area realize the costs and benefits of such events.
2. Due to the delicate nature of the interviews we promised all interviewees total confidentiality.
3. Those who might be concerned about the relatively small number of interviews will be reassured by the fact that the observations expressed by these informants were remarkably consistent. In all three cases the interviews were not stopped so much because of a lack of time or resources but rather due to the fact that they had become mostly repetitive.
4. The law and order frame did resonate much better in the Israeli press (Roeh and Nir, 1993; Collins and Clark, 1993; Wolfsfeld, 1993).
5. The army justified the bans by arguing that the presence of reporters tended to increase the level of violence. Indeed, most of the television reporters who were interviewed acknowledge that the cameras did have an effect on the level of protest violence.
6. Such cameras were in fact distributed to Palestinians during later stages of the *intifada*.
7. Due to the dependency of journalists on elected officials one might argue that a multi-party system offers somewhat more independence for journalists than a two-party system.
8. It is noteworthy that [at the time this chapter was written, in 1992] the claims about the influence of the media on the *intifada* had all but disappeared. The *intifada* continued in a rather different format and the Western media rarely covered it. The fact that the *intifada* continued without much media coverage did not, however, negate the possibility of media influence in the early stages of the protest. It merely reinforces the idea

that the news media is not the sole reason for violence and that the relative centrality of the media is always subject to change.

9. Those who disagree with this conclusion point to the fact that many very violent demonstrations also occurred without the news media. This is certainly the case but does not contradict the argument being made here for two reasons. First, the press is only one of the factors that can have an effect on the intensity of protest and the fact that demonstrations also occur for other reasons does not discount its importance. Second, the level of violence used by soldiers is likely to increase when the news media is absent, and this is still a media effect. This is an especially important point to bear in mind when one attempts to measure the amount of violence on the basis of the number of dead and injured among protesters. Where possible, therefore, researchers should attempt to distinguish between the effects of the news media on protest violence and on the violence carried out by the police or the military.

10. There is an important distinction between the electronic media and the print media in this regard. Most of those interviewed argued that the electronic media have a much greater effect on protests. We would offer two explanations for this phenomenon. One is that the electronic media, especially television, are seen as more powerful and therefore people are more likely to respond to their presence. The second explanation is that protesters understand the need to give television some type of action to film.

11. Part of the reason for this regulation was concern that relatives might learn about the casualties from the news media before the military could inform them.

12. It could be argued that the media helped the U.S. government maintain this high level of international support but that would not be an *independent* effect.

13. Other reasons given by the correspondents were that they were much more willing to accept such restrictions when Israel was involved in a genuine war and that one could hardly complain when the Americans were doing the exact same thing in the Gulf. It should also be remembered that it was considered dangerous to travel far from home during the war for one never wanted to be too far from a sealed room.

14. Those who would mock the Iraqi strategy should bear in mind that both France and the U.S.S.R. proposed peace plans that accepted the link between the two issues. It should also be remembered that Saddam Hussein received more favorable coverage in many non-Western countries, such as Jordan and India.

15. The Nexis archive was used to conduct a search for all articles (including editorials) in which the words Palestinian(s) and Iraq (or Saddam Hussein) were found within 30 words of each other during the actual war. A similar procedure was used for the other results which are presented below.

16. There were also a number of articles about the arrest of Sari Nusseibeh, a Palestinian leader accused of supplying Iraq with information about the location of SCUD attacks on Israel.

17. The Israelis did supply the news media with considerable amounts of information about Palestinians "dancing on the roofs." This became a major story in Israel, but was understandably less salient in the American press.

18. The Syrians also exploited the situation to move further into Lebanon while the Russians carried out an attack on Latvia.

References

Ahluwallia, M.M. "The Press in India's Struggle for Freedom, 1858–1909. *Journal of Indian History*. 38: 599–604 (1960).

Alexander, Y., and Picard, R.G., eds. *In the Camera's Eye: News Coverage of Terrorist Events.* New York: Brassey, 1990.

Alinsky, S.D. *Rules for Radicals.* New York: Vintage, 1971.

Barrier, N.G. *Banned.* London: Allen & Unwin, 1976.

Bennett, W.L. *News: The Politics of Illusion.* New York: Longman, 1990.

Brown, J.M. *Gandhi and Civil Disobedience.* Cambridge, U.K.: Cambridge University Press, 1977.

Collins, C.A., and Clark, J.E. "Structuring the Intifada in A-Far Jerusalem and The Jerusalem Post," in A. Cohen &. G. Wolfsfeld, eds., *Framing the Intifada: People and Media.* Norwood, NJ: Ablex, 1993.

Fialka, J.J. *Hotel Warriors: Covering the Gulf.* Washington, DC: The Woodrow Wilson Center Press, 1991.

Gamson, W.A., *The Strategy of Social Protest.* Belmont, CA: Wadsworth Press, 1990.

Gamson, W.A., and Stuart, D. "Media Discourse as a Symbolic Contest: The Bomb in Political Cartoons." *Sociological Forum*, 7: 55–86 (1992).

Gamson, W., and Wolfsfeld, G. "Movements and Media as Interacting Systems," *The Annals of the American Academy of Political and Social Science*, 528: 114–125, 1993.

Gannett Foundation. *The Media at War: The Press and the Persian Gulf Conflict,* 1991.

Gans, H.J. *Deciding What's News: A Study of CBS Evening News, NBC Nightly News, Newsweek and Time.* New York: Pantheon Books, 1979.

Garrow, D.J. *Protest at Selma.* New Haven: Yale University Press, 1978.

Gervasi, F. *Media Coverage: The War in Lebanon.* Washington, DC: Center for International Study, 1982.

Gitlin, T. *The Whole World Is Watching.* Berkeley: University of California Press, 1980.

Glasgow University Media Group. *War and Peace News.* Philadelphia: Open University Press, 1985.

Goldenberg, E. *Making the Papers: The Access of Resource-poor Groups to the Metropolitan Press.* Lexington, MA: Lexington Books, 1975.

Hallin, D. "Hegemony: The American News Media from Vietnam to El Salvador, A Study of Ideological Change and Its Limits," in D. Paletz, *Political Communication Research.* Norwood, NJ: Ablex, 1987.

Hallin, D. *The Uncensored War.* New York: Oxford University Press, 1986.

Herman, E., and Chomsky, N. *Manufacturing Consent.* New York: Pantheon, 1988.

Knightley, P. *The First Casualty.* New York: Harcourt Brace Jovanovich, 1975.

Lederman, J. *Battle Lines: The American Media and the Intifada.* New York: Henry Holt and Company, 1992.

Lipsky, M. *Protest in City Politics,* Chicago: Rand McNally, 1970.

Makovsky, D. "Media Impact," *The Jerusalem Post Magazine* August 25, 1989: 4, 5, 10.

Mandelbaum, M. "Vietnam: The Television War," *Daedalus: Journal of the American Academy of Arts and Sciences,* Vol. 111, Number 4, (1982).

Morrison, D. E., and Tumber, H. *Journalists at War: The Dynamics of News Reporting During The Falklands Conflict.* London: Sage, 1988.

Olien, C.N., Tichenor, P., and Donohue, G. "Media Coverage and Social Movements," in C. T. Salmon, ed., *Information Campaigns: Balancing Social Values and Social Change.* Beverly Hills, CA: Sage, 1989, p. 139–163.

Paletz, D.L., and Boiney, J. "Researchers' Perspectives" in D.L. Paletz &. A.P. Schmid, eds. *Terrorism and the Media.* Newbury Park, Calif.: Sage, 1992.

Paletz, D.L., and Entman, R.M. *Media, Power, Politics.* New York: The Free Press, 1981.

Patterson, O. "An Analysis of Television Coverage of the Vietnam War," *Journal of Broadcasting,* 28: 397–404, (1984).

Picard, R. G., and Sheets, R.S. Terrorism and the News Media: A Research Bibliography, Part I. *Political Communication and Persuasion,* 4: 65–85, (1987a).

Picard, R. G., and Sheets, R.S. Terrorism and the News Media: A Research Bibliography: Part II. *Political Communication and Persuasion,* 4: 141–152, (1987b).

Roeh, I., and Nir, R. "Reporting the Intifada in the Israel Press: How Mainstream Ideology Overrides 'Quality' and 'Melodrama.'" in A. Cohen and G. Wolfsfeld, eds. *Framing the Intifada: People and Media.* Norwood, NJ: Ablex, 1993.

Ryan, C. *Prime Time Activism: Media Strategies for Grassroots Organizing.* Boston, MA: South End Press, 1991.

Schattschneider, E.E. *The Semi-Sovereign People.* New York: Holt, Rinehart, and Winston, 1960.

Sharkey, J. *Under Fire: U.S. Military Restrictions on the Media From Grenada to the Persian Gulf.* Washington, DC: The Center for Public Integrity, 1991.

Schorr, D. "Ten Days that Shook the White House," *Columbia Journalism Review,* July/August, 1991: 21–23.

Shoemaker, P.J. "The Perceived Legitimacy of Deviant Political Groups," *Communication Research,* 9: 249–286, (1982).

Shoemaker, P.J. "Media Treatment of Deviant Political Groups," *Journalism Quarterly,* 61: 66–75, 82, (1984).

Tichenor, P., Donohue, G., and Olien, C.N. *Community Conflict and the Press.* Beverly Hills, CA: Sage, 1980.

Twentieth Century Fund. *Battle Lines: Report of the Twentieth Century Fund Task Force on the Military and the Media.* New York: Priority Press, 1985.

Wolfsfeld, G. "Introduction: Framing Political Conflict," in A. Cohen and G. Wolfsfeld, eds., *Framing the Intifada: People and Media.* Norwood, NJ: Ablex, 1993.

Wolfsfeld, G. "Media, Protest, and Political Violence: A Transactional Analysis," *Journalism Monographs*, Number 127, (1991).

Wolfsfeld, G. *The Politics of Provocation: Participation and Protest in Israel.* Albany, New York: State University of New York Press, 1988.

Wolfsfeld, G. "Collective Political Action and Media Strategy: The Case of Yamit," *Journal of Conflict Resolution,* 28: 1–36, (1984a).

Wolfsfeld, G. "The Symbiosis of Press and Protest: An Exchange Analysis," *Journalism Quarterly*, 61: 550–556, (1984b).

The Dilemma of Access

Frederick Schauer[1]

With the drumbeats of war come the drumbeats of the press. Predictably and insistently, the onset of war brings demands from the press for more access to military operations, more access to the theaters of war, more access to military personnel, and more access to information about military operations. Under current legal doctrine, however, any such access at all is not guaranteed by the First Amendment, a fact that prompts the mainstream press to make their case more in the courts of public and political opinion than in courts of law. This strategy for securing access has, not surprisingly, frequently been successful, for few political figures achieve political success without constantly heeding the old adage never "to argue with the fellow who buys ink by the barrel." Yet although press access to the machinery of military combat is more available in fact than it is as a matter of judicially recognized legal or constitutional right, the availability of access turns out to be more complex than is often appreciated. More particularly, the unavoidable physical capacity and technological limitations of press access to armies, to military transport, and to the theaters of war are such that press access will almost invariably turn out to be a privilege for the mainstream press. A major consequence of this is that the availability of access to the mainstream press but not (or at least less) to others is likely—at the same time that it provides more information to the public—to entrench mainstream views even further. This entrenchment of mainstream views by virtue of their privileged access will at the same time exacerbate the marginalization of those harsh criticisms of war and military operations that are in times of war in any event more likely to be stifled. Access is thus typically a two-edged sword, simultaneously providing the public with the information it wants and needs while further depriving that same public of a genuinely robust debate about the nation's military endeavors.

I. The Basic Legal Doctrine

Traditionally, First Amendment doctrine has operated as a shield and not a sword.[2] What speakers, writers, and publishers may speak about, write about, or publish with their own resources and their own initiative, with no support or assistance from the state, is virtually unlimited. Although the First Amendment as currently interpreted does allow some restrictions on speech, the restrictions on speech that are permitted are far fewer than exist anywhere else in the world. In extreme cases, civil or criminal actions against libel,[3] incitement to violence,[4] obscenity,[5] child pornography,[6] fighting words,[7] misleading commercial advertising,[8] and invasion of privacy[9] are countenanced, but the fact that the scope of such permissible limitations is far narrower than is the case in even the most open of other liberal democracies is strong evidence of the power of the American negative First Amendment. If the issue is simply the negative[10] First Amendment—whether and when the state can punish or otherwise restrict people from what they would say, write, or publish using only their own resources—describing the American First Amendment as absolute or unlimited is, to be sure, an exaggeration, but it is not much of an exaggeration.

When we turn to the positive First Amendment, however, things appear quite different. If the issue is the extent to which people can speak, write, or publish with their own resources, American First Amendment doctrine looks quite strong, but if the issue is the extent to which the First Amendment requires the state (or certain large non-state entities, such as, say, broadcasters) to provide positive assistance for the activities that the First Amendment negatively protects, the situation is quite different. Not only does the First Amendment not require non-governmental entities to provide space or time to those who would wish to speak,[11] but it also does not, in general, require the state to assist in the process of speaking, writing, newsgathering, or publishing.[12]

The lack of a strong positive conception of the First Amendment is manifested in numerous ways. Perhaps most prominently, the First Amendment does not require that speakers, writers, publishers, or journalists be granted exemptions from laws of general application. This is most controversial in the context of reporters' claims for exemptions—privileges—from generally applicable requirements that citizens disclose information useful to law enforcement authorities.[13] Yet although a significant majority of states have by statute or regulation provided such exemptions,[14] the existing constitutional doctrine as developed by the Supreme Court is such that these exemptions remain largely a matter of legislative or regulatory grace rather than one of First Amendment entitlement.[15]

Much the same applies to access to official documents, to government operations, and to governmentally controlled locations. With the exception of streets, parks, and sidewalks, the traditional public fora,[16] speakers have no constitutionally compelled claim on governmentally owned or controlled premises as a place to engage in First Amendment activities.[17] And with the exception of traditionally open judicial proceedings,[18] neither journalists nor the public at large may rely on the First Amendment in support of claims of access to government records, government operations, or government proceedings.[19] As the Supreme Court has put it, "neither the First Amendment nor the Fourteenth Amendment mandates a right of access to government information or sources of information within the government's control."[20] To the incessant consternation of reporters and others, virtually nothing in the existing judicially created First Amendment legal doctrine compels the Freedom of Information Act, state or federal sunshine laws, or any other form of constitutionally mandated affirmative access to the precincts of the state. Justice Potter Stewart neatly encapsulated the strength of the negative First Amendment and the virtual absence of a positive First Amendment by announcing, off the bench, that "[t]he Constitution itself is neither a Freedom of Information Act nor an Official Secrets Act."[21] As long as the First Amendment remains primarily a negative and not a positive right, a shield and not a sword, press and public access to government operations remains largely not a matter of legal or constitutional right, but instead almost completely a matter of legislative, administrative, or executive grace.

The First Amendment's negative strength and positive weakness is plainly reflected with respect to the First Amendment dimensions of press coverage of issues of war and national security. Highlighted most prominently by *New York Times Co. v. United States*[22]—the case of The Pentagon Papers—the First Amendment under existing judicial interpretations provides extraordinarily strong protection for those who would, even in time of war, criticize the government,[23] criticize the war,[24] give comfort to the enemy,[25] suggest violence against national leaders,[26] mock the military,[27] desecrate national symbols,[28] urge disobedience to law,[29] and even disclose official secrets.[30]

As with First Amendment doctrine generally, however, the strength of the negative First Amendment is to be contrasted with the slimness of the First Amendment's positive guarantees. Access to military bases,[31] to military information, to military personnel, and to the front (or even rear) lines is not guaranteed by current judicial understandings of the First Amendment, or so the courts have generally concluded.[32] Although courts have recently been generous in interpreting existing precedents in ways that increase access to tribunals and other judicial or quasi-judicial proceedings,[33] apart from plausible extensions of the constitutional right of access to judicial proceedings, and apart from the occasional lower court's tentative expressions of a qualified right of access even outside of judicial proceedings,[34] it remains generally the case on the existing doctrine that what access the press has remains a privilege to be granted by the government much more than it is a right to be demanded by either the public or the press. Indeed, it might be fair to note that the existing shape of the legal doctrine shapes press reaction itself. Here as in many other areas in which claimants have a choice of taking their claims to judicial, policy, or political areas, when the law is plainly in one's favor, the venue of choice tends to be the courts. But when, as with the case of access to military operations, the

262 Terrorism, War, and the Press

existing law is heavily against the claims and when the likelihood of the judiciary changing that law is small, the strategy of choice is more likely to be political and rhetorical than legal, a phenomenon that helps to explain what appears to be a high ratio of press anger to press litigation about denial of access or about insufficient access. And although the First Amendment has thus recently served more as a rhetorical prop than as a legal foundation for successful litigation, the results would seem to indicate that this strategy has been far from unsuccessful.

II. Revisiting *The Nation*

Although the government is not required to grant press access to military operations as a matter of existing First Amendment judicial interpretations, it generally does so, presumably for a complex array of prudential and theoretical justifications. This access, of course, is rarely as much as the press desires, and press claims to access to the arenas of war are usually embellished with cries of outrage coupled with interpretations of First Amendment doctrine and historical practice that are somewhere between generous and fabricated. It is interesting to note, for example, that fewer than thirty journalists were present at the invasion of Normandy on June 6, 1944, and that the number of accredited journalists accompanying American troops in most recent operations has been in excess of 1500.[35]

Although press anger at perceived or actual denials of access is, not surprisingly, a focus of frequent press attention, what is less noticed, and certainly less noticed by the press itself, is a First Amendment risk of granting the very access that the press often claims is commanded by the First Amendment. In order to explore this, it is worthwhile looking back a dozen years to one of the more important yet unresolved press access controversies during the war in the Persian Gulf. As is well known, much of the press access during the Gulf War was channeled through press pools, by virtue of which selected members of the press were given relatively wide access to front line operations and locations, on the understanding that the selected members would share their information with those reporters not part of the pools, and on the understanding, endorsed by no less a journalist than Walter Cronkite,[36] that greater access to military operations necessarily entails greater censorship by virtue of the increased awareness of planned military maneuvers that greater access almost inevitably brings.

Not surprisingly, the journalists selected for the press pools were representatives of the major national mainstream media, and reporters from smaller, more marginal, or less mainstream publications were either totally excluded or treated in less favorable ways. As a consequence of this exclusion, a group of left-of-center periodicals, news services, radio stations, writers, and journalists—*The Nation*, *Harper's*, Pacific News Service, *The Guardian*, *The Progressive* magazine, *Mother Jones*, *The L.A. Weekly*, *The Village Voice*, *The Texas Observer*, Pacifica Radio News,

Sydney Schanberg, E.L. Doctorow, William Styron, Michael Klare, and Scott Armstrong—brought suit against the Department of Defense.[37] These plaintiffs claimed a general right of access to military operations, a claim with which the trial judge expressed some qualified sympathy. More significantly, however, they also claimed that the differential access by virtue of which they were excluded from venues available to major media players constituted a form of viewpoint discrimination, among the clearest forms of First Amendment violation.[38]

The significance of this latter claim should not be underestimated. For a claim of unlawful First Amendment discrimination to exist, there need be no positive right in the first instance. As a matter of constitutional law, municipalities need not open their city council proceedings to the public, but if they choose to open those proceedings to Democrats but not Republicans, or only to those who have not or will in the future refrain from criticizing the city council, the discrimination on the basis of point of view constitutes an independent First Amendment violation even though a total exclusion would have been entirely constitutionally permissible.[39]

So too, *The Nation* and its confederates argued, with respect to press pools and other forms of limited access to military operations. The military could have closed all of its operations to everyone, the plaintiffs in the *Nation* case could have conceded for the sake of argument, but even so, opening access to friends but not foes, to the right but not the left, to sympathizers but not to critics, amounted to the independent First Amendment violation that we label viewpoint discrimination.

The speedy termination of the Gulf War prevented the claim from ever being adjudicated. Because the war was over by the time Judge Leonard Sand actually decided the case, he ruled the claim moot, and dismissed the suit on mootness grounds without ever reaching the merits of *The Nation*'s contentions. Not surprisingly, this angered the plaintiffs, but, more importantly, likely pleased the mainstream media whose members had enjoyed privileged access under the pool system. To the consternation of the plaintiffs, *The New York Times, Washington Post, Wall Street Journal,* and the major networks had refused to join *The Nation*'s lawsuit.[40] This reluctance of the mainstream media to side with the less mainstream plaintiffs[41] should come as no surprise. Given that members of the mainstream media were instrumental in setting up the pools and selecting their members (just as they are instrumental in determining what kinds of journalists obtain access to the Congress and to the White House[42]) and given that among the stated criteria for pool inclusion was being a "major publication[] with a long history of covering the military,"[43] it should come as no surprise that the pool system—and indeed any pool system operated by other than a random selection lottery—would have the effect of pitting the mainstream media against the more marginal media. That the comparative beneficiaries of the pool system did not eagerly align themselves with the comparative victims was only to be expected.

III. Differential Access Today

It is possible that the formal pool system will turn out to be a historical anomaly. The pool system was a product of the controversies surrounding press access in Panama and Grenada, and in its purest form it was perhaps restricted only to the Gulf War in 1991. As it has turned out, the controversies surrounding the pool system were such that the type of press pool employed in the Gulf War will not be used again. Already in 2002, especially in the context of Afghanistan, we see signs of somewhat broader access,[44] although not surprisingly we continue to see demands by the press for even greater access.[45]

Yet the elimination of some aspects of the formal pool system does not eliminate the basic problem that the pools, however imperfectly, were designed to address. There are only so many seats on a military aircraft, only so many places that can be given to reporters on a ship of war, and there are only so many reporters who can accompany any military unit without significantly impairing its military effectiveness. And as long as access is thus logistically, physically, and technologically limited, some method of deciding which reporters and which news outlets will get that access remains inevitable.

Consider, for example, the similarity between the issues raised in the *Nation* case and the issues raised very recently in a case entitled *Getty Images News Services Corp. v. Department of Defense*.[46] Unlike *The Nation*, *Mother Jones*, Pacifica Radio News, and their compatriots, the Getty News Services did not represent a particular point of view, and did not represent a point of view especially likely to be unsympathetic to the military. Getty News Services, however, did have the disadvantage of being comparatively small, and thus found itself excluded on that ground from the Department of Defense National Media Pool and excluded on that ground from what it believed was its rightful share of places on military flights to the detention center in Guantanamo Bay. Like *The Nation*, Getty argued that its exclusion represented a constitutionally impermissible form of First Amendment discrimination against smaller news outlets.

Because Getty was included in much of what it demanded prior to the resolution of the suit, its legal action was, like *The Nation*'s, dismissed on procedural grounds relating to standing to sue and to mootness. Nevertheless, the facts uncovered in its lawsuit are revealing. In allocating necessarily limited coverage opportunities, the Department of Defense stressed that it desired a "mix of the media,"[47] with a particular "emphasis on those media organizations reaching a broad audience."[48] Just as with *The Nation*, the consequence of limited access was to privilege the larger news organizations to the detriment of the smaller ones. And just as with *The Nation*, it should come as no surprise that the large news organizations were not among the challengers to the system.

It is not a logical truth that the largest news organizations must be the most centrist. It is possible that large organizations get that way by catering to the full range of political opinion, and that smaller organizations are small because they are, say, dull, rather than because they are iconoclastic. Nevertheless, whatever the logical possibilities may be, it would be astonishing to discover that a preference for "media organizations reaching broad audience" would not turn out to have the effect—possibly intended and possibly not—of privileging more centrist organizations and marginalizing those organizations representing less mainstream and more extreme positions.

The issue turns out to be remarkably similar to the issue presented whenever a political debate is planned.[49] Under one model of a political debate, the debate should be limited to the most "viable" candidates, with those substantially less likely to win being excluded in order to ensure both that there is sufficient attention to the major candidates and that the debate itself not be a vehicle by which minor or "fringe" candidates become more viable than their ability to secure preliminary electoral or financial support would justify. And under another model of a political debate, minor party or other "fringe" candidates will be included, and the debate not limited to the most viable candidates, partly because of the inappropriateness of allowing the debate organizers to determine who is viable and who is not, and partly because of the way in which a debate can be the vehicle in which the voters will be exposed to the widest array of people, personalities, and political opinions.

So too with access to the theaters of war. Under circumstances of physically or technologically limited access—the First Amendment can neither expand the size of a transport aircraft nor add bunks to an already crowded ship of war—granting privileged access to *The New York Times, The Washington Post, The Wall Street Journal, USA Today, Time, Newsweek, People,* ABC, CBS, NBC, CNN, and Fox will ensure that the largest number of people will have the greatest amount of information about a war and the manner in which it is being waged. But this privileged access, necessarily in a world of scarce physical space and scarce technological resources at the expense of smaller and less mainstream news organizations, will also ensure that the range of opinion heard will be narrower, the extent of criticism more constrained, and the style of that criticism less shrill. Simply by virtue of what makes the mainstream the mainstream, maximizing the extent of information will have the almost inevitable tendency to minimize the diversity of reported opinion, and, especially on matters relating to war and national defense, minimize the extent of strongly expressed negative opinion.

As with the dilemma of the political debate, there is no easy answer to this dilemma of access to military operations. When the cameras are off and the notebooks put away, officials of the largest news organizations will argue with some persuasiveness that it is not the job of access to make marginal opinions more mainstream than they in fact are, and will argue as well that claims of equal access without regard to size or audience are arguments for designing an access system so that less popular views get more attention than their popular support would otherwise justify. And in response to these arguments from the mainstream press, representatives of smaller or less centrist organizations will typically attribute the audience size of centrist news organizations less to genuine popular support for those centrist views or the centrist programming of those organizations and more to monopoly power, market failure, historical licensing preferences, and the various other pathologies that make the marketplace of ideas no less susceptible to breakdown than any other marketplace.

In the context of military access, there is no easy answer to this dilemma. As long as access remains a scarce resource, and it is hard to see how it could be otherwise, there are decisions that must be made about how that scarce resource should be allocated. Allocating it to the largest news outlets will increase the information available to the public, but it may do so at the expense of fostering the kind of robust and wide-ranging debate that is as much a goal of the First Amendment as is increased availability of information about government operations. Conversely, ensuring that *The Nation* and its ideological compatriots (as well as those well to the right of the mainstream, although this is likely to be much less of a problem in the context of military operations) have the access necessary to make their voices vivid may widen the scope of debate, but at the expense of greater, even if narrower, information being available to the widest possible segment of the population. At times, as with *The Nation*'s lawsuit a decade ago and Getty News Services' within the last few months, the courts will be the arena for struggling with this dilemma, in part because both access to information and the breadth of political debate are goals fostered by the First Amendment. More often, however, this dilemma will stay out of the courts, in part because the traditional deference of the courts to military decisions makes the likelihood of successful litigation small. Yet even when the arena is not the courts, the dilemma still exists, and it is important to remember that access, like most other goods, does not come without a price.

Endnotes

1. Frank Stanton Professor of the First Amendment, John F. Kennedy School of Government, Harvard University. This material was first presented at the Shorenstein Center's Washington Press Briefing on Terrorism on November 28, 2001.

2. The metaphor of sword and shield is a common one in the context of considering the positive and negative dimensions of the First Amendment. See, for example, *Miami Herald Publishing Co. v. Tornillo*, 418 U.S. 241, 251 (1974); Steven H. Shiffrin and Jesse H. Choper, *The First Amendment: Cases—Comments—Questions* (St. Paul, Minnesota: West Publishing Co., 2d ed., 1996), p. 365–86; Anthony Lewis, "A Public Right to Know About Public Institutions: The First Amendment as a Sword," *Supreme Court Review,* vol. 1980, p. 1ff.

3. *New York Times Co. v. Sullivan.* 376 U.S. 254 (1964).

4. *Brandenburg v. Ohio*, 395 U.S. 444 (1969).

5. *Miller v. California*, 413 U.S. 15 (1973).

6. *New York v. Ferber*, 458 U.S. 747 (1982).

7. *Chaplinsky v. New Hampshire*, 315 U.S. 568 (1942).

8. *Central Hudson Gas & Elec. Co. v. Public Service Comm'n*, 447 U.S. 557 (1980).

9. *Zacchini v. Scripps-Howard Broadcasting Co.*, 433 U.S. 562 (1977).

10. Here I borrow the conventional terminology of positive and negative rights and liberties. See, most prominently, Isaiah Berlin, "Two Concepts of Liberty," in *Four Essays on Liberty* (Oxford: Oxford University Press, 1969), p. 112–72.

11. *Miami Herald Publishing Co. v. Tornillo,* 418 U.S. 241 (1974), rejecting arguments made, most prominently, in Jerome Barron, "Access to the Press—A New First Amendment Right," *Harvard Law Review,* vol. 80 (1967), p. 1641ff. For more contemporary versions of the same argument, see Cass R. Sunstein, *Democracy and the Problem of Free Speech* (New York: Free Press, 1993); Owen Fiss, "Why the State,?" *Harvard Law Review,* vol. 100 (1987), p. 781 ff. Although legislation or regulation requiring access may not violate the First Amendment when applied to the domain of broadcasting, *Red Lion Broadcasting Co. v. FCC,* 395 U.S. 367 (1969), such access is even with respect to broadcasting not guaranteed by the First Amendment itself. *Columbia Broadcasting System, Inc. v. Democratic National Committee,* 412 U.S. 94 (1973).

12. See David Lange, "The Speech and Press Clauses," *UCLA Law Review,* vol. 23 (1975), p. 77ff.; William W. Van Alstyne, "The Hazards to the Press of Claiming a Preferred Position: A Comment on Some New Trends and Some Old Theories," *Hofstra Law Review,* vol. 9 (1980), p. 1ff.

13. See David Murasky, "The Journalist's Privilege: Branzburg and Its Aftermath," *Texas Law Review,* vol. 52 (1974), p. 829ff.

14. Many of the statutes are collected in *Matter of Roche,* 411 N.E.2d 466 (Mass. 1980).

15. The leading case is *Branzburg v. Hayes,* 408 U.S. 665 (1972), rejecting the argument that a reporter's privilege was required as a matter of constitutional law. The Supreme Court reached a similar conclusion regarding search warrants in *Zurcher v. Stanford Daily*, 436 U.S. 547 (1978). The basic holding of *Branzburg* was reaffirmed in *University of Pennsylvania v. EEOC,* 493 U.S. 182 (1990). In practice, however, the qualified nature of

Justice Powell's concurring opinion in *Branzburg*, a vote necessary for the existence of a majority, has opened the door in lower courts for limited arguments for a qualified First Amendment reporter's privilege. Jerome A. Barron and C. Thomas Dienes, *Constitutional Law* (St. Paul, Minnesota: West Publishing. 6th ed., 2003), p. 336.

16. *Schneider v. New Jersey*, 308 U.S. 147 (1939); *Hague v. CIO*, 307 U.S. 496 (1939). See also Geoffrey Stone, "Fora Americana: Speech in Public Places," *Supreme Court Review*, vol. 1974, p. 233ff.; Harry Kalven, Jr., "The Concept of the Public Forum: Cox *v.* Louisiana," *Supreme Court Review*, vol. 1965, p. 1ff.

17. *Houchins v. KQED*, 438 U.S. 1 (1978); *Pell v. Procunier*, 417 U.S. 817 (1974); *Saxbe v. Washington Post Co.*, 417 U.S. 843 (1974).

18. See especially *Richmond Newspapers, Inc. v. Virginia*, 448 U.S. 555 (1980). Also relevant are *Press-Enterprise Co. v. Superior Court*, 478 U.S. 1 (1986), *Globe Newspaper Co. v. Superior Court*, 482 U.S. 596 (1982), and *Press-Enterprise Co. v. Superior Court*, 464 U.S. 501 (1984).

19. See *Zemel v. Rusk*, 381 U.S. 1 (1965).

20. *Houchins v. KQED, Ibid.*, p. 14.

21. Potter Stewart, "Or of the Press," *Hastings Law Journal*, vol. 26 (1975), p. 631ff., p. 636.

22. 403 U.S. 713 (1971).

23. *Cohen v. California*, 403 U.S. 15 (1971).

24. *Bond v. Floyd*, 385 U.S. 116 (1966).

25. *United States v. Robel*, 389 U.S. 258 (1967).

26. *Watts v. United States*, 394 U.S. 705 (1969).

27. *Schacht v. United States*, 398 U.S. 58 (1970).

28. *Spence v. Washington*, 418 U.S. 405 (1974).

29. *Yates v. United States*, 354 U.S. 298 (1957).

30. *New York Times Co. v. United States*, 403 U.S. 731 (1971).

31. *Greer v. Spock*, 424 U.S. 828 (1976).

32. For overviews, see Lisa L. Turner and Lynn G. Norton, "Civilians at the Tip of the Spear," *Air Force Law Review*, vol. 51 (2001), p. 1ff.; William A Wilcox, Jr., "Media Coverage of Military Operations: OPLAW meets the First Amendment," *Army Lawyer*, vol. 1995, p. 42ff.; Kevin Kenealey, Comment, "The Persian Gulf War and the Press: Is There a Constitutional Right of Access to Military Operations?" *Northwestern University Law Review*, vol. 87 (1992), p. 287ff.; [Student] Note, "Assessing the Constitutionality of Press Restrictions in the Persian Gulf War," *Stanford Law Review*, vol. 44 (1992), p. 675ff. See also William E. Lee, "'Security Review' and the First Amendment," *Harvard Journal of Law and Public Policy*, vol. 25 (2002), p. 743ff.

33. See *Detroit Free Press v. Ashcroft*, 303 F.2d 681 (6th Cir. 2002). The fact that a somewhat different result was reached in *North Jersey Media Group, Inc. v. Ashcroft*, 308 F.3d 198 (3d Cir. 2002), also dealing with post–September 11 deportation hearings, indicates that Supreme Court resolution of the issue is likely.

34. See *JB Pictures, Inc. v. Department of Defense*, 86 F.3d 236 (D.C. Cir. 1996); *Flynt v. Rumsfeld*, 180 F. Sup. 2d 174, 175–76 (D.D.C. 2002).

35. See Turner and Norton, *op. cit.* note 32. See more generally Peter Young and Peter Jesser, *The Media and the Military: From the Crimea to Desert Strike* (New York: St. Martin's Press, 1997).

36. See *Electronic Media,* February 25, 1991.

37. *The Nation Magazine, et al. v. United States Department of Defense,* 762 F. Sup. 1558 (S.D.N.Y. 1991).

38. *R.A.v. v. City of St. Paul,* 505 U.S. 377 (1992); *Texas v. Johnson,* 491 U.S. 397 (1989); Susan H. Williams, "Content Discrimination and the First Amendment," *University of Pennsylvania Law Review,* vol. 139 (1991), p. 615 ff.

39. The point was recognized in the specific context of journalist's access by (then) Judge Warren Burger as long ago as 1959. *Frank v. Herter,* 269 F.2d 245, 247–48 (D.C. Cir. 1959).

40. See Jonathan Mandell, "Panel Tackles Role of Media During Gulf War," *Newsday,* May 9, 1991, p. 70.

41. See also Rich Brown, "War of Words on Coverage Continues," *Broadcasting,* March 25, 1991; Craig LaMay, "Media in Gulf War—Outwitted, Outflanked, Outmaneuvered," *The Record,* April 5, 1991, p. B07; Tom Wicker, "Marketing the War," *The New York Times,* May 8, 1991, p. A23.

42. The issues in the context of access to Congress and the White House are remarkably similar to those I explore here, for mainstream press control of press credentialing for the legislative and executive branches of the federal government has produced controversies when the journalist-dominated credentialing bodies have determined that neither advocacy publications nor non-profit Internet publications were entitled to press credentials. See *Schreibman v. Holmes,* 1999 US App LEXIS 25159 (D.C. Cir. 1999); *Consumers Union of United States, Inc. v. Periodical Correspondents' Association,* 515 F.2d 1341 (D.C. Cir. 1975). Indeed, in the recent case of *United Teachers of Dade v. Steiheim,* 213 F. Sup. 2d 1368 (S.D. Fla. 2002), a Florida federal court held unconstitutional the exclusion of a union newspaper from access routinely granted to other newspapers.

43. See Eric Neisser, "A Civil Liberties Review of the War in the Persian Gulf," *New Jersey Law Journal,* March 28, 1001, p. 28.

44. See Lee Hill Kavanaugh, "Soldiers in Chaotic Land Kindle Harmony at Home," *Kansas City Star,* December 9, 2001, p. A1; "Reporters Accompany Marines; First Allowed by Pentagon to Cover Combat," *Commercial Appeal,* November 27, 2001, p. A6.

45. For example, *Flynt v. Rumsfeld,* 180 F. Sup. 2d 174 (D.D.C. 2002), following the *Nation* case in tentatively suggesting the possibility of a qualified right to access. 180 F. Sup. 2d at 175–76.

46. 193 F. Sup. 112 (D.D.C. 2002).

47. 193 F. Sup. 2d at 115.

48. 193 F. Sup. 2d at 115–16.

49. For a rare case in which this very issue has reached the Supreme Court, see *Arkansas Educational Television Comm'n v. Forbes,* 523 U.S. 666 (1998). For analysis, see Frederick Schauer, "Principles, Institutions, and the First Amendment," *Harvard Law Review,* vol. 112 (1998), p. 84ff.

U.S. Government Secrecy and the Current Crackdown on Leaks

Jack Nelson

In the never-ending sparring match between the government and the news media, no subject produces more friction than the practice of leaking classified information. Government officials—at least those who don't leak—denounce the practice. They say it can damage intelligence operations and reduce the government's ability to detect and deter terrorists or other enemies.

Journalists, on the other hand, say they couldn't do their jobs without the leaks. Almost all leaks come from government officials, they point out. And, in an era of managed news and wholesale classification of government documents, such back-channel information is often the only way the public can gain an understanding of what its government is thinking and doing.

Not surprisingly, the debate over leaks has become increasingly heated since the 9/11 terrorist attacks and the showdown with Iraq over giving up any chemical and biological weapons and abandoning its quest to develop weapons of mass destruction. Defense Secretary Donald Rumsfeld called for jail terms for leakers and President Bush joined him in denouncing them. An intelligence official even suggested sending "swat teams into journalists' homes" if necessary to root out reporters' sources.

Ironically, government officials and military officers, from the president on down, routinely authorize leaks for policy or political purposes. On October 20, 2002, Senator Bob Graham of Florida, then Senate Intelligence Committee Chairman, accused the Bush administration of selectively disclosing classified information that corresponds more closely to its political agenda than to national security concerns. In a November 17 (2002) article, for example, *The New York Times* reported the reason government officials confirmed a secret report about monitoring Iraqis in the United States to identify potential terrorist threats was "an apparent attempt to rebut critics in Congress and elsewhere who have complained in recent days that American intelligence agencies are failing in their war on terrorism."

There are many motives for disclosing secrets, of course. Some leaks come from so-called whistleblowers who want to expose what they see as government wrongdoing or inefficiency or mistakes. Some are designed to stir opposition to a pending action. Leaks are also used to launch trial balloons; that is, to float planned policies or decisions in the news media as a way of testing public or political reaction. Leaks are frequently used to shape or spin news coverage. And some officials use leaks to settle political scores or even to curry favor with reporters they think may prove useful.

Today, the basis for taking any legal action against leakers of classified secrets dates back to the Espionage Act of 1917. The statute provides that any person who has information "relating to the national defense and has reason to believe it could be used to harm the United States and willfully transmits the information to an unauthorized recipient" could be subject to prosecution and a 10-year prison sentence. In addition, the government must show an intent to harm the United States or benefit a foreign power—no easy thing to prove. As a result, the ongoing debate centers on attempts to enact a much more sweeping law that would provide for prosecution of anyone who leaks any classified information regardless of intent or damage to national security.

Even before 9/11, proponents of tougher anti-leak laws were on the verge of victory. In fact, in 2000, for the first time in history Congress passed a bill covering the unauthorized disclosure of all forms of classified information. So sweeping was the legislation that leaking patently harmless information could draw up to three years in prison whether or not there was an intent to help a foreign government. The press was caught napping while Congress debated the issue, mostly in secret. Only an unprecedented, last-minute lobbying campaign by media executives and a late flood of editorial columns and news articles persuaded President Clinton to veto the measure, which his administration had supported.

Over the years, the sparring between the press and the government has sprung from what former Senator Daniel Patrick Moynihan has called "a culture of secrecy." Its roots go back to World War I and World War II, and grew tremendously during the Cold War—when the real and imagined dangers of communist subversion combined with the threat of nuclear war raised concern over national security to previously unimagined levels.

Now, despite the end of the Cold War, the number of documents being stamped secret by the government has soared. The total classification actions during the George W. Bush administration's first fiscal year set an all-time record, according to a November 18, 2002, report by the Information Security Oversight Office—the agency charged with overseeing the classification system. In part, the huge surge in classified documents may be attributed to increased national security concerns in the wake of 9/11. However, the Bush administration had a predisposition to secrecy before the terrorist attacks that suggests greater secrecy has become part of the government mindset regardless of the actual sensitivity of the material being classified.

The huge trove of secret information actually encourages leaking. As Justice Potter Stewart said in the Pentagon Papers case, "When everything is stamped secret, nothing is secret." As a result, leaking has been such a routine way of doing business in Washington for so many years that even some government officials say the government would have trouble functioning without some classified information being disclosed to the press.

This discussion paper looks at the long and continuing struggle over the scope of laws to punish leakers and discusses as well the mushrooming of secrets over the years. It also examines efforts to speed up the job of declassifying hundreds of millions of pages of classified material. Finally, it examines the work of an unprecedented group of government and press representatives who meet periodically in off-the-record sessions to discuss ways to protect the most sensitive national security secrets without abridging the public's right to know what its government is doing.

The work of the group—known simply as the "Dialogue"—is the one bright spot for the public's right to know in an administration steeped in secrecy. Working quietly with no public notice, the group contributed to a decision by Attorney General John Ashcroft not to seek a more sweeping anti-leaks law in 2002. The threat of future legislation has not receded, however. In his October 22, 2002, letter to Congress announcing his decision, Ashcroft declared the administration would work with Congress if it should choose to pursue the more sweeping statute.

Even more troubling, the Patriot Act, the Homeland Security Information Act, and the Homeland Security Act, all passed in the aftermath of 9/11, will create a whole new category of secrets and officials empowered to classify information. The new system will encompass virtually all agencies of the federal government and will require huge numbers of state and local government officials, as well as corporate officials who do business with the government, to sign sworn statements they won't disclose classified information.

Historical Overview

Openness in government, as opposed to secrecy, was seen as a democratic value when President Woodrow Wilson was inaugurated in 1913. Beginning in the 1880s, for example, the State Department began publishing an annual review called "Foreign Relations" that was known for its candor. In his book, "Secrecy," Moynihan quoted State Department historian William Z. Slany: "The question of secrecy appears rarely to have risen in the editing of the published documents."

But World War I changed government attitudes about secrecy and press access to defense information. Much of today's structure of secrecy took shape in about 11 weeks in the spring of 1917 while the Espionage Act was being debated by Congress and war hysteria was at a fever pitch. No one fanned the fear of war more than Woodrow Wilson.

In his 1915 State of the Union address, with war clouds on the horizon, Wilson warned of some U.S. citizens of foreign origin "who have poured the poison of disloyalty into the very arteries of our national life. . . ." The government, he said, needed more laws to address the problem and should enact them quickly because "such creatures of passion, disloyalty, and anarchy must be crushed out."

Never before or since has a president spoken in such harsh, vitriolic terms about some of the country's own foreign-born citizens. As the Commission on Protecting and Reducing Government Secrecy, chaired by Moynihan, reported in 1997: "Even during the Cold War, when there were indeed persons of foreign birth living in the United States and actively involved in seditious activities on behalf of the Soviet Union, no president spoke like that. . . . But the telling fact is that the intensity of fear and yes, loathing of those years was never equaled later."

Wilson called specifically for legislation that would make it a crime to disclose all national defense secrets to unauthorized persons. Even though the Senate passed an espionage law in 1916 that included that provision, opposition to it quickly mounted. The debate continued even after war was declared on April 4, 1917. Opponents declared the provisions would amount to prior restraint censoring newspapers on what they could publish and would delegate unlimited power to the president to decide what defense information could be published.

The debate was especially heated in the Senate where William E. Borah, Republican of Idaho, referred to the Sedition Act of 1798—an antecedent of the Espionage Act—as he attacked the pending bill: "Once before in the history of the government we undertook to establish something in the nature of an abridgement of speech and of the press. It was a complete and ignominious failure. It did not serve the objects and purposes of those who fathered it. It accomplished nothing in the way of that which they desired it to accomplish."

Despite heavy lobbying, by President Wilson, Congress dropped the anti-leaks provision before passing the Espionage Act, which became law on June 15, 1917. Though less sweeping than Wilson desired, it banned the unlawful obtaining of national defense information and the unlawful disclosure of such information to a foreign government or its agents. It also included a provision punishing certain "seditious or disloyal acts in time of war."

The Espionage Act has been amended several times over the years to cover disclosure of secret codes or disseminating unauthorized photographs of military installations and equipment. Since 1950, penalties have been added at various times for those who violate the statute, also to update the list of protected information, such as adding spacecraft, satellite systems, and other advanced technologies. Yet, the government has caught few leakers.

The Case of Samuel Loring Morison

The legislative history of the Espionage Act clearly shows that Congress's original intent was to punish spies, not those who disclose information to inform the public. However, in two exceptional cases, the government has used the act to prosecute civilian employees for unauthorized disclosure of classified information that clearly had no connection with espionage.

The first case involved the 1971 "Pentagon Papers" when former Defense Department official Daniel Ellsberg and Rand Corporation analyst Anthony Russo were charged with leaking classified information on the Vietnam War to *The New York Times.* That case never established a legal precedent for the prosecution of leakers because a federal judge dismissed it on grounds of prosecutorial misconduct. He based his decision on the disclosure that the "plumbers," a secret intelligence group connected to the Richard Nixon White House, had subjected the defendants to break-ins and wiretaps.

The second exception involved Samuel Loring Morison, a civilian analyst with the Office of Naval Intelligence in Suitland, Maryland—the only person ever convicted under the Espionage Act for leaking secrets to the press. A Navy veteran who served in Vietnam, Morison was convicted in federal court in Baltimore in October, 1985, for violating the act by giving three classified photographs of a Soviet ship under construction to *Jane's Defense Weekly,* a private British publication. The jury also found him guilty of "unauthorized possession" of military information for keeping secret documents in his home and two counts of theft of government property for removing the photographs and documents from the naval center in Suitland.

The fact that Morison had been working at *Jane's* part time with the approval of his superiors in Naval intelligence complicated the case. The government argued that he was trying to improve his chances of getting a full-time job by providing the photographs and that the quality and resolution of the photographs showed a reconnaissance capability previously unknown to the Soviets. Morison's defense was that the photographs did not reveal anything the Russians didn't already know.

The conviction of Morison, grandson of the distinguished naval historian and author Samuel Eliot Morison, alarmed the press and many of its advocates. They argued that if the conviction were upheld on appeal, the press would be stifled in reporting many government matters it covered routinely and reporters would be subjected to subpoenas in search of their sources and might even be prosecuted as a party to an illegal act. Justice Department prosecutors countered that while they hoped the verdict would send a clear signal that classified material should not be leaked, they respected First Amendment concerns and had no plan to hamper the media in its coverage of government.

The press was not mollified. Major print and broadcast media, as well as numerous news organizations and First Amendment groups, filed a lengthy brief supporting an appeal by Morison, arguing that "whatever one might think of government officials who release confidential or secret information to the press, it seems clear that leaking is not the same as espionage, and it is not the same as theft. . . . Congress has been sensitive to the valuable informative role of press leaks, and has repeatedly rejected proposals to criminalize the mere public disclosure of classified or defense-related information. Samuel Morison's conviction, if upheld, will overrule these careful judgments of Congress. It will restrict an important source of public information . . . and it will expose journalists and government officials alike to the threat of criminal prosecution for activity, which, no matter how offensive to those in power, has never been viewed as criminal."

However, a three-judge panel of the U.S. Fourth Circuit Court of Appeals, in a unanimous decision, upheld Morison's conviction and two-year prison sentence. In its opinion, the panel stressed that while its decision did not mean that news organizations could be prosecuted for publishing government secrets, it did not rule out that possibility.

Despite First Amendment issues and the concerns expressed by Morison and the media, the Supreme Court refused to hear the case on appeal. Nevertheless, so far the government has not used the Morison case as a legal precedent to subpoena or prosecute reporters or even to prosecute government employees for unauthorized disclosures. Nor has the case slowed the torrent of leaks to reporters, which includes not only the daily disclosures regarding policies, but more sensitive matters concerning sources and methods and other national security information.

Morison applied for a pardon in 1998 and Moynihan, writing in his former capacity as chairman of the Commission on Protecting and Reducing Government Secrecy, sent a passionate letter to President Clinton supporting the application. He observed that the commission had stressed that in the eighty-one years since the Espionage Act had passed, Morison was the only person ever convicted of passing on classified information. Singling out Morison for prosecution appeared "capricious at best," declared Moynihan, who argued that what was remarkable was not the crime, but that Morison was the only one convicted of something that had become a routine aspect of government life: leaking information to the press in order to bring pressure to bear on a policy question.

Although the CIA strongly objected, President Clinton pardoned Morison on January 20, 2001, his last day in the Oval Office. The pardon outraged Senator Richard Shelby, an Alabama Republican and leading proponent of clamping down on leaks. He said it would do nothing to curb a torrent of leaks and only underscored the need for new legislation that would make unauthorized leaks a crime. But First Amendment advocates hailed the decision and accused the Reagan administration of having inappropriately turned the Morison matter into a test case of whether the Espionage Act applied to all unauthorized disclosures of classified material to the media.

Mushrooming Government Secrecy

In many respects, the United States Government remains remarkably open, particularly when compared to foreign governments. It is not unusual, for example, for foreign academics or journalists to be denied access to government records in their own countries, only to find what they are looking for in the United States archives. In a 1987 20th Century Fund report, "Leaking: Who Does It? Who Benefits? At What Cost?" Elie Abel noted that few governments in Europe or elsewhere "allow reporters to forage for news in the corridors and offices of sensitive governments, as the United States does every day."

At the same time, acting in the name of national security, federal officials increasingly are curbing reporters' physical freedom to "forage for news in the corridors and offices" of government buildings, even though they carry government-issued press credentials. And each year the mountains of documents fenced off from reporters by secrecy classifications grow larger.

There are no laws on the books establishing procedures for classifying or declassifying documents. For most of the government's history, individual agencies developed their own ad hoc policies. Beginning with President Truman, however, uniform policies have been established through presidential orders for all agencies except the Atomic Energy Commission, which has its own legal procedures. But it wasn't until the Nixon administration that a serious attempt to deal with declassifying documents was made.

Surprising as it may seem for a president obsessed with secrecy, Nixon issued the first executive order requiring a systematic review of records for possible declassification. His order required the review after records had been classified for 30 years or more. The declassification became a monumental task, according to Steven Garfinkel, who was a 26-year-old attorney with the General Services Administration when the new policy was issued.

His superiors instructed Garfinkel to review a huge supply of World War II documents stored in the National Archives in Suitland, Maryland, and see if they could be declassified. "I walked into this stadium size room," he recalled in an interview, "and it was a mess, lined with shelves and shelves and boxes and boxes and it was all junk. It was declared to have permanent historic value, but it would have been better to throw it away. It was all the basic procurement that had been done during the war to buy for the military. I went through a couple of boxes and I said, 'this is nuts, I'll be here the rest of my life if I look at all these boxes.' So I said, 'this room is declassified' and went back to my job."

Garfinkel, who probably knows more about government secrets than any-body, later served for 20 years as director of the Information Security Oversight Office (ISOO), a small, little-known agency established during the Carter administration to oversee classification and to promote declassification as soon as possible consistent with national security concerns. He cites his first declassification experience as an example of how government often classifies huge amounts of documents and leaves them in storage long after they could possibly be sensitive. Such over-classification, he said, "becomes a big deal in time because sensitivity decreases over time, information becomes known, events change and yet stuff could lay around for decades and decades that should be declassified."

Under a 1978 executive order by President Jimmy Carter, government officials for the first time were ordered to consider the public's right to know in classifying information and were instructed to use the lowest level of clearance when in doubt. Even that did little to slow the build-up of documents. And the build-up even got much worse when President Ronald Reagan signed a 1982 executive order rescinding those provisions and essentially encouraging more classification of materials.

A significant change came only after President Clinton issued an executive order in 1995 aimed at holding classification to the minimum necessary and promoting as much declassification as possible consistent with national security. Garfinkel worked out the policy change with the help of two Clinton aides—John Podesta, who would later became Clinton's chief of staff, and George Tenet, a national security official who would become CIA director.

Clinton's Executive Order 12958, which became effective October 14, 1995, and remains in effect, resulted in the declassifying of more than 900 million pages of documents through fiscal 2001—more declassification than occurred under all previous presidents combined, according to Garfinkel.

Among the order's provisions aimed at keeping secrecy to a minimum is one that states when there is doubt about the need to classify information, it should not be classified, contrary to the previous presumption in favor of classification. The order also limits the duration of classification of most information to 10 years, except for documents that might reasonably be expected to reveal sources or methods or that deal with the development of weapons of mass destruction. It also provides for automatic declassification of all information more than 25 years old with exemptions for a series of specific national security concerns.

Each of the major classifying agencies—including Defense, State and Justice departments—now has in place an infrastructure for declassifying records, something almost none of the agencies had prior to Clinton's order. And they have continued to declassify unprecedented numbers of records with permanent historic value. In fiscal 2001, for example, 100,104,990 pages were declassified, compared to

11,452,930 in fiscal 1994 before the Clinton order was issued. In fact, J. William Leonard, who succeeded Garfinkel as ISOO director after Garfinkel retired in January, 2002, reports that the declassification system continues to churn out so many millions of documents that it exceeds the ability of agency systems and resources to process the records for public access.

At the same time, the pace of classifying records continues to accelerate dramatically. The total of all classification actions reported for fiscal 2001 increased by 44 percent to 33,020,997, with the Defense, State, and Justice departments accounting for 96 percent of the actions. As Leonard noted in a letter to President Bush accompanying the ISOO annual report, the agency does not expect the upward trend in classification to change "particularly in light of the current global war on terrorism."

Looking ahead, the ISOO reported it is "reasonably clear" that the automatic declassification program will be affected by the September 11 terrorist attacks "if only in the number of resources dedicated to it." The agency urged that staffs assigned to handle declassification be maintained because each year huge amounts of classified information becomes subject to automatic declassification.

If staff capabilities are not maintained, the ISOO reported, "another mountain" of older secrets will arise to choke the system. In fact, organizations that monitor government secrecy report that there already has been a significant slow-down in the pace of documents being declassified under the automatic declassification system.

Clinton Pressed to Veto a Bill He Supported

Surprisingly little attention was paid when Senator Shelby introduced his anti-leaks legislation in the form of an amendment to the 2000 intelligence reauthorization bill. Except for a debate on public television's "NewsHour with Jim Lehrer" on June 29, 2000, the measure attracted little news coverage, largely because the Congressional debates were taking place behind closed doors. And although the media had repeatedly won battles over similar legislation in the past, that summer the issue was not on the radar screens of the Newspaper Association of America and other major media groups.

The Lehrer show featured a debate between Senator Shelby and Scott Armstrong, an investigative journalist and strong advocate of openness in government. Armstrong argued that the bill would do nothing to stop authorized leaks by top government officials to influence policy, but that it would intimidate whistle-blowers and others in government who want to expose inefficiency and wrongdoing. Shelby declared that the bill was designed to ban disclosures of classified information that damages national security, not to protect the wrongdoings of politicians. And he pointed out that the Senate Intelligence Committee, which he then chaired, had unanimously endorsed the bill and said he was working with the Clinton administration to get its support.

Armstrong, who would emerge as a leader of a campaign against the anti-leaks amendment, asked Shelby why his legislation was necessary. The senator replied the information was classified, but he would tell Armstrong if he would come by his office. Armstrong asked him if the law he was advocating wouldn't make that illegal—a suggestion that seemed to stun Shelby. Later, he thought Shelby was uncomfortable defending his measure against arguments it could lead to investigations and wiretaps of journalists. Armstrong says he left Washington for a summer-long business trip thinking Clinton would never support the measure and Congress would not pass it.

While Armstrong was away from Washington, Shelby was adroitly pushing his legislation. The CIA was working hard to get it passed, too. In particular, the agency was upset over repeated leaks of national security secrets, especially to Bill Gertz of the right-wing *Washington Times*. He had infuriated intelligence agencies for years with articles citing secrets, many based on intercepted communications. Jeffrey H. Smith, a Washington lawyer and former general counsel of the CIA, said in an interview that Gertz's stories "drove people at the CIA absolutely nuts because he was just writing things and never asking if his stories can do any harm. And they did do harm."

Gertz had cited numerous classified documents in a book, *Betrayal,* as well as in the *Washington Times,* in criticizing Clinton's foreign policies toward China, North Korea, and Russia. In the book, published in 1999, Gertz wrote that "dissidents and patriots" in the intelligence community were so angry at Clinton's "betrayal of American security" that they "responded in the only way they knew how: by disclosing some of the nation's most secret intelligence."

CIA Director George Tenet had expressed anger at Gertz's reporting and had publicly complained that the executive branch "leaks like a sieve." It was Tenet who had encouraged Shelby to introduce his anti-leaks amendment in the first place. And now Tenet was enlisting support from other administration officials. Attorney General Janet Reno had opposed an early version of the measure, but joined Tenet in supporting it after some minor changes.

In October, Armstrong returned to Washington, where he is executive director of the Information Trust, a non-profit group that promotes openness in government. He was casually thumbing through *The Washington Post* of October 13 when a headline on page A5 jumped out at him: "Congress Passes Bill to Punish Leaks." It was a perfunctory, 236-word story with no by-line, no doubt based on an Associated Press story. It quoted Representative Nancy Pelosi, California Democrat and member of the House Intelligence Committee, as calling Congress "foolish" for giving the executive branch a blank check for prosecuting leaks cases. Buried inside

The New York Times was a short Associated Press story that included the same Pelosi quote. Neither the *Post* nor the *Times* had even bothered to staff the story.

The intelligence bill, including the Shelby amendment, had passed Congress by voice vote while the press had paid little attention to either the legislative process or the outcome. "I couldn't believe it at first," Armstrong said in an interview. "Never any hearings in the House, never any real hearings in the Senate, and the whole bill passed by voice vote!"

Armstrong, who called the Shelby amendment "the most draconian thing to happen to the First Amendment in our lifetime," started working the phones. First, he telephoned First Amendment advocate groups, such as the American Society of Newspaper Editors and the Society for Professional Journalists, seeking an explanation for why the bill had passed. They told him they had lobbied against the Shelby amendment, but the major media had done little to oppose it.

Next, hoping to spur a drive to get President Clinton to veto the intelligence bill, he telephoned Jeffrey Smith, the former CIA general counsel, who had represented Armstrong when he headed the National Security Archives, and Boisfeuillet Jones Jr., publisher of *The Washington Post*, where Armstrong had been an investigative reporter. Jones acknowledged in an interview that he and the National Newspaper Association had been caught off guard by the legislation's passage and needed to go into "high gear" to drum up support for a campaign if they were going to have any chance of persuading Clinton to veto a bill he had supported.

Jeffrey Smith thought the Shelby amendment was less threatening than Armstrong did but said he thought it could be "chilling" nonetheless. He noted that Kenneth Bacon, the Assistant Secretary of Defense for Public Affairs, was especially upset about the measure and feared that if it became law, information he might pass on to journalists on background could subject him to prosecution. Bacon, who made his views known to the White House, also told *The Washington Post* the measure was "disastrous for journalists . . . disastrous for any official who deals with the press in national security, whether at State, the NSC or the Pentagon."

Smith said he agreed with Bacon's sentiments because when he was in the State Department during the Nixon administration, he had seen Secretary of State Henry Kissinger instruct a senior official to do a backgrounder with reporters and when the story came out and was criticized for including classified information, Kissinger wrote the official a letter admonishing him for leaking the information and made the letter a part of his file. "That was disgraceful," Smith said.

Opponents of the amendment found an ally in John Podesta, the White House Chief of Staff. Like Reno, he had objected to an earlier version, which he criticized as being overly broad. In an interview, he said he thought after he raised his objections, the issue had been put on the back burner, but in any case he lost track of it. Following his objections, the proposal had been narrowed, but the Justice

Department, Office of Management and Budget, and the White House had all signed off on it and then sent it to Congress, confirming the President would sign it if Congress passed it.

"We just didn't do our homework," Podesta, now a Georgetown University law school professor, acknowledged. "All of a sudden, the bill passed with the negotiated amendment in there, slightly narrower than the original, but well on the way to an official secrets act."

Since the bill, as passed by Congress, bore the administration's imprimatur, Podesta found it awkward to be lining up support for a veto. And he thought persuading Clinton to veto a bill he had earlier endorsed and that was supported by the CIA and Justice Department, was a long shot. But Podesta had a history of supporting First Amendment causes and felt bad about letting the intelligence bill slip through with the Shelby Amendment attached. So he began seeking support for a veto from senior officials. He ultimately found allies in Sandy Berger, Clinton's national security advisor, Secretary of State Madeleine Albright, and Defense Secretary William Cohen.

Meanwhile, Jones, the *Post* publisher, had been joined in the lobbying campaign by Arthur O. Sulzberger Jr., publisher of *The New York Times*; Tom Johnson, then Chairman and CEO, CNN; and John F. Strum, President and CEO, NAA. They sent a letter to President Clinton arguing that the Shelby Amendment would, in effect, create an official secrets act of the kind that had always been rejected by this country, and they urged the president to veto the intelligence bill.

Their letter pointed out that Congress had enacted a variety of laws to punish disclosure of specific types of classified information, such as communications intelligence, atomic weapons, and covert agents, but added: "Congress has resisted demands for a broad officials secrets act even in the face of serious threats to the nation's security—including the outbreak of World War I, the attack on Pearl Harbor in World War II, and the Cold War that followed. In 1985 and thereafter, the CIA has proposed substantially similar legislation through Intelligence Authorization acts, but the proposals have been rejected each and every time." (See Appendix I for the text of the letter.)

Podesta said while the press was especially sensitive about weighing in on the government it covered, in this case it was not journalists, but media executives who were doing the lobbying." It was a different level," said Podesta, "and it was clear to the president that this was no third tier issue. He knew he needed to understand the law, the substance of the bill, and agency viewpoints. When I discussed it with him, he said he could get back to me later."

Opponents of the measure felt strongly they should also try to persuade the Justice Department to change its position on the legislation or to at least soften its support for it. Since it would be inappropriate for working journalists to be involved in the lobbying, Armstrong sought media executives for that mission, too, but executives with a strong editorial background who would have credibility with Justice Department lawyers when laying out the bill's likely impact.

The clock was ticking when Armstrong, Bill Kovach, former editor of *The Atlanta Constitution* and a long-time *New York Times* reporter and editor, and Ben Bradlee, a senior news executive and former editor of *The Washington Post*, met with about 15 Justice Department lawyers in the Attorney General's Conference Room on Friday afternoon, November 3. If Clinton failed to veto the bill by the end of the following day, it would automatically become law.

Kovach, who also had served as curator of the Nieman Foundation, felt uncomfortable lobbying the government on a piece of legislation. "It's not the kind of thing I would want to do," he said in an interview, "and I didn't want to get involved. I recommended other folks for it but there wasn't much time and it was a really serious issue so I agreed to do it." Bradlee wasn't thrilled to be involved either and said in an interview he didn't see how their arguments could be of much help since most of the time "things just don't work like that." But for two hours the trio made their case to the Justice Department lawyers that the anti-leaks legislation was bad for the press and bad for the government.

The Justice attorneys conceded that passage of the legislation could mean reporters would be drawn into leaks investigations, but suggested they could write regulations that would protect reporters. They conceded little else, however, and the journalists felt that most of the attorneys didn't understand the way leaks had become so commonplace in the way the government operated. The attorneys, it seemed clear to them, didn't realize that when a Secretary of Defense speaks for the record, a reporter might interview 10 other officials on what he said and those officials, to help explain or verify or amplify the Secretary's statements, might well use classified information.

The journalists left the session feeling certain Reno would continue supporting the legislation. And they felt sure Clinton would sign it the next day. That would mean any official who leaked any classified information, no matter what the motive or intent, could be subject to prosecution.

That had been Kenneth Bacon's concern at the Defense Department. And it was a concern of Strobe Talbot at the State Department. Talbot, Deputy Secretary of State and former *Time* Magazine editor and correspondent, thought the Shelby Amendment was "unbelievably pernicious for all kinds of reasons." In an interview, he recalled attending an interagency meeting in the White House's Roosevelt Room where the issue was discussed shortly before Clinton's veto decision. Bob McNamara, the CIA general counsel, made what Talbot thought was a "pro forma" argument for the bill, but Attorney General Reno strongly advocated it.

Talbot, who is now President of the Brookings Institution, told the other officials that he was constantly in the position of using classified information to provide background for reporters on foreign trips by the Secretary of State. If Clinton signed the intelligence bill, he said, whether the Shelby Amendment could be used to prosecute him for such activities "would have to depend on the good sense and good will of the people enforcing the law. And there would certainly be the potential you could have more than a letter of reprimand in your file. You could be prosecuted."

On Saturday morning, November 4, the last day the bill could be vetoed or would become law, Talbot went to the White House and delivered the same message to President Clinton, a long-time friend. Talbot told the president the State Department would have trouble functioning if the measure became law and urged him to veto it. Talbot recalls Clinton saying he was listening to both sides and would fully understand the issue before making a decision.

Later that day Armstrong, dejected about prospects the intelligence bill would be signed, tried without success to reach Podesta by telephone at the White House. A short while later Podesta telephoned him with the news: Clinton had vetoed the bill and sent Congress a message saying the anti-leaks provision was overbroad "and may unnecessarily chill legitimate activities that are at the heart of our democracy."

"I agree that unauthorized disclosures can be extraordinarily harmful to the United States national security interests and that far too many such disclosures occur," Clinton said. "Unauthorized disclosures damage our intelligence relationships abroad, compromise intelligence gathering, jeopardize lives and increase the threat of terrorism." But he went on to say the Shelby amendment posed dangers to liberty that outweighed security concerns. And, in an unusual admission for a president, he noted that his own administration's deliberations that led to congressional approval of the intelligence bill "lacked the thoroughness this provision warranted, which in turn led to a failure to apprise Congress of the concerns I am expressing today." (See Appendix II for the text of the veto message.)

Talking to Jones, *The Washington Post* publisher, after vetoing the bill, Clinton also made an unusually candid admission: "We let that one slip by us."

Clinton's veto infuriated Shelby. The Senator angrily told the Senate: "After 8 years of subordinating national security to political concerns, the Clinton-Gore administration now exits on a similar note. Three days before the election, in the face of hysterical, largely inaccurate, but extremely well-timed media lobbying blitz, the president overruled his national security experts and vetoed this bill over a provision to reduce damaging leaks of classified national security information."

Shelby accused media organizations and others of having "conjured up a parade of dire consequences that would ensue" if his amendment had become law. But he contended it would not have eroded First Amendment rights and "would not have silenced whistle blowers who would continue to enjoy current statutory protections, including those governing the disclosure of classified information to appropriate congressional oversight committees."

Shelby Plows Ahead

Still upset that the measure he had fought for so hard had been killed by Clinton, Shelby brought up the amendment again in 2001. Now the new Bush administration was in place, and both President George W. Bush and Attorney General John Ashcroft routinely employed and defended secrecy and vehemently criticized unauthorized disclosure of classified documents. At the same time they were also aware of the controversial nature of the proposed legislation. Moreover, they knew that news media executives had campaigned heavily the year before in persuading Clinton to veto the measure and that media interests were now fully mobilized for the new challenge.

Executives of local print and broadcast media from around the country bombarded their members of Congress and administration officials with calls opposing the amendment and newspapers published editorials denouncing the legislation. And they used Republican intermediaries to quietly lobby top White House and Justice Department officials.

Shelby sought the support of Bush and Vice President Cheney but got no commitment. An intelligence committee aide, according to *The Washington Post*, said Shelby was told the administration's position was being worked on. Some sources said administration officials discouraged Shelby from going forward. And the *Post* quoted John Martin, former Internal Security Chief of the Justice Department, as saying current law was sufficient to cover people who provide classified information to unauthorized persons, including the press.

Martin, who had handled the leaks prosecution of Samuel Loring Morison, said the problem with leaks had not been the lack of statutory sanctions but the lack of will on the part of agency heads and Cabinet secretaries to enforce security regulations. He reckoned that if the amendment became law and was enforced "you could relocate the capital from Washington to Lewisburg, Pennsylvania (site of a federal prison)" because "the biggest leakers are White House aides, Cabinet secretaries, generals and admirals, and members of Congress."

On September 5, 2001, the Senate Intelligence Committee again took up the Shelby amendment. Tenet and Ashcroft were scheduled to testify, but so were several well-prepared opponents: Floyd Abrams, a lawyer representing *The New York Times*; Don Oberdorfer, former long-time national security reporter for *The Washington Post*; Blaine Harden, a lawyer representing Jones, the *Post* publisher; and Philip B. Heymann, a Harvard Law School professor and former Deputy Attorney General, who had supervised a number of investigations of leaks while at the Justice Department.

The Bush administration, however, had been unable to reach a firm consensus on the measure. A senior intelligence official told reporters the administration just didn't want to take on any additional political problems at the time. Moreover, Justice Department attorneys were divided on how to proceed. Ashcroft told the committee the Department needed more time to study the issue. The committee dropped the anti-leaks amendment, then approved the intelligence bill without hearing testimony from the witnesses. And it instructed the Justice Department to study the issue of leaks and report back to the committee in six months.

If the anti-leaks measure had come up a week or so later—in the aftermath of the 9/11 terrorist attacks when national security concerns dominated Washington's political agenda—the committee undoubtedly would have endorsed it. And Armstrong and other leading opponents say that under those circumstances they have no doubt the full Congress would have passed the restrictions too.

The intelligence appropriations bill Congress ultimately passed called for Ashcroft to appoint an inter-agency task force to analyze protection against leaks, including criminal and civil penalties, and to determine whether additional laws were needed. The task force included officials of the Justice, Defense, State, and Energy departments, as well as officials from other agencies that handle classified information.

Media and Government Dialogue

With that formal review underway, Armstrong and Smith, the former CIA general counsel, embarked upon an extraordinary venture that they had been planning for several months and that they hoped would head off any additional anti-leaks legislation. They enlisted media executives and government officials to engage in an informal, ongoing dialogue about the issue of protecting government secrets without infringing on the right to report on the government.

The discussions of this unofficial body, called simply "Dialogue," generally are off the record, but several of the participants, including Armstrong and Smith, who function as facilitators, agreed to discuss its sessions and its aims with the author of this chapter.

The Dialogue sessions have been held over dinner at Washington's Metropolitan Club periodically—usually once every several weeks—for the past year. They have received virtually no publicity, but have attracted some of Washington's top journalists, as well as some of the government's senior intelligence officials. Officials from the Central Intelligence Agency, National Security Council, National Security Agency, and Defense Department, as well as several congressional aides, have taken part in the sessions. (For a list of those attending, see Appendix III.)

From all accounts, both sides have considered the meetings constructive, although some are more enthusiastic than others in assessing the Dialogue's impact. The best evidence of positive impact is that members of Attorney General Ashcroft's task force on leaks consulted with Dialogue participants before drafting his report to Congress of October 30, 2002, which concluded new anti-leaks legislation was not needed at that time, although it recommended the administration take steps to crack down on unauthorized disclosures of classified information.

Several participants said one of the most significant achievements of the Dialogue meetings, aside from weighing in on Ashcroft's decision not to seek anti-leaks legislation, has been a recognition on both sides of the need for the media and the government to be educated about both the dangers and the values of leaks. "National security leaders need to understand that some leaks are good for democracy and the country even though others are bad," says Jeffrey Smith. "The press needs to understand more about the sensitivity of national security leaks. Everybody understands you don't publish that the 82nd Airborne is planning to land somewhere, but not everyone understands that it's a national security problem to report that Osama bin Laden's cell phone calls have been intercepted."

Bill Harlow, CIA public affairs officer, agrees the Dialogue meetings could be educational for both sides. He points out there are times when a news article about sensitive issues can be written without changing its thrust or doing any national security damage if journalists are willing to check with intelligence officials. Often, agreeing to change just a few words is all it takes, he said. "There is value in sensitizing editors to those facts," he said, "but I'm not overly convinced how much good it does because there are too many players, too many editors involved."

In fact, although Harlow thinks the dialogue has been of some value, he is not as sold on it as some of the other participants. Unfortunately, he said, there is too much of government representatives waving their hands and complaining about leaks and press representatives waving their hands and complaining about the over-classification of records. "And they're both right," he said. "They're all reasonable people, but coming to common ground on the issue is difficult."

That's true because both sides approach the issue from such different perspectives. There are instances where the media is irresponsible in using classified information that might endanger national security while the government keeps far too many secrets that have little or nothing to do with national security. Media representatives at the Dialogue meetings insist that responsible journalists have no interest in disclosing secrets that might compromise national security or in some way endanger lives.

Nobody wants the intelligence agencies to know less or to be prevented from getting information valuable for their analysis, they say, and responsible journalists will negotiate with the agencies to try to find a way to write articles based on leaks without disclosing information that might be damaging. On the other hand, intelligence officials insist that too often the press will publish articles based on government secrets either without checking with them or without agreeing to withhold information the government considers damaging to national security.

A senior government official, who has taken part in the Dialogue sessions, found them "extraordinarily constructive," but the official, who declined to be further identified, wondered whether the meetings would have been so constructive had it not been that they have taken place since the 9/11 terrorist attacks. "To the degree that journalists participated," he said, "they were talking about the need to protect sources and methods, understanding we had just been attacked by terrorists and journalists had lost one of their own in Daniel Pearl (*The Wall Street Journal* reporter killed by terrorists in Pakistan). They felt personally they needed to engage in how they can still get information out to the public so the public can understand what the government is doing, but at the same time not give away the government's ability to continue collecting intelligence."

Individual cases of tension between the press and intelligence agencies sometimes are discussed in detail at the Dialogue sessions. At one meeting, a case was discussed that Harlow found especially disturbing. It showed how failing to find common ground can inflict hard-to-heal bruises on news organizations and intelligence agencies. He cited a *Los Angeles Times* story of January 15, 2002, that reported the CIA was recruiting Iranian/American businessmen in Los Angeles to act as informants after returning from trips to Iran.

CIA Director George Tenet telephoned Dean Baquet, the *Times* managing editor, and urged that the story be withheld on national security grounds. "It's rare for a director to do that," Harlow said, "but they decided to publish it anyway. The plan to use the Iranian Americans to bring back intelligence had worked quite well, but not since the *Times* story. It was a one-day story in the *Times*, but got much bigger play in Iran. The press can't have it both ways, criticizing us for not knowing things and then making it harder for us to find out things and do our job. Now, an Iranian ex-patriot going to Iran is going to find he is under much greater scrutiny."

For its part, the *Los Angeles Times* contends Tenet did not make a compelling case to withhold publication. In an interview, Baquet said that after receiving a message from the CIA that the story was harmful to an ongoing investigation, he did withhold the story a day to give Tenet a chance to make his case. But Baquet said that when Tenet called him, he was vague and argued in principle that the *Times* shouldn't write about ongoing operations and investigations because it would hurt them. "And it struck me that what they were doing in the community was well known and they were kidding themselves if they thought it wouldn't get out," Baquet said. He made the decision to publish, he said, after consulting with other editors who agreed Tenet had failed to make a compelling case.

In spite of such clashes, journalists generally agree that since 9/11, they have become more sensitive to national security concerns about leaks. Two journalists who attend the Dialogue sessions—Doyle McManus, Washington Bureau Chief of the *Los Angeles Times,* and Don Oberdorfer, *The Washington Post*'s former national security correspondent—said those concerns are stressed at the Dialogue sessions. McManus said, "things have changed, but not as radically as some portray it. We still apply largely the standards about what to publish that we did prior to 9/11, we're just more sensitive now because it's like the difference between peacetime and war."

Oberdorfer, now journalist in residence at Johns Hopkins University School of Advanced International Studies, took a somewhat different point of view. He said there was an assumption by journalists going into the Dialogue meetings that there was a serious problem of some leaks causing damage to national security. "I'm not sure that same assumption would have been there two years ago, but after 9/11 journalists felt that way."

One of the major concerns about leaks cited often at the meetings involves Bill Gertz, the national security correspondent of *The Washington Times*, an arch-conservative newspaper that vehemently opposed the Clinton administration. Gertz has used over 200 highly classified documents in articles and books since 1996, according to a tabulation this year by the CIA. And much of his reporting has been severely critical of the Clinton administration.

Jacob Heilbrunn, writing in the June 21, 1999 *New Republic,* said Gertz gets his stories—usually buttressed by classified documents—from "disgruntled conservative military and intelligence officers within the bowels of the Pentagon and the CIA." Gertz has said he's not concerned about his sources' motives when they give him classified information. It's not unusual for reporters to take that view of sources, of course, since many officials have reasons of their own to talk to the media.

Gertz's use of classified records based on intercepted satellite communications has been especially galling to intelligence agencies because they say it alerts foreign interests to the fact the United States can monitor their communications and perhaps read their codes, giving them the chance to alter both. For example, in 1999, Gertz reported that national security intercepts indicated that Chinese secret agents had notified China that the American bombing of the Chinese embassy in Belgrade during the NATO war on Yugoslavia had not been accidental, as the United States claimed, but had been deliberate.

Those are the kind of stories, intelligence officials say, that make it possible for foreign agents to figure out how the United States gets its information and to deny it the capability of doing it in the future. In Afghanistan, once al Qaeda and Taliban leaders discovered how easily their cell phone conversations could be intercepted, they became much more circumspect in using those phones, according to intelligence officials.

In an interview, Gertz acknowledged that his articles based on leaks "usually drive them crazy, especially issues related to communications intercepts." "I'm not in the secrecy business," he said, "I'm in the news business. It's not our job to keep secrets, it's their job. I don't clear my stories with the government." At the same time, he insisted that he tries to be responsible and normally goes to the CIA when dealing with sensitive classified information "and if they have security issues, I tell them, have your boss call my boss, and sometimes they do, sometimes they don't."

He said the intelligence agencies were trying to demonize him and that the focus on him was political. "Clearly there are official leaks all over the place," he said, "and officials who talk to *The New York Times* and *The Washington Post* are rewarded."

Intelligence officials, however, also cited cases where they criticized *The Washington Post* and *The New York Times* for using stories based on leaks that they said caused national security damage. One involved a *Post* story based on a satellite communications intercept of a message from Osama bin Laden. Another was a *New York Times* story in the mid-1990s dealing with how the CIA was using unsavory characters as "assets" or informers overseas to help fight terrorism. The CIA's Harlow recalls that the agency was able to persuade the *Times* to delete the name of an asset, but that the *Times* story described him in some detail. "The asset disappeared shortly thereafter and his family believed terrorists killed him," Harlow said. "We lost a good asset."

Despite such cases, government representatives at the Dialogue sessions have generally indicated that they have no big problem with the way most of the press handles national security issues most of the time. And with the exception of some Defense Department representatives who take a harder line about leaks, government representatives have indicated they support the system of negotiating with the press over national security concerns so that the press can write its stories and the government can protect its most sensitive secrets.

Ashcroft's interagency task force on secrets thought enough of the Dialogue that when the task force was still in existence more than half its members participated in some of the sessions. In fact, the task force's chairman, Patrick Murray, Associate Deputy Attorney General for National Security, described the nature of the final report at a Dialogue meeting long before Ashcroft sent it to Congress on October 22, 2002. The report had been scheduled to be sent to Congress much earlier, on May 1, after six months of study and deliberations. But a government official said it was delayed by two factors: The report was slow to work its way through the task force's various agencies and there was no demand from Congress to speed up the process.

Task force members who have attended the Dialogue meetings view them as constructive for the most part and suggest they should be continued, especially since press/national security issues are likely to increase as the government presses its war on terrorism. An earlier draft of the Ashcroft report called the Dialogue a "positive development toward achieving a change in the cultural attitude about the need to continue to safeguard classified information, and the media's desire to inform the public of the workings of its government without doing damage to the public's security." But the comment was deleted from the final report.

The Ashcroft report recommended a series of administrative measures designed to tighten controls on classified information and to identify and hold accountable any persons who engage in unauthorized leaks, if they can be found. It also would provide that individuals being investigated for unauthorized disclosures be required to execute affidavits swearing under penalty of perjury they have not engaged in such acts.

The report concluded that current statutes provide a legal basis for prosecuting those who engage in unauthorized disclosures, but left open the possibility of pursuing a broader statute in the future. Should Congress choose to pursue a criminal statute that covers in one place all unauthorized disclosure of classified information, it said, "the administration would, of course, be prepared to work with Congress."

Armstrong, although disappointed that the final report was less definitive in dismissing any new anti-leak legislation, said that in the context of Shelby's sweeping legislation on unauthorized disclosure, he considered the report a victory. "In the context of the media's ongoing dialogue with the government over unauthorized disclosures and secrecy," he wrote in an e-mail to colleagues, "I consider it just a beginning. We will have to remain engaged on these issues for the foreseeable future."

Media and First Amendment watchdogs are even more alarmed by the passage of several bills since 9/11—the Patriot Act, the Homeland Security Information Act, and the Homeland Security Act—all of which expand government secrecy. Armstrong says the Dialogue sessions have become more relevant than ever since the new system under these acts "would effectively become an official secrets act that could be used to intimidate and punish leakers much as had been intended with the original secrets act proposed by Senator Shelby."

Conclusion

The war on terrorism and the showdown with Iraq clearly have given a greater sense of urgency to the issue of unauthorized disclosure of sensitive national security secrets. Journalists such as those attending the Dialogue sessions say they clearly are more concerned now about the dangers of such disclosures.

Those who monitor government secrecy have been rethinking the issue as well. Steven Aftergood, executive director of the Federation of American Scientists' Secrecy Project, says that before 9/11 he viewed the secrecy policy as part of a game in which the government kept secrets indiscriminately and he responded by disclosing them indiscriminately. "But 9/11 made it clear there are people out there looking for creative ways to kill Americans," he said. "That made me and a lot of other people see secrecy in a new light. Before, I believed I should vacuum up all the secrets I could and make them available on the Internet. Now I have to first determine whether the material disclosed can be used by terrorists."

9/11 also has brought about a greater willingness by both the media and the government to discuss the issues. The Dialogue sessions are the best example of that. But Doyle McManus of the *Los Angeles Times* is perhaps correct when he suggests the degree of change could be exaggerated. For one thing, people and institutions find it hard to give up old habits and attitudes. Also, the fundamental reason the problem persists is that both sides have good and compelling reasons for holding fast to their positions.

The situation is more clear-cut when it comes to military secrets or information that could endanger lives. Since 9/11, a fairly strong consensus seems to have developed within the news media that such information usually should not be disclosed. Yet recent reporting on battle plans for a war in Iraq illustrates the complexity of the problem.

The reports may in fact have given Iraq's Saddam Hussein insight into United States military thinking and capabilities. But to the news media, it seemed necessary to reveal these plans to a public which had not focused on how seriously the Bush administration was preparing for war or what the scale and price of such a conflict might be. Moreover, even though the Pentagon denounced the stories as a serious breach of national security, they clearly were based on "plants" or "controlled leaks" by the Bush administration, according to both Brent Scowcroft, who served as President George H. W. Bush's national security advisor, and former Senator Warren Rudman, a New Hampshire Republican and ex-chairman of the President's Advisory Board on National Security.

Another nettlesome problem is that neither side always acts in a disinterested manner. News organizations are highly competitive and sometimes their drive to be first to disclose major news can outweigh concern for disclosing sensitive secrets. As for the government, it's obvious that political leaders frequently use secrets to serve them, not the public.

In today's climate, leaks undoubtedly will become an even more burning issue. With the war on terrorism raising serious concerns about violations of press freedom and other civil liberties, the news media and the government should continue the Dialogue sessions to broaden understanding on both sides. Dialogue meetings make it easier for both sides to avoid knee-jerk reactions. Also, the more sophisticated the news media's understanding of the problems, especially when dealing with sensitive intelligence, the greater the media's ability to avoid needless damage.

All this requires a greater willingness on the part of government agencies to deal with reporters and editors in more sophisticated, forthright ways, however. Officials who hold the media at arm's length and exploit secrecy for political purposes should not expect the media to just roll over when they make demands to withhold classified information.

Senator Shelby's anti-leak legislation undoubtedly will surface again. He has vowed to press for it until it becomes law and several Bush administration officials have said they would actively pursue such legislation. It's up to the news media to be ready for the challenge. Reporters and editors need to pay much more attention to the whole issue of leaks and classified information than they have in the recent past. Never again should the news media be caught napping when Congress is considering legislation that threatens the public's right to know about its government's operations.

The need for vigilance by the press is even greater today because of the Bush administration's excessive reliance on secrecy. Even before 9/11, it was predisposed to secrecy. To cite but a few examples, Bush refused to disclose the names of those who consulted with his energy task force, and he issued an executive order to prevent access to records of previous presidents. He also has denied congressional access to routine government information and fostered restrictions on the Freedom of Information Act.

Since 9/11, the administration has greatly expanded its secrecy policies, restricting the media's ability to cover war, military tribunals and proceedings involving terrorism and immigration. (Details of Bush's myriad secrecy policies are included in a 60-page report the Reporters Committee for Freedom of the Press issued on the first anniversary of 9/11.) Today's atmosphere of fear over war and terrorism, as Lucy A. Dalglish, the Reporters Committee's executive director, says, "induced public officials to abandon this country's culture of openness and opt for secrecy as a way of ensuring safety and security."

APPENDIX I

The text of media executives' letter to President Bill Clinton.
October 31, 2000

BY HAND

The President
The White House
Washington, DC 20500

Dear Mr. President:

As leaders of major news organizations, we take the unusual step of writing to express our concern—in fact, alarm—over a provision in the Intelligence Authorization bill recently passed by Congress. For the first time in our nation's history, a law would criminalize all unauthorized disclosures of classified information—in effect creating an "official secrets act" of the sort that exists elsewhere but that has always been rejected in this country. This provision shatters the delicate balance that has been achieved in this country between the public's right to know and the legitimate demands of national security. We therefore urge you to veto it.

The specific provision at issue, Section 304, would make it a felony for a government employee to reveal any properly classified information to any unauthorized person, regardless of whether any harm to the national security results. Even individuals who do not actually know they are revealing classified information could be prosecuted if they had "reason to believe" the information was classified.

Of course, the government has a duty to preserve national security secrets. And over the years, Congress has enacted a variety of laws to punish disclosure of specific types of classified information (e.g., communications intelligence, atomic weapons, covert agents). But Congress has resisted demands for a broad official secrets act even in the face of serious threats to the nation's security—including the outbreak of World War I, the attack on Pearl Harbor in World War II, and the Cold War that followed. In 1985 and thereafter, the CIA has proposed substantially similar legislation through Intelligence Authorization acts, but the proposals have been rejected each and every time.

The legislation now before you would change the kind of society that we have become. It would alter the way in which government officials deal with the press, the way in which the press gathers and reports the news, and the way in which the public learns about its government. On a daily basis, government officials—variously described as whistleblowers, "senior State Department officials," or even "sources close to the President"—disclose government "secrets," which sometimes are classified.

The motives of those who disclose what has been classified may be honorable or dishonorable, and the immediate effect of publication may be harmful or beneficial—or these matters may be fairly open to debate. But the overall effect of disclosures concerning the affairs of government is to enhance the people's ability to understand what the government is doing and to hold the government accountable. Any effort to impose criminal sanctions for disclosing classified information must confront the reality that the "leak" is an important instrument of communication that is employed on a routine basis by officials at every level of government.

The laws on the books strike a balance—imperfect, to be sure—between the public interests in preventing harm to the national security, on the one hand, and preserving free discussion of governmental affairs, on the other. This legislation simply goes too far. The mere fact that a document is classified, even properly classified, does not mean that its disclosure is harmful to national security. Over 7 million documents (not pages) are classified each year, and billions of pages remain classified from past years. As the bipartisan Commission on Protecting and Reducing Government Secrecy noted in 1997, the ordinary rule for those in a position to classify is to "stamp, stamp, stamp." That Commission, which was tasked with proposing ways to strengthen the protection of legitimately classified information, never endorsed criminalizing the leaking of classified information.

Section 304 would empower the government effectively to silence a broad range of important news reporting. Consider these subjects that came to light when classified information was disclosed to journalists:

- The Pentagon Papers;
- Details of the Iran-Contra affair;
- Government radiation and biological warfare experiments on unwitting Americans;
- Safety violations in nuclear weapons manufacturing processes and nuclear power plants;
- Lapses in security creating vulnerability to espionage, such as the case of CIA agent Edward Lee Howard;
- Waste, fraud, and abuse in the defense industry;
- The efficacy of particular weapons systems, such as Star Wars;
- Human rights abuses in Latin America, Asia, and Africa.

As these examples illustrate, press leaks, even of classified information, can serve as a vital source of information about public issues and the operation of government. Yet each of these stories could have resulted in criminal prosecution under Section 304. And despite the assurances from the legislation's sponsors, journalists themselves may fear the possibility of prosecution by overzealous authorities for aiding and abetting the release of classified information. Certainly, journalists could face subpoenas, search warrants, telephone taps, and review of their phone records to identify the culprit. The net effect would be censorship and self-censorship among journalists, sources, and whistleblowers alike.

There is no warrant for legislation of this kind. The government has ample power to deal with those who engage in the unauthorized disclosure of confidential information. It can remove security clearances and fire employees for unauthorized disclosures. It can bring criminal prosecutions under existing criminal statutes that cover particular concerns. If needed, Congress can enact further, specific legislation after appropriate hearings—legislation that focuses on particular types of grave concerns rather than all classified information.

At bottom, legislation that criminalizes all disclosures of classified information is anathema to a system that places sovereignty in the hands of the people. That, at least, has been the prevailing view for the first two and one-quarter centuries of our nation's existence. If we are about to embark on a new era of criminalizing all leaks, let there be public hearings and a full review by the House and Senate Judiciary Committees, and let a well-informed consensus emerge. An addition to an authorization bill is not the proper vehicle for so fundamental a change in the public's right to know.

We urge you to veto this bill, and we thank you for considering our views on this matter.

Sincerely,

(The letter was signed by Tom Johnson, Chairman and CEO, CNN; Boisfeuillet Jones Jr., Publisher and CEO, *The Washington Post*; John F. Sturm, President and CEO, Newspaper Association of America; and Arthur O. Sulzberger Jr., Publisher, *The New York Times* and Chairman, The New York Times Company. It was copied to John Podesta, White House Chief of Staff, who delivered the letter to President Clinton.)

APPENDIX II

Clinton's message vetoing the Intelligence re-authorization bill.
November 4, 2000

STATEMENT BY THE PRESIDENT

TO THE HOUSE OF REPRESENTATIVES:

Today, I am disapproving H.R. 4392, the "Intelligence Authorization Act for Fiscal Year 2001," because of one badly flawed provision that would have made a felony of unauthorized disclosures of classified information. Although well intentioned, that provision is overbroad and may unnecessarily chill legitimate activities that are at the heart of a democracy.

I agree that unauthorized disclosures can be extraordinarily harmful to United States national security interests and that far too many such disclosures occur. I have been particularly concerned about their potential effects on the sometimes irreplaceable intelligence sources and methods on which we rely to acquire accurate and timely information I need in order to make the most appropriate decisions on matters of national security. Unauthorized disclosures damage our intelligence relationships abroad, compromise intelligence gathering, jeopardize lives, and increase the threat of terrorism. As Justice Stewart stated in the Pentagon Papers case, "it is elementary that the successful conduct of international diplomacy and the maintenance of an effective national defense require both confidentiality and secrecy. Other nations can hardly deal with this Nation in an atmosphere of mutual trust unless they can be assured that their confidences will be kept . . . and the development of considered and intelligent international policies would be impossible if those charged with their formulation could not communicate with each other freely." Those who disclose classified information inappropriately thus commit a gross breach of the public trust and may recklessly put our national security at risk. To the extent that existing sanctions have proven insufficient to address and deter unauthorized disclosures, they should be strengthened. What is in dispute is not the gravity of the problem, but the best way to respond to it.

In addressing this issue, we must never forget that the free flow of information is essential to a democratic society. Justice Stewart also wrote in the Pentagon Papers case that "the only effective restraint upon executive policy in the areas of national defense and international affairs may lie in an enlightened citizenry—in an informed and critical public opinion which alone can here protect the values of democratic government."

Justice Brandeis reminded us "those who won our independence believed . . . that public discussion is a political duty; and that this should be a fundamental principle of the American government." His words caution that we must always tread carefully when considering measures that may limit public discussion—even when those measures are intended to achieve laudable, indeed necessary, goals.

As President, therefore, it is my obligation to protect not only our government's vital information from improper disclosure, but also to protect the rights of citizens to receive the information necessary for democracy to work. Furthering these two goals requires a careful balancing, which must be assessed in light of our system of classifying information over a range of categories. This legislation does not achieve the proper balance. For example, there is a serious risk that this legislation would tend to have a chilling effect on those who engage in legitimate activities. A desire to avoid the risk that their good faith choice of words—their exercise of judgment—could become the subject of a criminal referral for prosecution might discourage Government officials from engaging even in appropriate public discussion, press briefings, or other legitimate official activities. Similarly, the legislation may unduly restrain the ability of former Government officials to teach, write, or engage in any activity aimed at building public understanding of complex issues. Incurring such risks is unnecessary and inappropriate in a society built on freedom of expression and the consent of the governed and is particularly inadvisable in a context in which the range of classified materials is so extensive. In such circumstances, this criminal provision would, in my view, create an undue chilling effect.

The problem is compounded because this provision was passed without benefit of public hearings—a particular concern given that it is the public that this law seeks ultimately to protect. The administration shares the process burden since its deliberations lacked the thoroughness this provision warranted, which in turn led to a failure to apprise the Congress of the concerns I am expressing today.

I deeply appreciate the sincere efforts of Members of Congress to address the problem of unauthorized disclosures and I fully share their commitment. When the Congress returns, I encourage it to send me this bill with this provision deleted and I encourage the Congress as soon as possible to pursue a more narrowly drawn provision tested in public hearings so that those they represent can also be heard on this important issue.

Since the adjournment of the Congress has prevented my return of H.R. 4392 within the meaning of Article I, section 7, clause 2 of the Constitution, my withholding of approval from the bill precludes its becoming law. The Pocket Veto Case, 279 U.S. 655 (1929). In addition to withholding my signature and thereby invoking my constitutional power to "pocket veto" bills during an adjournment of the Congress, to avoid litigation, I am also sending H.R. 4392 to the House of Representatives with my objections, to leave no possible doubt that I have vetoed the measure.

William J. Clinton

APPENDIX III

The following are the names of those who have attended Dialogue meetings in 2001 and 2002.

Government officials: John Bellinger, general counsel of the National Security Council; Robert Dietz, general counsel, National Security Agency; Judy Emmel, Public Affairs Officer, National Security Agency; Bill Harlow, CIA Public Affairs Office; Richard Haver, Assistant to the Defense Secretary for Intelligence; Fred Manget, Deputy General Counsel, CIA; Mark Mansfield, CIA Public Affairs Office; Bob McNamara, CIA General Counsel; Stanley Moskowitz, CIA Congressional Liaison; Patrick Murray, Associate Deputy Attorney General for National Security; Powell Moore, Assistant Secretary of State for Legislative Affairs; Anna Perez, National Security Affairs; Richard Schiffrin, deputy general counsel, Department of Defense; and Paula Sweeney, CIA General Counsel's office.

Former Government officials: Hodding Carter, head of the Knight Foundation and former Secretary of State for Public Affairs; Boyden Gray, Washington lawyer and former counsel to President George H. W. Bush; John Martin, Washington lawyer and former head of the Justice Department's internal security; and John Podesta, Georgetown University law professor and former White House chief of staff in the Clinton administration.

Congressional observers: Vicki Divoll, general counsel of the Senate Intellignce Committee; Chris Healey, senior counsel of the House Permanent Select Committee on Intelligence; and Tim Sample, staff director of the House Intelligence Committee.

Media representatives: Tom Bettag, Executive Producer, ABC's "Nightline"; Patrick Butler, vice president, *The Washington Post*; David Cloud, National Security Correspondent, *The Wall Street Journal;* Peter Copeland, Washington Bureau Chief, Scripps-Howard News Service; Daniel Klaidman, *Newsweek* Washington Bureau Chief; Bill Kovach, former editor, *The Atlanta Constitution,* and former curator, Nieman Foundation; Doyle McManus, *Los Angeles Times* Washington Bureau Chief; Greg Miller, *Los Angeles Times* National Security Correspondent; Paul McMasters, ombudsman, Freedom Forum, and former associate editor, *USA Today*; Don Oberdorfer, former *Washington Post* national security correspondent; Frank Sesno, former CNN Washington Bureau Chief; and George Wilson, *National Journal* national security correspondent.

Co-conveners and facilitators: Jeff Smith, Washington lawyer and former general counsel, CIA, and Scott Armstrong, former *Washington Post* reporter, director of Information Trust, and founder of National Security Archive.

The Contributors

Tim Cooke is the head of broadcasting at BBC Northern Ireland and is responsible for commissioning and scheduling all television, radio and online programming. Previously, he ran the BBC's newsgathering operation in Northern Ireland. He was a Shorenstein Fellow in the spring of 1998.

Andrew J. Glass is managing editor of *The Hill* newspaper in Washington, D.C., and the retired Washington bureau chief of Cox Newspapers. He began his journalism career in 1960 as a business and financial reporter for the *New York Herald Tribune* and covered the White House and Congress for *The Washington Post* and *Newsweek*. Glass was a Shorenstein Fellow in the fall of 2001.

Nik Gowing is the main program anchor for the BBC's 24-hour international TV news and information channel, BBC World, produced by BBC News for a global audience that now numbers more than 210 million in 200 countries. Before joining the BBC, Gowing was a foreign affairs specialist and presenter at ITN for 18 years; his reporting from Bosnia was part of the Channel Four News portfolio that won the BAFTA "best news coverage" award in 1996. He was a Fellow at the Shorenstein Center in 1994.

Jack Nelson, a Pulitzer Prize winner and former Washington bureau chief of the *Los Angeles Times,* has written two books and co-authored three others, including *The Censors and the Schools,* written while a Nieman Fellow at Harvard. He was a founder and long-time Steering Committee member of the Reporters Committee for Freedom of the Press. Nelson was a Shorenstein Fellow in the fall of 2002.

Frederick Schauer is the Frank Stanton Professor of the First Amendment at the John F. Kennedy School of Government, Harvard University. Schauer is a Fellow of the American Academy of Arts and Sciences and has been awarded a Guggenheim Fellowship. He is the author of *The Law of Obscenity; Free Speech: A Philosophic Enquiry; Playing by the Rules: A Philosophical Examination of Rule-Based Decision-Making in Law and in Life;* and the forthcoming *Profiles, Probabilities, and Stereotypes.* Schauer has been affiliated with the Shorenstein Center since 1990.

Nachman Shai was a Fellow at the Shorenstein Center in the fall of 1996. He was media advisor to the Israeli embassy in Washington (1981–83) and later, media advisor to the Israeli defense minister (1983–85). He became chief IDF spokesperson in 1989 and continued in that role during the Gulf War. Nachman Shai recently retired as the chairman of the board of the Israel Broadcasting Authority and is now Senior Vice President of the United Jewish Communities and Director General of UJC/Israel.

Ramindar Singh wrote his chapter as a Shorenstein Fellow at Harvard in the fall of 2001. In an earlier Harvard incarnation he was a Nieman Fellow (1981–82). He has been editor of the *Sunday Times of India*, *The Times of India, Delhi* and managing editor of *The Pioneer*. He has launched three newspapers and is currently president of IN Mumbai TV channel in Bombay. He hosts a popular weekly interview program called "Charcha," which in Hindi means "discussion."

Matthew V. Storin was editor of *The Boston Globe* from 1992 to 2001. During his 36-year journalism career, Storin covered Congress and the White House and served as Asian Bureau Chief as the Vietnam War concluded and Cambodia began to fall apart. He is now an associate vice president at the University of Notre Dame. Storin was a Fellow at the Shorenstein Center in the spring of 2002.

Gadi Wolfsfeld is a professor at the Hebrew University in Jerusalem in the Department of Political Science and the Department of Communication. He also serves as director of the Levi Eshkol Institute for Economic, Social and Political Research and has previously served as chair of the department of communication and as director of the Smart Family Institute of Communication. His most recent book is entitled *Media and the Path to Peace* (Cambridge University Press, forthcoming). Wolfsfeld was a Shorenstein Fellow in 1992.

Index

A

ABC News, 16, 49, 51, 71, 77, 141, 263
Abel, Elie, 277
Abkhazia, 152
Abrams, Floyd, 285
Access, press, dilemma of, 259–266
    Differential access, 264–266
    Legal doctrine, 259–262
Ackerman, Mike, 6
ACLU, see American Civil Liberties Union
Adair, Johnny, 98–99, 101–102
Adams, David, 106
Adams, Gerry, 90, 93, 95, 107
Aden, Yemen, 3, 9
Adie, Kate, 200–201
Afghanistan, 3–6, 9, 11–14, 17, 28, 30,
    32–36, 39–42, 45, 47, 53, 55, 57, 71, 152,
    264, 289
        See also Kabul; Northern Alliance;
        Taliban
Aftergood, Steven, 72, 291
Agency for Toxic Substances and Disease
    Registry, 73
Ahmici massacre, 165, 181–184
Aideed, General, 190–192
Alagiah, George, 144
Albright, Madeleine, 154, 160, 195, 282
Algeria, 152
Al HaMishmar, 132
Allison, Graham, 7, 19, 181, 194–195
al-Saud, Alwaleed bin Talal bin Abdul Aziz,
    72
Amir, Ayaz, 31–33, 36, 39
al Qaeda, 11, 61, 64, 289
        See also September 11
AMA, see American Medical Association
Amanpour, Christiane, 20
Amazon.com, 72
American Airlines Flight 587, 52
American Civil Liberties Union (ACLU), 69
American College of Emergency Physicians,
    79
American Data Technology, Inc., 48
American Medical Association (AMA), 79
American Prospect, 60
American Society of Newspaper Editors, 281

Amnesty International, 169
AM News/Talk, 52
Angola, 152
Annan, Kofi, 154
Anonymizer.com, 69, 71
An Phoblacht/Republican News, 88
AP, see Associated Press
Arafat, Yasser, 113
        See also PLO
Arens, Moshe, 113, 116, 118, 123–124
Argonne National Laboratory, 74
Arian, Asher, 120
Armed conflicts, television coverage of, see
    Television coverage
Armitage, Richard, 31–32, 39
Armstrong, Scott, 263, 279–281, 283–284,
    286, 291
Army Corps of Engineers, 73
Arnett, Peter, 242
Arria, Diego, 177, 180–181
Ash, Timothy Garton, 21
Ashcroft, John, 58–60, 62, 73, 273, 285–287,
    290–291
Ashkelon, 117
Assam.com, 72
Associated Press (AP), 49, 143, 239, 280–281
Atlanta Constitution, 283
Atlanta Olympics, 3, 6–7
Atlantic Monthly, 21
Atomic Energy Commission, 277
Atta, Mohamed, 63, 78
Attitudes toward U.S., coverage of, 20–21
Aum Shinrikyo, 3
Azzam Publications, 71–72

B

Bacon, Kenneth, 281, 283
Baghdad, 3, 149, 185, 242
        See also Iraq
Baker, James, 153
Balladur, 197
Banja Luka, 171
Baquet, Dean, 288
Barlow, John Perry, 65
Barone, Michael, 52